THE BATTLE FOR SANSKRIT

Praise for *The Battle for Sanskrit*

'For the past sixty years my primary activity has been to interpret Sanskrit and sanskriti. Indeed, Malhotra and I are sailing in the same boat. This book provokes a debate between the "insiders" and "outsiders" of our heritage. It exposes that many outsiders pretend to be insiders, but their hidden agenda is to convince ignorant Hindus that the Vedas are myths and that the traditional claims are nonsensical. They pretend to know our traditions even better than our highest exponents. Unfortunately, most insiders are either blissfully unaware of these subversive projects or are living in isolation and afraid of debating them. Malhotra's work is designed after the traditional method of purva-paksha and uttara-paksha which makes it very interesting and thought provoking. I strongly recommend this work to all Indologists, traditional pandits, historians, philosophers and ordinary seekers.'

– DAYANANDA BHARGAVA, Recipient of President's Award, former Head of Department of Sanskrit and Dean of Faculty of Arts and Social Sciences, University of Jodhpur; presently Chairman, J.R. Rajasthan Sanskrit University, Jaipur.

'This book calls upon traditional scholars to get out of their silos, and calls upon opponents to join the conversation as interlocutors. It is a remarkable work of systematic argumentation that provides a forceful defence against the onslaught of Western scholarship. Serious scholars will benefit from its remarkable insights, boldness and uprightness. I highly recommend it as a preparation for strategic debates.'

– S.R. BHATT, Chairman, Indian Council of Philosophical Research, HRD Ministry, Government of India; Former Head of Department of Philosophy, Delhi University.

'Rajiv Malhotra belongs to that rare breed of Indian scholars who have been working in the area of Indic civilization for a long time. In this incisive and exhaustive work he brings forth the critical role of Sanskrit, and ignites a meaningful discussion on a long neglected area. I wish the book all success.'

– R. VAIDYANATHAN, Professor, Indian Institute of Management, Bangalore.

'Westerners consider themselves very progressive when meddling in Indian affairs. The values they now defend, such as egalitarianism and feminism, are different from what prevailed in the West during the colonial age, but the underlying spirit of "civilizing the savages" is the same. They now try to wrest control of Sanskrit studies from the "oppressive, reactionary" traditionalists, and increasingly succeed with the help of native informers eager for the status and money that Western academics can confer. Once upon a time, the colonizers brought prized artworks to museums in the West, claiming that these were safer there than in the care of the irresponsible natives. Now, their successors try to carry away the *adhikara* (prerogative) to interpret Sanskrit texts, so as to make Hindus look at their own tradition through anti-Hindu lenses. For the first time, Rajiv Malhotra analyses the stakes involved for Hindu civilization, which risks losing control over the backbone of its historical identity, and the power equation in the production of knowledge concerning Sanskrit and the dharmic tradition. He proposes a research programme that Hindus will need to carry out if they are to face this sophisticated onslaught. This path-breaking book maps a battlefield hitherto unknown to most besieged insiders.'

– KOENRAAD ELST, Indologist.

'This book provides extensive ground work for traditional scholars, sadhaks, writers and awakened minds to understand the serious threats against Indian civilization. The author's fearless exposition is driven by his indomitable will, persistence and vigour, long swadhyaya, and cool and patient mind. Works of this calibre appear rarely in a generation. Future scholars will be grateful to Rajiv Malhotra for this wakeup call to retain the sacredness of Sanskrit and its association with Indian life.'

– DEEPIKA KOTHARI and RAMJI OM, Filmmakers of *History of Yoga*.

'Rajiv's work is a timely response to the discourse by Western academics, and exposes the need for Indian scholars with a deep understanding of our languages and culture, working with original texts, to counter the flawed narrative and create an Indian narrative.'

– T.V. MOHANDAS PAI, Chairman, Aarin Capital Partners

'Having gone through the pages of this book, I highly recommend that every traditional scholar and Western Indologist should study it and engage the issues it raises. The author provides a solid response to the prejudices against Indian civilization, and his remarkably systematic approach is commendable.'

– RAMESH KUMAR PANDEY, Vice-Chancellor, Shri Lal Bahadur Shastri Rashtriya Sanskrit Vidyapeeth.

'While an army of Western scholars has been hurling criticisms and throwing challenges against Indian heritage for two centuries, there has hardly been a commensurate response from the heirs of our heritage. This is largely due to gaps in knowledge at our end: the Sanskrit pandits are often ignorant of nuanced English and Western frameworks and paradigms; and the modern westernized Indians are culturally illiterate and lack the competence to respond. This book bridges the gaps and enables traditional pandits as well as the Indian literati to comprehend Western Indology from an Indian perspective. It also exposes how westerners have manoeuvred by capturing Indian resources to perpetuate their biased verdicts. The book makes it possible to have dialogues as equals. The responsibility now lies squarely on traditional Indian scholars to take on the issues between insiders and outsiders which this book has framed. Rajiv Malhotra's contribution consists of this valuable role as a prime initiator of this dialogue.'

– K.S. KANNAN, Former Director, Karnataka Samskrit University, Bangalore.

'*The Battle for Sanskrit* has immense potential to equip and arm Vedic insiders with the required knowledge not just to battle the outsiders but, more importantly, to preserve their own sanskriti based on its indigenous principles. I humbly request all Sanskrit lovers, scholars and practitioners of Vedic traditions to read this book and join the suggested "home team" for serious intellectual exchanges on the issues concerned.'

– SAMPADANANDA MISHRA, Director, Sri Aurobindo Foundation for Indian Culture, Sri Aurobindo Society, Pondicherry.

'*The Battle for Sanskrit* wrests open a main gate to the predominantly Western-constructed citadel known as Indology. Who can remain silent or, worse, collaborate, in the face of groundless allegations that Indian elites are promulgating Sanskrit and its traditions for political gain, thus perpetuating a so-called Sanskrit-born social abuse? As the linguistic key to the highest wisdom of humanity, Sanskrit studies must escape captivity enforced by academic guardians who over-zealously wield the club of Western theoretical methods. The author, besides exposing the colonial baggage still colouring the Western approach to India's Sanskrit heritage, also shines his torch, in fairness, upon the large platoon of Indian sepoys colluding to help keep the Sanskrit potentiality in check. A salient point this book offers us is that the Western approach to Sanskrit is often weighed down by "political philology" – cultural biases, hegemonic filters. Superbly presenting the positive correction to this imbalance, the author advocates our seeing through the lens of "sacred philology".'

– H.H. DEVAMITRA SWAMI, Spiritual Leader and Author of *Searching for Vedic India*.

'This is an important book to ignite the much-needed conversation on Sanskrit, its past and its future. Rajiv Malhotra opens a new ground by evaluating what Western Indologists have been writing about our traditions. It is time for the scholars to wake up and give responses impartially. I commend the author for arguing against the view that Sanskrit is oppressive or dead. Every serious scholar of Indology should read this book and join the intellectual discourse on our heritage.'

– UPENDRA RAO, Chair, Special Centre for Sanskrit Studies, Jawaharlal Nehru University, New Delhi.

'Rajiv Malhotra deserves kudos for his insightful book, *The Battle for Sanskrit*, which is a much-needed intervention that gives insiders a seat at the table as equals. Rather than Western Indologists and their Indian supporters becoming defensive, they should welcome this book as an opportunity for honest exchanges. The issues raised here are too important to be ignored any longer. The direction that this battle takes can have far-reaching consequences on approaches to science, technology, social studies and economics. The pompous edifice of Western Indology that has been built over a long time will not crumble overnight. It is now up to the traditional scholars and practitioners to heed the author's call and develop solid intellectual responses (uttara-paksha) to the challenges.'

– HRISHIKESH A. MAFATLAL, Chairman, Arvind Mafatlal Group of Companies; Chairman, BAIF Development Research Foundation.

'This book's meticulously gathered information, and its coherent arguments presented in a lucid and engaging style, will easily make our traditional and modern scholars realize that they can no longer rely on Western scholarly endeavours, however profound and painstaking they may be, for achieving a resurgence of Indian civilization. A book that absolutely must be read, by anyone who cares for the resurgence of *Bharatiya-samskriti*, which is deeply embedded in Sanskrit!'

– K. RAMASUBRAMANIAN, Professor, IIT Bombay

'Sanskrit can no longer be the concern of only the traditional pandits. Modern methods of analysis, interpretation and communication have to be brought in and we have to rebuild our own universities – inspired as much by Nalanda as by Cambridge – with science, philosophy, humanities, in fact all knowledge, created, pursued and taught on the same campus. As an unabashed lover of Sanskrit, I welcome this debate that Rajiv Malhotra has brought out into the open about the status of Sanskrit studies in the world, including in particular its homeland, India. This book should trigger a discussion on the scientific qualities of Sanskrit, in particular the tradition's emphasis on empiricism, and on the similarities and differences between Indian and Western approaches to knowledge.'

– RODDAM NARASIMHA, eminent aerospace scientist and recipient of Padma Vibhushan.

'The knowledge system which has developed in relation to ancient India since the middle of the eighteenth century was (and still is) dominated by Western scholarship. The so-called consensus in this field was essentially a matter of agreement among Western scholars, with Indians playing only a subsidiary role. The situation should have begun to change in the light of the new power equations since the mid-twentieth century. The fact that it has not yet significantly done so is due to several factors operating in the background, the most important of which is the deplorable unwillingness among Western scholars to take note of the viewpoints of an increasing number of Indian professionals. It is basically a confrontational situation, if not that of war. The Western academic institutions dealing with India are full of "experts" who are basically anti-India. Rajiv Malhotra, a well-known independent scholar, has long been known for his deep perception of this problem and his clear, well-argued analysis and criticism of it. I have always been an avid reader of his columns and books. In this volume he throws new light on the power network behind Sanskrit studies in the West. This is a book which will long be cherished by the rational elements among the Indian and Western Indologists.'

– DILIP K. CHAKRABARTI, Emeritus Professor of South Asian Archaeology, Cambridge University.

THE BATTLE FOR SANSKRIT

Is Sanskrit political or sacred, oppressive or liberating, dead or alive?

Rajiv Malhotra

HarperCollins *Publishers* India

First published in hardback in India in 2016 by
HarperCollins *Publishers* India

P-ISBN: 978-93-5177-538-6
E-ISBN:978-93-5177-539-3

2 4 6 8 10 9 7 5 3 1

HarperCollins *Publishers*
A-75, Sector 57, Noida, Uttar Pradesh 201301, India
1 London Bridge Street, London, SE1 9GF, United Kingdom
Hazelton Lanes, 55 Avenue Road, Suite 2900, Toronto, Ontario M5R 3L2
and 1995 Markham Road, Scarborough, Ontario M1B 5M8, Canada
25 Ryde Road, Pymble, Sydney, NSW 2073, Australia
195 Broadway, New York, NY 10007, USA

Typeset in 11/14 Adobe Jenson Pr
By Saanvi Graphics Noida

Printed and bound at
Manipal Technologies Ltd, Manipal

Dedicated to our purva-paksha and uttara-paksha debating tradition. With gratitude to the purva-pakshins (opponents) I have learned from. May we engage in this intellectual yajna with mutual respect.

Contents

Introduction: The Story Behind the Book

There is a new awakening in India that is challenging the ongoing westernization of the discourse about India and the intellectual machinery that produces it. Serious readers, regardless of their ideological affiliations, would benefit from open and honest discussions between experts on opposite sides. Rather than having two separate monologues, it is better to bring together both sides of such encounters into dignified conversations with mutual respect. However, any such conversation requires each side to be well informed about the other. Unfortunately, this is often not the case today on several key topics.

Although the westernized side has systematically studied the traditional Indian side's texts and practices, the reverse has not been the case: traditional Indian experts using their own categories and frameworks have not adequately studied the scholarship being produced by Western and westernized Indian scholars. My work is a humble attempt to fill this knowledge gap in the traditional camp.

In each book, I take up a specific important topic with the hope of informing the traditional scholars so they can participate in the discourse as equals.

This book seeks to wake up traditional scholars of Sanskrit and sanskriti (Indian civilization) concerning an important school of thought that has its base in the US and has started to dominate the discourse on the cultural, social and political aspects of India. This academic field is called Indology or Sanskrit studies (or more broadly, South Asian studies). From their analysis of the past, the scholars of this field are intervening in modern Indian society with the explicitly stated view of detoxifying it of 'poisons' allegedly built into Sanskrit and its texts. Often, they interpret India in ways that the traditional Indian experts would outright reject or at least question. I will start with the episode that intensified my monitoring of this field and led to this book.

In August 2014, I suddenly became aware of an unprecedented threat to the integrity of the Sringeri Sharada Peetham (started by Adi Shankara in the eighth century CE), one of the most sacred institutions for Hindus. (Peetham in Sanskrit signifies 'seat'. In this case it is a high seat which the Shankaracharya occupies to perform the duties, responsibilities and rights for protecting the tradition represented by the peetham.) There was a serious risk of a profound and systematic distortion of the teachings and mission of the peetham, as well as a distortion of sanatana dharma more broadly. I immediately stopped all my other work to investigate this and intervene. From that moment onwards, my energies have been channelled into dealing with this urgent matter.

I will begin with a brief account of how this extraordinary peetham began, and then summarize the dramatic events that unfolded starting about a year ago to potentially undermine it. This book is an outgrowth of those events. The crisis it addresses is much broader and deeper than the implications for one institution; it is a crisis that threatens to undermine the foundations of authority more broadly in Hindu dharma.

The Sringeri Sharada Peetham (often abbreviated as Sringeri Peetham) is one of the oldest centres of learning in Vedanta and considered one of the most important institutions in Hinduism. Adi Shankara, the renowned sage, walked across India to revive sanatana dharma. He debated and defeated the competing philosophies that dominated the discourse at the time.

According to traditional accounts, one of his most significant debates was with Mandana Misra, a prominent scholar in Purva-mimamsa philosophy, a philosophy that emphasizes a ritualistic and literal interpretation of the Vedas. Mandana Misra graciously requested that Shankara pick the judge for the debate as Shankara was much younger and Misra wanted to make the terms of the exchange as equitable as possible. Shankara chose Mandana Misra's wife, Ubhaya Bharati, as the judge, because she was known to be intellectually very sharp. She was equal to her husband in all aspects and Shankara knew she would be impartial.

The debate was held over eight days. Finally, Mandana Misra conceded defeat and Ubhaya Bharati showed her true form as Devi Saraswati, and her mortal body disappeared.[1] She granted Shankara's request that she would re-manifest at a place where he invoked her. Shankara then initiated Mandana Misra, and they proceeded to Sringeri where the first of four peethams was set up.[2]

At Sringeri, Shankara invoked Devi Saraswati to manifest as Sharadamba. This is how Sri Sharada Devi, a manifestation of Saraswati, the Goddess of Wisdom, became the presiding deity of that institution. Hence its name Sharada Peetham. Shankara then appointed Mandana Misra – renamed Sri Sureshwaracharya – as the first acharya of the Sringeri Sharada Peetham. This lineage has remained unbroken to this day.

Over the years, due to the presence of Sharada Devi and the erudition of its acharyas, Sringeri became famous as a centre of spiritual power and traditional learning. Many century later, the famed and powerful Vijayanagara Empire was founded under the guidance of the twelfth acharya of Sringeri, Jagadguru Sri Vidyaranya.

Such is the illustrious lineage and prestige of the Sringeri Peetham. There is no Vatican or Pope in Hinduism, owing to its decentralized nature. However, Sringeri is one of a handful of institutions that has comparable importance, being an unimpeachable body of learning and austerity. It is therefore critical that the integrity and credibility of Sringeri remain uncompromised.

Unfortunately, as the events I am about to disclose will show, Sringeri now runs the risk of potentially losing its integrity, all because of some short-sighted choices under consideration by some of its administrators in the USA and India. If their plans were to succeed, Sringeri would find itself in the ruinous position of having relinquished the name and legacy of its founder, Adi Shankara, and of perverting the values of erudition that are its hallmark. Most shamefully of all, such a move would place Shankara's legacy in the hands of the very same forces that have published volumes of academic writings undermining the sanatana dharma tradition.

In each of my previous books, I have taken on the leaders of specific schools of thought that are in effect misrepresenting Hinduism, in terms of its true history and its principles. Even though such whistle-blowing creates tensions with the individuals and institutions being exposed, I consider it necessary that the public be well informed and that important debates take place openly and transparently.

The US-based academic genre of Sanskrit studies that I critique in the present volume as being detrimental to Sringeri Peetham in particular, and Hinduism more broadly, has been on my radar for more than a decade. As early as 2005, at the World Sanskrit Congress in Bangkok, I had raised red flags about the work of its leader, Sheldon Pollock, a prominent American Sanskrit scholar. I described how he placed part of the blame for European racism and Nazism at Sanskrit's door. More specifically, he had written extensively claiming that 'brahmin elitism' was a factor in shaping the ideologies of British colonialism and German Nazism, and that social oppressiveness built into Sanskrit had contributed to the legitimation of genocide. Chapter 4 explains this further.

The present saga erupted in August 2014. It was then that I learned that a group of wealthy non-resident Indians (NRIs) in the New York area had teamed up with the top administrative leaders of Sringeri Peetham in India and representatives of Sringeri Peetham in the USA to set up a university chair in the name of Adi Shankara. It was to be called the 'SVBF Adi Shankara Chair in Hindu Religion and Philosophy'. (SVBF stands for Sringeri Vidya Bharati Foundation, which is the official institution representing the Sringeri Peetham in the US.)[3] They had already collected $4 million for the chair, which was to be created at Columbia University.

The plan was to set up three other chairs in various other universities in the US. Someone close to the group of donors told me that as soon as this precedent with the Adi Shankara Chairs had been achieved, the door would be open to approach other Hindu lineages for establishing similar chairs across the US. These chairs would serve as official ambassadors of diverse Hindu movements. For instance, there could also be chairs in the name of Sri Ramanujacharya, another great exponent of Vedanta.

To appreciate why such chairs would undermine our tradition, the reader needs to understand the proposed terms of the Adi Shankara Chair at Columbia. Two committees were being formed to manage this chair. One was the Academic Committee, consisting of scholars from Columbia, to be headed by Sheldon Pollock. The second was the Donor and Advisor Committee, which would represent the various financiers and administrators of Sringeri Peetham. All the funding would come from the Donor and Advisor Committee. The selection of the scholar to occupy the chair would be made by the Academic Committee, which would have *sole control* over the selection, academic content and activities of the chair. The donors would have no veto right or say in the matter; they would merely be informed of the selection after it had been made.

This is a common way to make donors feel good about themselves, and to allow them to enjoy some public limelight without having any meaningful influence over the actual discourse. To put it bluntly, it is a way to co-opt people by giving them importance, while keeping them out of all matters of substance. The implications have to be understood carefully.

These chairs would be established in the name of Sringeri Peetham. The professors associated with them would therefore be speaking to the world with the voice and authority of Sringeri. The whole objective of establishing the chairs would be to represent Shankara's teachings to the modern world. In my opinion, if the content and subject matter produced and taught under the aegis of such a chair represent views as seen from outside the tradition that oppose some of the core principles of sanatana dharma (as I will argue in this book), such a chair would certainly compromise the Hindu tradition in general, and Sringeri Peetham in particular.

The name, power and sanctity of Sringeri have been carefully safeguarded for more than a thousand years. The adhikara (authority) to represent the peetham and speak on its behalf has always rested solely with the acharyas, who are groomed from childhood to assume this responsibility. They are required to lead lives of austerity and devotion and spend their time studying the traditional texts. They have received the mantras and powers of the lineage unbroken since Adi Shankara in the tradition of transmission from guru to disciple.

It would be the height of irresponsibility to give up control of the teachings and brand name of Sringeri to outside interests. This would be especially alarming if it were done without a thorough investigation into the backgrounds and agendas of those being put in charge – equivalent to haphazardly giving away the intellectual property, trademark and custodianship of the peetham to some alien third party.

Upon learning this, I immediately approached the lead donor to offer my perspective on the risks. I explained the importance of carrying out a process that investors call 'due diligence' before any commitment is made. I explained my background in corporate due diligence and my subsequent experience over the past twenty years in analysing how some prominent Western scholars represent (or misrepresent) Hinduism today. However, the concerns I expressed and the suggestions I offered were not welcome. I was told that the Adi Shankara Chair at Columbia was, for all practical purposes, a 'done deal' and that it would be formally announced within six weeks, i.e., in October 2014. I was further told that the Shankaracharya of the Sringeri Peetham had personally blessed it and that, according to the rules, the deal could therefore not be retracted or renegotiated by Sringeri. I expressed my doubts as to whether the Shankaracharya had been made aware of *all* the relevant information and issues before giving his blessing.

All I asked of the wealthy donors was that they carry out at least the same degree of due diligence that they would conduct in any of their business deals. Before signing any strategic investment, a businessman's professional training requires that he study the other party's products, strategies and management philosophy, as well as the industry and its market dynamics. I informed them that I had done similar analyses of Hinduism studies and India studies in academia. Using my professional expertise, I had examined them as a specialized knowledge industry.

I asked the donors why they would not exercise *at least* as much caution when acting on behalf of dharma and the Sringeri Peetham as they would when making personal business investments. After all, their purported motive for such donations was to help the legacy of Adi Shankara and enhance the fame and prestige of the peetham. Given the contentious nature of the way Hinduism has often been depicted within Western academics, this ought to be a matter of concern to them.

It became immediately apparent that they had not done any research or due diligence whatsoever. They were simply relying on the general media perception that the scholars who would be in control of the chair were reputed to be popular and enjoyed prestige and clout amongst Western academics. I was shocked that the top donor (a high-ranking NRI in the US financial industry) used Sheldon Pollock's public relations interview in *India Today* as his background check on Pollock.[4] I pointed out that no competent investor would agree to a deal relying merely on the other party's PR machinery and the self-serving opinions of that party's own circle of associates. What is needed in such cases is a rigorous analysis carried out by someone who is independent and outside this circle. No such analysis had been done in this instance.

The lead donor defended Pollock and wrote to me: 'With all due respect, we found Professor Pollock highly enthusiastic and excited about the CHAIR at Columbia ...' I was deeply troubled by the implications of this initiative, in part because of the cavalier attitude taken towards this important decision, and in part because of what I already knew of Sheldon Pollock's work on Sanskrit. He is undoubtedly a brilliant scholar. However, some of his key publications undermine the traditional understanding of sanskriti (Indian culture and civilization) in significant ways. In an e-mail, I gave the following advice to the lead donor:

> My advice is that before the deal gets formalized, you should bring in an experienced independent industry consultant of your choice (autonomous from the parties concerned), who can help address such issues as the following: What are *your* goals in setting up the chair? What are the benchmarks for evaluating the output you expect? What is the track record of the parties involved in producing such outputs in the past? Please have someone review the content that has been produced on Hinduism and Sanskrit by the Columbia faculty in the past, and see if this agrees/conflicts with the intellectual positions of Sringeri Peetham. (I am developing a paper that points out serious conflicts between the ideological positions of these academic scholars and those of Sringeri.) If the goal is to promote Adi Shankara's philosophy, it would require an expert in Vedanta. It is important to note that the methodologies routinely used in the Western academy to study Hinduism do not coincide with the methods sanctioned by our tradition. Therefore, which methods/criteria will be used by them to evaluate Shankara – Indian or Western? You might want to have an independent report written on the major projects on Hinduism previously done at Columbia. I have been involved in some of these situations. For instance, there were tensions between Swami Dayananda Saraswati's ashram in Saylorsburg (Pennsylvania) and Columbia University's Hinduism program a decade back. This was due to research approaches which the Hindu side considered biased and denigrating.[5]

What I got back from the lead donor was a list of his prior philanthropic experience where he had raised millions of dollars per project. However, none of these projects was related to Hinduism or Indian philosophy in any manner. My advice had fallen on deaf ears.

I felt confident that although the financial donors seemed unconcerned, the intellectual leaders of Sringeri Peetham based in the US would provide me with a good avenue to express my concerns. Therefore, I reached out to the main leader of the Sringeri Peetham at its US affiliate, SVBF, offering to share my insights before anything was officially signed or announced. I suggested a personal meeting, but he referred me back to the leading financial donor. The lead donor, however, told me they were getting very close to signing the deal and that it could not be delayed any more.

By this time, word had spread among my social media followers as to the impending potential crisis. This, in turn, sparked a firestorm, and many hundreds of people started directly calling and writing to Sringeri Peetham in India to protest.

The lead donor was upset by all this negative publicity and wrote to me cancelling a lunch meeting we had planned. He wrote: 'I have to call off our luncheon. ... In the context of some postings, and other mails floating around against Columbia University, an institution I adore and respect personally, and in whom I have the greatest faith and confidence, I came to the conclusion that it is the right thing to do.' With this meeting cancelled, there was an impasse that prevented me from expressing my concerns directly to the relevant parties.

The logjam was broken when I met Ravi Subramanian and his wife in Canada. They are among the major donors and supporters of Sringeri Peetham in North America and were extremely courteous and willing to listen to my concerns. As genuine devotees of the Sringeri Peetham, they were the first persons associated with Sringeri who understood the serious implications of the issues I was raising. Ravi immediately grasped the urgency of having independent scholars with a traditional perspective review the works of Sheldon Pollock. During my visit to his home, he called the main US-based leader of Sringeri (i.e., SVBF based in New Jersey) and requested him to meet with me.

Meeting with the US-based Sringeri leader and one of the major donors

As a result of Ravi's intervention, I had a meeting in New Jersey with the US-based head appointed by Sringeri Peetham. He appeared to be sympathetic to my concerns. He heard me out carefully and politely expressed his appreciation for the sincerity of my investigation into the matter. He offered to facilitate my planned visit to Sringeri Peetham.[6]

I suggested that they should be in no hurry to sign the chair contract with Columbia University as the interests of Sringeri Peetham and the Vedanta tradition are too important to get compromised in haste. I recommended that their contract with Columbia must specify some minimum qualifications required of any candidate for the chair. These qualifications should include knowledge of tarka, vyakarana, mimamsa and the primary texts of all the schools of Vedanta. The scholar should also be an active disciple of a recognized guru from the Vedanta lineage and under his ongoing guidance. He or she should also comply with the traditional lifestyle required of someone serving as a role model for students. Because the purpose of the chair would be to propagate the ideas and ideals of Adi Shankara, such an ambassador should uphold and embody the values of Adi Shankara.

I requested that they delay their decision for a few months and wait for my 'kshetra analysis'. The term 'kshetra' means field or theatre of activity, and in this case it is the field of Hinduism studies which I have been analysing as a sort of knowledge industry consisting of producers, distributors, packagers, consumers, institutions, investors and so forth. The issues analysed by me are important for practising Hindus of *all* lineages. These points apply broadly to the entire spectrum of studies related to Indian civilization, and not just the writings of Sheldon Pollock, although he is the best example of these issues. My goal was to trigger debates among the parties representing different views. The head of SVBF appeared to be receptive to these ideas.

However, sitting next to him at our meeting was one of the project's financial supporters who had driven from New York to attend the meeting. He was visibly annoyed with me and implied that I had ruined his 'deal' to set up the Columbia chair. He noted that thousands of e-mails and hundreds of phone calls to Sringeri had registered outrage at the planned deal with Columbia University. My response was that he and the other donors should be grateful to me for raising these issues because the due diligence I proposed would save the Sringeri Peetham much embarrassment. Otherwise, had they proceeded rashly as planned, the Hindu community would be scandalized when they read my critique of the academic scholars put in control of the Sringeri legacy. I was saddened that the donor seemed more concerned about protecting his personal relationships in New York's financial circles than about protecting the legacy of Shankara.

The donor said that he was a fifth-generation follower of Sringeri Peetham. He considered me a meddlesome outsider to the Sringeri tradition, whereas according to him he was the one qualified to speak for it. What followed during the meeting was a sort of mini-debate on Vedanta. Since the points he raised are commonly heard among some Vedanta experts, it is important that I summarize them below along with my responses.

He argued that our tradition is extremely strong, so it does not matter if scholars attack it. The qualities and competence of the professors appointed to represent the tradition could not taint the purity of the tradition. It was unimportant whether the scholar occupying the chair agreed or disagreed with Shankara's ideas or lifestyle. I was worrying unnecessarily, he felt.

His view shows a woeful ignorance on the purpose of dharmic education and the role of the scholars in charge. I responded by asking why Sringeri Peetham had such strict rules on the behaviour and conduct of the acharyas. Since the tradition is so strong, how would it matter if its teachers were qualified or not? Why, I asked, is there the principle of 'adhikari bheda', according to which an individual must be competent and worthy before being appointed to such a role? The entire lineage of Sringeri is based on adhikari bheda and the careful transmission of knowledge from guru to disciple. How can a professorship be established as the official ambassador of Sringeri Peetham without similar considerations about whether he or she has the appropriate adhikara?

The issue was not whether Hinduism or the teachings of Adi Shankara can sustain critique. Indeed, such critiques are necessary and healthy. Rather, the issue was that, in this case, the critique would be put forth *with the imprimatur of Sringeri Peetham*. The peetham should shoulder the responsibility for *answering* the critics, not sponsoring them! The proposed chair would serve as a mutt (branch) of the peetham and its research output and teachings would be seen as an official representation of Adi Shankara's teachings. An analogous situation would be for the Vatican to officially lend its name to a wholesale reinterpretation of Catholicism by some independent non-Catholic institution.

The financial donor then raised another point, one about which many Hindu intellectuals are confused. He said that since Shankara's teachings are the absolute truth, they are unassailable. The absolute truth cannot be toppled by anyone. Therefore, it does not matter what anyone teaches, good or bad.

His underlying point is valid: the absolute truth cannot be overturned by false claims. But his extrapolation based on this point is flawed. It does not follow that because the ultimate truth is unassailable, false claims should therefore be allowed to proliferate in the world. I pointed out that going by his logic, Adi Shankara should not have bothered to traverse the four corners of India twice to debate against various distortions of dharma and wrong teachings. Why did he take the trouble to debate scholars of competing philosophies? The truth was always the truth, long before Shankara, so it was unnecessary for him to debate it at all. Why does Sringeri Peetham even exist as a centre for the careful and accurate transmission of his teachings if getting them right does not matter in the first place?

I argued that Sringeri Sharada Peetham is important precisely because it debates against falsities in order to convince people of the truth, and because it does so openly and courageously. The truth itself is never vulnerable. What is vulnerable is the state of knowledge or ignorance of human beings, especially our youth, who are being exposed to so many falsehoods.

The realm we live in is the relative or mundane realm called 'vyavaharika'. The basis of dharma consists of living righteously in the mundane realm while staying connected to the absolute realm. The logical corollary of the donor's position would be that it is okay to violate the laws of society or one's personal ethical conduct because such violations have no impact on the absolute truth. This is obviously a complete misreading of our tradition.

I pointed out that, thanks to such attitudes as this man was representing, we have become dependent on westerners to interpret us and to speak for us, and we request them to give us fair treatment. It is sad that we have lost our capability to 'reverse the gaze' and come back with a rejoinder. Adi Shankara would never have accepted such a lopsided state of affairs.

Just as Adi Shankara did in his time, we must fully understand the kshetra with which we are engaging, i.e., the academic kshetra of Hinduism studies in this case. This requires that we do purva-paksha (systematic study of the opponent's positions) of the state of affairs in the academic kshetra. I have been doing this in my own humble way to the best of my abilities for the past twenty years on a full-time basis.

I left very unimpressed by the thinking of such leaders who now speak for Sringeri Peetham. Regardless of their claims of pedigree, it troubled me that such minds seem to set the strategic direction of a great institution.

Meeting with Sheldon Pollock

Soon after having these discussions with the NRIs who were organizing the Columbia chair, I suddenly received an e-mail from Sheldon Pollock inviting me to meet with him. This was a surprise because our previous e-mail exchange had been five years earlier, and that exchange did not end positively. He had then refused my request to interact because he was concerned about my criticism of his 'Death of Sanskrit' paper. Indeed, I had characterized his writings as being against the interests of Hindus because of his views supporting the foreign Aryan theory, his position that Sanskrit was dead and his persistent characterization of Hindu tradition as rife with social abuses. But such disagreements ought not to be taken personally.

I accepted his invitation and we had a pleasant meeting at a local coffee shop in Princeton. He was charming and gave me a detailed biography of all his achievements as a pre-eminent Western scholar of Sanskrit today. After citing his impressive list of publications and awards, he turned to me and asked: 'How could you think I hate Hinduism when I have spent my entire life studying the Sanskrit tradition? How could someone possibly hate the tradition that he has devoted his life to studying? Only a person in love with the tradition could work so hard to understand it.' This logic would certainly have impressed the vast majority of Indians he deals with. The mere fact that a famous westerner is working so hard to study our tradition is enough to bring awe into the minds of many Indians.

However, my response was different from what he might have anticipated. I told him he must have heard of certain American academicians who are considered Islamophobic (a well-known term referring to those who hate Islam). He replied, 'Of course there are those scholars.' Then I pointed out that Islamophobic scholars spend their entire lives studying Islam. By Pollock's logic, their long-term investment in Islamic studies ought to make them lovers of Islam. Nevertheless, they hate Islam and they study it diligently for that very reason. Their careers are made by studying a tradition with the intention of demolishing it and exposing its weaknesses. Similarly, I said, there are scholars in many disciplines who study some phenomenon for the purpose of undermining it, not because they love it. People study crime in order to fight it. There are experts on corruption who want to expose it, not because they love corruption. There are public health specialists who study a disease with the intention of being able to defeat it. Therefore, I argued, it was fallacious to assume that merely studying Sanskrit made him a lover of sanskriti (the Indian civilization based on Sanskrit).

To his credit, he instantly appreciated the point I was making. Then I told him that a scholarly-style assessment of his works could only be done by reading and analysing his writings thoroughly. That he has spent many decades studying Sanskrit and its texts does not by itself constitute any sort of favour to the tradition. After all, many evangelists studied our tradition in order to find its weaknesses. Colonial Indologists were among the most accomplished Sanskrit scholars of their time, yet their loyalty was to their own civilization.

Therefore, I explained to Pollock, it was desirable that an important figure like him be evaluated based on the merits of his works and nothing else. I had the experience of evaluating several Western scholars who specialize on India and had already planned to evaluate his works also. This evaluation, I pointed out, should not be taken personally at all, but as something Indian scholars have done with each other for centuries. I explained that the tradition of purva-paksha was central to

Indian intellectual methods and that this tradition ought to be revived. Unfortunately, hardly any serious purva-paksha is being done today, not even on prominent Western Indologists such as him. Many well-known thinkers owed their fame to the debates concerning their work, and not to blind cronyism.

He agreed about the importance of such work in principle, but asked if he and I could 'work something out', in the sense of finding common ground rather than being opponents. I responded that I would love to explore ways of working together but that that could only be explored *after* my investigation on his works was completed and published. He had the advantage of having spent over thirty years researching and writing on my tradition, and with the benefit of resources from major institutions and prestigious endorsements. I, on the other hand, had only just started to develop a response to his views. I deserved some time to finish my review before we could sit down and discuss how to work in cooperation going forward.

He said he had worked closely with traditional Indian scholars and listed several names. But when I asked him to name a single traditional Indian scholar who had written an extensive critique of his major works, he acknowledged this had not happened. He was quick to point out that this was not his fault because he had never stopped anyone from writing critiques. I agreed that obsequious Indian attitudes towards westerners and especially towards Western Indologists were a colonial hangover for which he cannot be blamed. Many Indians who have the competence to do such critiques are inside the intellectual milieu of universities, think tanks or media, and dare not go against the tide. They depend on Western academics for institutional backing in their careers. They are unlikely to break ranks and write objective critiques.

We then moved on to discuss the Adi Shankara Chair at Columbia that was being finalized with the official backing of Sringeri Peetham. He claimed that this had been something the NRIs and the people at Sringeri wanted to do and that he had merely 'offered help to facilitate' it at Columbia. I asked if he was a practitioner of sadhana based on Shankara's teachings; he frankly admitted that his was strictly an *objective* study of the tradition as an outsider and not as a practitioner from within the tradition.

We discussed the issue of potential conflict when the occupant of the chair takes positions that undermine the very tradition that has backed and funded the chair. Pollock said such conflicts are normal in the interest of academic freedom and that the donors cannot interfere with the autonomy of the scholars. I then listed a few contentious positions *he* has taken in his own work on Sanskrit that Hindus would find very disturbing. I did not want to delve into details at the time. I told him that my findings on the serious contradictions between his work and the tradition ought to be consolidated first, and then he, as well as traditional scholars, would be in a better position to debate their respective views. In a sense, I was facilitating a debate which had not taken place concerning the study of Indian civilization.

I complimented him on the amazing range of awards he had received from Indians, such as the Indian government's Padma Shri Award, India's highest Sanskrit award, and *India Abroad*'s Friend of India Award. I noted the way Narayana Murthy (the Infosys billionaire) had showered him with millions of dollars, thereby boosting his prestige as the most powerful scholar in the field of Sanskrit and Indian vernacular languages. He was modest and said he felt honoured by this appreciation but pointed out that he had not solicited this fame and that it came to him at the initiative of the Indian side. He related anecdotes like, 'I was surprised one day to receive a call from the Indian embassy informing me of their decision to give me the award ...'

I mentioned my concern that some of his students have become prominent critics of Hinduism. I also mentioned his team's distaste for Narendra Modi, for Samskrita Bharati's spoken Sanskrit initiative, and for various other pro-Hindu individuals and organizations. I had no problem with criticisms that were backed by facts and logic, but Pollock's group tended to sensationalize. He said that such fights were being carried out by his students and not by him. I said that several political petitions against Hinduism, Modi, etc., had been *personally* signed by him, including petitions to the US government authorities condemning

India on human rights grounds. He was uncomfortable and remarked that as a 'concerned scholar' about the plight of 'certain communities' he speaks out for them. I decided that it was best to let all the facts come out in my analysis before opening up the debate further. We agreed to get back in touch when my work was published and then continue the conversation.

I found Sheldon Pollock to be remarkably well informed about Sanskrit and sanskriti, as well as on modern Indian politics in which he takes strong positions. I also found him to be a worthy opponent with whom to engage, and doing so has expanded and sharpened my own thoughts. What I take exception to is his allowing himself to be positioned as a spokesperson for Sringeri Peetham, a central institution of Hinduism, his lack of self-awareness about the ways in which his own assumptions and world view prejudice his analyses of Sanskrit and sanskriti, and his failure to fully disclose the ideology and agenda that underlie his scholarship when soliciting support from the faith community.

Surprisingly, Pollock acknowledged knowing about some of the contents of the letters I had sent confidentially to the Shankaracharya of Sringeri. Earlier I had found out that the NRIs involved in setting up the chair also mentioned receiving copies of the letters I had sent to Sringeri. I felt disturbed that there was a potential security leak in Sringeri Peetham itself. The loyalties of such persons ought to be completely to the peetham, and not to a third party.

Trip to Sringeri Sharada Peetham

Disturbed at what appeared to be the compromised position of the administrative leadership at the Sringeri Peetham, I decided I should visit the Shankaracharya of Sringeri personally and present my case. The dilemma was how to go about arranging such a direct contact, given that the official channels may have been compromised. The head administrator of the Sringeri Peetham in India was already on board with the Columbia deal. He had visited the US and had been impressed by the scholarship on Sanskrit and Vedanta he found there. In fact, in my travels in India I find many traditional Indians who consider Western Indologists superior to Indian ones.

This is when Rama Shankar, a Chicago-based lady who had been following my work for over a decade, approached me to offer assistance. Through her personal connections with the Shankaracharya of Sringeri for many decades, she was able to quickly arrange a private, confidential meeting with him that bypassed the normal channels. Along with a Bangalore-based supporter (Dr T.S. Mohan), a Toronto-based supporter (Sunil Sheoran) and Rama Shankar's nephew, I visited Sringeri for an overnight stay. While waiting for the meeting with the Shankaracharya, I met a young swami who is a follower of Swami Dayananda Saraswati. This young swami told me that my campaign against the Columbia chair had become high-profile, and had stirred up a lot of disturbance among many senior acharyas. He was sympathetic to the issues I had raised and offered his support in the future.

The meeting with the Shankaracharya went well. The head administrator of the peetham had heard about my visit at the last minute and was already sitting in the room when I entered. Nevertheless, I was able to have an open-minded and direct conversation with the Shankaracharya. He blessed my earlier books that I had brought with me and heard out my concerns in detail. After listening to the examples I cited concerning academic biases, he said these Western scholars do not understand Vedic knowledge. He was appreciative of my concerns.

I was in no position to make anything resembling a 'demand' on him. It is his right to decide as he pleases. My only request was that the decision regarding Columbia be put on hold, so that my written report could be made available for review by Sringeri Peetham's own scholars who could then make their independent, objective assessment. The Shankaracharya did not formally commit to this, but his response hinted a favourable posture. One of my main reasons for writing this book is to fulfil my promise to the Shankaracharya.

Who will control our traditions?

At the time of this writing, no announcement had been made about the deal between Sringeri Peetham and Columbia University being signed, but I know that lobbying continues to target Indians as a source of funding for American universities. Attractions include incentives like prestigious board positions, visibility with the upper echelon of American society, 'networking opportunities' to make deals for their businesses and opportunities for family members.[7] All this is normal in business; but should such motives be fuelling the study of sanatana dharma?

One of my persistent objections to the way this drama has unfolded is the failure of the Sringeri Peetham's administrative leaders and the NRI donors to open up this discussion to the public, and to the community whose interests are at stake. In the true spirit of Adi Shankara, there ought to be public debates on the pros and cons of making such a move, and on the issues and principles at stake before commencing any specific negotiation. The entire Hindu community is a stakeholder in this, and not just a few officials with formal posts along with moneyed and well-connected elites.

The problems Pollock and his school of thought have raised about Sanskrit and Hindu traditions are important ones, and our tradition can indeed become stronger by engaging with them. Those who criticize our tradition certainly deserve a hearing in the spirit of the purva-paksha system. As outsiders, they are able to see certain aspects that insiders cannot see.

At the same time, we have a right to defend our principles especially when these are misrepresented. That obligation falls heavily on the Sringeri Peetham because its core mission lies in safeguarding the interests of the sacred traditions that have been its legacy for more than a thousand years. Adi Shankara spent his life studying and understanding the positions of his opponents and then systemically defeating them. It is the dharma of the Sringeri Peetham to uphold and adhere to Shankara's model of rigorous scholarship, learning, critical engagement and abiding defence of dharma and the Vedas. It should not be handing over the contemporary understanding of this tradition and its adhikara, wholesale, to those who are not aligned with dharmic principles and who seek to present them as fundamentally flawed.

As I will show in considerable detail in this book, the Vedic traditions are under assault from a school of thought whose fundamental assumptions are dismissive of the sacred dimension. If, out of naivety, we simply hand over the keys to our institutions and allow outsiders to represent our legacy, then any chance of genuine dialogue will be lost. Furthermore, because of the enormous prestige and power of Western universities, an inadequate view of the Sanskrit tradition will become accepted by the public.

This is, then, an epochal moment for Sringeri Peetham and for dharma more broadly. Our institutions and leaders must decide whether they will become intellectual followers whose discourse will be outsourced to Western scholars, or whether they will retain their swaraj and credibility as the authoritative voices for dharma. We cannot allow a return to the days when the East India Company co-opted gullible and opportunistic Indians to serve as its sepoys and used them to gain control over the seats of authority in our society.

Let me be clear that *I do not desire my criticisms in this book to silence those who criticize our tradition*. On the contrary, I hope my opponents will engage my views, and I encourage them to make their positions clearer. This book might perhaps even persuade them to be a little more self-critical about their work and a little more open to dimensions of Hinduism they have dismissed. I am a staunch proponent of intellectual freedom.

I also wish to differentiate between descriptive and prescriptive scholarship. Descriptive writings simply describe how things are, or were, without demanding any change. On the other hand, prescriptive works want to intervene in the state of affairs with a strategy to bring change. The Western scholars I take to task have gone too far in *prescribing* change and are more like political activists representing a foreign world view seeking to dismantle and topple Indian sanskriti in its present form. I wish they would not engage in aggressive campaigns to shift the adhikara from Indian paramparas (lineages) to new Western-headquartered paramparas.

We are at a dangerous pass when it comes to debates on culture, religion and violence in India. Hinduism is being tarred with the brush of caste-based racism of sorts. Those who cherish Sanskrit traditions as a living force often feel that the ground is giving way under their feet. They are thrust into a false opposition between tradition on one side and 'progress' on the other. I reject this dichotomy for I see our tradition as a resource for progress.

One of my main criticisms of a certain group of scholars is that they unabashedly privilege their own left-wing lens as the only legitimate way of viewing our traditions. They drag in Indian politics and sensational acts of violence in order to whip up followers while remaining blind to their own allegiances. They often control the means of knowledge production in their fields to such an extent that the threat to intellectual freedom should be laid at *their* door! They operate in such a way that those who represent insider views of various dharma traditions often cannot even get a proper hearing.

What is at stake?

I want to highlight what is at stake in this battle, which the later chapters will elaborate further. What stands out is that the sacred dimension of Sanskrit is the target of Western Sanskrit studies. Hindus have had a deep connection with Sanskrit at several levels as illustrated below:

1. **Meditation mantras:** The primordial vibrations were discovered by rishis and comprise the fabric and building blocks of Sanskrit. Many of them are used for specific meditation practices. Their importance derives from the large body of evidence accumulated by practitioners over the centuries that they produce effects which ordinary sounds do not. Sanskrit is therefore indispensable for adhyatmika purposes (inner sciences) and the pursuit of embodied knowing.[8]

2. **Yajna mantras:** Many rituals and practices involve Sanskrit mantras chanted with specific intonations and in precise steps. Hindus subscribe to the efficacy of these rituals, and consider the

Sanskrit mantras used therein as non-translatable. By this, I mean they cannot be replaced with synonymous words even in Sanskrit, let alone words of another language that might appear to have a similar meaning.

3. **Discourse in metaphysical domains:** Sanskrit is the medium in which Indian metaphysics (darshana or philosophy) is conceived and transmitted, and thus is part of a long tradition of creative innovations in many intellectual disciplines.
4. **Grammar of the civilization:** Sanskrit's non-translatable categories are the genetic code or the grammar in which the civilization (sanskriti) is expressed. This integral unity of Sanskrit and sanskriti is reflected across such diverse realms as architecture, dance, theatre, sculpture, poetry and so forth. Thus, the structures of Sanskrit are mirrored in several domains as well as in its literature.
5. **Discourse in physical sciences, mathematics, medicine, linguistics, etc.:** The enormous libraries of Sanskrit texts comprise an impressive body of knowledge pertaining to both worldly and transcendental domains. Much of this knowledge has yet to be understood and appreciated by modern society.
6. **Living language for cultural production and ordinary communication:** To this day, *Natya Shastra* continues to be used as a means for teaching dance and music. New kavyas (poetry, literature) and music are constantly being composed. Spoken Sanskrit, which was never destroyed, has actually assumed greater importance of late, thanks to the revival efforts of such organizations as Samskrita Bharati.
7. **Meta-language of Indian vernaculars (Prakrits):** The decentralized and dynamic Sanskrit–Prakrit architecture has formed the foundation of India's unity (Sanskrit's role) and diversity (Prakrit's role) for several millennia. Overall, the formal (Sanskrit) and informal (Prakrit) genres of Indian language have

always coexisted and developed in harmony. There is a reciprocal flow of influence between Sanskrit and the Indian vernacular languages. Compromising Sanskrit's integral connection to the vernaculars makes the vernaculars open to takeover by Western ideologies, which is fast happening already.

In Chapter 2, I will explain the opposing school of Sanskrit studies which I have called 'American Orientalism'.[9] That school dismisses or sidelines some of the above dimensions of Sanskrit, either explicitly or implicitly. It often regards these as antiquated or mystifying, or as mere smokescreens deployed to obscure or justify abusive social, economic and political practices. Hence this particular genre of Orientalists takes the following stances:

- Mantras for meditation and yajnas are pejoratively branded as meaningless 'hymnology' controlled by brahmins for nefarious purposes.
- Some of the structures embedded in Sanskrit and sanskriti are seen as socially oppressive and abusive against Dalits, women and Muslims.
- The shastras on philosophy as well as secular/worldly domains of analytical knowledge are sidelined as unimportant for study, or even labelled as dangerous.
- Spoken Sanskrit is seen as a movement to perpetuate the elitism and social oppression allegedly built into Sanskrit. The Indian government's efforts to revive Sanskrit are criticized as dangerous to the 'downtrodden', whom the Orientalists want to 'save' from the oppressive structures they perceive in Sanskrit.

In effect, it is precisely those qualities that make Sanskrit a priceless legacy for Hindus that the new Orientalists are neutralizing and negating. I show why the reasoning and processes that define their idea of reviving Sanskrit are in effect threatening it as a living language. The table below highlights some of the key battles at stake.

Usage of Sanskrit	View of Insiders	American Orientalism View	Potential Harm by American Orientalism
Mantra for Meditation	Sanskrit mantras used for meditative purposes. Seen as vibrational qualities beyond conceptual meanings.	Sanskrit mantras can be replaced. Their religious undertones reflect oppressive structures. Mantra chanting is hypnotic and maintains hierarchy and abuse.	Destruction of Hindu cosmology's place for vac (vibration). Loss of key adhyatmika (inner sciences) methods.
Mantra for Yajna	Vedic yajnas play important roles and need specific mantras.	Primitive, superstitious, hypnotic and socially abusive.	Loss of traditional rituals.
Metaphysical Discourse	Language for philosophy, logic and support systems.	This discourse is irrational and irrelevant today.	Hindus will become more intellectually dependent on, and subservient to, the West.
Grammar of the Civilization	Sanskrit is the template of Indian culture, such as architecture, dance, theatre, sculpture, poetry, etc.	This contains abusive elements; it originated separately from native cultures and languages; brought by foreign Aryans.	Alienating Indians from their roots.

Usage of Sanskrit	View of Insiders	American Orientalism View	Potential Harm by American Orientalism
Discourse in Sciences and Other Vyavaharika Fields	Natural sciences, mathematics, linguistics, medicine, ethics, political thought, etc.	Not acknowledged. Available for digestion into Western civilization.	Loss of unique intellectual capital embedded in Sanskrit shastras for problem solving. Loss of claim to Indian heritage's contributions, which are reformulated as Western knowledge.
Fresh Cultural Productions and Ordinary Communications	*Natya shastra* for performing arts. New compositions in music, literature and political kavya. Spoken Sanskrit.	This is elitist usage, and a ploy to Sanskritize the masses into accepting a socially abusive system.	Denial of Sanskrit in India will cut off Hindu culture's roots, just like the impact of Persianization and subsequent anglicization.
Meta-language of Indian Vernaculars	Bidirectional flow with vernaculars is due to the decentralized architecture of sanskriti.	Sanskrit was disconnected from vernaculars until the brahmin–king nexus conspired to impregnate vernaculars with abusive structures for exploitation.	'Breaking India' strategy at work to divide Indians and fragment identities.

Assault on Sanskrit goes mainstream

The reader should not think that this book deals with esoteric matters of concern to only a few scholars. Chapter 10 shows that the slanted views of Western Indology have dispersed well beyond academics, and now infect many organs of Indian society. The following point-form summary attests to this:

- Prominent leaders of the USA-based Sanskrit studies movement occupy powerful academic positions, from where they control the editing and annotating of many influential works of Sanskrit. These works are prescribed in universities where Sanskrit and Indian culture are taught.
- Several bright young Indians with elitist positions have already been trained in this approach to Sanskrit studies. These young scholars are deployed in key posts in India and elsewhere. They control many journals, conferences, dissertation committees and other forums that shape the approach to Sanskrit and sanskriti.
- Many institutions have been infiltrated, and new ones have been created by this movement. These scholars have garnered high-profile awards. The prestigious Murty Classical Library, which plans to translate 500 volumes of Indian-language works into English, is an example of the enormous power controlled directly by this group.
- Mainstream media in India and the USA, overawed by this group of prestigious individuals who project themselves as saviours of our heritage, have neither the background nor the courage to ask the pointed questions required. In fact, I find many instances of prominent channels of TV, print and other media being used for the widespread dissemination of their ideas. Such ideas have also permeated the school curricula in several countries.
- Besides the direct impact and dissemination by the outsider group of scholars, the indirect echoing of their ideas by mainstream authors is also on the rise. Many echoing authors are naive and have failed to examine the implications of their support.

- The groups of scholars I am discussing are politically very active. They have supported numerous petitions that attack Hindu institutions and leaders. They also lobby in Indian political circles, exerting influence through the media, and canvass privately as well.

Finally, I want to make it clear that I wish to entertain no acrimony in this disagreement. Nor do I claim to have written an error-free, authoritative analysis of the other side. Rather, I have produced a 'red flag' list of issues that ought to wake up serious Hindu intellectuals and prompt them to investigate these points for themselves. More scholars should enter these debates. Given the very short time frame I had in which to publish this, I am well aware that a great deal more needs to be done. But this book is a new beginning because there has been no similar contestation from the insider perspective on this matter until now.

We need a friendly exchange with the opposing side in order to better understand their positions. The result would be a segmentation of the issues along the following categories. These are not mutually exclusive categories:

1. **Agree to disagree:** These are issues where the other side would *accept* my representation of their position, i.e., it would *agree with* my purva-paksha. In these cases, our mutual disagreements would be based on a proper understanding of each other. They are entitled to their views just as we are to ours. These would become topics for mutually respectful debates in order to balance out the discourse.

2. **My interpretation of their position deemed flawed:** These are issues where the opponents would find my characterization of their views erroneous. In other words, my purva-paksha did not depict them properly, thereby necessitating modifications on my part. The result would be to improve our understanding of the outsider camp's positions. This clarification would be important because their writings are often too convoluted and couched in technical jargon which few traditional Hindu scholars can understand. I

would like to make the outsiders' positions more accessible to the insiders.

3. **Disagreement among Hindus:** These are issues where many Hindus would side with the outsiders. This should generate a healthy internal debate amongst Hindus. The outsiders would have provided us the provocation to make us think harder and, therefore, my book would help Hindus in their self-understanding.

Each of these categories can lead to a fruitful manthana (churning) for the sake of expanding our knowledge with the help of each other. Once such a dialectic is set in motion and managed with integrity and mutual respect, it could open many minds on both sides. I repeat that the stands I take on various issues are primarily for the sake of highlighting the 'red flag' items. I am interested in further deliberations on these complex issues. I also wish to clarify that I do *not* consider all Western scholars as 'outsiders', nor all Indians or Hindus as 'insiders'. These are provisional terms to get the conversation started.

My suggestion to the reader is that s/he should first read the Conclusion chapter that concisely articulates the final takeaway messages of this book. It lists a set of debates I want between the insiders and outsiders on a range of issues raised in this book. After reading the Conclusion, the rest of the book comes into focus more easily.

1

The Hijacking of Sanskrit and Sanskriti

Why this book matters

Sanskrit has been the heartbeat of Indian civilization for several thousand years. It could even be said that sanskriti, the culture that arose from India, has Sanskrit embedded in its DNA. Put another way, Sanskrit provides the vocabulary in which the Indian civilization is encoded. Even those who do not explicitly use Sanskrit often draw upon its knowledge through other means, such as philosophy, bhakti or meditation, or use another Indian language based on Sanskrit structures.

One would think, then, that a major takeover of Sanskrit studies by people whose work tends to discount or undermine a number of its core traditional values would not go unnoticed. Unfortunately, such a takeover has been under way, and the intellectual forces that challenge the traditional view of Sanskrit and sanskriti are winning the battle, not only at the academic level but also among the wider public. The problem is that those who should be defending the traditional point of view against this assault are blissfully unaware of the onslaught and pitiably ill-equipped to deal with it.

This book contrasts two entirely different world views concerning Sanskrit. Its purpose is to articulate the differences between them so as to facilitate debate. Such debates are imperative, and not enough have taken place. But first, we must define the rival 'camps' on either side of the issue and clarify their respective positions. How do we characterize the two sides? The side I oppose consists of those who see Sanskrit as a dead language, worthy of being relegated to a sort of intellectual museum. As self-appointed custodians of this museum, they would 'sanitize' Sanskrit, cleansing it of what they see as its inherent elitism and oppressive cultural and social structures. Once Sanskrit has been 'detoxified' in this manner, its custodians intend to put it on display as an exotic and nostalgic artefact from the past epoch of South and South-east Asia. A very important part of their interpretation is to deny or sideline its sacred dimension and to focus only on its secular usage.

The other side consists of people like me who want to see Sanskrit regain and retain its power as a living language. We want to celebrate it for its enduring sacredness, aesthetic powers, metaphysical acuity and ability to generate knowledge in many domains.

The first camp is led by a new breed of Western scholars of Sanskrit (and their Indian followers) who have seized control at elite institutions of Sanskrit studies. They occupy prominent perches in Indian high society and mainstream media, and have infiltrated many centres of learning.

The second camp includes not only traditional scholars and pandits but also ordinary Hindus who value their cultural heritage and wish to see it studied and promoted as part of their dharma.

For ease of communication, it is helpful to assign names to these two camps. At times I will refer to these camps as 'outsiders' and 'insiders', respectively. I am well aware that this is a simplistic way to characterize them, but it serves as an effective starting point.

- The *outsiders* are mostly westerners and Western-trained Indian scholars who approach our culture from 'without'. The label does not refer to the race or ethnicity of any of these scholars but to the fact that the theories they use were formed in the context of Western history; indeed, these theories are a part of what I have previously termed 'Western Universalism'. As a result, the outsiders' orientation towards Sanskrit prompts them to ignore, even attack, the sacred domain of Sanskrit and sanskriti. At various times in this book, I refer to these outsiders as the 'Western' camp or the 'social sciences' camp or 'non-practitioners' or the 'secular' camp. Each of these is an approximation and not to be taken as some absolute or literal term.

- The *insiders* are those who see the world using the traditional lens through which Sanskrit and its texts have been studied and transmitted for centuries. They see sacredness as a central and integral feature of the tradition, one that brings meaning to the lives of large numbers of people. Sometimes I refer to these insiders as 'traditionalists' or 'practitioners' of Sanskrit-based faiths or the 'sacred' camp.

In academic jargon, the insider perspective about a faith has been called 'emic' and the outsider perspective has been called 'etic'. I am also aware that many scholars are in neither camp and some are in both camps to some extent. However, I will focus on these two poles of the spectrum in order to get some debates off the ground.

Many insiders practise a faith or adopt a perspective in which Sanskrit is foundational. They see Sanskrit as serving a liberating purpose in their lives. The academicians who are outsiders, by contrast, are typically not serious practitioners of a Sanskrit-based faith. Many of them see the Sanskrit-based cultural tradition as too readily lending itself to be used as a tool for the exploitation and oppression of people; hence their approach to it is heavily political. They could easily see claims of Sanskrit's sacredness as a justification for domination by a power elite, taking their cue from Marx's characterization of religion as 'the opium of the masses'. They view most traditionalists today as either ignorant or in collusion with regressive communalist politics.

Unfortunately, many traditionalists live in silos. They tend to dismiss the views of the opposing ideological camp, seeing them as irrelevant to the 'real' tradition. They are unaware of, or indifferent to, the fact that they are the objects of study from the 'outside'. Some of them are so naive and insecure as to feel flattered when representatives of the Western elite show an interest in them. In addition, the scholars using the 'outsider' lens are highly vocal and public in championing their point of view whereas the insiders often prefer to remain private about their allegiances and shy away from defending their tradition even in important forums.

Those who do not practise a Sanskrit-based faith might make the valid claim that Sanskrit has had other uses besides the sacred ones. It would follow that Sanskrit-based faiths should not be considered a definitive, central characteristic of Sanskrit; nor should the practice of such a faith be a qualification for those studying it. Nobody 'owns' Sanskrit and so those who use it for purely secular purposes also have the right to call themselves 'insiders' of a certain kind, if only because they have taken the trouble to learn to appreciate the language and its texts. There is merit in this view. It appears logical and fair.

However, one cannot ignore that a major asymmetry exists between these two types of approaches to Sanskrit. The non-faith/secular users see it as just another language in which one can order a cup of chai, for instance. Hence, if Sanskrit were to vanish from active use, the loss incurred would be of relatively little consequence; after all, plenty of other languages are available for such mundane purposes. In other words, the outsiders are not critical stakeholders and would have little to lose if Sanskrit were to die. A dead Sanskrit, ensconced in a museum, would still be available for academic study, and this would not necessarily affect their world view or lifestyle in a serious way.

On the other hand, those whose faith and entire world view depend on the special place given to Sanskrit have an entirely different kind of stake in this debate. For them, there is no substitute. The very sounds of Sanskrit comprise non-translatable vibrations, which are taken to be the very fabric of reality. The narratives on which their practice is based get their meaning from Vedic principles.

In other words, while the 'secular' camp (i.e., the outsiders) would have little to lose if Sanskrit were to die, the 'sacred' camp stands to lose their foundation.

Admittedly, dichotomies such as 'insider vs outsider' and 'traditional vs Western' are intrinsically fuzzy. Let me make it clear again that while I have used these terms, I do not see such distinctions based on national or ethnic identities. They are merely shorthand ways of indicating different word views. I will provide a sharper and more detailed characterization of the two opposing camps in the next chapter. But for the moment, this vocabulary of differentiation helps get our discussion started.

It is important not to stereotype the camps by exaggerating their positions. In any debate, the opponents tend also to share a few commonalities, and there are always individuals who straddle the fence by adopting some positions from one camp and some from the other. Persons with a foot in each camp include some Western-trained Indian elites, who might seem at first to be 'insiders' to the tradition, but who are profoundly conditioned by Western theories and assumptions. At the same time, many reputable scholars in academia, despite their Western training, do value Sanskrit as a living tradition which transmits sacred truths. Then there are traditional Sanskrit pandits and Hindu practitioners who also share concerns with the outsiders about social hierarchies and injustices and actively work to address them. However, despite the existence of these crossover cases, the secular position still remains dominant in the academic discourse, as this book will demonstrate.

I do not come at this project from a neutral point of view. I am a Hindu practitioner, an 'insider', so to speak, who values Sanskrit and its culture, in particular its philosophical gravitas, capacity for self-critique and its role as the substratum of our sanskriti. I believe that scholars representing the traditional view deserve a seat at the table when its future is being discussed. In other words, I defend Sanskrit not as a language of the past, allegedly tainted by a notorious association with social oppression, but as a vital and living medium with immense potential for fostering justice and liberation.

I have also been immersed in Western culture for decades, studied its social sciences and academic culture, and I have engaged with the rising concern about the troubling direction Sanskrit studies have taken in the West. This book faces an uphill battle. The academicians I critique rule the day and, in my view, tend to see Sanskrit as a vehicle of political domination. Their camp is grounded in the Western academic study of Sanskrit, and their views have spread widely among leading Indian universities, media, intellectuals and wealthy patrons. They have also won over several traditional Sanskrit scholars and institutions. The Indian government has showered them with prestigious awards. They enjoy a huge advantage of resource asymmetry over the proponents of the tradition. They are disseminating their discourse into mainstream society through a variety of channels.

The Sanskrit traditionalists are more dispersed and less well resourced. They are for the most part practitioners of various forms of Hinduism and they tend to cluster in 'like-minded' groups where they feel safe with one another. Unfortunately, many of them are ignorant of the battle that is being waged overtly as well as covertly, and hence they are unwittingly complicit. I sent drafts and overviews of this book to some persons who I felt would be supportive, only to discover that several of them vehemently opposed the very idea of investigating this new elitist school of Sanskrit studies. Their general attitude is that we should instead be grateful to those westerners who are 'taking the time to study us'.

A lot of traditional scholars are oblivious to the fact that their 'adhikara' (authority) as experts on Sanskrit is being systematically eroded. Many outsiders have appointed themselves as new authorities for the interpretation of Sanskrit traditions. Their tentacles penetrate deep, not only into the psyche of young scholars but also into several traditional and modern institutions. This book is meant, in part, to serve as a wake-up call for insiders, to force them out of their slumber and isolation.

Many of those I refer to as outsiders will claim that *they* are the real defenders of Sanskrit, while people like me are chauvinists who are hijacking the tradition for political ends. Indeed, the outsider camp will commonly charge their opponents with chauvinism as a ploy to drag in the straw dogs of communalism and identity politics. I do not accept their premise that my commitment to my Hindu tradition is intrinsically oppressive to others. Of course, the tradition should be subject to critical analysis, with all voices represented, but the domination of such discourse by the outsider voice is counterproductive.

Highlighting the disputes between the two intellectual camps

The following is a partial list of some of the major issues that differentiate insiders and outsiders. The list aims to clarify the positions of these camps.

Sanskrit and the realm of the sacred

Scholars wearing the Western lens regard support for the sacredness of Sanskrit as a smokescreen for elitist and oppressive views. They reject the 'paramarthika' aspects of the tradition (those dealing with transcendence/sacredness) as being primitive and abusive. They ascribe greater priority to the 'vyavaharika' texts (those concerning worldly activities and which deal with secular and mundane matters such as politics and the arts).

Traditionalists, of course, consider the sacredness to be built into Sanskrit and attach great significance to its paramarthika aspects. They feel that paramarthika and vyavaharika cannot be decoupled as together they comprise an integral unity. They note that vyavaharika elements have enriched the daily lives of ordinary people by providing ways of accessing the paramarthika realm. For instance, Hindu dance (such as Bharatanatyam), puja and meditation are worldly activities that can serve as pathways to transcendence.

Sanskrit and social oppression

The social sciences camp of Sanskrit studies asserts that the Vedas and the Sanskrit language are inherently hierarchical and oppressive, citing built-in mandates that restrict their use to the brahmin elite.[1] They sometimes refer to this phenomenon using terms such as: 'toxicity', 'barbarism', 'social abuse', 'oppression', 'poison' and so forth. I shall cite examples of the use of such terms, and I shall use them interchangeably to convey the general sense of accusation with which they approach Sanskrit's deep structures, including its grammar and texts. Despite the efforts from within the Indian tradition to introduce changes that address such concerns, these structures are seen as being entrenched in the tradition. Therefore, the outsiders argue, Sanskrit needs to be thoroughly purged of its Vedic assumptions and structures.

Traditionalists disagree with this depiction of Vedic heritage and with the sweeping allegations against Sanskrit. They see the language and its legacy as unique tools for liberation available to all humans. Although insiders are also critical of social oppression, they do not see Sanskrit as being its vehicle, nor do they believe that Sanskrit culture requires the kind of wholesale revision and purgation that the Western scholars prescribe.

Sanskrit and the oral tradition

The scholars I criticize base their analysis primarily on written texts. They dismiss oral traditions as unreliable and unfathomable sources. Indeed, they actively disparage the oral tradition as a brahmin conspiracy to monopolize higher learning and as a ploy to conceal knowledge. This camp claims that writing came to India only as a result of the Buddhist intervention to end the monopoly of brahmins.

The traditional camp sees orality as a primary mode of transmission. Orality was indeed a higher form of language than writing for some purposes. In fact, Sanskrit mantras are understood as corresponding to vibrations (far subtler than the outward sounds) serving as keys to higher states of consciousness. Writing, being an external form and practice, is intrinsically less subtle than the inner vibrational form of the language. As a result, traditionalists consider the use of Sanskrit prior to the written form as important. They want the revival of Sanskrit to include the oral tradition.

Sanskrit and the vernaculars

The current fashionable view in the West is that Sanskrit was brought to India by foreigners called Aryans, and that these Aryans imposed

Sanskrit upon the indigenous population. Consequently, it is believed that Sanskrit lacks a common origin with Indian vernaculars. According to this view, there has always been tension between Sanskrit and the vernaculars for power and prestige. Moreover, the flow of influence is claimed always to have been primarily one-way: from Sanskrit to the vernaculars. The spread of Sanskrit across Asia is claimed to have been driven by the need of kings and brahmins to deploy it for the political purpose of controlling the public.

The subsequent resurgence of vernaculars, according to this model, was also due to royal patronage. By the twelfth century, before the Turkish invasions, the Indian kings had decided that vernaculars were a better vehicle for domination and for warding off threats from the populace to overturn their oppressive policies. It was for this reason that Sanskrit 'died', i.e., it perished because it lost its elitist support, which was the only reason for its existence in the public square. Part 2 of Pollock's book *Language of the Gods...* is a detailed argument on this. I summarize Pollock's thesis in Chapter 7. Also, the whole theory of 'aestheticization of power' explained in Chapter 6 was designed by Pollock to systematically argue this very point.

Traditionalists, by contrast, believe Sanskrit originated organically within India itself and is not the result of any foreign conquest. Furthermore, its relationship with the vernaculars has, in their view, always been bidirectional and reciprocal in terms of influence. The spread of Sanskrit and sanskriti, the culture, was not just a matter of top-down patronage but also of bottom-up demand, due to its effectiveness in bringing meaning to people's lives.

Sanskrit genres of shastra and kavya

Sanskrit texts encompass a variety of genres, among which are 'shastra' and 'kavya'. Shastras are texts of knowledge systems across a vast range of disciplines – medicine, mathematics, philosophy, chemistry, architecture, farming and so forth. Kavyas, on the other hand, are literary and artistic texts, including works of poetry and drama, as well as epics and folklore. Shastras arise out of, and are deeply intertwined with, the metaphysics of the Vedas. Kavyas are less formal and hence more accessible at the popular level.

Unfortunately, many current proponents of secularized Sanskrit argue that shastras are little more than repositories of knowledge that were extrapolated from the Vedas and hence constrained by the perceived limitations of their source. Since they must perforce comply with what secularists see as a primitive (and abusive) Vedic cosmology, they lack creative freedom. This outsider view says that shastras cannot produce real progress, because people lost in the shastra realm lack agency to create 'history' as it is defined by the West. Since shastras are derived from Vedic metaphysics, they must be regarded as unscientific and tainted with the same backwardness as is found in the Vedas. Many Western-trained scholars explicitly sideline the shastras and espouse a selective focus on kavya for their Sanskrit studies. Although the kavya genre is also seen as tainted with Vedic structures, it is the product of at least some degree of creative freedom. This argument is advanced to justify interpretations based on their favourite themes: social oppression and resistance to that oppression.

Traditionalists treat these two genres as symbiotic and not mutually exclusive. In fact, many kavyas describe the same knowledge as the shastras do but in a poetic form, and many shastras systematically analyse the content of the kavyas. One should not, according to traditionalists, eliminate the shastras; they contain precious knowledge pertaining to many disciplines, and a case can be made for their relevance today in diverse fields. Indian poeticians have unequivocally declared that the Vedas, the Puranas, itihasas and kavyas have a common and single aim although their modes are different. The Vedas are seen like kings' (prabhu) utterances, the Puranas are like friends' (mitra) utterances, and kavyas are like the utterances of a beloved wife (kanta).[2] But their message is similar.

The impact of Sanskrit on Europe

The camp that this book critiques holds that European Indologists adopted Vedic ideas of social hierarchy and oppression and introduced these into Europe during the colonial era. They claim it was Sanskrit that supplied Europeans with support and inspiration for their racist biases.

Later on, German Indologists learned from Sanskrit texts supportive rationales for violence against those who were different and deemed 'inferior'. These Sanskrit structures of discrimination were introduced into Nazi thinking and helped them develop their policy of holocaust against the Jews. I deal with this in Chapter 4. Pollock's famous paper 'Deep Orientalism', which I cite, makes this point. In fact, Grunendahl's rebuttal cited is on this point.

In response to this view of the outsiders, the insiders note that European Indologists had brought with them their own past conditioning, laden with racism and prejudice against those who were seen as different, and that they often misread and misinterpreted Sanskrit texts. They submit that the blame for their inherent bigotry should not be projected onto Sanskrit. One must also mention the numerous benefits Europeans have derived from the study of Sanskrit texts – benefits which they initially acknowledged but which later got digested and appropriated into their own historical narrative.

Ramayana interpretation

One of the leading initiatives of the outsider camp is to interpret the literature of Sanskrit as encoding socially abusive attitudes and ideas. For instance, a prominent exponent of the outsider perspective, Sheldon Pollock, has done extensive work on the Ramayana. He considers it a code in which 'proto-communalist relations could be activated and theocratic legitimation could be rendered'; the Ramayana, for such a scholar, is the 'mytheme par excellence' whose impact is to promote 'reactionary politics'.[3] He argues that the divinization of kings in the Ramayana grants them the moral authority to surpass all social rules and limits, which in turn empowers them to commit atrocities. His translation is considered an important reference in the West and among English-speaking Indian scholars. The section titled 'The divinization construct' in Chapter 5 explains this.

Furthermore, he alleges that in the Ramayana, Ravana and the rakshasas are cast in the role of dangerous 'others' and that this portrayal has instilled among Hindus a tendency towards bigotry that was later projected on to Muslims in order to stir up violence against them. According to this view, the combination of divinizing the king and demonizing the 'others' offers tacit justification for rabble-rousing violence against Muslims today. Pollock's team thus alleges that hatred towards outsiders is built into the Ramayana.

Traditionalists disagree and see the Ramayana and the Mahabharata as sacred texts of a sacred past, as holding great appeal for all audiences and peoples, and as encoding ethical messages for positive living even today. They do not see them as endorsements of violence or as 'othering' any class or race. Any powerful text can be misused in ways that were not originally intended, as Pollock himself acknowledges on rare occasions. This caveat is often forgotten in the currently fashionable scholarly literature on the important texts of Hinduism, especially by those who call themselves the Indian left.

Divisiveness within Indian society

The Western-trained camp employs social science theories to identify and accentuate differences between various kinds of Indians. Besides 'caste conflict', a favourite theme is to exaggerate the contrast between Buddhist and Vedic world views. Scholars of this camp often claim that the rise of Buddhism forced Sanskrit to come down from its pedestal into the 'world of men'; the idea was to make it more open and less oppressive, although with mixed results. They also depict sanskriti as having been tainted throughout by the male oppression of women.

Traditionalists recognize the existence of tensions but see them as residing within a broader continuum that has also included harmony and reciprocity. Most importantly, traditionalists believe that sufficient resources exist within the tradition to address such issues. They disagree that the tradition is fundamentally flawed or that Western intervention is necessary for its repair.

The revival of Sanskrit

Western-trained scholars habitually congratulate themselves for championing the 'revival' of Sanskrit. But what do they mean by 'revival' and how are they pursuing it? What they are in fact advocating is an academic project in which Sanskrit is systematically cleansed of its supposed taints of hierarchy, social oppression and elitism. In practice, they advocate erasing its sacred principles. Such a 'detoxified' Sanskrit is to be presented in the medium of English, on the terms dictated by these scholars and through the channels they control: the westernized academia, the museum, the publications and outlets of learned societies, and the occasional cultural showcase. In the meantime, efforts by Indians to promote Sanskrit as a spoken language are being ridiculed. Pollock's *Tehelka* interview is an example.

When these outsiders use the term 'classical language' to refer to Sanskrit, the tacit analogy they proffer is with dead Western languages of high culture, namely Latin and ancient Greek. When Western scholars study old languages using linguistic, philosophical and social theories, they construct an understanding of those ancient civilizations that is consonant with their Eurocentric world view. To take Sheldon Pollock's work again as an example, he deploys a 'tool' he calls 'liberation philology' to liberate Sanskrit from its supposed shackles of oppressiveness. His chosen term is in fact a reference to a movement called 'liberation theology': a Christian (primarily Roman Catholic) movement of the 1960s and 1970s that sought to purge Christianity of socially regressive thought and deploy the analytical tools of Marxism to advance social justice.[4] Pollock – a child of that era – seeks to position himself as the champion of those he claims were the victims of exploitation by 'classical' Sanskrit.

Traditionalists have an entirely different interest in the study of Sanskrit and yet they are unfortunately ignorant of the other camp's hidden agenda for 'reviving' Sanskrit. Traditionalists advocate the revival of Sanskrit as a living force, one which does indeed originate in antiquity but nonetheless is adaptive, useful and appropriate to the communication and development of new bodies of knowledge today. Sanskrit is both old and new, and the traditionalists perceive these qualities as belonging within a single continuum without any contradiction. I propose a status for Sanskrit equivalent to that of Mandarin, Arabic and Persian today; these are ancient languages with established continuity of usage and value in the present.

Furthermore, Sanskrit in the traditional view is best studied using methods compatible with its function as a sacred language. These methods do not exclude its important and established role in worldly (secular) affairs. Traditionalists are not in general averse to the critical study of Sanskrit or to using tools of philology and history for this purpose. However, they do not approach it *exclusively* through the lens of politics; rather, they see it *also* in the context of dharmic practice and spiritual realization.

I also feel that westerners should not do the 'revival' of Sanskrit on our behalf, but that we must do it ourselves. Of course all the help we can get should be welcomed, but it must be under our control, and the hub of such activities must reside in India within our traditional institutions. It would be dangerous to outsource the revival of Sanskrit to westerners for a number of reasons. For one thing, it would further increase our dependence on outsiders to 'take care of us' as though we are children looking for foster-parents. This parent–child relationship was called the 'civilizing mission' and the colonialists used it as their rationale for governing India.

One must note that when the British first arrived in India they did not do so as colonizers, and that many of them were very friendly at an individual level, and were favourably inclined towards Indians' best interests: the proverbial 'good cops'. However, their personal success in 'helping' Indians also had the effect of empowering the British system, including its imperialistic power structure. Once in place, this system assumed different colours in its long stay in India, and numerous 'bad cops' came to power because the foundation already established by the preceding 'good cops' allowed them to do so. (The notion of 'good cops' and 'bad cops' is further explained in the next chapter.)

If Indians were to do this revival of Sanskrit themselves, it would help create a broad cultural ecosystem within the country that would grow enduring roots over time. This would empower a much larger number of scholars in the long run, and it would be integrated with civic society in a variety of ways. Rather than sending our bright youth to places like Columbia and Harvard to study Sanskrit, it would be far better (and more cost-efficient) to establish world-class Sanskrit studies in

India. The best centres for the research and study of Mandarin, Arabic and Persian are in their respective homelands, and are integrated with their societies. If India can host world-class institutions for fields like information technology, why can it not achieve the same in Sanskrit and sanskriti studies?

I am reminded of Reverend C.F. Andrews, a great friend and supporter of Mohandas Gandhi's struggle against British rule. He lived in India for many decades as part of the freedom struggle and Gandhi respected him for his infallible loyalty to India's cause. However, Gandhi eventually requested Andrews to go back to England. Why? Because Gandhi felt that in order to be effective and sustainable, India's freedom must be won by Indians themselves. The satyagraha ought to be a process of inner transformation. I feel the same way about decolonizing the studies of Sanskrit and sanskriti: we must develop self-sufficiency in these within India, and *then* export our own version to the rest of the world.

Where is the home team?

Every tradition faces similar challenges from time to time, and its adherents must consider how to maintain its viability in new epochs. On the whole, this is a healthy process. A tipping point, however, comes when opponents begin to dominate the discourse so overwhelmingly that the defenders of the tradition simply capitulate. Sanskrit studies are facing this risk right now.

In order to ensure Sanskrit's survival so that it may flourish anew, traditionalists need to assemble what I have called a 'home team' to represent their views and restore balance. The 'home team' would consist of those who work towards seeing Sanskrit flourish as a living language, and also as a pathway into the transcendent realms of experience (and the knowledge systems based on them).

We have excellent intellectual resources for mounting such a team. In terms of methodology, we have the traditional practices of purva-paksha (examining the opponent's position) and uttara-paksha (developing a response). These practices go back many millennia and were used by the great debaters of our tradition. They demand taking the time to appreciate an opposing position, to understand it as much as possible from within the opponent's world view, and then to develop a response rooted in one's own world view. Unfortunately, nobody has undertaken to do this with respect to the current dominant school of Sanskrit studies, not even to the preliminary extent that I have attempted in this book.

Therefore, such a home team is nowhere to be seen. Some of the troubling questions are as follows: Why have no traditional scholars conducted such an exercise during all the decades in which the view of Western social science has been developed and promoted, and why are none doing so even now when that view has achieved widespread acceptance and endorsement? My conversations with traditional pandits reveal that they have only a superficial awareness of what Western social science scholars and their Indian leftist collaborators have been up to. Indeed many traditionalists aren't even aware that the opposition exists! Whereas the outsiders have been honing and refining their views for decades, the traditionalists have barely begun to recognize the problem they face. The outsiders are sophisticated, well funded and able to draw from centuries' worth of prior Western experience in managing similar inter-civilizational encounters.

The traditional Sanskrit scholars are, for the most part, completely unprepared to tackle such issues. The Western social sciences and philological positions are articulated in heavy, complex and sometimes jargon-ridden English. Their matrix lies in theories that traditionally educated Indians have rarely heard of. These theories are based on Western historical experiences that Indians know about only vaguely (if at all), and from a distance. Such theories originated in response to the crisis of modernism in Europe in the twentieth century: a catastrophic internal collapse of values that led in turn to predatory capitalism and fascism. The social sciences have drawn on literary and cultural theories that were developed to analyse this crisis. However, these are now being applied to India in a blanket fashion, at times with no regard for the differences in historical context between India and the West.

Those few traditional scholars who want a seat at the table of international Sanskrit studies would first have to spend years studying complex Western theories. By then, however, they might become so immersed in the perspectives of Western thought as to have forgotten or discarded their traditional methods of understanding. The Western camp presents a mountain of information, all analysed in terms of its own world views and with purposes that traditionalists find strange and antithetical to their interests. It is natural for traditional Indian scholars to be overwhelmed and baulk at evaluating such a huge and systematic body of work. I was disappointed that an internationally renowned Indian expert in Sanskrit drew a complete blank when I asked him basic questions regarding a prominent Western Indologist's major work. He had no clue about such details but was in awe of the Indologist, based solely on his 'reputation'.

The traditional scholars prefer to pursue the studies using the methods that evolved over the centuries, rather than grapple with the new-fangled Western methods. Among other things, they really do not consider work based on these Western theories to constitute useful or genuine knowledge. After all, they reason, the West is not bothered about Sanskrit itself but is concerned only with the political and social dimensions of its history. What, they ask, is the point of studying such things at all? It is but a waste of time, for the ultimate purpose of studying Sanskrit is only to learn what the tradition itself was intended to teach. This attitude has led many traditionalists into self-isolation.

As this book will show, the secular camp has definitely infiltrated the apparatus of formal Sanskrit studies worldwide. Its exponents control many of the important international conferences on Sanskrit, the prestigious chairs of research activity, the best-paid academic jobs, the availability of grants for research work and so forth. In other words, they influence the means of knowledge production. As a result, many scholars who would be qualified to carry out due diligence regarding the Western school of Sanskrit studies are enmeshed in a conflict of interest that prevents them from performing such controversial work. Some of the important traditional scholars have been co-opted by Western Indology. There are those who dance between conflicting postures depending on the audience they are facing at a given time.

Many top Indian scholars of Sanskrit enjoy Western – most notably American – patronage in one form or another. Their careers are often underwritten by American largesse. They are frequently invited to places like Columbia and Harvard universities which brings them more prestige back home in India. The support increases their brand value among peers and boosts their careers. Consequently they become even more loyal to their Western sponsors and are less prone to question them. It is difficult to expect such individuals to involve themselves in the formation of such a home team as I have described. Some have given me leads and pointers to help with my own work but often under the condition of anonymity.

Worse still, many traditional Indian scholars have told me they actively *support* the work of the outsiders, who they say have done yeoman service to our tradition, whereas, according to them, the insiders have neglected to work in this area. Some traditional scholars of this variety are simply bowled over by the fact that a few white men and women have learned enough Sanskrit to read out slokas in public, and feel flattered by the praise such westerners routinely lavish on the beauty of the language. These individuals tend to close ranks with the Americans. They accept the Americanized discourse because it is seen as more sophisticated.

This raises the question: What about those modern (and westernized) Hindus who *are* concerned about these issues and who *do* have the English language skills and Western education to grapple with this work? They know postmodernism theory, are familiar with European and American secularist and leftist critical thought, and can read densely written English materials. Their difficulties, I find, are the opposite of those our traditional scholars face: They lack even a rudimentary understanding of the Sanskrit tradition, metaphysics and cosmology it would take to respond to the theoretical sophistication of the other side. As a result, these potential defenders of a traditional point of view cannot adjudicate what the Western-trained scholars write. They are also sometimes shamed by the fact that others know so much more about their tradition than they themselves do. Hence they turn to anyone who appears to give them English-language access to this tradition: something they have been denied by the Indian education system.

Frequently, these westernized Hindus are simply unaware that India even possessed such a distinguished Sanskrit tradition until some Western-trained specialist happens to mention it. The new discourse falls on their ears like a revelation, fascinating them because it charts the unknown territory of their own history. A number of modern Hindus also feel that Western-trained scholars, whatever their flaws and limitations, will 'package' Sanskrit thought in such a way as to make it presentable in international forums: something traditional pandits have not been able to do. The process of re-packaging our tradition for worldwide acceptance instils pride.

Unfortunately, such well-meaning supporters of the tradition fail to see that Sanskrit thought becomes seriously compromised in the process. In most cases, they cannot even evaluate what is being delivered. They have a shallow understanding of the real treasures of Sanskrit and sanskriti, and they cultivate an aura of sophistication by joining the chorus of support for Western interpretations.

One must acknowledge that the Western Sanskrit studies camp has cultivated a highly skilled ability to be poetic in their popular lectures and interviews, using careful words of praise. For instance, they often praise kavya as valuable but often remain silent on shastra/knowledge; acclaim Sanskrit's revival but do not extend this to spoken Sanskrit; celebrate vyavaharika texts while omitting mention of paramarthika texts.

While the traditionalists are sensitive to instances of blatant attack, they fail to 'read between the lines' when the subversion is subtle or when the insinuation is by omission. Often they miss the nuances in the discourse, hence they cannot see through the fine rhetoric employed by the outsider camp.

Although the Sanskrit tradition has met with many challenges in the past, the situation now is more dangerous than ever. For the first time, American scholars of Sanskrit have co-opted Indian billionaires, received Indian government awards and endorsements and become the darlings of the mainstream Indian media elite. In effect, the outsiders have infiltrated some of the most sacred, established and renowned traditional Sanskrit centres of learning.

In sum, few today are engaged in responding to the outsiders. Those who have the necessary knowledge do not wish to object. Those who understand the problem and wish to object are ill-equipped with the required knowledge.

Offering my humble attempts

This book is my modest effort at applying the principles of purva-paksha and uttara-paksha. I have studied the principal writings of a few prominent Western Indologists and attempted to understand their assumptions, evidence, detailed arguments and conclusions. I have tried to present a reasonable first approximation with simplicity and clarity. Just as Western scholars use 'native informants' in India to help them decode Indian culture and gain deeper insights, so also I could be seen as a sort of 'native informant' in the reverse direction who is explaining American thought and culture to Indian traditional intellectuals at a deeper level than they can easily access on their own. My main contribution has been to crystallize some perspectives and working definitions. I point out the red flags which can help Indian scholars distil the discourse and take it forward. I also offer rebuttals in several instances, at times giving the worst case view of an opponent just to challenge the traditional scholars to take note of it.

My goal is to present in a way that is simple enough to be understood by my target readers. It has been no easy task to read a few thousand pages of complex writings, to identify the issues that are relevant for my project, to summarize and synopsize these in order to make them accessible to non-experts in Western theories, and to attempt to remain as true and authentic as possible. I have used my discretion to decide where to place emphasis and to interpret through a lens that practising Hindus can relate to.

Western scholars claim the licence to reinterpret Indian texts on the basis of the well-known postmodern notion that 'the author is dead'. This means that the reader supplies his or her own context and lens through which to interpret; whatever the original author might have intended to express is unimportant to adhere to and might not be relevant in the reader's context. I claim the same prerogative: to superimpose my own interpretative lens on Western scholarship. I do not claim that mine is 'the' universal way to see things, but my work serves its purpose as long as enough traditional scholars benefit.

I consider my interpretation a starting point only. There are many shortcomings in my purva-paksha and uttara-paksha that arise from my own limitations. In the time available for writing this book, I could read only a subset of Pollock's vast corpus of work. My conclusions might have to be counterbalanced by his other writings where he often takes stands that differ from the ones I have read. I must give him this benefit of doubt. However, my principal objective is to raise awareness about the need to engage in this debate. My purpose will have been achieved as soon as a critical mass of responses from the traditional side begins to appear. In essence, I want to inspire the beginnings of a home team.

2

From European Orientalism to American Orientalism

In the previous chapter, I described two camps with distinctly different approaches to the study of Sanskrit: that of 'insiders', for whom it is a highly valued, living tradition, and that of 'outsiders', for whom it is largely a dead language encoding oppression and mystification. In this chapter, I first provide some historical background for the evolution of the outsider approach to Sanskrit and sanskriti. I will then introduce its chief academic champion, whose work will be the focus of the remaining chapters.

I use the term 'American Orientalists' to refer to an important group of scholars with their base in the USA who pursue Sanskrit studies through a secular lens. This lens uses social sciences, postmodernist thought and philology and largely excludes the sacred dimension. I refer to their lens as 'American Orientalism'; through it they filter out certain features of Sanskrit and sanskriti, while sometimes exaggerating certain other features. The fundamental assumptions and theories shaping this lens are axiomatic for its proponents, and yet the implications have not been examined adequately. My reference to 'American' in this genre of Orientalism will become clear later in this chapter as I explain how American history played a role in shaping it.

Once again, I wish to clarify that this lens is not the only outsider lens. I am well aware of the diversity of views from outside the tradition, but for this project, I have selected this view as the target of my critique; towards the end of this book it will become clear why this particular lens deserves to be studied. I also wish to make it clear that I do not consider every American scholar to be in this camp: it is not about ethnicity but about a certain focussed viewpoint that I will describe.

Origins of Orientalism

The term 'Orientalism' was formally introduced by Edward Said in 1978 to describe the European lens through which non-European cultures were analysed and depicted during the colonial era.[1] His thesis can be summarized as follows:

- Colonial powers compartmentalized East and West as categories divided by rigid distinctions. Orientalism is 'the way that the West perceives – and thereby defines – the East'.[2]
- To contrive and enforce such distinctions, Orientalists constructed a positive identity for themselves based on the idea of 'Western values' and juxtaposed stereotypes of non-westerners against this.
- They justified such distinctions by using theories that were considered as scientific truths. Inherent in the process of domination is the need by the dominant culture to rationalize its domination.

The term 'Orientalism' as used in South Asian studies refers to the construction of a languid and passive India from the Western perspective. Orientalism was intimately related to colonialism and one may think of it as an intellectual cousin of colonialism.

The Orientalist view of India is not always an overtly negative one. Often, it appears 'positive' and romantic. However, being founded on an implicit sense of the West's superiority, it is nonetheless projected with a patronizing attitude. Indians are conceptualized as 'children' whom Europeans must 'raise' so that they become civilized adults in the European sense. Indian culture is often treated as a patient needing to be 'cured' by Western intellectuals, who in turn feel proud to act as doctors. Many Orientalist studies have been framed in terms of westerners helping Indians in need.[3] Rudyard Kipling, whose writings won him the Nobel Prize for literature, captured this Orientalist image of India perfectly when he poked fun at his fellow English for taking the view that 'India, as everyone knows, is divided equally between jungle, tigers, cobras, cholera, and sepoys.'[4]

Both Indian and Western scholars have extensively criticized the European approaches towards India that prevailed during the colonial era. This genre of criticism is at the heart of the academic field called 'post-colonial studies'. One of its aims is to point out many kinds of biases in European Indology, the Western academic field that studies Indian civilization and culture. And yet, despite their rigorous criticism of colonialism and the Orientalist thinking it spawned, post-colonial scholars still largely limit themselves to regurgitating a standard list of charges against the now-dead British Empire. I consider it important to extend post-colonial studies into the present American era.

In this chapter, I will trace the historical context of Orientalism in the following three stages:

A. **European Orientalism:** First, I will explain the rise of European Orientalism in the context of the European colonization of India.

B. **American frontier view:** Next, I will discuss the experiences that the Europeans had in America after the so-called 'discovery' of America by Christopher Columbus in 1492. 'A' and 'B' will be explained as separate and parallel phenomena at first.

C. **American Orientalism (today):** Bringing these two experiences together, I will propose my insight that, after the Second World

War, the USA assumed the mantle of leading the West and that this has resulted in the rise of what I call American Orientalism.

The diagram below shows these three lenses.

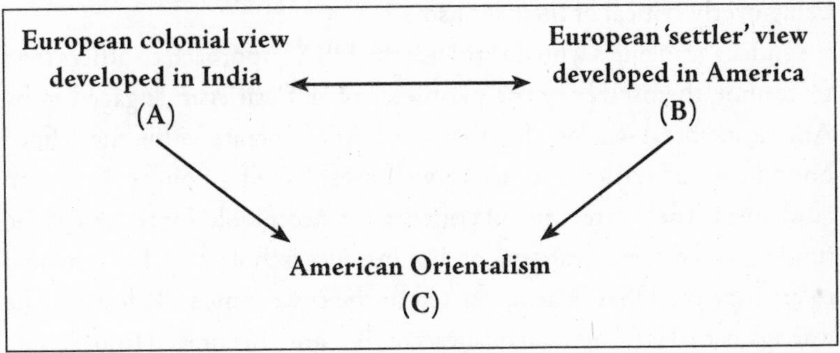

The first two kinds of Orientalisms (in India and America, respectively) emerged in parallel and were different from each other due to the nature of the encounters that shaped them. In the seventeenth century, at about the same time as the East India Company was founded to engage India (A), the first English settlements in America began to consolidate. The English encounters with the Native Americans and subsequently also with African slaves shaped the European views of non-Europeans (B).[5] Each successive encounter the Europeans had with the outside world further refined these lenses. Considering the parallel progression of European encounters (in America and India, respectively), it becomes clear that the colonial lens used in India was a refinement derived from colonial lenses being used elsewhere. Many of the intellectual mechanisms the colonizers used in India had already been tried and tested in America, Africa and Ireland.

The end of the colonial era did not end the use of Orientalist lenses by Western scholars. The new kind of Orientalism (i.e., American Orientalism) was born and it must be studied as a phenomenon by itself. The USA's intellectual institutions are highly influential in shaping opinions across the world. Many post-colonial scholars wrongly assume that their sweeping critiques of European Orientalism apply to the USA in general terms, without much need for specific adjustment in the

American context. Hence, they do not see any need to analyse American attitudes towards Indian civilization separately. There is also a political sensibility at work here. Most post-colonial scholars, who now owe their funding and careers to American institutions, find it prudent to avoid being overly critical of their sponsors.

Indian academics who do criticize the USA's approach to others tend to confine themselves to the perimeter of self-criticism engaged in by American liberal scholars. In other words, they operate within the defined boundaries of criticism that are well-established amongst American academics. These categories of criticism are 'acceptable' for those seeking funding and career advancement. For instance, scholars are freely invited to criticize the USA in areas related to the environment, Palestine, 'the war against Islam', social inequality, etc., but are discouraged from raising issues specific to the American posture on Hinduism. Indians serving the American intellectual establishment are often unconsciously aware of the ideological boundaries they must respect.

It is time the biases of American scholars towards Indian civilization were reviewed separately from the critiques of European Orientalism. It is true that all westerners share a great deal in common with each other. However, this is an oversimplification, and it is important to appreciate the differences between European and American views of various non-white peoples. My reason for using the term 'American Orientalism' is to highlight the new kind of Orientalist lens through which Americans see India, which is distinct from the earlier lens of European Orientalism.

To begin this discussion, I will explain the historical background and lens of European Orientalism. Then I will do the same for the American frontier lens. Subsequently, I will show how these merged into what is now American Orientalism. I will conclude this chapter by introducing Sheldon Pollock as the leading protagonist of the genre of American Orientalism.

The rise of European Orientalism

The modern European experience of India began with the arrival of the Portuguese in the late 1400s. This incursion triggered an avalanche of

European encounters with India involving trade, conquest, evangelism and, at times, various forms of cultural genocide.

The British East India Company was formed in London in 1600. After engaging in trade with the subcontinent for over a century, it began making forays into the political realm. Soon it had established a solid power base that continued to expand with the takeover of one Indian kingdom after another.

Even as they purported to respect the culture of India, many British intellectuals rationalized the East India Company's governance of India as a grand mission to civilize her primitive peoples and rescue them from the deficiencies of their own culture. Their real motive, of course, was to expropriate wealth on a scale unprecedented in world history. Alongside and often in support of these mercantile interests, Christian missionaries compiled massive records documenting the allegedly oppressive and abusive nature of the Hindu tradition. What resulted was a system of colonial power, administered by what could be seen as a collusion of British men who were the equivalents of vaishyas (businessmen), kshatriyas (rulers) and brahmins (intellectuals).

Sir William Jones, the European Orientalist

The British pioneer who is widely credited for having launched the genre of Orientalism focussing on India was Sir William Jones (1746–94), the great eighteenth-century Orientalist. A marble frieze located in the chapel of University College, Oxford, reproduced on the cover of this book, shows him sitting on a chair, writing at a desk while three learned pandits are seated at his feet, wearing traditional clothing. Two are gazing down, and one is looking upward as if a bit lost. The inscription below hails Jones as the man who 'formed a digest of Hindu and Mohammedan Laws'.

Contrary to what the sculpture suggests, it was Sir William Jones who 'sat at the feet' (if not literally, at least in the sense of being the pupil) of learned pandits in India for a few years to study Sanskrit grammar, poetics, logic, metaphysics and jurisprudence. He wrote letters home about how fascinating and yet how complex and daunting it was for him to learn these Sanskrit materials. Interestingly, the pandits knew their texts by heart and did not need notes or printed texts! This has been explained in Franklin (2011) which I have relied upon greatly.

As a result of this brief immersion, Jones declared himself the 'Justinian of India', modelling himself after the famous emperor who had codified Roman law. The truth is that he translated and interpreted into English only a tiny tip of the massive iceberg of ancient Indian literature. Yet the monument conveys the impression of Jones as 'law-giver' and the pandits as 'native informants' supplying him with raw data and taking instructions from his teachings.

The profound asymmetry of epistemic prestige in any East–West exchange of knowledge represented by this monument continues to this day; only now, it is the Western Indologists who play the role of the 'giver of human rights'. Columbia and Harvard have replaced Oxford as the central sites for Sanskrit studies.

Sir William Jones accumulated a large number of prestigious awards and honours from the British monarchy, Oxford University and the East India Company where he was employed. He founded the first society of Orientalist scholars, and his work launched brand new fields of inquiry in the West. He is considered one of the pioneers in the field of philology. His complete works were published in thirteen volumes and covered a wide range of topics.

Under the auspices of the British East India Company, Jones was appointed judge of the Supreme Court in Bengal. He was also asked to address such questions as: Who are the Indians and what is their place in history and the world today? How do they relate to the British ruling over them? How should the British govern them? Jones's arrival in India as the first great scholar working for the Company suddenly made such a project feasible.

Warren Hastings, the governor of Bengal from 1772 to 1785, who appointed William Jones, felt that British policies in India should be made to appear consistent with Indian traditions as that would legitimize colonialism. Indians would be told that they were being governed by their own laws. This became one of the motivations for the study of Sanskrit texts; the agenda was to claim to have 'discovered' the laws by which Hindus ought to be governed.

Jones's Oxford friend, Nathaniel Brassey Halhed, had earlier compiled *The Code of Gentoo Laws* in 1776. This was the first British-sponsored compilation of a legal treatise claiming to be based on Sanskrit texts. Although it received an enthusiastic reception in Britain, it has been heavily criticized by Indians. Madhu Kishwar explains the problems:

> In order to arrive at a definitive version of the Indian legal system that would mainly be useful for them, the East India Company began to recruit and train pandits for its own service. In 1772, Warren Hastings hired a group of eleven pandits to cooperate with the Company in the creation of a new digest of Hindu law that would govern civil disputes in the British courts. The Sanskrit pandits hired to translate and sanction this new interpretation of customary laws created a curious Anglo-Brahmanical hybrid. The resulting document, printed in London under the title, *A Code of Gentoo Laws, or, Ordinations of the Pandits,* was a made-to-order text, in which the pandits dutifully followed the demands made by their paymasters. Though it was the first serious attempt at codification of Hindu law, the text was far from accurate in its references to the original sources, or to their varied traditional interpretations.[6]

This so-called book of Hindu law was a mishmash of ideas compiled by a group of pandits from an assortment of texts. The pandits were hired by the British to serve as native informants. It failed to achieve its purpose. Therefore, Jones decided that he would personally translate the large *Manusmriti* text.

Jones also had a personal dilemma that he wanted to resolve by developing a book of Hindu laws. A major contradiction in his life was that on one hand he actively supported the American revolt against British imperial rule, and yet on the other, he was a key functionary in helping the British rule over Indians. Michael Franklin, in his biography of William Jones, has noted this duplicity: 'How does a lawyer who values liberty above all end up as part of a global machine of world subjugation?' Jones argued: 'I shall certainly not preach democracy to the Indians, who must and will be governed by absolute power.'[7] In Britain, then, he was a radical intellectual championing liberty and freedom of his fellow whites in America whereas in India he supported despotic British rule.

Franklin says that to deal with this contradiction, Jones maintained that British India was ruled by a peculiarly British despotism modelled upon enlightened Mughal governance.[8] His work tried to make it seem that British rule in India was in accordance with traditional Indian laws. The British were merely continuing the laws that had earlier existed in India.

Jones embarked on a serious project to master Sanskrit rapidly and use it for this purpose. He started his study in 1785 at Krishnanagar, near the University of Nadia, arguably the most distinguished centre of Sanskrit learning in Bengal at that time. He lived in a bungalow on a riverbank, and the local maharaja helped him find a pandit. The teacher, though not a brahmin, imposed upon Jones the strict purification rules applicable to a student of Sanskrit. He ensured the lessons were held in a separate room, specially tiled with white marble and ritually cleansed with Ganga water. Jones respected his teacher and appreciated the place he stayed for his studies. In less than a year, Jones declared his knowledge of *Manusmriti* was sufficient for him to arbitrate in legal disputes.[9]

Warren Hastings claimed that he had established a political and cultural 'system' for producing knowledge of India, the goals of which were to reconcile Indians with their imperial masters, 'free the inhabitants of this country from the reproach of ignorance and barbarism' and absolve the British colonial employees from accusations of 'moral turpitude'.[10] Thus began an entire era of studying India with the purpose of codifying it for the West. This study would make India understandable in the West's frameworks and help the British govern and control it.

The impulse to systematically categorize everything Indian resulted in oversimplification, reductionism and even caricature. Jones and his followers hastily drew conclusions that were often based on flawed data. The 'idea of India' that emerged in the European imagination was a sort of mummification of a vast subcontinent.

Another reason for his work on Sanskrit texts was that, unlike Islam, Hinduism was older than Judaism and did not easily fit into the time frame of the Bible. This posed a threat to the established Western notions of the origins of civilizations, and the origin, for that matter, even of the world. Jones set about to find a solution that would be consonant with both Europeans and Indians. He decided to interpret Hinduism to make it fit into the main Biblical requirements.

He translated and interpreted numerous Sanskrit texts, and wrote an original theory of world history showing how the ancient Hindus were located in the race scheme as described in the Bible's book of Genesis. His interest in the ethnology of the jatis (mistranslated as castes) also started with the desire to understand the relationship between Indians and the races mentioned in the Bible.[11] His entire project was intended to defend the Bible by showing that the Hindu texts fitted into the Mosaic account of the history of ancient people. Jones wanted to prove that Sanskrit literature was a distant echo of the events of early history as recorded by Moses.[12]

As has been mentioned in Franklin (2011) and Trautmann (2004), which I summarize here, as also dealt with in my book *Breaking India*, Jones also explored Vishnu's ten avatars using Biblical equivalents and found ways to accommodate certain floods mentioned in Indian texts with the Biblical flood. He rejected those Hindu elements that did not conform to the Bible, one example being his dismissal of the theory of the yugas and kalpas on the grounds that these Indian time cycles are in terms of millions of years whereas Biblical time is extremely short by comparison. He analysed many Puranas, always with the intention of showing how they validated Biblical geography and history. Puranas, he felt, belonged to the pre-Christian pagan era of humankind. Whatever portions of Indian texts failed to dovetail into the Biblical framework were dismissed as myths, and what did fit was magnified and accepted as history.

In this manner, Jones seized every possible opportunity to boost his interpretation of Hindu ethnology with the goal of demonstrating that Hindu scripture fortified Christian truths, and he used this as evidence against those Europeans who were sceptical of Christianity. Hence, Sanskrit became useful for defending Christianity against its critics back home in Europe. The ancient wisdom found in Sanskrit texts was given great respect in the context of humanity's shared heritage, and selectively appropriated and used as evidence to argue in favour of

Christianity. India was thus digested into the Biblical world view and given a favourable place in it.

Jones also saw Hinduism as the living cousin of the religions of the ancient Greeks and Romans, and tried to force a relationship between the pagan divinities of Greece and Rome and those of Hinduism. His ambition was to digest the knowledge of Sanskrit texts for the Western world's consumption. He saw Sanskrit as a civilized European language surpassing Latin and Greek in its grammatical sophistication.

Jones assumed the role of convincing Europe that in ancient times India had achieved an advanced culture, but that it had subsequently declined (just as ancient Greece and Rome had). Like these, however, it still had some valuable elements left. He thus presented Europeans with the enormous challenge of dealing with a dark-skinned people who had an ancient and 'exquisitely refined' civilization. This contradicted European thinking about their own superior place in the history of the world. Jones influenced British imperialism by encouraging at least some semblance of respect for its Indian subjects.[13]

The impact of his work was huge because it influenced other scholars long after his death. For European intellectuals of the next few generations, he articulated with clarity and authority a world view that seemed compelling and unlike any other available at the time. Indeed, he was the architect who laid the foundations for the field of Western Indology and Orientalism. He launched a century of romanticized narratives with a positive spin on a fantasized 'Orientalized' India, and is rightfully considered one of the foremost pioneers of Orientalism. European universities especially in Britain, Germany and France entered the gold rush of Sanskrit studies, initiating what has been called the 'oriental renaissance' of European intellectual history. His sympathy with Indian thought is noteworthy, and he broke ranks with his English contemporaries who showed blatant contempt towards Indians.[14]

Jones always ensured that the new admiration for Hinduism he was promoting would reinforce Christianity and not undermine it. There was no doubt in his mind that Christianity was the only true religion, and that Europe since the times of the ancient Greeks had surpassed India in rationality and refinement. In science, Asians were 'mere children'.[15] He and the Orientalists that followed would at times even modify Hinduism to protect it in Christian eyes. For example, because Hinduism has sacred images which are very offensive to Christians, the Orientalists theorized that these images were later additions by brahmins, and not a part of the original essence of Hinduism which was compliant with monotheism.

In effect, Jones and the Orientalists that followed him were domesticating Hinduism, making it safe for Europeans to accept a modified version of it with some degree of respect.

Both the European intellectual camps (those romanticizing Indian culture and those denouncing it) studied Sanskrit texts and interpreted them according to their respective needs. The anti-Hindu camp was represented by the evangelicals and the utilitarians whose chief architects were men like Charles Grant and James Mill. Both camps typically agreed on the superiority of European civilization to that of the Indian, and both had profound influences on the future course of Indology. Jones's work was later cited by scholars (for example, Max Müeller's well-known theory of Aryan invasion) to prove that Indian civilization had arrived from 'foreign Aryans', and has become the standard history of Indology.

These debates were not limited to India or Hinduism, but were part of much bigger debates concerning competing European ideologies and theories about their own ancient histories. Sanskrit and its texts provided valuable fodder for these intellectual battles among Europeans. Franklin writes that Jones and his colleagues were 'appropriating Sanskrit culture just as efficiently as Robert Clive and his generation had appropriated Indian wealth'.[16]

The American frontier

In order to understand what is different about the American Orientalist lens (as compared to the European Orientalist lens), we need to discuss the unique experience of what became known as the 'American Frontier'. This was an intense, prolonged experience that has no parallel in the history of any other modern nation; one that ended up shaping the American mindset in a way that makes it fundamentally different from that of Europeans.

Despite many shared aeons of prior history, the past few centuries have produced an American culture that is very different from those that exist in Europe. For that matter, the various European peoples – English, Irish, Dutch, Germans, French and so on – all have histories and cultural experiences that differ from one another. There certainly exists a definite locus that we can refer to as the 'West', which is distinct from the 'non-West', and it is sometimes quite appropriate to use these categories as they are commonly understood. However, for our present purpose, it is important to make further distinctions within the category of the 'West' itself.

Modern European nations, unlike their American counterpart, were formed without having to dislocate any natives from their lands. But white settlers arriving in America had to evict the natives of the soil in what turned out to be a prolonged and violent affair. Likewise, their enslavement and persecution of Africans left an indelible stain on the American psyche. Hardly any other modern nation has undergone such trauma at the very heart of its formation as a sovereign country. These cataclysmic encounters – with both Native Americans and African Americans – scarred the collective American consciousness.

As the USA expanded further by invading Latin America, the Caribbean, numerous Pacific islands such as the Philippines, and other countries farther afield, each successive encounter with the 'other' proved unique, and each has left its own signature imprint upon the American mindset. Many legends of American heroism were born, taught in schools, and presented in mainstream works of literature and entertainment, becoming reinforced in their mythic status with each passing generation.

It is pointless to debate whether the American kind or the European kind of encounter was worse in terms of the effect on the people who were destroyed. Comparative moral judgements are hard to make. What we must note here is that the scars and collective memories left in the American subconscious are *distinct from* those held in the psychological basement of Europeans.

Some historians have characterized the history of America since the seventeenth century in terms of the images of 'us' and 'them' developed by the first European settlers who came to the New World. The identity and sense of selfhood of these settlers were continuously defined and redefined in contrast with the non-Europeans whom they dominated. Indeed, we can follow this historical process by tracing the evolving terminology by which the white Americans designated themselves:

- At first, the Europeans called themselves 'English' and the Native Americans were known as 'Indians'. The early literature uses these terms as normative.
- Soon, however, European settlements in America also had new immigrants from Germany, France, Holland and other non-English countries in Europe. Hence, the term for selfhood was changed to 'Christians', and the Native Americans were referred to as 'heathens'.
- Over time, the Christian missionaries were successful in converting many Native Americans, who could no longer be branded as heathens. By this point, African slaves were being imported in large numbers to operate the lucrative plantations that funded American prosperity. These slaves were labelled 'blacks'. In contrast, Americans of European descent began to refer to themselves as 'whites'. Many laws of this era referred to blacks and whites as normative categories, as did the popular literature.
- Later on, when it became politically incorrect to use terms like 'black' and 'white', it was claimed that 'race science' had located the origin of all European peoples in the Caucasus Mountains near Turkey. Henceforth, the term 'Caucasian' replaced 'white' in the US immigration laws and popular culture. This term continues to persist, despite the fact that the Aryan invasion theory, on which the notion of 'Caucasian' origin is based, now lies thoroughly discredited. Only very recently has the term 'European American' been adopted in its place, although it remains common even now to refer to people of European origin as Caucasians.

Throughout the period from 1600 to 1900, American literature referred to territories captured by white Americans as 'settlements'; these areas were considered 'civilized'. The boundary between these settlements and the lands that had not yet been claimed as part of civilization was referred to as 'the frontier'. The zone beyond 'the frontier' was seen as a dangerous place where many kinds of 'savages' lived (who were, ironically, the true natives of the land). The territory was also highly precious to capture. However, only brave men with frontier expertise and courage could venture into it. Such men were referred to as 'frontiersmen', and their heroic representations are an iconic part of the imagery of the Wild West. They were masculine, tough, rugged, intelligent and had mastered survival skills in dangerous circumstances.

The frontier also symbolized an alluring, exotic locale. It was full of astonishing landscapes, animals, cultures and opportunities that differed hugely from anything in Europe. Frontiersmen who returned to their settlements after embarking on adventures often became legends, and their stories were turned into the folklore of the frontier.

I have written extensively on the frontier as America's defining myth, and on the broader implications of this perspective for the way India is being seen. The ideas I present are well established in American history and have been discussed by numerous scholars. The reader is referred to my writings for details; I provide a brief summary of the key features below.[17]

According to historians of the frontier myth, the frontiersmen were sometimes conceived as 'good cops' or 'bad cops'. The first group represented those who were overtly friendly towards the Native Americans; the second comprised those who fought them openly. Both kinds of frontiersmen were important in capturing and 'taming' the frontier so that it could be incorporated into the white settlements.

The good cops made friends with the natives and even lived amongst them, at times marrying into their tribes and adopting their languages and customs. They reported their discoveries to the white settlements, providing valuable information about the frontier, just as the English anthropologists were reporting back home in England about their explorations of India. Good cop frontiersmen sometimes went forth as missionaries to convert the heathen natives. At times they even fought on the side of the natives against the whites, both militarily and to help negotiate 'peace treaties'. The ultimate test of a good cop was his ability to win the trust of the natives, and the extent to which he could gain acceptance as one of them.

The bad cops ventured to openly annihilate or subjugate the natives, either alone or in small groups, and later in large armies. Their images and narratives of the frontier characterized native culture as oppressive, unjust and primitive. The good cops also perceived negative qualities in the natives, but their accounts tended to romanticize the same.

Ultimately, both the good cops and the bad cops served the long-term interests of white expansionism. The former often managed to make the natives pliable and vulnerable, that is, more trusting and accommodating of the whites. At times, they would outright dupe the natives. It was not unusual for a good cop to capitulate eventually to the bad cop's pressure, claiming that he could not help the natives any further, or that the 'deal' being offered by the bad cop was the best available, and hence should be accepted. This 'frontier thesis' is standard in writings of American history. The multiple volumes by the historian Richard Slotkin explain this in detail.

Besides this 'external' frontier populated with natives, there was the 'internal' frontier of African slavery. The external frontier with the natives was a geographical space outside the boundaries of the white settlement, while the internal one was defined by a different sort of boundary – it comprised a locale where enslaved African-Americans lived within the perimeter of the settlement. Americans, over the past few centuries, have incorporated both the external and the internal frontiers into their collective psyche.

American literature is filled with many images of frontier 'savages' who are classified as either 'dangerous' or 'noble'. The former refers to those who must be dealt with using physical violence; which is to say they must be killed, enslaved or otherwise oppressed. The latter are portrayed as cute, exotic and are even romanticized, but ultimately there is no doubt as to their inferiority. Those savages who revolted were dangerous while those who collaborated were noble. The goal was to destroy the dangerous ones while assimilating and co-opting the noble ones.

Atrocity literature and American Orientalism

'Atrocity literature' is a term coined by cultural historians to refer to a certain kind of myth-making about the frontier. It is a form of propaganda based on exaggerating the dangers emanating from the stereotypical 'savage' and promotes fables of the frontier's strangeness and exotica. In my view, American Orientalism, at many points, both draws on and fosters this kind of literature about India.

Atrocity literature has the following characteristics:

- Its core consists of myth-making geared towards portraying the other side as 'dangerous savages', particularly if they were seen as a threat to 'innocent' white folks.
- It often applies the image of the 'savage' to those deemed 'idol worshippers', 'primitive', 'lacking in morals and ethics', 'prone to violence' and so forth. The trio – lack of aesthetics, lack of morality and lack of rationality – became a construct that is found frequently in this literature.
- Its narratives about dangerous non-westerners were formulated and repeatedly used to incite support for violence against the 'savages'. The whites were expected to respond harshly to the 'savages' whenever conflicts erupted, and pre-emptive strikes initiated by whites were generally justified as reasonable measures.
- It often stereotypes 'savage' culture as being oppressive towards its own women, children and lower social strata (those described as 'subaltern' groups in modern academic discourse); hence, the violent civilizing mission by white Americans is represented as a humanitarian endeavour in the larger interest of 'savage' societies.

This kind of atrocity literature became a popular genre which gave intellectual sustenance to the doctrine of America's 'manifest destiny': the destiny of a chosen people sanctioned by the Bible to receive dominion over the earth. In turn, manifest destiny fed more expansionism and reciprocally increased the demand for such supportive literature.

The atrocity literature genre thrives on half-truths, on selectively choosing facts and observations bereft of context, and stitching them together into a narrative that plays on the reader's psychology and preconceived stereotypes. Such literature seeks to foster a sense of heightened urgency in dealing with what it defines as 'savagery'. The 'other' culture in question may or may not have committed all the alleged atrocities ascribed to it in any given situation. The truth, in all probability, was never as one-sided as atrocity literature portrays it, with typical exaggeration and sensationalization of carefully curated facts. In the American case, whites were spared all the blame for their massacres and enslavement of non-whites, and their aggression against the latter was held to be just and unavoidable.

The imagery used at the time suggested that the Biblical Eden (the white people's space) was under threat of violation by evil savages from the frontier. Once this idea had been established in the popular mind, atrocity literature served the purpose of justifying the harsh subjugation of peoples beyond the frontier because it had been accepted that they did not deserve to be treated like civilized human beings. In many instances, this led to large-scale violence.

Images drawn from atrocity literature were not only commonplace in popular literature, theatre, and later American cinema, but were also officially codified in American laws. The frontier vocabulary of atrocity literature was used openly in discussions in the US Senate and Congress. There was no compunction about using such terms as 'savage' to refer to non-westerners.

In the twentieth century, African-Americans began to strongly protest against these sorts of depictions and stereotypes of themselves. Many Latin American/Hispanic scholars are now doing the same in an effort to correct various horrible images of their cultures and ancestors. For instance, in many schools and towns across America, Christopher Columbus is no longer celebrated as a hero, and the genocides his expedition precipitated against the natives stand exposed. Columbus Day, though an official holiday of the Federal government, is not commemorated in many places in the USA because of the new awareness of Columbus as a major abuser of human rights. Likewise, the Japanese (and recently the Chinese as well) have fought back against the racist depictions they once suffered in American literature and popular culture.

Scholars from India, however, have unfortunately become complicit in fostering atrocity literature directed against their own civilization. They have not adequately objected to the common Western images of India as a place of rape, ritual sacrifice, immolation of widows and ruthless exploitation of Dalits and others. They prefer to evade such depictions and wilfully ignore that such literature is used to justify American interventions. Some Indian scholars even actively join in this American Orientalist attack against Indian civilization. Many of them suffer from a complex and a tendency towards opportunism; others are motivated by high idealism and a justifiable desire to correct the injustices and abuses which do occur in Indian society (as in all societies, including Western ones).

The rise of American Orientalism

In the foregoing pages, I have discussed two separate historical events that have merged to form what I call American Orientalism. The diagram used earlier in this chapter shows them as 'A' and 'B', respectively. The rise of American Orientalism ('C') was fed by the USA's ambitions for international expansion after the Second World War; the USA replaced Europe, particularly Britain, as the new superpower. From the mid-twentieth century onwards, American evangelical, political and academic interests converged to develop an image and a narrative that would justify interfering with and demanding subservience from other countries, including India. This narrative is made up, in part, of atrocity stories of the kind I have discussed. The convergence of interests underpinning this narrative has a colonial past; the constructs created in the colonial era continue to be leveraged as a source of poignant images and frameworks for studying India. The power of such frameworks has become highly amplified and their leverage in international power politics has increased considerably.

To make matters worse, the image of India projected by American Orientalism is now being propagated, and even strengthened, by many of the English-speaking elite within India. This large-scale appropriation of Indians is a recent American innovation; the British Orientalists did not allow as large a number of Indians to occupy top positions in their intellectual apparatus as the Americans have.

Some American scholars have, no doubt, reflected critically on this stereotyping of India. Below are three significant samples of such self-reflection:

> The social sciences used in India today have developed from thought about Western rather than Indian cultural realities ... All social sciences develop from thought about what is known to particular cultures and are thus 'cultural' or 'ethno-' social sciences in their origins. All are initially parochial in scope. Since thought originating outside of Europe and America has not yet been recognized or developed as 'social science', the world has thus far had to manage with ethnosocial sciences of only one limited, Western type. (Marriott)[18]

> India seen as a mirror image of the West appears otherworldly, fatalistic, unequalitarian and corporate. It is as though we would be less ourselves, less this-worldly, masterful, egalitarian and individualistic if Indians were less what they are. (Rudolph)[19]

> American selves, operating largely within the categories of sexuality, race, and illness, projected onto Indian Others traits that seemed loathsome or illicit: Indians were, among other things, unsanitary, disorderly, promiscuous, and primitive. (Rotter)[20]

The following is a remark from the late L.M. Singhvi, a prominent Indian intellectual who fought hard against such scholarship:

> My anguish is that many Indologists of Indian origin dignified colonial Indology by their own endorsements in the name of objectivity and out of misplaced deference for the colonial masters and mentors. There was thus an array of antagonists and protagonists who made Indology look like the battlefield of Kurukshetra with only a few on the side of India who desisted from denouncing and denigrating India and its past. The battle continues even now on home ground by homegrown warriors, many of whom won and acquired their scholarly spurs and genes from their colonial mindset in the West. Even after the advent of freedom, official Indologists have remained prisoners of the colonial past which

in my opinion has only a bleak future. On one side of the battle array we find the Eurocentric regiments including many Indian foot soldiers; on the other side of the battle array we find a few friendly European scholars as well as a small number of Indians, often anguished but nevertheless edifying and eloquent, with some of them unduly diffident and apologetic.[21]

American Orientalism appropriates the Indian left

After Independence, Indian Marxists working under Soviet patronage internalized the Marxist discourse and used it to reinterpret Indian history along the framework of class warfare. They depicted upper-caste Hindus as the exploiters, while low-caste Hindus, women, Muslims and other minorities were depicted as the exploited. A watershed event occurred when the Soviet Union collapsed. Starting in the early 1990s, the Indian left suddenly found itself without a grand patron. At this point, the USA decided to appropriate various kinds of intellectual assets from within the former Soviet camp – both to prevent them from falling into the wrong hands in future, and to reap the benefits of using them for the USA's own purposes.

Just as nuclear scientists from the former Soviet Union were recruited by the CIA to work in the US or other Western countries, India's leftists too were appropriated by such agencies as the Ford Foundation to serve the American academies in the humanities. These were well-educated, articulate and often self-alienated Indians, available for hire as mercenaries. Beginning in the 1990s, the US universities became a major destination for Indians of this persuasion.[22]

This was also the time when the field of post-colonial studies, recently launched by the publication of Edward Said's *Orientalism*, began to gain ground. Grants were plentiful in this new academic field. The genre of post-colonial scholarship not only channelled many bright young Indians towards ultimately serving American interests, but also served to assuage Western guilt over past colonial oppression, becoming the 'brown' equivalent of Black Studies in America.

As enterprising Indian scholars quickly learned, a sure path to rapid advancement in this field was to produce research demonstrating that exploitation was built into Indian society. Using tools they had been taught in the West, such scholars generated reams of socio-political analyses fundamentally geared towards framing some Indians as having been the exploiters of other Indians throughout history. Their construction of Indian society as inherently exploitative was naturally useful to the Western patrons, insofar as it diverted attention away from Western exploitation around the world.

Indians in post-colonial studies were indeed encouraged to criticize the old empire of Britain, as well as Indian society itself; yet, implicit in the very term 'post-colonial' is the idea that Western colonialism was a problem of the past. On the other hand, the critiques of India made by these scholars foster the perception of an ingrained Indian tradition that has continued to perpetuate social injustices in the present. Gradually, the blame for social problems has shifted from colonialism to India's own sanskriti.

Each time new theories, largely based on social sciences, were developed by the academic left in the West, they were imported and mimicked by the Indian left for the study of Indian society's internal exploitations. This occurred during the era when Indian intellectuals such as Romila Thapar and Irfan Habib rose to prominence in India, while in parallel, West-based Indian intellectuals, including Dipesh Chakrabarty, Partha Chatterjee, Homi Bhabha and Gayatri Spivak, garnered acclaim overseas.

The social sciences approach to India has since become dominated by an offshoot of post-colonial studies known as 'subaltern' studies. The scholars claiming to speak for India's voiceless people describe themselves as subalternists. Their commonly stated mission is to champion the local and the indigenous in a manner that is often reminiscent of the 'good cops' of the American frontier. This may be seen as the Indianization of atrocity literature as a genre.

What is most important to note is that this lens does not see Sanskrit and Hinduism in a positive light as resources for the natives of India. Nor does it recognize the history of India's oppression under foreign Islamic, Christian and Marxist elements. Instead, it reverses the picture and presents Sanskrit and Hinduism themselves as the prime causes of oppression against the poor and dispossessed among Indians.

Who, then, are the 'real' natives of India? According to subalternists, they consist of Dalits, women, Muslims and other marginalized communities who have allegedly been oppressed by Hinduism. It is proclaimed that such groups need urgent help from activist scholars. Indeed, the very reason they are described as subaltern is that they supposedly do not have a voice of their own, providing a justification for activist scholars to ventriloquize their voice and champion their rights. The scholarly discourse purveyed by the subalternists emphasizes salvaging the cultural authenticity of the subalterns from the clutches of Sanskrit and sanskriti hegemony.

However, when trying to represent themselves as authoritative critics of traditional Indian society, Indian leftists faced one major roadblock: they lacked adequate knowledge of Sanskrit and sanskriti. This made them vulnerable to the charge that their research was based on colonial Indologists' biased interpretations. Traditional Indian scholars could easily point out the numerous errors that arose from their distorted understanding of traditional texts. This proved a serious handicap for Indian leftists when confronting their Hindu opponents. Over the past few decades, this gap has been filled by a group of politically charged American Sanskrit scholars with Marxist commitments. They have successfully fused their Sanskrit capabilities into the leftist lens on India. This fusion is at the heart of the American Orientalism phenomenon. It is important to note that this systematic study of Sanskrit is not being driven by any kind of shraddha in the traditional sense.[23] Rather, it is driven by a political agenda as the later chapters of this book will explain.

The scope of American Orientalism is vast and covers many kinds of approaches to India. This book centres only on one important subset: the American Orientalist approach to the study of Sanskrit and sanskriti. I focus on their project of wanting to detoxify Sanskrit's alleged oppression of others, for which a popular term of very recent coinage is the 'de-saffronization' of Indian culture in the broadest sense.

The diagram that follows depicts the historical background of the rise of American Orientalism which I have summarized already.

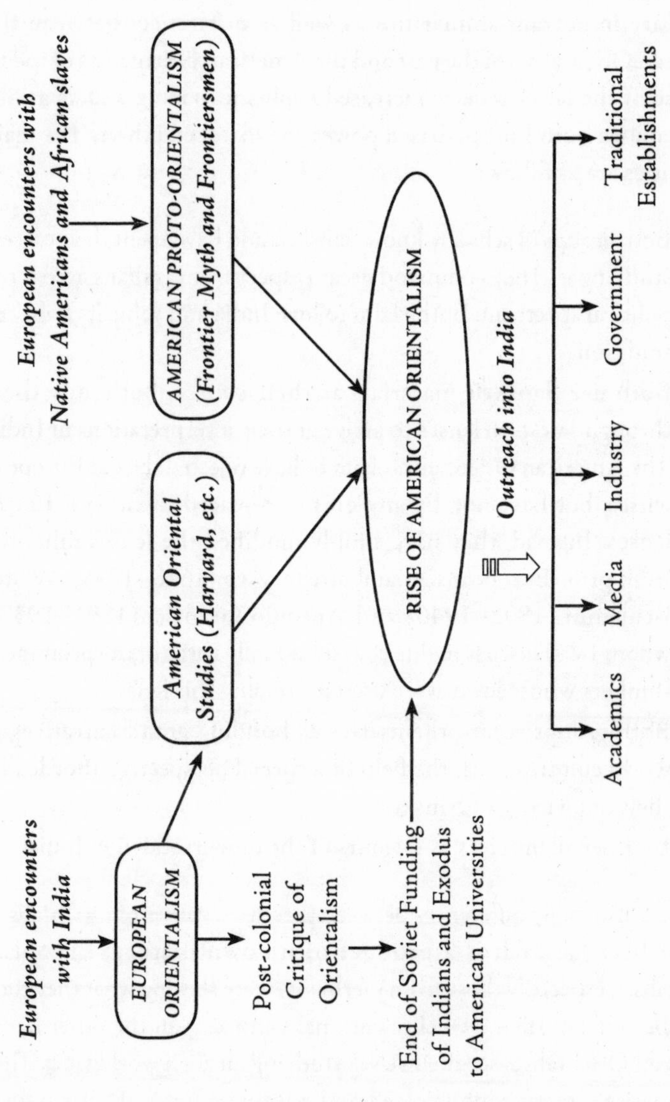
European encounters with India
EUROPEAN ORIENTALISM
Post-colonial Critique of Orientalism
End of Soviet Funding of Indians and Exodus to American Universities
American Oriental Studies (Harvard, etc.)
European encounters with Native Americans and African slaves
AMERICAN PROTO-ORIENTALISM (*Frontier Myth and Frontiersmen*)
RISE OF AMERICAN ORIENTALISM
Outreach into India
Academics
Media
Industry
Government
Traditional Establishments

Comparing European Orientalism and American Orientalism

There are important similarities as well as differences between the European Orientalists of the past and the American Orientalists of today. The rise of the latter reflects increased sophistication as well as a shift in geopolitics from Europe-based power to US-based power. The main similarities are as follow:

1. Both groups of scholars know Sanskrit and have spent their careers studying it. They command great respect from Indians across the political spectrum. Both claim to love India and value its Sanskrit tradition.
2. Both use Sanskrit materials as their source, but study them through Western lenses to arrive at their interpretations of India. The American Orientalists claim to have rejected the old European lenses, but have not, by any means, replaced them with Indian lenses. Instead, they have simply modified the lenses inherited from prior Europeans. Giambattista Vico (1668–1744), Walter Benjamin (1892–1940) and Antonio Gramsci (1891–1937), whom I will discuss in due course, are only three of the prominent thinkers whose ideas were used in shaping this lens.
3. Both groups regard themselves as building grand narratives of world cultures, with the help of a special perspective afforded by their knowledge of Sanskrit.
4. Both see themselves as saviours of the downtrodden in India.

There are also many differences between these two genres of Orientalism, in part because each is a product of its own history. European Orientalists, especially those from Germany, were seeking what they took to be the roots of their *own* elite national cultures. On the other hand, American Orientalists see themselves studying an alien world view. They also practise a more sophisticated and advanced form of Orientalism than their European predecessors. Below is a table that highlights these contrasts.

European Orientalists	American Orientalists
Views shaped by encounters with Asians, largely Indians.	Views previously shaped by encounters with Native Americans and African-Americans.
Linked to the colonial enterprise; clearly branded as 'outsiders' to India.	Decoupled from European colonialism and imperialism, although funded by American capitalism and global cultural hegemony. Skilfully camouflaged as 'insiders' in the minds of many Indians.
Did not have large numbers of Indians trained by them in their team as scholars.	Many Indians under their tutelage and patronage are involved as scholars.
Had limited access to original Sanskrit texts.	Have far greater access to Sanskrit texts.
Did not get support from wealthy Indians or traditional Hindu centres of learning.	In close alliance with some Indian billionaires and supported in traditional centres.

Impact of American Orientalism on the study of Sanskrit

In Chapter 1, I described the differences between the perspectives of Indian traditional scholars and American Orientalists, referring to them as 'insiders' and 'outsiders', respectively. The table that follows summarizes these differences. It explains how both camps claim to champion Sanskrit even though their ultimate goals are diametrically opposite. In fact, each side accuses the other of hijacking Sanskrit.

Sanskrit Traditionalists	American Orientalists
Sanskrit is sacred and central to the tradition, spiritual practice and world view of scholars.	Sanskrit is beautiful as a language but not necessarily central to the scholar's world view or spiritual practice.
Sanskrit viewed from a traditional perspective using theories from within Sanskrit itself.	Sanskrit viewed from a Western social sciences perspective wearing 'secular' lenses.
Sanskrit seen as a great asset for humanity at large.	Sanskrit seen as also being oppressive for many large communities, most notably Dalits, Muslims and women.
Revival of Sanskrit should be multifaceted, as: (1) a spoken language, (2) a medium for rituals and meditation (paramarthika), (3) a vehicle for producing new knowledge relevant to the everyday material realm (i.e., shastras for use in vyavaharika) and (4) a living repository of oral and written kavya that bridges paramarthika (sacred) and vyavaharika (worldly).	Sanskrit should be embalmed as a dead language within the confines of academic studies. The goal of its ongoing study, by modern scholars trained in Western theories, should be to 'exhume' and exorcise the 'barbarism' of social 'hierarchies' and 'oppression' of women embedded within it since its beginning.

The diagram that follows shows the impact American Orientalism has had on the study of Sanskrit.

- The four boxes at the top are historical causes that have led to the rise of American Orientalism.
- The eight boxes that result from American Orientalism indicate the consequences of this important new genre. These points will be discussed in later chapters.

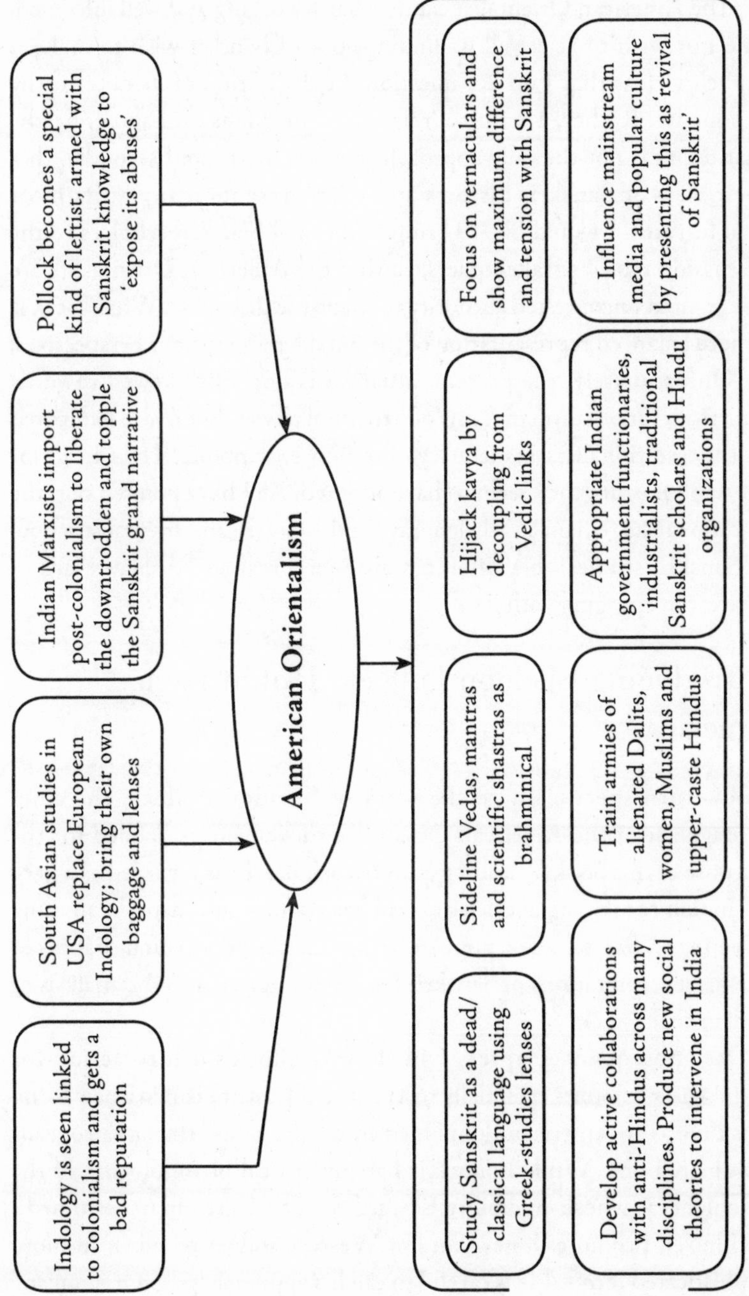
Indology is seen linked to colonialism and gets a bad reputation
South Asian studies in USA replace European Indology; bring their own baggage and lenses
Indian Marxists import post-colonialism to liberate the downtrodden and topple the Sanskrit grand narrative
Pollock becomes a special kind of leftist, armed with Sanskrit knowledge to 'expose its abuses'
American Orientalism
Study Sanskrit as a dead/classical language using Greek-studies lenses
Sideline Vedas, mantras and scientific shastras as brahminical
Hijack kavya by decoupling from Vedic links
Focus on vernaculars and show maximum difference and tension with Sanskrit
Develop active collaborations with anti-Hindus across many disciplines. Produce new social theories to intervene in India
Train armies of alienated Dalits, women, Muslims and upper-caste Hindus
Appropriate Indian government functionaries, industrialists, traditional Sanskrit scholars and Hindu organizations
Influence mainstream media and popular culture by presenting this as 'revival of Sanskrit'

The American Orientalist camp is hard-working and well informed. I do not wish to reject all its findings out of hand. I wish to make it explicitly clear that I do not question the dedication of its noteworthy exponents. Rather, I wish to 'relativize' their lens and show, firstly, that theirs is not the only approach that has merit; and secondly, that their view of Sanskrit distorts and misrepresents many of its most vital features. I would like to bring traditional Sanskrit scholars to the discussion table as stakeholders, so that the American Orientalists are not granted uncontested authority to shape the discourse. What I seek is a more balanced representation of the outsider and insider perspectives.

Unfortunately, the present situation is not only skewed towards American Orientalism in terms of structural power, but is also hampered by the traditionalists' inadequacy of response, symbolized by a head-in-the-sand posture they seem to have adopted. As I have pointed out, the traditionalists remain largely ignorant of the American Orientalist school of Sanskrit studies; they often trivialize its threat and display a lack of interest in engaging with it.

Introducing Sheldon Pollock: Pandit from America

I now turn specifically to the work of Sheldon Pollock, the chief protagonist of the American Orientalist movement as defined for the purpose of this book. A leading Sanskrit scholar, he is regarded as a hero by Indian secularists and leftists. He has trained and inspired an army of young Indian scholars, popular writers, and other opinion shapers to use his interpretations of Sanskrit for a new approach to the analysis of Indian society.

As subsequent chapters will show, Pollock's call to action for Indologists amounts essentially to a return of Orientalism in a new form, this time as an American-dominated enterprise rather than a European-dominated one. While Pollock is harshly critical of Indologists of the colonial era (whose credibility Edward Said had already undermined), he himself promotes a new kind of Western influence, albeit in more sophisticated terms. He is careful to call his approach 'post-Orientalism' in order to make it seem free from the baggage of Orientalism. Nonetheless, in his work one can detect the underlying drive towards intellectual hegemony. I am not alone in making this point. At least one European Indologist accuses Pollock of relocating Orientalism 'to the "New Raj" across the deep blue sea' (a reference to the USA).[24]

Pollock scolds the old European Orientalists for being too romantic about India. Their work, he says, is filled with fantasy of India's religion and metaphysical transcendence. He seeks to remedy this by making Indology reflect what he perceives as the reality of India. He describes the old Orientalist fantasy as follows:

> ... highly commodified, scientistically packaged, and aggressively marketed contemporary forms, continue to nourish one of the most venerable orientalist constructions, the fantasy of a uniquely religion-obsessed India (and a uniquely transcendent Indian wisdom), and how this fantasy in turn continuously reproduces itself in contemporary scholarship ...[25]

He himself, as we shall see, is determined to secularize the study of Sanskrit. This entails rejecting any 'uniquely transcendent Indian wisdom', or in other words, utterly purging Sanskrit studies of their sacred dimension. I show in the chapters that follow how he is in effect championing Orientalism in a brand new package. His research lives under the broad umbrella of South Asian studies, one of many disciplines initiated after the Second World War by US government agencies to protect US interests in the Third World.

I focus on Pollock as opposed to a broad review of multiple scholars for the following reasons:

- To set a debate in motion against a powerful school of thought, one must dissect and respond to its very best minds and works, and not engage its weakest or most vulnerable scholars. This has also been the traditional Indian approach to debate since ancient times. Pollock deserves to be considered the foremost contemporary exponent of American Orientalism.

- By naming Pollock as the leader, I invite him, his students and his collaborators to have open-minded conversations and debates with the goal of achieving a better mutual understanding. In effect, this book starts a sort of debate with the American Orientalist camp on their approach to Sanskrit studies.
- My focussed approach allows me to drill deep into the American Orientalist writings and offer my perspective. I can be concrete instead of making abstract generalizations.
- Pollock's writings inform a whole generation of scholars as well as mainstream media personalities, many of whom regard him as the pre-eminent authority on Indian heritage. Therefore, by engaging his scholarship singularly, the debate will be taken to the top of their hierarchy.

This approach of debating the opposing side's leader is consistent with my previous books. In each of them, I have addressed *one* big issue, an issue that was not being addressed adequately until then. I did this by taking on the most powerful leader(s) of the opposing side. All I wish to do here is start a conversation on an important issue where none exists presently.

Academic background and accomplishments

Sheldon Pollock studied Latin and Greek classics at Harvard and this grounding has influenced his subsequent approach to Sanskrit. After acquiring his PhD in Sanskrit studies from Harvard under the famous Indologist, Daniel Ingalls, he spent the next few decades working diligently on a variety of Sanskrit texts. His publications cover a vast canvas of topics in Sanskrit studies, one that has been rarely matched by Western scholars.

His first major study was on the Ramayana in the 1980s. In it, he consciously differentiated himself from fellow Western Indologists. He criticized scholars who romanticized the Sanskrit tradition, and argued for the use of his 'political philology' method to interpret Sanskrit texts. He made considerable effort emphasizing that his approach was radically different from those of Ingalls and the major German Indologists, in that he did not share their goal of representing the insider's perspective on Sanskrit.

Pollock has been consistent in his view that the ethical responsibility of Sanskrit scholars today compels them to play an activist role. To him, this involves firstly exposing the oppressiveness he sees within the Sanskrit tradition, and secondly eliminating it by re-engineering the tradition. He is a self-declared outsider in the sense I use the term, having not espoused any spiritual practice within the tradition. He has never claimed shraddha in the traditional Hindu sense.

I list some of the highlights of his impressive career in order to illustrate his amazing reach and importance:

- He is a fellow of the prestigious American Academy of Arts and Sciences, and is currently a chaired professor at Columbia University in Middle Eastern, South Asian and African studies.
- His publication *The Language of the Gods in the World of Men: Sanskrit, Culture, and Power in Premodern India* (2006) won the Coomaraswamy Prize from the Association of Asian Studies, as well as the Lionel Trilling Award.
- He has been awarded a Distinguished Achievement Award by the Mellon Foundation.
- At a 2008 conference entitled 'Language, Culture and Power' organized in his honour by his students, some of the most respected Indologists participated to pay him tribute.
- He was general editor of the Clay Sanskrit Library, for which he also edited and translated a number of volumes.
- He has been joint editor of *South Asia Across the Disciplines,* a collaborative venture of the University of California Press, the University of Chicago Press and the Columbia University Press.
- He is currently the principal investigator of 'SARIT: Enriching Digital Collections in Indology', supported by the National Endowment for the Humanities/Deutsche Forschungsgemeinschaft Bilateral Digital Humanities Program.

- One of his initiatives was the Ambedkar Sanskrit Fellowship Program at Columbia, which aims to establish an endowment to fund graduate studies in Sanskrit for students from historically disadvantaged communities.
- He directs the project 'Sanskrit Knowledge Systems on the Eve of Colonialism', in which scholars examine the state of knowledge that was produced in Sanskrit before colonialism.
- He is also editing a series of 'Historical Sourcebooks in Classical Indian Thought' while working on another book, titled *Liberation Philology*, for Harvard University Press.

A celebrity with many constituencies

These awards and recognitions have sealed his status in the eyes of most Indian intelligentsia as one of the few remaining scholars with the adhikara (authority) to interpret and speak about Sanskrit texts. Today, Pollock is widely celebrated both within India and amongst Indians abroad. Some examples of this recognition are listed below:

- The president of India awarded him the Certificate of Honour for Sanskrit, and separately the Padma Shri for his distinguished service in the field of letters.
- He has been featured as one of the star figures at the Jaipur Literary Festival over the last seven years, and is routinely invited to high-profile conclaves and seminars in India to help interpret India's traditions for the academic elite.
- He is frequently interviewed by *Tehelka* news magazine and India's NDTV network, and has received *India Abroad*'s Person of the Year award.
- He was the keynote speaker at the golden jubilee celebrations of the Centre for the Study of Developing Societies in Delhi.
- He serves as a juror on the committee that awards the Infosys Prize for Humanities and Social Sciences. One of the most prestigious feathers in his cap is his position as general editor of

the Murty Classical Library of India (Harvard University Press). I will examine this position in detail in a later chapter.

Pollock is important and interesting to many kinds of constituents, each with their own reasons for appreciating him:

- The *Indian left* sees him as a priceless ally in exposing Hindu chauvinism by providing evidence of oppressiveness encoded within Sanskrit tradition. For them, he is a worthy successor of D.D. Kosambi (the late Marxist Indologist) and far better equipped with updated Western social theories. They lionize him as a creator of new Marxist lineages.
- *Western academics* see him as a unique scholar of intellectual history, his credentials bolstered by an access to Sanskrit that few of his peers possess. He is also a novel exponent in the application of Western social theories to Sanskrit-based cultures. Those Western scholars with sympathies for the sacred dimensions of Sanskrit might find themselves marginalized.
- *Wealthy Indians* see Western Indologists as vehicles for obtaining a seat at the high table of global prestige. Association with Pollock opens doors for them to serve on esteemed boards, giving them the proud sense of finally having arrived into the same league as the Rothschilds and the Rockefellers. Some of his benefactors might seek more mundane rewards, such as access to high-level networking.
- *Indian Sanskrit scholars* believe that Pollock's elevated profile brings prestige to their field of study, which has otherwise been largely neglected by modern, sophisticated people. They perceive him as doing them a favour by serving as their ambassador.
- *Traditional Hindu organizations* are, in some cases, in awe of him, because of his international affiliations. By virtue of his presence, their tradition at least nominally secures a seat amongst the global elite. A good example of this phenomenon has been the desire of the administrators at Sringeri Sharada Peetham,

established by Adi Shankara, to anoint him as a sort of ambassador for their legacy.

- *The Indian government, media and public intellectuals* tap superficially into his work as a source of one-liner wisdom. Pollock seems to provide an easy bandwagon, as it were, on to which they can jump without having to know much in the way of depth.
- *Naive Hindus* feel proud that their heritage is being championed by an American from a prestigious university, and celebrate him for bringing their tradition into the limelight.

Reliance on Western theories

While he often asserts that he studied Sanskrit under traditional gurus many years ago, Pollock's present allegiances and sources do not indicate active affinity with such an approach. He claims that he wants to use theories and perspectives on how the tradition viewed itself in the past. However, his writing frequently compares alternative interpretations by diverse Western thinkers while positioning himself as the arbiter of their views.[26] He tends to select those which he can use to support his framework. At the macro level, he often relies on theories originated by Europeans like Vico, Gadamar, Habermas and Benjamin, to name only a few. His closest interlocutors seem to be either westerners or Western-trained Indians.

Mapping Pollock's major works

Pollock is a prolific writer. His voluminous writings are frequently impenetrable to the layperson, demanding a lot of effort to understand. In the course of examining a couple of thousand pages of his published work, I have noted some red flags from the traditionalist's point of view. These will be dealt with in greater detail in the subsequent chapters:

1. **Decoupling Sanskrit and its shastras from the Vedas:** He maintains that Sanskrit must be studied as a window into the history and present structure of India's social oppression. He

does not concern himself with its usage to produce and transmit knowledge contained in the shastras, which are analytical texts in such fields as mathematics, astronomy, medicine, philosophy, etc. Nor is he interested in its utility for practitioners of sanatana dharma as a means of transcendence to higher states of consciousness. This is a position he adopted early in his scholarly career.

2. **Politicizing kavya (literature) and decoupling it from the Vedas:** Pollock develops his Sanskrit theories around kavya, which he characterizes as creative expression that was driven for political purposes. He seeks to disconnect kavya from the Vedas with the claim that kavya originated only through the practice of writing literary texts and only with the help of Buddhists opposing the Vedas. He dismisses those who say Sanskrit was already there, and hence so was kavya. He calls them chauvinists and says they 'have long sought to provide an infinitely receding history to Sanskrit *kāvya*, or at least a very long genealogy leading back into the Vedic period'.[27] In effect, he secularizes kavya by removing its paramarthika (transcendental) dimensions. He also conveniently reduces the rasa aspect of kavya to something secular. As per tradition, rasa also encompasses the aesthetic conceptualization of mental states used in bhakti and other spiritual traditions as a link between the mundane and the divine, i.e., a bridge connecting vyavaharika (the worldly) and paramarthika (the transcendent).
3. **Interpreting the Ramayana as a project for propagating Vedic social oppression:** A large volume of his work centres on the Ramayana. He claims that the Ramayana, in conveying a theme of the divine king (Rama) who must kill the demonic enemy (Ravana), embodies Vedic structures that are oppressive. Pollock argues that, since the twelfth century CE, the Ramayana has served as a weapon for inciting violence by Hindus against Muslims. According to this interpretation, the Hindu rulers saw in themselves the embodiment of Rama's role as a divine king with extraordinarily sanctioned powers; meanwhile, the

role of demonic enemy in the Ramayana was projected on to the Muslims. Furthermore, he asserts that even in recent times, this reactionary potential within the Ramayana continues to be invoked for instigating anti-Muslim fundamentalism in the Hindu communities in India. This has been explained in Chapter 5.

4. **Rise of the pan-Asian Sanskrit cosmopolis:** Pollock explains the dramatic and peaceful expansion of Sanskrit across much of Asia as a political project to strengthen the royal power of kings with the help of brahmins. By implication, a brahmin–king nexus was the driving force that caused Sanskrit to thrive across Asia for nearly a thousand years.
5. **Death of Sanskrit and the rise of vernaculars:** He claims that Sanskrit had died as a living language by about the twelfth century, and that it has not been used to produce new content since then. The cause of its death was the structures of abuse that were built into it, as well as the rise of the vernaculars. He emphasizes that the 'death of Sanskrit' was caused by Hindu kings; it was not the fault of Muslim invaders or British colonizers, who he claims tried to revive it.
6. **Dangerous impact of Sanskrit on Western thought:** Pollock argues that German Indology was not altogether misled in finding support in Sanskrit for its violent fascist and racist ideology. He explains that elements within the Sanskrit tradition did indeed support this ideology. Thus, the study of Sanskrit made its own contribution to the Nazi holocaust of the Jews. Pollock appears to implicate Sanskrit for having infected colonial Indology, as British rulers claimed to merely continue the practices encoded within Indian traditions. By implication, they cannot be given the entire blame for perpetuating a despotism that was already in place; they were being faithful to Indian traditions.

In my analysis of Pollock's work, I also take note of what he chooses not to say. For his silences reveal a great deal.[28]

Call to Sanskrit scholars to adopt his lens

Pollock's overall goal, stated clearly in numerous writings, is to revolutionize Sanskrit studies by moving them away from their traditional Hindu roots where Sanskrit is seen as a sacred language. He beseeches scholars to adopt his secular social and political positions as well as to change the future course of Sanskrit studies. Therefore, he wants them to expose and eradicate what he sees as the socio-political abuse built into Sanskrit and its texts. It is this type of 'revival' that he wishes to bring about in Sanskrit studies.

It will become clear that his overarching mission is to invigorate the *study* of Sanskrit, but not the *active use* of it. He wishes Sanskrit to be perceived as a dead language, to be studied by his protégés with this perspective, much as a fossil encased in a museum is studied by palaeontologists. His is a bold, courageous and clever initiative with huge implications.

He describes his approach as 'liberation philology' in a clear reference to the tradition of 'liberation theology': a left-wing interpretation of Catholicism that emphasized economic and political justice and became widely popular throughout Latin America in the 1960s. In so doing, Pollock imparts his own spin on to the practice of philology, demanding that the thrust of this academic discipline be to effect social change. This sort of activism, he writes, would bring about an 'inclusivist, species-wide community' to replace the divided, nationalistic, economically and socially unjust world in which Indians now live. Pollock's liberation philology constitutes a strictly atheist approach to interpreting Sanskrit language and texts, wherein the main purpose of examining them is to 'uncover' the hidden political themes he reads into them and thus liberate the downtrodden from oppression.[29]

Pollock is an accomplished scholar whose clearly declared intention is to gain control over the study of the Sanskrit tradition. One of his goals is to critique and expunge what he sees as deeply entrenched static social hierarchies, barbarisms and poisons. I do not see anything inherently wrong with this intention by itself; most Hindus welcome improvements and the evolution of their culture. The issue worth debating is that

Pollock sees these ills as deeply rooted in the Vedas themselves and as requiring the abandonment of core metaphysical and sacred perspectives. In establishing this method of interpretation, Pollock has founded an enduring legacy in Western academics.

Work positioned as an original grand narrative

Pollock has an ambition to fit Sanskrit into his own universal theory of how languages developed. He aims to develop a grand narrative of languages and cultures out of his work on Sanskrit. This is evident from his declaration that his main book could easily have carried another subtitle: 'A Study of Big Structures, Large Processes, and Huge Comparisons.'[30] He sees himself as a Western theorist who supersedes prior Western thinkers in having developed a revolutionary way to understand both the East and the West. For Pollock the Sanskrit tradition is a resource to be mined for ideas that will fuel such projects.

To establish a status and authority commensurate with undertaking such ground-breaking work, he bombards the reader with heavy Sanskrit textual references. He goes through a data mining expedition through Sanskrit literature, carefully picking writers and quotations that support his thesis. He refers to his interpretations as 'data' and insists that they 'clearly' lead to certain conclusions. Such words inspire confidence and give the impression that his research is exhaustive, balanced and impartial. They also suggest that the conclusions are the only rational ones possible. Such displays of erudition are bound to impress his academic peers, highlighting his knowledge of the exotic East.

Yet, at the same time, he makes it clear that he is distant from and critical of the Sanskrit tradition and holds an objective position. Consequently, as we shall see, he succumbs to a pitfall common to many who attempt far-reaching sweeps through vast territories: connecting random data points to claim a pattern of causation, one that is at times incoherent and filled with inconsistencies.

Collusion with the Indian left

In the course of this work, it became clear to me that much of the problem Hindus would find in his work has to do with his collaboration with the Indian left. He serves them as their foremost supplier of knowledge about Sanskrit and its texts. In return, they disseminate his ideas widely into Indian society. Pollock and the Indian left comprise a symbiotic pair with considerable gravitas. This partnership has achieved a great deal in injecting certain subversive ideas into the mainstream. Therefore, his work cannot be evaluated in isolation, and neither side can be successfully dealt with without the other.

In other words, it is not only what Pollock writes that matters; it is also important to see how it is being received by his intellectual and political supporters in India. His work does not arrive on a blank slate in India. It is received in a pre-existing intellectual context that is loaded with divisiveness and anger against Hindu traditions. The Indian left has made him their mascot on certain matters. They are being inspired by his theories, and he has created a hegemonic discourse that serves as the foundation on which others can confidently produce their own extrapolations.

He is associated with many Western and Indian scholars who could easily be seen as Trojan horses that have infiltrated deep within Indology and South Asian studies. They smuggle ideologies into the mainstream that appear balanced and even positive on the surface, but beneath this façade they often contain materials that undermine the tradition. I shall point out many such examples in this book.

This raises the following question: Is he being appropriated by the Indian left for helping them in their struggle for political power? To answer this question, I will use Pollock's important theory called 'the aestheticization of power' that is summarized in Chapter 6. This theory says that the cunning brahmins supplied the popular literature that helped to spread the political power of the kings. In other words, his theory claims that kings sponsored brahmins who, in turn, supplied the intellectual and popular works to help the kings politically. Can we not also apply this theory to say that Pollock is playing a role similar to what the brahmins are alleged to have played? The Indian left is clearly working with him closely to boost their own political power. His work on Sanskrit supports them ideologically. How is this any different than the aestheticization of power that he accuses the brahmin–kshatriya nexus of carrying out?

We should not a priori assume any such 'conspiracy theory'. We should start examining the matter by giving Pollock the benefit of doubt. Let us say that he might have exported his theories to India with a neutral mindset, and presented both sides of each issue with equal weight. It could be surmised that the predispositions of the Indian left are what colour his works as anti-Hindu in certain instances. In such a scenario, he has innocently and unconsciously allowed his work to be used by the left to disrupt an equilibrium in India's internal fault lines.

Though I am open to consider such a scenario, I must say that there is plenty of evidence presented in this book that shows his explicit and profound commitments to bring social and political interventions in India. He sees himself as a political activist; he also asks other Indologists to channel their work in order to bring social transformation. Hence, he cannot be assumed to be completely innocent of his motives. He is culpable to the extent he knows (or ought to know) that his work lends itself to be deployed in ways the Hindus would regard as Hinduphobic.

Finally, I point out in this book several instances where he is projecting Western universalism – perhaps unconsciously – not of the modern kind but of the postmodern kind. Postmodernists become angry when I accuse them of serving Western universalism, because their project purports to do the exact opposite. However, in *Being Different* I have supplied my arguments claiming that postmodernism, in fact, is a newer and more insidious form of Western universalism.

Return of the Charvakas

One way of seeing Pollock in terms of traditional Sanskrit categories would be to locate him in the Charvaka school of thought. Tradition uses this category to describe those who are completely closed to transcendence (paramarthika), and hence closed to the sacred realm.[31]

This school espouses a strictly materialistic view of the world, and condemns the Vedas and the practices of yajna and puja as magical buffoonery. It may be helpful for those immersed in traditional categories to see Pollock in this light, and to locate him as a new kind of Charvaka pandit.

Indian tradition does not ban books or consider any point of view blasphemous. I am not attempting to silence Pollock by casting him in these terms but rather to illuminate his work. In fact, Sanskrit scholars hold the Charvaka pandits in high esteem for their intellectual rigour. Charvaka is the first school of thought discussed in *Sarva Darshana Sangraha*, a compendium of all major schools of Indian philosophy.

'Sanskrit is dead. Long live Sanskrit studies'

Pollock routinely speaks of the need to 'revive' Sanskrit. It is quite understandable that most of the westernized Indians (and some traditionalists) are moved with pride at such rhetoric. However, many of his admirers have not delved beneath the surface of his scholarship to understand what exactly his idea of 'revival' amounts to: the reinvigorated *study* of Sanskrit as if it were the embalmed, mummified remnant of a dead culture.

Put simply, Pollock's activism thus far has been to revive Sanskrit *studies* but not Sanskrit itself or its culture. Its implications are that Sanskrit is to be repeatedly and vehemently declared a dead language; and its scholars must subscribe overwhelmingly to a persuasion moulded by his political philological methods. Although he does not say this explicitly, the implication is that it must *not* be studied experientially as a guide to sacred living. The spiritual dimension of Sanskrit must be quarantined to protect society from its negative aspects, and the scholars trained in using his lens should be put in charge of managing that quarantine.

Clearly, Pollock does not seem to regard the expertise of insiders as serving much useful purpose beyond facilitating the first stage of language acquisition; indeed, his project hinges upon decoupling the study of Sanskrit from traditional Hinduism. While he expresses love and regard for Sanskrit, he is not sensitive to the Hindu sacred tradition's perspectives.

A worthy critic and discussant

A few days before I finalized this book's manuscript, I had further meetings with Sheldon Pollock in which I wanted to be open and upfront with him about the general nature of my critical inquiry. These were candid and friendly meetings in which both sides felt we could benefit from cooperation and wanted to move forward positively. As a result of these personal conversations, I have developed a deeper appreciation for his sincerity in pursuing his work on India.

He told me that he would like to be seen as 'a critical friend of India' who is appreciative of many aspects of India. I pointed out to him certain specific issues in his work that would definitely trouble practising Hindus. Although he does not like my characterization of him as anti-Hindu, my point has been that if equivalent things were written about Islam, most Muslims would call that Islamophobic. Why, then, should Hindus not be entitled to a similar discretion in deciding what constitutes Hinduphobia?

He replied that it is very important for us to hear such critical voices as his. He felt that most people say only what the other side wants to hear, and that very few persons say what is unpleasant to hear. Hence, his criticisms should be taken as coming with friendly intentions. After our meeting, he e-mailed me a quote from the Ramayana to this effect. I would like to cite that verse:

> It is easy to find men, my lord, who will always say what is pleasing. But how difficult to find one who will say—let alone hear—what is necessary though displeasing.[32]

I agree with him that we can benefit when outsiders criticize us. I told him that I consider him a worthy discussant whose criticisms ought to compel us to respond. My book is only a preliminary beginning in that direction. He has spent most of his adult life studying India and certainly takes its Sanskrit traditions very seriously. He is arguably the hardest working and most influential Western Indologist I am aware of today.

I wish to use an analogy with vaccination: We must treat Pollock's work as an injection containing both subtle and not so subtle foreign attacks on our sanskriti. Our traditional scholars are like the body's immune system and they need to generate antibodies to defend and respond. This is what is called the uttara-paksha (response). Such debates and argumentation make the sanskriti stronger as a result. He is right that we can use his criticisms for constructive outcomes.

At the same time we must also safeguard against allowing a heavier attack than we are prepared to defend at this point in time. We do not want to capitulate by allowing our vulnerabilities to remain exposed. This means we must also construct firewalls to protect the entry of dangerous forces into our fragile institutions, especially when our own people are still so confused about the dynamics of this intellectual Kurukshetra. Some of the dangerous viruses are being imported into our traditional institutions by our own people serving as naive carriers.

It is true that similar criticisms are also found against Christianity, for instance. But Christian seminaries have armies of well-trained scholars who give a strong response. For every anti-Christian scholar of substance who has been writing for several decades, one expects to find pro-Christian voices to dissect the criticisms and offer rejoinders. The same can be said of Chinese scholarship that routinely responds to the West on China's own terms and by using Chinese traditional frameworks and idioms.

Therefore, I explained to him, it is not his criticisms that trouble me as much as the lack of thoughtful responses by our traditional scholars. This, as he has reminded me frequently, is not his fault, but our own. Clearly, we ought to strengthen our internal mechanisms, and this book is intended to stimulate us into action.

It is important to clarify that only a small portion of the American academicians are Orientalists; it would be incorrect to project my critique of Orientalists on to the general community of academic scholars of the social sciences and humanities. However, the influence of Pollock's group is significant in academics, media, education and public opinion. Hence, his works must be discussed in detail, which has not been adequately done prior to this book.

Comparing two pioneering Orientalists: Sir William Jones and Sheldon Pollock

I close this chapter with a brief comparison between the two eminent figures in the Western study of Sanskrit that I have discussed separately above: Sir William Jones, the nineteenth-century judge, and Sheldon Pollock, the twenty-first-century entrepreneur of scholarship.

I find the parallels between Jones's project and that of Sheldon Pollock illuminating, both in terms of their similarities and differences. Just as Jones was, Pollock is a serious student of Sanskrit who has gone to great lengths to master its corpus wherever possible. Like Jones, he interprets this body of work at times on the terms of Western culture. Both of them arouse Western interest while preserving an underlying sense of Western superiority in terms of social justice and political organization.

A key difference between William Jones and Sheldon Pollock is that the former appreciated Hinduism's sacredness and wanted to 'domesticate' it within the Biblical framework, whereas Pollock explicitly rejects the domain of the sacred as backward and obscurantist. Therefore, while Jones applied the Biblical lens to study Indian culture, Pollock applies a secular Western lens that derives many features from postmodernism. While Sir William Jones was an Orientalist for the modern period, Pollock is a postmodern Orientalist.

Both depend on Indians as native informants, but in different ways. Jones used mainly traditional pandits, whereas Pollock also collaborates with the elitist westernized Indians. And of course, while Sir William Jones was an unabashed supporter of the economic imperialism of his times, Pollock is critical of corporate capitalism.

A monument to honour Pollock would not look like the one for Jones on the front cover of this book. Pollock himself would be depicted as a pandit, addressing the Americanized elitist Indians, media leaders and politicians sitting on sofas around him. They would be taking notes from his dictation. But he too, like Jones, would be seen to be giving to the Indians a comprehensive, critical and 'modern' account of their heritage, history, political thought and, most of all, liberating them from problems inherent in their own traditions.

While Sir William Jones claimed to be giving the Hindus their laws, Sheldon Pollock presents himself as giving the Indians their human rights.

3

The Obsession with Secularizing Sanskrit

In much of Pollock's work, his idea of secularization involves rejecting or sidelining what the tradition refers to as 'paramarthika', or the realm of transcendence. The corresponding term 'vyavaharika' refers to the mundane, worldly realm of daily life, and this is his area of focus.

However, our tradition sees these two realms as one whole, a single integral/organic unity. We are not asked to pick one and reject the other. In fact, many vyavaharika activities – such as dance, music, yoga, karma, bhakti and so forth – are also paths to the divine. We always start the journey towards the paramarthika from the vyavaharika.

The paramarthika realm, the realm of the transcendent/spiritual/sacred, is central to the entire Vedic tradition, and rejecting it is tantamount to the distortion of that tradition. In effect, what he is saying is that Sanskrit and sanskriti ought to be separated from Hinduism, that they should be 'de-Hinduized'. He does not say this explicitly, but this is the effect of his position to make Sanskrit and sanskriti secular. If such a trend were to continue, only the vyavaharika realm would be included and texts and structures relating to the sacred dimension of life would be eliminated.

The reader will be amazed, if not shocked, at the magnitude of this project to secularize Sanskrit and its culture. And yet, this fundamental agenda has not been brought to light for the mainstream public to understand clearly. This chapter will discuss step by step the following interpretations of Sanskrit and sanskriti by Pollock, and the interventions he proposes:

- **Against transcendence:** He uses the Italian thinker Giambattista Vico to conclude that texts which focus on transcendence represent a primitive culture, and uses Marxist ideas to conclude that transcendence camouflages the oppressive power relations of caste.
- **Against ritual/yajna:** He sees these as mechanistic, hence impeding creativity and freedom.
- **Sidelining of oral tradition:** He gives hardly any weight to the oral tradition as that would challenge a number of his assumptions. For Pollock, the history of Sanskrit begins when written texts begin. He finds the oral tradition frozen in 'hymnology' and lacking in progress. Hence, his history of Sanskrit skips the oral tradition.
- **Rejection of shastra (knowledge systems):** This follows from the first two points; since shastras rely on Vedic metaphysics, he finds them tainted and wants to sideline them. His focus is on kavya – written poetry, fiction, etc. – with emphasis on political usages.
- **Sanskrit grammar as toxic:** Pollock insinuates there are structures for social hierarchy embedded in Sanskrit grammar. Thus, the grammar of Sanskrit is held to be a dangerous device used to deny social justice. I discuss this in the sections 'Is it fair to blame Sanskrit grammar' in Chapter 4 and 'Grammar as a form of political power' in Chapter 7.
- **Political analysis of kavya:** He finds kavya interesting to study because he claims it is decoupled from the Vedas. Kavya can

produce historical change, he says, because it is a *political* device. He earlier downplayed the role of rasa in the arts for the purpose of transcendence, and recently acknowledged it as a later development.

Integral unity of Hindu metaphysics

Most spiritual traditions are founded on the notion that beyond the ordinary world there is a higher reality that we cannot perceive with our limited senses. In Hindu cosmology, this higher reality is referred to as paramarthika, or by various other terms, such as 'Brahman', 'Ishwar', 'Shiva', 'Devi', 'Paramatma', 'moksha', etc. Although each of these Sanskrit terms is unique and non-translatable, and has its own shade of meaning, the general sense of paramarthika is approximately conveyed by English phrases such as 'transcendental', 'higher states of consciousness', 'ultimate reality', 'supreme person', 'divine', 'sacred', 'spiritual', and so forth.

Hindus see both this paramarthika realm and the realm of vyavaharika as intrinsically intertwined and unified. Paramarthika is ultimate and independent whereas vyavaharika is dependent and contingent, but both are integrated. My earlier book *Being Different* describes the various ways in which Hinduism, Buddhism and other dharma systems have conceptualized the relationships between these realms.[1]

For insiders, the teachings of the Vedas offer a window into the paramarthika part of reality through a variety of approaches. These paths serve the cognitive capabilities and personal preferences of each individual. For example:

- Darshana (philosophy) is an intellectual method requiring analytical capabilities.
- Dhyana (meditation) is available without the need for analysis since it is entirely experiential.
- Yajna is an embodied performance combining mental, physical and vocal components.
- Bhakti is a way to channel one's emotions towards the divine.
- Kavya is literature that can be merely entertaining, or can also be a means for experiencing transcendence.

If paramarthika is the realm 'beyond', vyavaharika is the ordinary reality around us. Kapila Vatsyayan explains the multitude of ways in which Indian culture is permeated by the Vedic structures of ultimate reality:

> Classical Indian architecture, sculpture, painting, literature (kavya), music, and dancing evolved their own rules conditioned by their respective media, but they shared with one another not only the underlying spiritual beliefs of the Indian religio-philosophic mind, but also the procedures by which the relationships of the symbol and the spiritual states were worked out in detail.[2]

All Hindu schools and paths serve the purpose of helping the practitioner proceed from the vyavaharika realm to the paramarthika realm. Regardless of the specific path, the Hindu's starting point is the vyavaharika world, because that is where he is situated in a practical sense. And so, from our shared mundane starting point, a number of different paths or approaches can be opened up.

Among these is the path of bhakti, or devotion, which fosters an evolutionary progress towards higher states, culminating in the ultimate state of experiencing divinity. An advanced bhakta is guided to see Sri Krishna, for example, everywhere in his or her vyavaharika life. Every particular situation he or she comes across in daily life is to be seen as a part of the integral unity. The person's life as a householder, businessman, worker or professional is informed by this overarching journey towards paramarthika. The various bhakti practices teach the devotees to connect with this paramarthika.

Another path is that of tantra, which taps the intelligences built into our bodies and uses them for advancement towards higher realms. A serious Sri Vidya practitioner follows a strict regimen, beginning with a morning puja in a part of the home set aside as the devi's abode. The devi upasana has a daily, weekly, monthly and annual cycle of actions that are completely integrated into the practitioner's life. If the practitioner is a surgeon, then every time she raises her scalpel she is aware that it is the devi who gives her the shakti to carry out the intricate life-saving task at hand. She is able to go through the complex surgical procedure with perfect concentration and a smile on her face. In her world, she sees the devi as being with her all the way through. When she returns home in the evening, she does her chants and has a contemplative conversation with devi in her mind. In this manner, the integral unity of the world is experienced as a continuum containing both the vyavaharika (everyday life) and the paramarthika (transcendent).

Those who are inclined to do intensive work can follow the path of karma, the method of connecting with paramarthika, the transcendent, through selfless work for others.

For those whose tendency is towards aesthetic pleasure and play, the artistic disciplines of music, dance and theatre have been developed. The *Natya Shastra* provides a structured way of using aesthetics to make available the teachings of the Vedas by embedding the dharmic lifestyles in kavya (poetry), natya (theatre) and nritya (dance). Kalidasa (in *Malavikagnimitra*, 1.4) states that natya (a generic term which subsumes theatre) is a form of yajna (he uses the synonym 'kratu') and that it has been so declared by the rishis. The path of hatha yoga uses body disciplines. There are many systems of yoga; one of the best known is found in the Yoga Sutras of Patanjali.[3]

Those predisposed towards philosophy and abstraction can study Vedanta and practise jnana, the path leading to a cognitive shift. There are multiple sub-paths within Vedanta. The one taught by Shankara (and many other acharyas) has three steps: shravana (listening/reading to expand one's knowledge), manana (contemplation on the knowledge) and nididhyasana (cognitive shift even while carrying out daily activities).[4]

In this manner, different modes of study and practice were developed to ensure that the teachings of the Vedas reach various kinds of individuals, wherever the given individual happens to be on this vyavaharika–paramarthika continuum. It is a rich and comprehensive life that Hindus are asked to lead.

Not only were multifarious modes of study and practice developed, as described above, but the channels designed to disseminate them were just as varied. The tradition recognized the diverse levels of cognition of the general population and hence nurtured multiple transmission mechanisms to reach them. All these had the same objective: making the knowledge contained in the Vedas available to all.

For example, the Brahmanas are texts that include commentaries on the Samhita portion of the Vedas. These are examined and discussed in debates among scholars, and these debates get compiled into answers for frequently asked questions. They were designed for serious students of the Vedas. At a more popular level, *Natya Shastra* was a text developed to enable theatrical performances of itihasas. These were choreographed in such a way as to deliver Vedic knowledge packaged as entertainment. They were adapted for given localities, and included anecdotes that served as a bridge between paramarthika and vyavaharika. The shastras are texts of the various disciplines and branches of knowledge, and these were also composed in kavya form to help memorize and facilitate transmission.

Sanskrit texts are, in one way or another, vital to understanding these paths. In the first place, Sanskrit has a precise and highly refined terminology for identifying and analysing them. Almost all these paths rely, in varying degrees, on non-translatable Sanskrit terms.

Pollock refers to paramarthika and vyavaharika, but separates them in such a manner that he can choose one and completely reject the other. Whereas the tradition sees them as a unified whole, he places them in mutual conflict, and dismisses the paramarthika as a primitive idea. He ignores the sacred dimension of Hindu life that is expressed, analysed and taught in the texts of Sanskrit. His project to secularize has the effect of erasing many popular spiritual paths.

Traditionally, Hindus have read Sanskrit for the purpose of understanding the ideas of ultimate reality. Pollock wants to eradicate this particular motivation for studying the language. He repeatedly complains that Sanskrit studies have played into the hands of brahmins; hence he feels that the texts retain their oppressiveness. In fact, he sees the promotion of standardized Sanskrit grammar, rituals and devotional practices as sources of social abuse.

He wants to replace the sacred interpretation of Sanskrit with new philological studies that emphasize its politics. His focus is on empowering the downtrodden who he feels have been exploited by the Sanskrit tradition for centuries. Such a shift in focus requires a new lens for interpreting the old Sanskrit texts. However, Pollock has not explained why his political philology or liberation philology lens is superior to the way the Sanskrit tradition has interpreted itself. His rationale for rejecting traditional methods is that they somehow lead to social abuse.

Rather than using his political philology methods, traditional scholars learn from texts such as dharmashastras and Patanjali's *Mahabhashya* the answer to the following question: What is the standard for practising dharma? The answer provided by the texts is consistent: Follow the exemplars, the noble shishtas, those who live very simply but with high thinking, free from greed.

Unfortunately, Pollock's strategy serves to sabotage this lifestyle by provoking and rabble-rousing against the 'elites' even though the notion of elites in the West is hardly applicable to these shishtas. The irony we shall see later is that Pollock himself is a member of and represents the American elites with its Indian elitist extensions.

Discarding the transcendent/sacred aspects of Sanskrit

Pollock starts his magnum opus *The Language of the Gods in the World of Men* by taking up paramarthika and vyavaharika as a key pair from the Vedas. He correctly says that these categories or principles are central to the life of practising Hindus. However, he has a distorted understanding of both in so far as he juxtaposes them as antithetical to each other, and then superimposes the lens of Western theories on to this opposition. He sees these realms in mutual tension rather than holistically and organically unified.

Traditional scholars representing the 'insider' view appreciate the importance of *both* paramarthika and vyavaharika. If you exclude the former, the result is a materialistic world view devoid of the sacred. If you eliminate the latter, the result is a world view that is other-worldly and dysfunctional in the everyday world. Both are symbiotic and reciprocal in our tradition. Unfortunately, Pollock consistently sidelines paramarthika except to study it with the intention of exposing its intrinsic oppression; he is essentially secularizing the entire sanskriti.

In making this hard and fast distinction between the sacred and the secular, Pollock is following a methodology that has informed Western social science for centuries. He uses the ideas of Vico, a leading European thinker of the seventeenth century and one of the founders of European social thought. Vico developed an important European theory of imagination and myth, as well as social theories with notions of class struggle. He strongly influenced a number of other Western thinkers, including Marx, Habermas, Gadamer and various others whose theories Pollock cites as strategic resources.

Vico differentiated earlier societies from the European society of his time, by classifying nations into two stages of evolution. The early societies and nations were considered childlike in their level of rationality. Vico described this ancient period as 'the age of gods and heroes' filled with fantasy and creativity. The nations enjoying a more advanced stage of rationality were deemed to exist in the age of 'learned men', which applies to Europe. These two stages correspond to 'poetic' and 'philosophical' thinking, respectively.[5]

Pollock is influenced by Vico's theories in his own interpretation of the Vedas. There are two key points in his lens which are inspired by Vico: (1) the principle of treating the secular as separated from the transcendent and (2) the view that ancient texts and thinkers were pre-rational, mythically oriented, and emotional – and they lacked the rationality to develop and apply this principle to look at history clearly, a history driven by purely material acts.

Using such a classification of the stages of nations and peoples, Pollock implicitly assumes that Vedic ideas belong to the primitive stage of civilization. They are, then, the creations of theological poets who are not real philosophers in the European sense. They emphasize pure feeling – curiosity, wonder, fear and superstition – and reflect the childlike capacity of human beings. As Vico puts it, 'In the world's childhood, men were by nature sublime poets,' and hence such early nations must be 'poetic in their beginnings'.[6] The 'poetic' or 'metaphysical truth' that underlies such primitive societies is manifest primarily in fable, myth and the polytheistic religions. These truths were not based on empirical evidence of the external world whereas mature, rational European thought was.

Pollock comes across as a westerner wagging his finger at the Vedic rishis, whom he reductively sees as poetic/romantic and irrational. The early societies, according to him, were incapable of forming 'intelligible class concepts of things' and hence they explained natural phenomena personified as gods. By implication, the rishis could not explain nature rationally based on any empirical evidence, and so they conjured up Vedic deities as natural forces. Pollock refers to the 'long prehistory of Sanskrit' as a period of 'sacerdotal isolation', in which the Vedic rishis existed in a state of irrationality divorced from a logical understanding of the empirical world.[7]

He sees the rishis as pre-rational poets in the same way that westerners see ancient Middle East and Greece as representing the pre-rational childhood of their culture. This view forecloses consideration of the possibility that the rishis were in touch with a higher, not a lower, state of consciousness where the rational limits get transcended. Pollock writes that Vedic knowledge is meaningful only 'to the degree that it enunciates something that transcends the phenomenal and is thus inaccessible to observation, inference, or other forms of empirical reasoning'. Because of this, he argues, it is 'in fact, nonrational, if not irrational'.[8]

He does not consider super-rational states wherein reason *does* exist, but not in a way that is limiting.[9] In the traditional Hindu view, reason is only a subset of one's cognition. In other words, para-rational faculties can *also* get activated. Unfortunately, Pollock equates such states with irrationality. In the next section in this chapter, I will explain the difference between pre-rational and super-rational states. Many Western intellectuals, Pollock among them, are unfamiliar with, or else openly reject, the latter.

Pollock has completely sidelined the central premises of Vedic cosmology. His approach has merit only if you assume that these two realms, the paramarthika and the vyavaharika, can be disconnected from one another. However, from the traditional Indian point of view, they cannot be.

Pollock declares explicitly that his work gives primacy to vyavaharika only. He is clear about his reasons: vyavaharika texts give him access to human history whereas paramarthika texts do not. He calls paramarthika texts 'non-literature' and the vyavaharika texts 'literature'. He explains:

> This raises a point of method basic to this study, which might best be explained by the distinction Indian philosophers draw between paramarthika sat and vyavaharika sat, or what the eighteenth-century Italian thinker Vico called *verum* and *certum*. The prior term points toward the absolute truth of philosophical reason, the second, toward the certitudes people have at different stages of their history that provide the grounds for their beliefs and actions. It is these workaday truths, these certitudes, that are granted primacy in this book, in the conviction that we cannot understand the past until we grasp how those who made it understood what they were making, and why.[10]

To bifurcate these in an absolute sense, he asserts that these two kinds of texts had separate participants in terms of 'literary culture, writers, critics, and audiences alike'.[11] By studying the vyavaharika texts using his lens of political philology, he wants to uncover the character and historical development of Indian society in ancient times.[12]

To explain the two intellectual camps (of insiders and outsiders) better, I have coined the term 'sacred philology'. This term refers to analytical approaches of the insiders that see both paramarthika and vyavaharika as an integral unity. I will explain my term further in the Conclusion chapter. By contrast, the 'political philology' lens of Pollock is limited to the vyavaharika realm, and furthermore, it uses Western theories that were based on an entirely alien metaphysics and history as far as the Vedic system is concerned.

Pollock's research using political philology purports to uncover Vedic 'toxins', which for him have flowed through Sanskrit, and especially through Sanskrit grammar, into all the products emanating from that tradition.

Sidelining the oral tradition

Pollock equates the Vedic Sanskrit tradition, which is primarily expressed and taught orally, with paramarthika. He equates the new literary culture, which he claims arose after writing became widespread, with vyavaharika. Hence, his paramarthika/vyavaharika dichotomy maps on to his oral/ written split. Ancient oral Sanskrit, according to him, was used solely for 'mythic hymnology', which is his pejorative way of referring to Vedic rituals. This is why, he says, Sanskrit was strictly 'the language of the gods'. He then claims that only after the Buddhist influence did Sanskrit start to be written down. In this manner, the monopoly of the Vedic brahmins over knowledge was broken by Buddhist intervention. Thus, it became 'the language of men'. Once written down, Sanskrit was not limited to a secret or private code amongst brahmins, and it became available for vyavaharika purposes. This is what eventually led to the beginning of 'literature' or kavya as he sees it.

As I have shown, Pollock is consistent in differentiating two separate categories, and his thesis revolves around the tension between them. These categories are:

A. **Oral:** Not literature; paramarthika; language of the gods; used for mythic 'hymnology'.

B. **Written:** Literature; vyavaharika; language of men; cosmopolitan usage.

He claims that those who produced literature were conscious of this distinction between literature and what had earlier existed orally as non-literature. According to him, once literary culture started in India, the writers broke away from paramarthika, and made a 'methodological commitment to *vyavaharika*', because they knew that that was where 'a history of their culture and power must begin'.[13] The implication is that prior to written literature, the oral tradition lacked vyavaharika capabilities and did not have a sense of history or development/progress of society. The oral tradition and its paramarthika material, according to him, were pre-rational, poetic fantasy. It was incapable of innovation, limited in scope and monopolized by brahmin oppression.

In my view, the conflation that oral = paramarthika = irrational, and the corresponding one that writing = vyavaharika = rational, are both simplistic and erroneous. Traditionalists say that for thousands of years,

Hindus composed texts and transmitted them orally. They were creative and their compositions evolved over time. The validity of knowledge is independent of whether it is written down or not. But Pollock does not see this. His overemphasis on writing and his exclusion of orally transmitted knowledge imply that his work omits important materials. I shall cite a few examples to illustrate this omission.

Carnatic and Hindustani vocal music, for instance, cannot be eliminated from consideration on the basis that it is composed orally and taught orally. There is no writing required here. Yet the listening–vocalizing method of learning intricate ragas leads not only to musical excellence but eventually also to transcendence. In this manner, over the centuries, thousands of new ragas have evolved, all of them orally, and all of them rooted in the Vedas. For the traditionalists, this is attested in the *Yajnavalkya Smriti*, which says that one who is an expert in playing the veena, and is knowledgeable in shrutis, jatis and the talas in musical terms, knows totality and attains moksha.[14]

On the other hand, Western classical music is taught from written scores. One cannot assume that writing is a universally necessary condition for the production and dissemination of worldly knowledge; rather, it is something peculiar to Europe in a certain historical era.

Pollock also fails to appreciate that great yogis have invested in embodied practices that do not require literacy. To be a yogi with enlightened experiences, one need not read any text at all. Similarly, great bhaktas do not need to be bookworms in order to achieve heightened states of divine experience. Dharmic ideas of higher states of consciousness are deeply connected with oral traditions. The key point concerns the notion of embodied knowing, which is where experiences of transcendence and oral traditions come together.

As I have repeatedly pointed out, dharmic traditions across the spectrum are built on the notion that all humans have the potential for what is nowadays being called 'supersensory experiences' or 'higher states of consciousness'. This potential has been discussed extensively in various dharma traditions, each of which has its own vocabulary. For instance, the Sri Chakra tradition is concerned with seven principal levels of consciousness, each with its own attributes. The term 'siddhi' refers to awakened ways of cognizing that are unavailable at the ordinary level of cognition.

In Rig Veda, the ultimate reality is conceptualized as a productive principle and a force of energy expressed as vac (speech) that is often personified as a goddess.[15] Vac is refracted into the fifty-two phonemes making it the linguistic matrix and model of both devavani (language of the devatas and of spiritual quest) and lokavani (people's language of everyday communication and exchange).[16] In the course of time, these two language streams blossomed into Sanskrit and Prakrit, respectively.[17]

In Kashmir Shaivism and some other systems traceable to the Vedas, vac (speech) has four levels, from the most external/gross to the most internal/subtle. These are as follow:

A. **Vaikhari** speech is where we hear external sound. When we converse with each other or hear someone speak, it is at this level. It is the gross level.

B. **Madhyama** speech is within one's mind. When I am thinking, I am talking to myself at this level of speech.

C. **Pashyanti** is unconscious speech in meditative states. There is a slight hint or inkling of a 'presence' inside, but it lacks form. Many mantra meditation systems take one to this level. There are volumes written on such systems, including Transcendental Meditation, Yoga Nidra and systems of tantra, to name a few. Beginners experience only level B, but more advanced practitioners transcend to this higher level. (As soon as one recognizes that one is having this experience, that experience is already over because the 'thought' of it has entered.)

D. **Para** level is connectivity and unity with the cosmic vibration (ritam), available only in deep meditation.

None of this is about organized 'religion', nor is it in conflict with science. In fact, the scientific exploration of consciousness is now overlapping with neuroscience and cognitive science. The idea of selfhood that is transcending the ordinary ego is increasingly accepted in scientific inquiry. Western scientists have entered this realm of investigation through their encounters with Hindu and Buddhist meditation and philosophical systems over the past half-century. The result has been an extensive effort to explore Indian spiritual discoveries using so-called 'new and original' Western vocabularies and frameworks. Not only are the Indian sources later sidelined, but worse still, these sources are seen as inferior to what the Western 'discoverers' have come up with.

An important confusion among many westerners dealing with this research is what is called the 'pre/trans fallacy'. Pollock is implicated in this fallacy (although he does not even bother to discuss it), and that is why he considers rishis as pre-rational. Let us further discuss the pre-rational, rational and post-rational states to clear this matter.

Pre-rational, rational and super-rational states

According to conventional Western frameworks, the following diagram illustrates the two states of human development, namely pre-rational and rational.

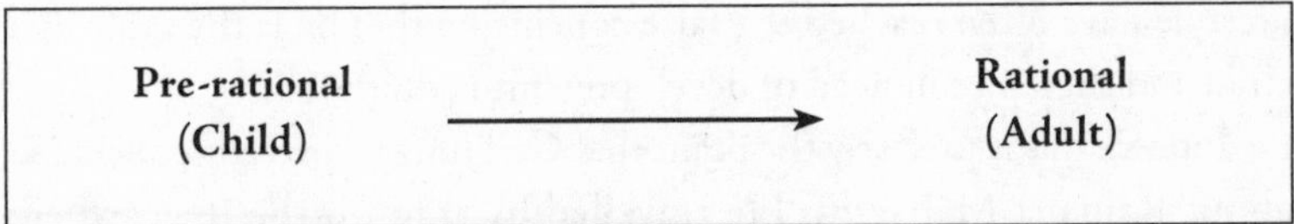

This refers to the model of human development which posits that children are in an early stage 'before the age of reason', whereas adults reach the rational stage, where their cognitive faculties culminate. Dharma-based metaphysical systems also acknowledge the unformed state of childhood and the transition to a more rational state in adult life.

However, dharma metaphysics adds a third dimension that is even higher than the rational adult state. This is called by various names, and the diagram below refers to it as the 'rishi' state of consciousness. In this state, the individual *has all the rational faculties but is not limited by them.* He is fully capable of logic, intellect, etc., but goes beyond what ordinary persons can cognize. Here the buddhi/intellect is more fully awakened.

The rishi state is a superset of the rational state and is not divorced from rationality.

Numerous Hindu and Buddhist explanations and descriptions are available concerning this state. These traditions differ from the Abrahamic religions precisely because they have processes designed to facilitate the evolution of consciousness towards this higher state.

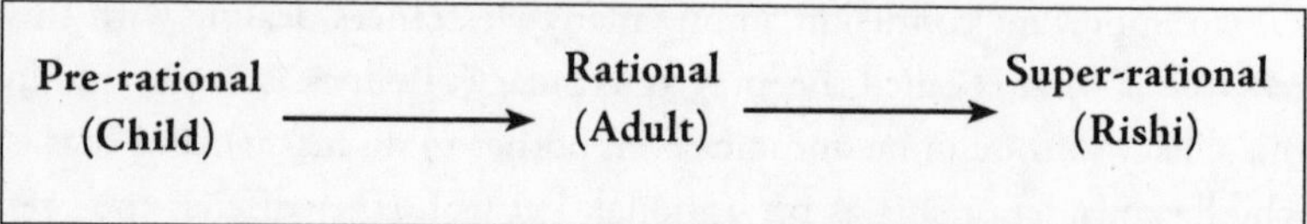

Here is the pre/trans fallacy: many westerners tend to assume that the child and rishi states are the same thing since both are different from the rational state. Both are different from the rational state and this gives the false impression of the two being the same. A rishi might be uninterested in so-called 'normal' adult rational ideas, and yet be fully able to work with them. However, westerners observing such a person's lifestyle have often reached the false conclusion that he is the same as a child and therefore in need of developing into adulthood.[18]

Indeed, this is precisely the point that Carl Jung incorrectly concluded about Ramana Maharshi. He travelled by train to the town where Ramana Maharshi lived but refused at the last minute to leave his train and visit the famous rishi. Basing his views entirely on what he had read and heard, Jung described Ramana Maharshi as being pre-rational, an escapist and other-worldly man and therefore unfit for an intelligent engagement.

Pollock falls into the very same fallacy, if only tacitly, believing that the rishis and the Vedic material that expresses their thought are 'pre-rational' when they are actually 'super-rational'. Only recently, thanks to their exposure to Eastern thought, have some Western cognitive scientists made a point of distinguishing between pre-rational and super-rational states.[19]

Other issues with sidelining the oral tradition

Human cognition is essentially a 'multimedia' system with various senses. However, only one of our senses, namely sight, is used in reading; and even sight has many functionalities that are not used in reading. Our vision is a sophisticated pattern-recognition system that is able to appreciate complex sights that are non-linear, three-dimensional and multicoloured. Vision processes motion too, and not merely static images. However, reading a text involves only one-dimensional, linear processing of mostly monochrome, static letters, and uses a small vocabulary of characters to be recognized. Which is to say, reading utilizes but a tiny portion of our cognitive system.

Our cognitive systems have evolved over millions of years of multimedia experiences. Our natural perception, cognition and experience are vaster and far grander than anything that reading can provide. To engage and know the world requires us to utilize our faculties to the fullest. The purpose of embodied practices is to open and expand – not contract – our faculties. Therefore, it is a big blunder to disown the non-literate dimension of our heritage and dismiss it as some kind of irrational fantasy, when in fact it is an amazing vehicle for knowledge.[20]

In India, the oral has been a creative laboratory for innovation, change and experimentation. Written, oral and embodied systems have thrived side by side, and reinforced one another. This has enabled our knowledge systems to be more contextual and relevant, enjoying greater freedom than in centralized societies.

I wonder if Pollock is unconsciously projecting his Judeo-Christian background where the earliest revelations (and hence the beginning of 'true' religion) come in the form of *written* stone tablets given by God to Moses. By contrast, the rishis did not receive written texts from any external deity. Nor can the highest human knowledge remain frozen in stone forever the way it is in the Ten Commandments.

Western ideas of culture and liberation have largely obliterated local knowledge and values across the globe. Could one not see Pollock's stance against the oral tradition as elitist? Many modern social scientists equate literacy with being educated, thereby discounting the knowledge base of the masses that is often embodied and not written.[21]

On one hand, Pollock's liberation philology project claims to liberate the Indian downtrodden from their abusive traditions. However, in contradistinction to this goal, it eschews the non-literate cultural production that arises naturally among ordinary people. He hobnobs with elites and writes using intricate Western theories that no ordinary reader can fathom. The main consumers for his works are a small subset of Western academics and their Indian students. It is no surprise that he is so dismissive of oral traditions.

The table below summarizes key differences between oral and written ways of knowing as per my views.

Oral/Embodied Knowing	Written/Disembodied Knowing
Hindu theories and practices show vac (speech) at levels more profound than external and mental speech. These are 'pashyanti' and 'para' levels, attained in meditation. Higher states of consciousness are embodied and trans-rational, not to be confused with pre-rational.	Intellectual knowledge and writing are limited to a lower level of knowing.
One-on-one direct communication, similar to guru–student or modern 'coaching', caters to individual needs.	Impersonal teaching through written texts, not easily customized for each individual's psychological configuration.
Not easily controlled by powerful institutions.	Controlled by media, academic publishing and higher educational institutions, all of which are vulnerable to top-down power.
Future of multimedia technology: non-linear cognition is consistent with the brains of animals, including humans.	Linear cognition, artificial reduction that is counter to our nature or to the world around us.

This general background helps us see that Pollock rejects the possibility of super-rational states and thus falls into the pre-rational/trans-rational fallacy. For him the verses of the Vedas are magical chants put together by men who were in awe of nature and expressed their wonderment by fantasizing about all sorts of gods. Such primitive men glorified the exploits of the gods as a way of coping with the vagaries of nature. This is why he sees the Vedas as having no legitimacy and serving no useful purpose.

Accusing yajnas of being linked to social hierarchy

Pollock's rejection of the oral tradition is also linked to the notion that its only use according to him was for the performance of rituals. This 'sacerdotal isolation' of Sanskrit, as he calls it, indicated its limited and exclusive nature; he sees this isolation as a strategy by Sanskrit speakers for perpetrating inequality and discrimination. He also implicitly claims that brahmins were incapable of innovating because they were stuck in mechanical Vedic chanting. Pollock marginalizes the significance of mantra and dismisses it as 'hymnology', a perfunctory repetition of meaningless sounds. He does not appreciate the vibrational function of mantra and its influence on embodied knowing.

Pollock's argument about how Sanskrit rituals led to social hierarchy goes as follows: In the early first millennium BCE, Sanskrit was used only as the language of the Veda. Brahmins performed their magical chants while doing fire rituals called 'yajnas'. They convinced the public that only brahmins could do these rituals and that the rituals were necessary for solving human problems. In return, the public was required to provide for and sustain the brahmins. This, Pollock claims, was how and why brahmins monopolized Sanskrit. They refused to teach the Vedas to non-brahmins, and therefore knowledge of how to use Sanskrit and perform yajna was not available beyond the chosen few.

An incorrect assumption being made here is that Sanskrit in the early period had no other use except for chanting the Vedas in rituals.[22] Pollock interchanges and equates three separate claims as one: exclusivity of Sanskrit, exclusivity of Vedas and exclusivity of performing yajnas. Therefore, he assumes, monopolizing the yajnas amounted to the monopolizing of all of Sanskrit.

When discussing the 'social monopolization' and 'discursive ritualization' of Sanskrit, he explains:

> At least two species of the language family usually called Indo-Aryan were in use as far back as we can see. One of these, Sanskrit, was a formal speech, viewed as correct by the custodians of the language and employed in particular contexts broadly related to *vaidika* ritual activity; the other was a demotic speech with what are usually called Middle-Indic characteristics.[23]

Demotic speech is defined as the speech of ordinary people used commonly for daily life. Pollock is saying that while brahmins used Sanskrit for their Vedic chanting, the rest of the population used a different, more colloquial, language. He claims that social restrictions on usage of Sanskrit by brahmins separated them from those who used everyday/demotic language. His theory of languages insists that these two languages were not equal or symmetrical in power, and that Sanskrit was hegemonic over the popular (demotic) languages. This point will be explained in Chapter 7 on the history of languages.

In addition, he claims that because the brahmins followed strict rules of ritual purity that were required for Vedic chanting, this in turn gave them another reason to discriminate against women and shudras. Thus, Pollock connects Sanskrit and its alleged monopolization by brahmins with what he says has been the unchanging social hierarchy in Hindu India.

Rejecting the shastras as Vedic dogma

For Pollock, shastras (texts of systematic knowledge) are also seen as tainted with Vedic cosmology. Hence, the study of them on their own terms is to be avoided. The study of shastras is to be carried out by scholars like him for the purpose of uncovering the social oppression built into them. Through much of Pollock's voluminous works, he displays a negative attitude towards shastras. He describes them as carriers of structures that deepen and maintain the Vedic hegemony, or else he ignores them altogether.

His case against shastras is articulated in one of his early papers, written in 1985. It presents a detailed analysis of his views on this subject. This paper was published in the prestigious *Journal of the American Oriental Society* in a special issue in honour of Pollock's teacher, the famous Harvard Indologist, Daniel Ingalls.[24] His extreme views on shastra provide insight into the deep-rooted prejudices and chauvinism of the West. The abstract at the beginning of the article states his position clearly:

> The understanding of the relationship of *śāstra* ('theory') to *prayoga* ('practical activity') in Sanskritic culture is shown to be diametrically opposed to that usually found in the West. Theory is held always and necessarily to precede and govern practice; there is no dialectical interaction between them. Two important implications of this *fundamental postulate are that all knowledge is pre-existent, and that progress can only be achieved by a regressive re-appropriation of the past.* The eternality of the *vedas*, the *śāstra* par excellence, is one presupposition or justification for this assessment of *śāstra*. Its principal ideological effects are to naturalize and de-historicize cultural practices, two components in a larger discourse of power.[25]

The following summarizes the points he makes in his paper:

- Since the Vedas are considered eternal and perfect, they are assumed to be the repository of all knowledge. Therefore, shastras are incapable of fresh creativity and progress as they are limited to whatever is contained in the Vedas.
- Shastras can merely restate or extrapolate from what is already in the Vedas, but they cannot utilize fresh insights from the empirical world. He calls this 'regressive'.
- No historical advancement is possible in the Western sense because shastras are incapable of producing anything new.

- Shastras discourage individual agency, unlike in the West where individual agency is emphasized. This means the behaviour of Indian people is driven by codified rules that emanate from the Vedas.

Pollock is unable to see that transcendence is the very fountainhead of creativity. For Hindus, a shastra can be a tool leading to transcendence, be it rasa in the performing arts, jnana in Vedanta, or samadhi in yoga. All these paths enhance creativity. Instead, he sees shastras as extrapolations from a structure of religious dogma that is deterministic and the cause of bondage; he sees this as leading to misery and the entrapment of people.

Pollock characterizes the shastras as frozen in time and decries the 'homogeneity with which they treated the subject over some two thousand years'.[26] Along with these shastra stipulations, the 'codification of behavior was represented across the entire cultural spectrum'.[27] This is what resulted in a normative (dogmatic) culture. In the process, creativity and intellectual progress were suffocated. According to him, shastras are meant to serve the purpose of domination, authoritarianism and cultural hegemony.

In this early paper, he establishes the shastras as a key culprit in the social abuses that he highlights in later work, stating:

> It was this attitude that prompted me to further study in the area of shastric regulation, conceived accordingly as an analysis of the components of cultural hegemony or at least authoritarianism. The question of domination remains in my view important for several areas of pre-modern India, the realms of social and political practices, for instance.[28]

Even art in India is constrained by rigid rules, he says, and refers to these rules as 'cultural grammars'. My own view is that every society has such rules. However, he feels that Indian shastras stand out compared to the texts of other cultures, because shastras offer the 'most exquisite expression' of how they can be used to regulate every aspect of human behaviour.

Pollock argues that the rules for Vedic rituals were not limited to the spiritual domain but also applied to secular life to constrain people's daily behaviour. This made them rigid and incapable of innovation. In other words, although peoples of virtually all cultures try to follow some rules of conduct, none has been as rigid or frozen as those living in a Vedic culture. He explains his position:

> Such cultural grammars exist in every society; they are the code defining a given culture as such. Classical Indian civilization, however, offers what may be the most exquisite expression of the centrality of rule-governance in human behavior. Under the influence perhaps of the paradigm deriving from the strict regulation of ritual action in vedic ceremonies, the procedures for which are set forth in those rule-books par excellence, the *Brāhmaṇas*, secular life as a whole was subject to a kind of ritualization, whereby all its performative gestures and signifying practices came to be encoded in texts. *Śāstra, the Sanskrit word for these grammars, thus presents itself as one of the fundamental features and problems of Indian civilization in general and of Indian intellectual history in particular.*[29]

According to him, westerners find Indian culture alien because Western civilization is built on freedom and is not shackled by such bondage.

Pollock's approach is often to start by praising the tradition, and those who do not read him closely will find plenty to celebrate. For instance, in the very same pages where he criticizes shastras for being codes for oppression, he also says that this collection of knowledge systems is 'a monumental, in some cases unparalleled, intellectual accomplishment in its own right – and extrinsically, with respect to the impact it has exercised, or sought to exercise, on the production and reproduction of culture in traditional India'.[30] What a closer reading reveals is that these monumental and unparalleled shastras are to be seen as a prison in which Hindus have trapped themselves. He believes that virtually every human activity of Indians has been affected by shastras and that every shastra is but a way to confine freedom:

> That the practice of any art or science, that all activity whatever succeeds to the degree it achieves conformity with shastric norms would imply that the improvement of any given practice lies, not in

> the future and the discovery of what has never been known before, but in the past and the more complete recovery of what was known in full in the past.[31]

He says, 'dharma is by definition "rule-boundedness"', and notes that, 'the rules themselves are encoded in *śāstra*'.[32] These rules have governed every aspect of human behaviour in India, having been codified as formal texts from an early date. They had to be mechanically learned and applied, without adequate reflection or debate, he says. Such grammars of behaviour control were 'invested with massive authority, ensuring what in many cases seems to have been a nearly unchallengeable claim to normative control of cultural practices'.[33]

In short, traditional Hindus are depicted in ways resembling robots, living in compliance with intricate rules which they cannot challenge or amend; this is said to be in part because the shastras were regarded as having come from the gods.

He explains that shastra can be of two kinds: apaurusheya (of transcendental origin) and paurusheya (of human origin). Then he says that even those composed by humans claim to be of divine origin. He gives examples of shastras viewing themselves as 'divinely inspired prototypes' or as 'exact reproductions of the divine prototypes obtained through uncontaminated, unexpurgated descent from the original'.[34] The earliest shastras, including those in secular fields such as architecture, astronomy and medicine, 'contrive for themselves' what Pollock sees as the 'mythological self-understanding' that they have descended from various gods.

Therefore, he writes, 'The Veda, the transcendent *śāstra*, subsumes all knowledge.'[35] Even secular shastra is a portion of this corpus emanating from the Vedas which is 'the basis of all activity'. Secular shastra is established as the basis for every aspect of human activity, and this is how it 'attained its incomparable legitimacy and claim to practical authority'.[36]

The implications are ominous: even the secular shastras are to be downgraded as part of Pollock's project to secularize Sanskrit. These shastras may appear secular in terms of the kinds of things they address, but they are driven by the Vedic substratum. Hence, Vedic poisons have permeated all the shastras.

Pollock also wants to show that shastras are a closed canon, and hence they deny us the ability to invent freely. He cites various traditional thinkers who gave lists of the shastras which they considered valid and he uses these lists to conclude that the shastra canon of all knowledge is closed. He says, 'The very notion of a finite set of "topics of knowledge" implies an attempt at an exhaustive classification of human cultural practices.'[37] I would suggest that one could draw the exact opposite conclusion from Pollock's data: the mere fact that so many authorities he cites gave *different* lists of shastras that they considered valid goes to show that the world of shastras is far from closed or fixed. There was a thriving production of new and original shastras that, in various ways, competed with each other, unbounded by the kinds of restrictions he sees.

The early Vedangas, he says, were descriptive texts which merely explained and elaborated on what was already in the Vedas. However, they were not prescriptive in the sense of legislating behaviour. Later on, things changed and each subsequent shastra transformed into 'a rigorously normative code, enabling it to speak in an injunctive mood'.[38] Shastras increasingly used the Vedic authority to shape the reality with which humans were required to comply.

In effect, although he does not use the term, he insinuates that Hindu culture is driven by dogmatic 'commandments' in the Vedas. Here he seems to be superimposing the Western religious idea of God's commandments carved in stone, and is searching for a similar function in the Sanskrit tradition. He would argue, of course, that the West liberated itself from Biblical injunctions when it entered the 'age of reason'. Indians have not been so progressive, in his view. This is one reason why he considers his work and that of his students to be so critical for the liberation of Indians.

An important part of his logic is to insist that the Sanskrit grammatical tradition provides the relationship between theory (shastra) and practical behaviour. He claims that the purpose of royal courts commissioning formal Sanskrit grammars is to restrict practice and make it depend upon theory, and this is a means of ensuring and enforcing that all cultural practice conforms to the Vedas. Even in sex, as explained in the Kamasutra, the shastras instruct the subject what to do and even how to feel the experience. (An individual must not allow his feelings and natural responses to lead the activity, he says.) Pollock repeatedly emphasizes this top-down nature of the flow of all knowledge in shastras. What he implies is that in all of this, there seems to be no consideration for people's actual lives:

> All knowledge derives from *śāstra*; success in astrology or in the training of horses and elephants, no less than in language use and social intercourse, is achieved only because the rules governing these practices have percolated down to the practitioners – not because they were discovered independently through the creative power of practical consciousness 'however far removed' from the practitioners the *śāstra* may be. ... Even the act of ascetic renunciation, which is in its very essence the withdrawal from the rule-boundedness of social existence, depends on the mastery and correct execution of shastric rules.[39]

He does cite some counter-examples showing that pragmatic considerations of experience were at times given importance. Kautilya is cited as saying that someone who knows only theory but lacks experience will come to grief, and encourages learning from men of experience. Similarly, in economics, a shastra recommends learning from those who are engaged in practical affairs. Manu is cited advising that we learn from common people. Dandin, the famous writer of the sixth century, is cited as saying he also observed actual practices to formulate his texts. The medical text, *Charaka Samhita*, asserts that the most dependable information is to be gained by direct observation: 'The wise understand that their best teacher is the very world around them.'[40]

However, in typical Pollock style, after acknowledging a few examples of texts that contradict his position (in order to appear balanced), he simply dismisses them: 'Such voices ... in any case are pretty much in the minority. The dominant ideology is that which ascribes clear priority and absolute competence to shastric codification.'[41] However, he has not given convincing reasons for sidelining these contrary examples. No evidence is cited that the creative and pragmatic camp was a minority and that the shastras were mechanisms for authoritarian control.[42]

The shastra constraints, he alleges, were not a later development; he finds them as early as the Ramayana and various Puranas. Many examples are cited by him to make it seem that people who thought for themselves or tried to compose their own shastras were severely reprimanded. Abhinavagupta, the great exponent of Kashmir Shaivism, is mentioned by him saying that one must never contemplate action according to one's own insights but must instead follow shastric injunctions.

It is the Bhagavadgita, says Pollock, which contains the 'most succinct statement of the doctrine'. He paraphrases Bhagavadgita 16.23–24 as follows:

> Whoever abandons the injunctive rules of *śāstra* and proceeds according to his own, will never achieve success, or happiness, or final beatitude. Therefore let *śāstra* be your guide in deciding what to do and what not to do. Once you determine what shastric regulation pronounces, you may proceed to action.[43]

After citing many such examples, he concludes:

> First, the 'creation' of knowledge is presented as an exclusively divine activity, and occupies a structural cosmological position suggestive of the creation of the material universe as a whole. Knowledge, moreover – and again, this is knowledge of every variety, from the transcendent sort 'whose purposes are uncognizable' [*adṛṣṭārtha*] to that of social relations, music, medicine (and evidently even historical knowledge) – is by and large viewed as permanently fixed in its dimensions; knowledge, along with the practices that depend on it, does not change or grow, but is frozen for all time in a given set of texts that are continually made available to human beings in whole or in part during the ever repeated cycles of cosmic creation.[44]

The dominant position in the West, according to him, has been the exact opposite. There, 'efficient practice precedes the theory of it'. Westerners are not frozen in any shastra-like dogma and instead are learning from practical experience. Nevertheless, he remarks condescendingly, Western

Indologists should not use the Western standard to judge Indians since the goal of Indology is not to understand India in terms of the pragmatic and freedom-loving West. That would be unfair. His goal, he claims, is just to understand

> how such things were understood in traditional India. This understanding, as should now be clear, *is diametrically opposed to that commonly found in the West,* and the formulation of it appears to have been an essential component in the mature Weltanschauung of traditional India.[45]

In spite of his disclaimer, there is Western chauvinism that comes out. The West was endowed by a 'peculiar constellation of representations' concerning time, history, etc. He is here referring to Western metaphysical assumptions about the nature of the cosmos. By implication he is saying that India was not endowed with these. Therefore, Indians have faced numerous 'ideological hindrances', he says. Their behaviour derives from the 'divine patterns' recorded in the Vedas. This is why they cannot progress based on people's 'experience, experiment, invention, discovery, innovation'. He explains further:

> The relationship of *śāstra* to practical activity may be patterned after the function of the vedas in, so to speak, cosmic 'practice', the creation of the material universe. ... Human action in general may thus be viewed as following the paradigm offered on the plane of cosmogonic speculation.[46]

Hence, he concludes that Indians are incapable of originality and of developing new insights. All this he spells out as follows:

> Indian intellectual history demonstrates that this conclusion was clearly drawn – that there can be no conception of progress, of the forward 'movement from worse to better,' on the basis of innovations in practice. Undoubtedly the idea of progress in the West germinated in a soil made fertile by a peculiar constellation of representations, about time, history, and eschatology. Whatever may be the possibility of the idea's growth in the absence of these concepts, it is clear that

> in traditional India there were at all events ideological hindrances in its way. If any sort of amelioration is to occur, this can only be in the form of a 'regress', a backward movement aiming at a closer and more faithful approximation to the divine pattern ... Logically excluded from epistemological meaningfulness are likewise experience, experiment, invention, discovery, innovation. According to his own self-representation, there can be for the thinker no originality of thought, no brand-new insights, notions, perceptions, but only the attempt better and more clearly to grasp and explain the antecedent, always already formulated truth. All Indian learning, accordingly, perceives itself and indeed presents itself largely as commentary on the primordial *śāstra*.[47]

Pollock asserts that even if in certain areas like mathematics and architecture, Indians have managed to achieve something creative, they did not see it as original. Instead, they saw it as merely recovering and renovating the prior knowledge:

> We may in fact characterize the ideological effects of the shastric paradigm more broadly as follows: First, all contradiction between the model of cultural knowledge and actual cultural change is thereby at once transmuted and denied; creation is really re-creation, as the future is, in a sense, the past. Second, the living, social, historical, contingent tradition is naturalized, becoming as much a part of the order of things as the laws of nature themselves: Just as the social, historical phenomenon of language is viewed by Mīmāṃsā as natural and eternal, so the social dimension and historicality of all cultural practices are eliminated in the shastric paradigm. And finally, through such denial of contradiction and reification of tradition, the sectional interests of pre-modern India are universalized and valorized. *The theoretical discourse of śāstra becomes in essence a practical discourse of power.*[48]

The final sentence is key to understanding Pollock's perspective: Shastra, he says, is Veda-centric and controls theory and practice; *this is how power is imposed top-down.*

His conclusion is that according to Indian tradition, all sciences have pre-existed without any human author, and there are no theories in the humanities developed freely by humans based on their own experiences. He cites a well-known passage from Vedanta that just as a clay pot pre-exists in the clay, so also all knowledge must pre-exist in something. Hence, just as the potter does not create anything new, so also we cannot create knowledge. He claims to have made a discovery here, and says that the social and political implications of this discovery have not been properly explained in Indian philosophical literature.

My attempt here is to draw the attention of the insiders to the main lines of the arguments presented by Pollock for rejecting the shastra literature. I do not intend to give a full-scale, point-by-point rebuttal. There are far too many sweeping assumptions in Pollock's analysis described in the foregoing. He does not seem to understand that dharma, shastra and indeed every teaching in the Indian tradition is meant to be interpreted in a given context and not as an absolute, as is often the case in Western thought. (I have argued in my book *Being Different* that shastra is not normative but contextual.) He constantly ignores this principle and sees every statement in shastra as akin to God's commandments in Western traditions. According to our tradition, a shastra is also meant to facilitate one's journey along a path leading to immensely creative states.

Plenty of scholars, both Indian and Western, have noted the remarkable amount of serious argumentation among Indian thinkers, long before the West began its critical thinking (which too was imported from the Greeks and is almost entirely absent in the Bible). No serious scholar of Indian shastras says they lacked progress from one era to another. Indian society in general has shown remarkable innovation in numerous domains of knowledge. For example, George Cardona, one of the most prominent Sanskrit scholars in the West, wrote an excellent paper showing the sharp critical thinking skills of early Sanskrit scholars across various disciplines. He writes: 'At no time in early and medieval India was there an absolute, thoughtless acceptance of tradition, even by different followers of a single tradition.' Arguing directly opposite to Pollock's position, he says, 'Nor are grammatical, exegetical or logical systems made solely as maidservants to Vedic tradition.'[49]

As far as his assertion that shastras stifled debate is concerned, I suggested earlier in this chapter that the proliferation of shastras that disagreed with each other should lead to the exact opposite assessment. Also, Pollock must compare this freedom with the dogmatic restrictions that prevailed in the same period in Western societies.

Infinity Foundation started an ambitious project to research and publish twenty volumes of the *History of Indian Science and Technology*, ten of which have so far made it to print. These show clearly the practical advancements from one period to the next in numerous fields such as metallurgy, civil engineering and the like. These advancements were empirically based and reflected practical experience. In fact, prior to the eighteenth century, when the British colonial system disrupted Indian industry, there is little doubt that India was considered (by Europeans' own accounts) to be far ahead of Europe in many practical/ vyavaharika domains. These included medicine, agriculture, metallurgy and textiles, to name a few. Indian contributions to mathematics are legendary. Pollock simply ignores all this evidence that would undermine his thesis.

More recently, there has been extensive Western appropriation of Indian knowledge systems in the mind sciences (cognitive science, psychology, neuroscience), as well as in healing, environmentalism, and other domains. I am also writing a book on the Hindu-Buddhist contributions that have transformed Christianity over the past century in profound ways. Arguably, in certain fields the shastra-based Indian tradition has shown far greater creativity, diversity and evolution of ideas than the supposedly progressive and historically determined West. The international success enjoyed by Indians in many creative fields today is further testimony to this heritage.

Using Buddhism as a wedge for secularizing Sanskrit

Pollock develops a new chronology of Sanskrit history to support his claim that the Buddhists started the programme of detoxifying Sanskrit. They did this, he says, by removing the Vedic influences and by developing literary and documentary (i.e., secular) uses for Sanskrit extensively for the first time. This is how it became transformed into a language useful for kavya. The diagram that follows shows the first major rupture of the Vedic tradition as claimed by Pollock. The main elements of this rupture are as follows:

- Vedas were brahmin-controlled and hence so was Sanskrit.
- Things changed when foreign nomadic tribes called Shakas and Kushans, among others, arrived from Central Asia and settled in northern India. They became Buddhists or else were strongly influenced by Buddhism, and they started producing works in Sanskrit. The Jataka tales of Buddhists were a result of this.
- This act of nastika writers (those who do not affirm the Vedas) adopting Sanskrit is what changed Sanskrit. The new writers in Sanskrit opposed brahminical hegemony and caste. Being secular people, they also rejected Sanskrit as the 'language of the devatas'. Hence, they sidelined mantras and Vedic rituals. A new kind of Sanskrit emerged that was free from brahmin tyranny. Literature flowered freely henceforth.
- Brahmins continued to practise their rituals and mantras on the sidelines, and this usage of Sanskrit is what Pollock pejoratively calls 'hymnology' – the mechanical parroting of hymns.[50]
- By claiming the above chronology, Pollock is implying that the Ramayana came after the Jataka tales of Buddhism.

The above assumptions are a part of Pollock's theory that Sanskrit became secularized by the Buddhists. I reject his notion of two different epochs separated by a Buddhist assault against the Vedas. According to him, the epoch before Buddhism was one in which the sole and exclusive use for Sanskrit was for the paramarthika realm, to the exclusion of the vyavaharika realm. After the Buddhist intervention to de-monopolize the control of Sanskrit by brahmins, he says, the opposite happened: the vyavaharika usage became dominant and sidelined the paramarthika. According to tradition, Sanskrit was always both the language of the gods (i.e., paramarthika) and used in the world of men (i.e., vyavaharika). This continued after Buddhism.

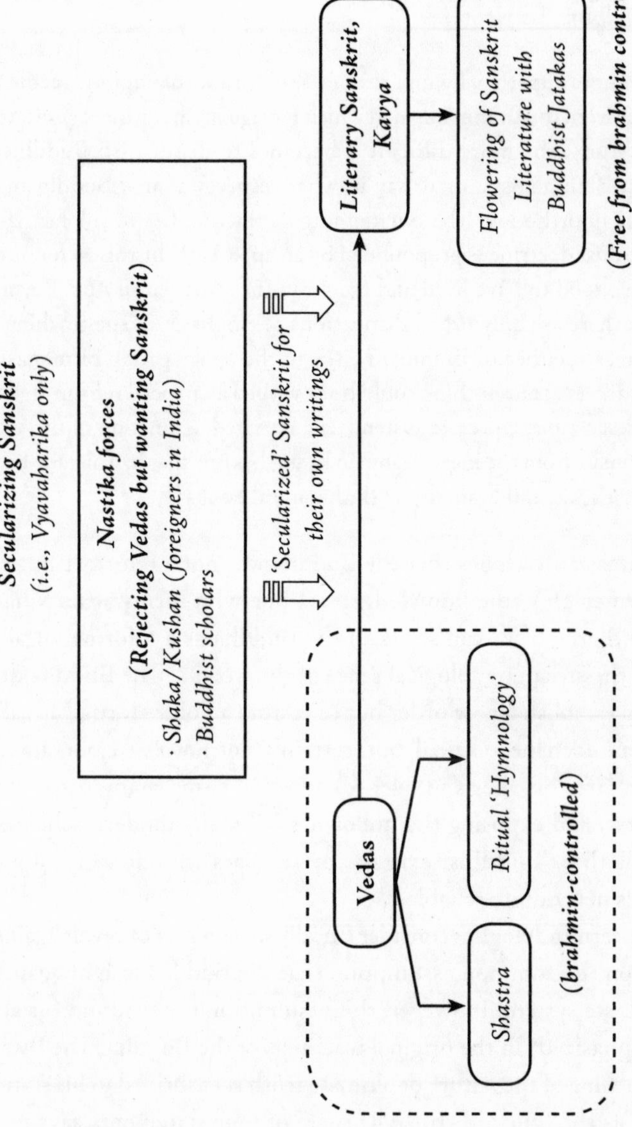
Secularizing Sanskrit
(i.e., Vyavaharika only)
Nastika forces
(Rejecting Vedas but wanting Sanskrit)
Shaka/Kushan (foreigners in India)
Buddhist scholars
'Secularized' Sanskrit for their own writings
Literary Sanskrit, Kavya
Flowering of Sanskrit Literature with Buddhist Jatakas
(Free from brahmin control)
Vedas
Ritual 'Hymnology'
Shastra
(brahmin-controlled)

Pollock's ideas are based on a cherished premise of Western Indologists that Buddha was opposed to the Vedas. This view was refuted many decades ago by Ananda Coomaraswamy. In his book *Hinduism and Buddhism*, he wrote:

> The more superficially one studies Buddhism, the more it seems to differ from the Brahmanism in which it originated; the more profound our study, the more difficult it becomes to distinguish Buddhism from Brahmanism, or to say in what respects, if any, Buddhism is really unorthodox. The outstanding distinction lies in the fact that Buddhist doctrine is propounded by an apparently historical founder, understood to have lived and taught in the sixth century BC. Beyond this, there are only broad distinctions of emphasis ... The teaching is addressed either to Brahmans ... or to the congregation of monastic wanderers ... but nothing could be described as a 'social reform' or as a protest against the caste system. The repeated distinction of the 'true Brahman' from the mere Brahman by birth is one that had already been drawn again and again in the Brahmanical books.[51]

Coomaraswamy argues that the Buddha was not a reformer but rather a *re*-former of Vedic knowledge, i.e., one who forms again what was already there: 'If we can speak of the Buddha as a reformer at all, it is only in the strict etymological sense of the word.'[52] The Buddha did not come to establish a new order but to restore an older form. He calls the Buddha's doctrine 'original' but 'certainly not novel'.[53] Coomaraswamy substantiates his thesis in over forty pages, citing many texts, chapter and verse, and exposing the hollowness of many modern scholars. He cautions that, 'Buddhist exegesis by scholars who do not know their Vedas is never quite reliable.'[54]

Western Indologists consider Buddhism as a sort of revolt against the Vedas on the common assumption that the Buddha fought against the varna/caste system. However, this assumption is not found (or at least not emphasized) in the original teachings of the Buddha. The Buddha's core teaching of the nature of ultimate truth is enshrined in his statement known as the fourfold truth. This set of four statements says nothing about varna, jati or the like. His teaching about the path to follow is called the eightfold path. Here too none of the eight steps he prescribes says anything about rejecting varna.

In fact, there is no record that Indian society on a large scale decided to abandon identities based on varna or jati as a result of the teachings of the Buddha. There is no core text attributed to the Buddha himself calling for a varna-free society. Nor did the Buddha make any outright denunciation of brahmins. We do not find any Indian text or texts written by Chinese visitors from the early period discussing any social revolution in India, nor any injunction from the Buddha or any king to overthrow the social system. The Buddha did not offer any such advice to any king either. This issue ought to be an important topic for debate. Appendix A offers some additional arguments that could begin such a debate.

Disconnecting kavya from Vedas and shastras

According to Pollock, the Buddhist intervention against Vedic hegemony and Sanskrit monopoly is what led to a new kind of written Sanskrit and this is how kavya began. It is the influence of Buddhism that enables him to separate kavya from the Vedic spiritual genres. I will now summarize his arguments that exaggerate the differences between kavya and Vedas and between kavya and shastras.

Pollock acknowledges that kavya has been considered by tradition to be the direct descendent of the Vedic mantra and an extension of the sacred domain. However, he insists, such traditional views are incorrect. Although there are 'some commonalities', kavya, according to him, was 'profoundly new' and 'fundamentally different' from Vedic ideas in so far as it was a vehicle for political power instead of sacred discourse. He emphasizes the differences between Vedas and kavya by citing the following points:[55]

1. The Vedas are not attributed to a single author, either human or divine, whereas kavya has an explicit author.[56]
2. The Vedas and kayva were always treated differently, and the Vedas were never read as 'literature' or as a political source.

He says that the Veda was never read as kavya and never cited in anthologies.

3. The rhetorical, discursive, aesthetic and affective purposes of kavya are different from those of the Vedas.
4. Unlike the Vedas, which do not have a beginning, the kavya, as a literary genre, has a beginning in the Ramayana which is called the adi kavya (first kavya).
5. Vedas were transmitted orally; kayva, in writing.[57] While the Vedas have traditionally been heard and learned in the oral form, he contrasts this with kavya and says that the 'one thing that could not be *kāvya* was the purely oral'.[58]

Thus, Pollock tries to separate kavya from the Vedas. He says there is a 'clear and untranscendable line dividing Veda from *kāvya*', and emphatically adds: 'Before the modern era, the Veda was never read as *kāvya*, never cited in anthologies, never adduced as exemplary in literary textbooks; in fact, the Veda was expressly denied to be *kāvya*.'[59]

In response, K.S. Kannan points out that the Atharva Veda makes a reference to kavya as something that never gets old, and never dies; the interpretations vary, some saying it is poetry, some saying it is the world that is metaphorically referred to.[60] Kannan also points out that the Vedas have been designated as a kavya in some inscriptions. Lord Shiva is praised as the poet whose kavya is the triad of the Vedas, thereby implying that the three Vedas are Shiva's kavya. Kannan has also compiled other extensive material to support this view.[61] Also, traditional Hindu dancers performing Bharatanatyam assert that their art is based on Bharata Muni's *Natya Shastra*, which in one of its first few verses (1.17) says it is based on Rig Veda, Sama Veda, Yajur Veda, etc.[62]

Besides creating a dichotomy between kavya and the Vedas, Pollock also creates mutual tension between kavya and shastra. He writes: 'The discourse of *śāstra*, or systematic thought, differs from the mantra, or liturgical formulas, and both differ from *kāvya* because each has a radically different intention and purpose.'[63] Pollock explains the principal difference between kavya and shastra in this way:

> At the high-water mark of Sanskrit literary theory in the eleventh century, the principal dichotomy in discourse was between *kāvya* and *śāstra*, or literature and science; a comparable distinction was operationalized in inscriptions by the use of one language for the expressive and imaginative, and another for the contentual and informational.[64]

Thus, he defines kavya as literature and shastra as science. These are Western categories which allow him to apply Western dichotomies of literature versus non-literature to Sanskrit texts. He writes:

> At the heart of the premodern Indian conception is a distinction not unknown to modern literary theory, though variously formulated: between expression and content, performance and constatation, imagination and information ... In general, then, there is broad enough agreement on the *differentia specifica* of literature and nonliterature to make modern Western distinctions largely unobjectionable for describing the history of South Asian literary cultures.[65]

Specifically, he says shastras are a genre of Sanskrit that claim to provide factual content. In sharp contrast, he maintains, kavya is that which expresses and performs what is imagined and cannot be verified. It is not information, per se, and hence corresponds to literature. Both of these are different from mantra, which is equivalent to liturgy in Western categories. He writes:

> The communication of new imagination, for example, is hardly less valuable in itself than the communication of new information. In fact, a language's capacity to function as a vehicle for such imagination is one crucial measure of its social energy. This is so in part because of the text-genre that above all others embodies imagination and its associated expressivity – called *kāvya* in Sanskrit or 'literature'.[66]

He is saying that there is no need to look at Sanskrit texts more broadly to find 'social energy'. Only kavya needs to be looked at because: (a) social energy may be measured by its new imagination; and (b) kavya contains the capacity to communicate such new imagination. Thus, if kavya can be shown to be static (which Pollock equates with Vedic) in its expression in any given period, then it is a reflection of a low level of imagination and social energy in that period.

Tradition disagrees with such absolute dichotomies. The epics and the Puranas act as shastras as well as kavyas depending on the context and audience. Kavya can have both dimensions: related to the Vedas (and hence a path to transcendence) or entirely secular for pure entertainment. However, Pollock insists that the former dimension is unimportant. His argument is that the sacred aspect cannot cause social progress because it is other-worldly. According to him, only secular literature can produce change in the real world. This is consistent with his dismissive attitude towards paramarthika and his valorization of vyavaharika only.

Tradition maintains that *both* these dimensions (sacred and secular) are important in kavya. In many texts it has been expressly stated that the goal of kavya and shastra are not different at all. For example, Kuntaka in his *Vakrokti-jivita* (roughly tenth century) clearly says that the key purpose of both kavya and shastra is one and the same.[67] Bhattanayaka (ninth century) proposed the metaphor of the Vedas, Puranas and kavya functioning as the king, the friend, and the wife: all designed towards the same unitary goal.

In fact, virtually every field of traditional knowledge of India has texts declaring their goal of attaining the four purusharthas (pursuits of life). Many kavis wrote bhakti literature invoking the paramarthika, while firmly living in the vyavaharika. Kalidasa straddles both domains, blending the two. For Hindus, kavya facilitates living in the vyavaharika and at the same time gaining access to the higher realm of existence. Tradition says that kavya is useful to present the Vedic truths through images, stories and mundane narratives. For example, Rama's life in the Ramayana presents profound ideas and principles in a user-friendly way. Kavya, itihasa and *Natya Shastra* exist at the popular level of expression and manifestation, and make the Vedic world view known for the benefit of common people of all varnas and stages of life.

Kavya can entertain and educate. It can also take us all the way to its culmination where it connects us with the realm of paramarthika, the transcendent. Some kavis write tragic-romantic kavyas, describing everyday joys, travails and tribulations, but their contemplative pointers to the paramarthika are never far away. Thus, kavya can be used as one of the most important bridges from the vyavaharika realm to the paramarthika realm, that is, from the mundane to the transcendent. This was the goal of all art, not just kavya. The flexibility of kavya makes it rich and concrete, with an unlimited variety that is contextualized for particular times, places, persons, situations and actions. Its subject matter is the human experience of life, accumulated over thousands of years.

The traditional view of kavya emphasizes the importance of *Natya Shastra*, ascribed to Bharata Muni. This seminal text underpins all the performing arts and poetry, and provides informal access to Vedic insights without requiring a formal study of Sanskrit texts. It is also esteemed as 'the fifth Veda'. (The itihasas and Puranas also style themselves as the fifth Veda.) Hence, *Natya Shastra* and other kavya theories based on it provide an unbroken continuum of access to Vedic knowledge from various starting points: from everyday usage in the arts to the experience of the highest consciousness explained in Vedanta.

On the other hand, one must note that there is nothing equivalent to kavya in the Abrahamic religions. That is because liturgy (worship) is, for the most part, disconnected from the performing arts. There was no equivalent Jewish, Christian or Islamic dance, epic or drama, etc., that would serve as a full-fledged pathway to God and be considered on par with the Bible/Quran and prayer. In fact, Western theatre and literary arts are largely of Greek and/or Roman origin, from the pre-Christian era of paganism. Even in the Greek tradition, theatre and arts did not serve the same paramarthika purpose that they serve in Hinduism.

The divide between Biblical theology/liturgy on the one hand and the performing arts on the other is what Pollock seems to have superimposed on to Hinduism. He sets out to decouple kavya from the Vedas, by grounding kavya on a foundation that is remarkably different from the way Hindu tradition sees it. His objective is to praise kavya for bringing in a secular world view and to keep it segregated from transcendence. He values kavya immensely for several reasons, including aesthetic ones, but he values it most highly for enabling a secular and political distance from transcendence.

Pollock does not accept the Hindu claim that people who are bhaktas, for example, and who chant the kavyas to connect them to paramarthika can be creative and inventive when it comes to 'worldly', mundane matters. Pollock finds such claims troubling, because they are deeply influenced by what he calls 'philosophical-religious aesthetics', i.e., they are too immersed in sanatana dharma.[68] He wants kavya to be read with an eye towards the social and political intentions of the kavya authors. More specifically, he wants to excavate what he believes is the oppression explicitly or implicitly contained therein.

A key element of kavya did not receive the central attention by Pollock for much of his career. This element is rasa, which means the feeling evoked in an individual combined with the emotional theme embedded in a work of art. The art could be visual, or heard as music or as a reading, or it could be experienced as being part of a performance. Only very recently did he adequately acknowledge rasa as one of the central components of kavya. This happened when he invited an important Indian scholar, Radhavallabh Tripathi, to Columbia University to serve as visiting professor and teach a full course on rasa.[69] Even after he began to appreciate rasa, he has not fully acknowledged its foundations in the early sacred texts.

4

Sanskrit Considered a Source of Oppression

The crisis of Indology and a novel solution

Edward Said's thesis in his book *Orientalism* in the 1970s exposed the role played by Western scholars in supporting the colonial powers in India and elsewhere. This book triggered a great deal of introspection and feelings of guilt among Western academicians who entered a state of crisis about their field. Many of them were afraid to perform their earlier role of interpreting India, because that project had become tainted as 'Orientalism' with racist implications.

Pollock describes the resulting state of confusion as intellectual 'impotence', writing: 'In a postcolonial and post-Holocaust world ... these traditional foundations and uses of Indology have disappeared' and led to a feeling of 'impotence' and 'loss of purpose'.[1] According to him, Indologists 'no longer know why they are doing what they do'.[2] He wrote these words in 1993 by which time Said's work had achieved a devastating effect on Western studies concerning others and on Indology in particular.

By then the new field of 'post-colonial studies' had emerged in the wake of Said's writings. A large number of Indians jumped into this field to criticize the West and its Indology. Unfortunately, they did not know much about traditional Indian discourse, and hence their critiques of the West were (and still are) based almost entirely on using the West's own theories and methods. Indian post-colonial studies later morphed into subaltern studies, in which the blame shifted from colonialism and Christianity to India's own caste system and Hinduism. However, the subalternist scholars continued to use Western assumptions and theories about the caste system. Hence, it was not a true reversal of the gaze (i.e., purva-paksha) through an Indian lens. The Indian scholars in this field still continue to use Western imported frameworks such as Marxism, post-modernism, anthropology, secularism, Western feminism, critical theory and so forth. I have criticized this as a way for elitist Indians to become 'white liberal' intellectuals, or at least pseudo-intellectuals.

In my view, traditional Indian scholars missed a great opportunity to lead the new field of post-colonial studies. They ought to have entered this field by doing purva-paksha on Western Indology using Sanskrit categories and theories for their analysis.

Western Indologists found themselves facing a new opponent: the post-colonial scholar. Indologists naturally became defensive and sought to redefine their field in order to create a new role for themselves. They wanted to reposition their field such that they would not be accused of engaging in Orientalism with the ingrained connotations of that time. This task was not easy because many of the institutions for which they worked had past colonial links. Furthermore, the idiom, theories and methods being used in their field had been developed in the colonial era and were associated with oppression.

Pollock saw this as an opportunity. In his seminal paper of 1993, he seeks to transform the field of Indology such that it would not be seen as something which helped oppressors. Instead, he would like Indology to be seen as a resource for saving India. He made a breakthrough by arguing that *Orientalism as such had existed in Sanskrit itself long before the advent of European Orientalism.* This was a clever ploy to boomerang the blame for oppression on Sanskrit itself and thereby exculpate the European Indologists.

According to his argument, Sanskrit texts contain certain specific structures and ideas which lend themselves to oppression. Western Orientalists did not originate these problems, he argued. They learned the structures of oppression from their study of Sanskrit. Throughout his work Pollock iterates that the 'indigenous discourses of power – the various systematized and totalized constructions of inequality in traditional India – might be viewed as a preform of orientalism'.[3] By 'preform' he means that Orientalism had already existed in a preliminary way in traditional India. The place to look for it would be the 'systematized and totalized constructions of inequality', a phrase by which he alludes to the caste system. This thesis becomes more explicit and assertive in his work, as I shall show below.

He wants to prove that Nazism and British Indology were merely building on the socio-political oppression that had always existed in Sanskrit language and texts, and in Indian society which contained and reflected those texts. He claims that 'the pre-existence of a shared ideological base among indigenous and colonial elites may have been one contributing factor to the effectiveness with which England consolidated and maintained its rule in India'.[4] The Indian brahmin elites were like internal colonizers, and the British did nothing new by stepping into their shoes. By characterizing Sanskrit in this way, in effect, he relocates certain sources of oppression within Sanskrit itself.

His new kind of Indology, which he calls 'post-orientalism', has thus been given a new gloss to look like a provider of solutions to oppression, rather than being a facilitator of oppression the way Orientalism was. Indologists now want to be seen as heroes liberating the downtrodden. The oppressor would no longer be seen as the West; it were the brahmins as a social group who were the original oppressors of India, and Sanskrit was their weapon. Pollock has thus become a great innovator within Western Indology. He has repositioned that discipline with an entirely new game plan, such that it is not seen aligned with the oppressor but as a supplier of human rights for the oppressed.

He is especially critical of those Indologists who romanticize pre-colonial India, because he feels they are complicit in perpetuating the abuses of Sanskrit. Under the heading 'Pre-Orientalist Orientalism', Pollock finds fault with those who claim that orientalist biases emerged out of colonialism, Christian evangelism, etc. He says Western and Indian Indologists wanting to blame colonialism for India's problem have become prone to idealizing India's pre-colonial past. The British are usually accused of hegemony, but he says this is better seen as emanating from the 'pre-colonial orientalism' of the brahmins. He identifies caste as the pre-colonial institution that deserves all the blame.

His study of India is driven by the question: 'Which of those forms of traditional domination that have existed in India remain sedimented in contemporary society?'[5] Once he has identified these forms of traditional domination, he can delete them and thereby sanitize the Sanskrit tradition of its poisons. He accuses his fellow Indologists of being complicit and ignorant of their own role, because they have been romanticizing Sanskrit too much:

> The colonial foundations of Indology may have given way, but neocolonial foundations have been built in their place. These await careful analysis, and our ignorance of our own role in the reproduction of power may account in part for the acute sense of confusion about our work some of us feel.[6]

He wants to teach how to do Indology 'beyond the Raj and Auschwitz', and proposes a radical post-colonial Indology that should 'challenge the residual conceptual categories' of Sanskrit. He goes on to say: 'In rejecting Eurocentrism, we have to be particularly watchful of its mirror image, "*third worldism*",'[7] which is just as bad. The West's oppressiveness and the third world's own oppressiveness are reflections of each other. In this way, he goes on to accuse Sanskrit of being not only as bad as colonial oppression, but indeed one of the primary sources of it.

Pollock refers to his characterization of Sanskrit as 'Deep Orientalism', the title of his paper. It is 'deep' because its original source lies within the linguistic structures of Sanskrit, which got expressed in Sanskrit texts and in the society based on Sanskrit knowledge systems.

He frames Indology in a new manner, as follows:

1. He first admits, following Said, that 'the whole project of humanistic scholarship, by reason of its capitulations and collusions, seems suspect.'[8]
2. He then provides a new purpose for Indology going forward – namely, to rescue Indians from aspects of their own sanskriti, which he says are the source of various societal ills.
3. He calls the producers of pre-colonial Sanskrit texts 'Indian orientalists' because they wrote and thought in a way that perpetuated these ills. Brahmins and Hindus in general thus used Sanskrit hegemony to justify their oppression of Dalits, women and Muslims for centuries. Therefore, the seed of oppression lies in Sanskrit's DNA, as it were.
4. He focusses particularly on texts prior to the Turkish invasion of India and argues that such writings establish and sustain social differences even today. The dating of the texts he selects is critical for him to be able to show that these problems are of Hindu origin.
5. He insists that Sanskrit caused problems not just locally but globally, wherever it was admired and studied. British Indologists, for example, appropriated the *already existing* hegemony of Sanskrit for their own colonial discourse. German Indology borrowed the arguments and structures from Sanskrit for German fascism, including the Holocaust. Pollock's paper 'Deep Orientalism' has this as its core thesis.
6. He calls on liberal Western intellectuals to intervene actively in Indian society and politics in order to eradicate the social poisons carried within Sanskrit.

Pollock defines the task of Indology going forward as follows:

> *One task of post-orientalist Indology has to be to exhume, isolate, analyze, theorize, and at the very least talk about the different modalities of domination in traditional India.* By all means one is eager to help in the project of reclaiming 'traditions, histories, and cultures from

> imperialism' (Said 1989: 219), but can we forget that most of the traditions and cultures in question have been *empires of oppression* in their own right against women, above all, but also against other domestic communities?[9]

His team of scholars is being asked to be cautious when they revive India's past traditions and cultures because these 'have been empires of oppression'. He acknowledges that such intervention is controversial but that such controversy is unavoidable:

> It is a perilous enterprise for the Western scholar to thematize the violence in the traditions of others, especially when they are others who have been the victims of violence from the West (though a culture's failure to play by its own rules, and evidence of internal opposition to its domination, are two conditions that certainly lessen this peril). Yet can one avoid it and still practice an Indology that is critical, responsible, and self-aware?[10]

The parenthetical remark in the above quote is very important to understand. It says that the West is somehow less prone to committing oppression nowadays because there is dissent and internal opposition. In other words, according to him, the westerners revolt rather than play 'by their rules', whereas Indians (being fatalistic and stuck in shastras) are bound by the rigid rules of their culture and lack the initiative to rebel against injustice or move past them.

This helps Pollock rationalize the intervention by Indologists. In other words, the humanistic liberal voices within the West are justified in intervening in India to help overcome the Sanskrit-based ideologies that have spawned 'empires of oppression' over a long time. The culprit, he says, has been Sanskrit:

> Sanskrit was the principal discursive instrument of domination in premodern India and in addition, it has been continuously reappropriated in modern India by many of the most reactionary and communalist sectors of the population.[11]

This oppressive deployment of Sanskrit continues today, according to him, as he writes:

> *Traditional domination as coded in Sanskrit is not 'past history' in India, to be sure.* Partly by reason of the stored energy of an insufficiently critiqued and thus untranscended past, *it survives in various harsh forms* (intensified by the added toxins of capitalist exploitation by twice-born classes) despite legislation designed to weaken the economic and institutional framework associated with it.[12]

Scholars have ignored all this, he laments. So the goal of Indology today, he says, should be to 'exhume, isolate, analyze, theorize, and at the very least talk about the different modalities of domination in traditional India'.

His analysis is based on an interpretation of the social restrictions on the use of Sanskrit in the early tradition. Access to Sanskrit, he points out, was reserved for 'particular orders of society'.[13] In his view, Sanskrit only became de-monopolized by the intervention of Buddhists, though even then it remained an instrument of political power. Kings used it to stabilize the culture and create a 'culture-power formation'.[14] They decided who could study it and for what purpose. He elaborates on this point as follows:

> It was a code of communication not everyone was entitled to use, and fewer still were able to use. It is not just that some people did and some did not employ Sanskrit, but rather that some were permitted to do so and some – the majority, who otherwise might have been able to do so – were prohibited. Given the nature of the primary sphere for the application of Sanskrit, it is not surprising that this constraint was formulated as a restriction on participation in the rituals and liturgical practices of the Sanskrit speech community, whose members called themselves Āryas.[15]

In effect, Pollock wants to resurrect Orientalism in the post-colonial era by reformulating it in new clothing. He wants to criticize non-Western ideologies, such as Sanskrit-based ones, which are 'a species of a larger discourse of power that divides the world into "betters and lessers" and thus facilitate[s] the domination ... of any group'.[16] Whereas the previous Orientalism was seen as facilitating domination over Indians, his new genre (that I call American Orientalism) wants to liberate them from their own internal oppression caused in part by the deep structures in Sanskrit.

His movement to secularize Sanskrit is therefore devoted to the purpose of re-engineering Indian society today. Pollock's 'liberation philology' seeks to turn the study of Sanskrit into socio-political activism to undermine those aspects of Sanskrit that he sees as Vedic or linked to Hinduism.[17] He describes liberation philology as a project of

> supplementing post-colonialism with post-capitalism, or a concern over past wrongs with a concern for future rights; and finding way[s] to meet, from our small philological locations as specific intellectuals, the obligation to construct 'a planet-wide inclusivist community'.[18]

Studying Sanskrit as a Greek classicist and postmodernist

As noted elsewhere, Pollock's earlier academic background at Harvard University was as a Greek classicist. Therefore, it is not surprising that he wants to study Sanskrit in the way westerners study Greek. He uses the tools of political philology developed in the West during the Enlightenment, when Europe undertook the study of classical Greek.[19] Pollock adopts this Eurocentric approach which studies the rules of language as carriers of political dominance, and extends it using the more recent postmodernist Western thinking.

An important idea in postmodernist thinking is that one need not consider any such thing as an 'original author's meaning'. The claim is made that the 'author is dead', and this allows each interpreter to superimpose his or her own context and lens. The context is to be found by examining the external social and political circumstances. Such an approach undermines the sacredness of Indian texts because the purpose, context and meaning as experienced by the rishis are declared irrelevant. Pollock's liberation philology method supplies the context of social exploitation. In essence, the context of the rishi's experience gets replaced by the context of social engineering.

Sparing English

One could just as well argue that based on an examination of past English literature and present British society, there is deep social prejudice embedded in the English language. Yet Pollock has no qualms about educating a new generation of Sanskrit scholars to use English as the medium for understanding and critiquing Sanskrit. In fact, his main project now is to translate Indian texts into English and thereby legitimize their reinterpretation by English-speaking elites.

Pollock likes to call himself a 'comparatist' (one who compares a topic across various civilizations), but a true comparative study would at least mention that oppression in one form or another is encoded into *all* ancient languages, from Latin to Arabic, Persian and Mandarin. He does not raise philological arguments to accuse the English language of all the atrocities committed by English-speaking peoples; nor, for that matter, does he raise arguments against Latin, Mandarin, Persian and Arabic languages with equal intensity.

As a matter of fact, many political regimes occasionally sought to regulate language or create a gold standard of grammatical and lexical correctness, just as the French Academy does today. The Portuguese banned the use of Konkani in Goa during the Inquisition and the colonial rule in the seventeenth and eighteenth centuries.[20] Numerous languages were banned in Europe as part of organized identity engineering. There is no evidence that Hindu kings practised acts of cultural violence that were equivalent to the English suppression of the Celtic languages or the American eradication of the languages of native peoples. In other words, his assault on Sanskrit and its sanskriti is selective and not applied to other civilizations with equal force.

The 'good cop'

Some Hindus think of Pollock as the proverbial 'good cop' in the lineage of other famous pioneers, such as Roberto de Nobili and Max Müller. Both de Nobili and Müller had mastered Sanskrit, and in the case of the former, Tamil as well. De Nobili, an Italian missionary in early seventeenth-century Tamil Nadu, wanted to adopt the bodily aesthetics of a Hindu sadhu. He went so far as to shave his head, retaining only a tiny tuft of hair, and wore a white dhoti and wooden sandals. He also wore a three-stringed thread across the chest, which he said represented the Holy Trinity: the Father, the Son and the Holy Spirit.

Max Müller was the Western Indologist credited with having single-handedly produced the most comprehensive volume of translations from Sanskrit into English. Pollock, for his part, is the latest editor of the Clay Library, which has produced forty-six volumes of translations of ancient Indian texts into English. These were published by New York University Press.[21] He is now taking similar projects to a new level as the editor of the Murty Classical Library, where he supervises the translation and interpretation of Indian literature into English. The goal is to translate 500 Indian books.

Exposing Sanskrit's 'poisons'

Pollock considers it important to examine the 'domination, exploitation, violence' encoded in Sanskrit. He says he is unconcerned about the actual mechanisms of force that were used and merely wants to 'establish some role for culture in legitimating force'.[22] In 2011, he again clarified his position by saying: 'Sanskrit ... offers at one and the same time a record of civilization and a record of barbarism, of extraordinary inequality and other social poisons.'[23]

He appears to see himself as completing the project that B.R. Ambedkar, the important social reformer, had started. Ambedkar was an Indian jurist, economist, politician and social reformer who converted to Buddhism and campaigned against social discrimination directed at Dalits, women and labourers. He was a principal architect of the Constitution of India. The main training that Ambedkar and other Indian reformers lacked, Pollock argues, was Pollock's theory of political philology. He considers political philology necessary for the proper study of Sanskrit texts in order to expose them as the cause of social inequality and injustice. Pollock seems to imply that had Ambedkar been educated in Pollock's methods he would not have so easily accepted the greatness of Indian civilization.

He claims that Sanskrit was the principal intellectual weapon for domination in ancient India, and that it is still being used in modern times by communalist and nationalist forces because it has not been sufficiently critiqued and expunged of its toxins.[24] At times he uses terms such as 'social power' when he wants to expose 'oppression'. He writes:

> Sanskrit knowledge presents itself to us as a major vehicle of the ideological form of social power in traditional India, and I want to look at this self-presentation and some of the questions that have been raised about its status as an 'orientalist construction'.[25]

The Vedas, he argues, contain an ideology of divine hierarchy. This ideology carried over into dharmashastra and other texts and was used to sustain India's social and political hierarchy. He quotes Burton Stein's argument:

> The ideology of divine hierarchy ... is an important part of the ancient knowledge of India, beginning with the post-Vedic Brahmana texts, with their neat order of social differences within a moral unity, and continuing through medieval dharmashastra texts, with their more messy, contingent and regionally varied codes.[26]

Pollock works very hard to explain the 'Vedic logic of discrimination' that has worked against the shudras and others. He notes that brahmins developed the lexicon, etymology, phonetics and metrics, grammar and the calendar sciences, all for the purpose of performing Vedic rituals. He observes that only the brahmins were taught these and concludes that this gave them power over others. This exclusivity came from the framework that determined who had the right to use Sanskrit and for what specific purposes. Through these entitlements, he says, some individuals and groups were considered morally superior to others.

He writes that the problem lies in the world view of the milieu of Sanskrit speakers in the early Vedic period, who enforced the special entitlements to ritual performances. These rights to perform rituals echoed as social power, thereby turning the Vedic discourse on yajna into a discourse on social power. Shudras were excluded from the Vedic rituals, even as listeners, he claims. Through this process, the brahmins created cultural inequality. He says this happened in the first millennium BCE. This unequal access was a form of colonization where one group of Indians colonized another, he says.[27] In rare instances, Pollock does admit that the ground reality was most likely different from his deterministic logic, and that the ritual restrictions did not get reflected in the non-ritual domains of society and power.[28]

His thesis is that after the Buddhists brought social liberation, the brahmins responded by developing the Purva-mimamsa texts in order to codify the prohibitions against shudras and others, because these restrictions were now being contested. Hence, formal rules were needed to restrict shudras. He examines the Purva-mimamsa text to prove the existence of this officially mandated social oppression in the tradition.[29] Later on, the Purva-mimamsa was challenged by a new school of thought called Uttara-mimamsa, one of whose champions was Adi Shankara. Pollock implicates Shankara as a caste-abusive person, giving the reason that the prohibitions against the shudras became even worse as a result of his work.[30]

He projects the gradation of rights to perform and participate in yajnas as a framework for prejudice in all domains of life.

Response: Debating varna

Flexibility of interpreting varna

The traditional interpretation of varna as a social construct is very complex and has been dynamic throughout the history of India. In fact, I will show below that the discourse on varna within the tradition has had tension and serious disagreements among the traditional authorities. I see this as a positive quality as it gives us the freedom and flexibility to innovate and not get frozen like some 'people of the book' have.

My view is that varna is a non-translatable term. Therefore, attempts to translate it and fit it into some rigid framework or grid have created distortion and confusion. I see it as a constantly negotiated and renegotiated term in Indian history. Indeed, this continual manthan (churning) has been India's method for social debate, change and progress amongst diverse voices and constituencies. By way of analogy, my book *Indra's Net* explained another pair of non-translatable terms that have also been repeatedly negotiated: astika and nastika.

Such dynamic Indian terms cause great discomfort to Western Indologists and their Indian social sciences followers, because it becomes problematic for them to try and control the discourse when the key terms are not easily fixed on a familiar template. By way of analogy, the Western notion of 'rights' is a complex and nuanced one with a dynamic history of its meaning. There is a distinction between civil, economic and moral dimensions of rights in the West. There is a complex history of rights concerning women, African-Americans, animals and so forth. Hence, no serious Western scholar would accept a simplistic and fossilized definition of what is meant by that term. It is a category that has been heavily contested and will remain contested. In fact, the process of such contestation is the mechanism by which the West progresses. The same is true for varna in the Indian context.

My purpose in this brief analysis is to criticize the prevailing notion that varna is something simple that can be equated with caste or race or privilege. To appreciate this complexity and dynamism, one must note that there are at least six levels of differences in the way varna has been seen by the tradition. These are as follows:

1. Different periods of history have had different views of varna.
2. A particular text's attitude on varna may differ from another text's views. For example, the positions adopted differ among *Arthashastra, Dharmashastra* and the Mahabharata.
3. Even within the same text there are many views expressed because the context changes. This indicates that the meaning and application of varna has been highly context-sensitive and not something absolute and homogeneous.
4. Depending on the person who is interpreting, there can be different interpretations of varna even for the same text. The various experts have not been in a stable consensus over time.
5. There have been gaps between theory and actual practice. This means that just because a certain position on varna may have

been more prevalent in the texts, or even as a consensus among prominent voices at a given time, it does not follow that this was how it worked in practice.

6. There have been numerous social challenges and reformations throughout India's history, as we shall see below. Also, one finds many kinds of anomalies. Individuals who 'ought to have been' classified in a certain varna as per the prevailing interpretation, have in practice often been classified differently. Such examples compel us to question the view of varna as a static classification system. Also, shudras are found to be building temples in which Hindus from all categories worship, even when the orthodoxy might disapprove of this. Furthermore, shudras have been rulers and leaders of armies.

All such dichotomies, challenges, contradictions and arguments about varna have taken place repeatedly in the past. Prior to very recent times, this dynamic was carried out entirely within India itself; it was not driven by any external power or with the use of imported ideologies. Therefore, it is unfair to assume (as is often being done today) that India needs foreign interventions to solve its social problems because it is frozen in time and incapable of addressing its own issues. Furthermore, all these movements, reinterpretations and changes have been from the grass roots; they were not the result of some king waging a war to impose and spread his new social or religious ideology by destroying the previous ones.

The fact is that change has been triggered from and fought by all strata of society and this was rarely a top-down process. All this makes it very difficult for Western social scientists to fit India into their pet theories. Nevertheless, they are compelled to promulgate 'universal theories' for their career advancement and because their dominant civilization wants to characterize varna as something static, canonical and homogeneous. This has led to a long history of Orientalists modelling Indian society using inappropriate theories.

Historical changes

In his book *Hindu Egalitarianism* Arvind Sharma develops the chronology of the way differential punishments based on varnas were perceived and implemented, into four major historical periods.[31] I have adapted his periodization as a framework for expressing my own insights. The four stages as adapted by me are as follow:

1. **The Vedic period:** The early period was represented by the Samhitas and there was no legal discrimination in terms of how people of different varna were treated under the law. In the later Vedic period from the Brahmanas to the Sutra period, there is some evidence of discrimination, but no evidence of it being enforced.
2. **The Smriti period:** Discrimination (especially in a legal sense) starts and there is evidence from which one may indirectly infer that it was implemented at times. (Ironically, Sheldon Pollock sees this period in terms of Buddhist interventions against the Vedas, claiming they attacked the caste system. The evidence provided by Sharma seems to indicate the opposite, namely, that the post-Buddha period is when the varna discrimination starts.)
3. **The medieval period, after 1200 CE:** Discrimination seems to have become dead. There were enough varna-related counter-discourses, intellectual and social revolutions and reinterpretations across India. In other words, for the past 1,000 years, these provisions do not appear to have been enforced, and discriminatory discourse has become superseded.
4. **The modern period, starting under British colonialism:** This is when for the first time varna gets manipulated into an official hierarchical caste system that is falsely stereotyped as the essence of Hindu society. This becomes formally mapped and codified into law through the use of the British censuses of India.

Discussing the early Vedic period, V.M. Apte says that the Rig Veda refers to the varnas in a way that cannot be considered discriminatory or hierarchical. He concludes that the brahmins did not constitute an exclusive caste or race and the prerogative of composing hymns and officiating at the services of the deities in the age of the Rig Veda was not entirely confined to men of priestly families. Even the other vocations such as being a poet or a physician were more flexible. Apte emphasizes that in the Rig Veda, there is not even a remote hint of prohibitions of inter-dining or intermarrying among the varnas; these are the prohibitions that have been considered the most serious forms of oppression in recent times.[32]

The hereditary nature of some occupations was not because of any Vedic restrictions but as a matter of practice similar to what is found in every part of the world where people like to teach their children their own profession. In olden times, there was less mobility across distances and there was a lack of public schooling; hence, training tended to be done at home by the parents. It was natural to pass on one's skills to one's progeny through a system of apprenticeship. Even today, the English-speaking elite in India enjoy privileges by birth, by circumstances, by the type of upbringing and by the social milieu in which a person is able to network.

In the later Vedic period, discriminations gradually emerge. However, it is not clear whether these are simply speculative recommendations in somebody's mind or whether they reflect the actual social reality at the time. Ram Sharan Sharma, a well-known Marxist and critic of Hinduism and the caste system, also agrees that it is unclear whether the discriminatory laws are to be taken very seriously in this particular period.[33]

In the subsequent Smriti period, it seems that some of the Smriti texts did influence the actual law. Some historians speculate that this was the period when foreign kings became established in certain parts of India, and as a result of this, or as a reaction to it, there emerged a practice to fix legal rights based on varnas. It could be that brahmins came up with such laws in order to limit the rights of the foreign kshatriya kings at the time. The exact nature of the social and political process is unknown and there are many speculations on this.

G.C. Pande, the noted Sanskrit scholar, says that only the *Dharmashastra* in the post-Vedic period started to pervert the original idea of varna by conflating it with jati. And this period is when the ritual superiority of the brahmins got converted into a more or less formal hereditary right of priesthood.[34]

P.V. Kane's interpretation of the *Dharmashastra* emphasizes that from about 1200 CE onwards, the interpretation of varna as jati/caste seems to have become marginalized in the formal sense. In support of this view, he cites a text from the south, dated around the year 1200 CE, another text dated around 1400 CE from the north, and another text of the 1500s dated from the east of India. Kane writes as follows: 'The discriminating provisions based on caste and the ascription of minor or grave sins had become a dead letter and were not being enforced by the kings of India by the twelfth century CE at least.'[35] This is when the rule of law formulated by the kings started taking precedence over earlier *Dharmashastra* texts; these laws were very diverse and varied from one king to another, and from one period to another.

Sharma gives numerous examples of individuals who stand out as counter-examples to the notion of a hierarchical social varna system. He gives examples of people from all parts of India, who either were transgressing this supposedly rigid hierarchy, or were actually honoured and openly accepted into positions that would violate such a hierarchy. This trend peaks in the fifteenth century when Kabir and Surdas become famous mystics in the bhakti movement who defied these caste hierarchical restrictions. But even before this, there were Jnaneshwara and Namdev in the thirteenth century, and Tukaram and Ramdas later on in the seventeenth century. Sharma also mentions the Lingayat movement in Karnataka in the twelfth century, where the orthodox varna boundaries got boldly challenged.[36]

All of these challengers started out as ordinary individuals who conflicted with and overcame the restrictions of orthodoxy that would prevent them from enjoying equal status. The fact that there was resistance from the orthodoxy is not surprising because such changes have always been contentious. In the case of Hindu history, the old and the new coexist in mutual tension; there is negotiation, argument and debate, which is creative and progressive. Moreover, they each learn to cope with the other, with both old and new going on in parallel, at certain times one prevailing over the other. The interpretations and practices are not fixed or uniform over either geographical space or time.

Unfortunately, what we are commonly told about varna, jati and caste today is the result of the damage done by Indologists over the past 200 years or more. The British census by Lord Risley described in my book *Breaking India* was the basis for creating the caste hierarchy on birth on a permanent basis. While some Western scholars promoted these interpretations claiming good intentions, others like J.S. Mill and Max Weber were blatantly Hinduphobic.

These Western ideas have been re-exported into India through the English language medium. A growing number of people among the Indian well-educated elite, people who see themselves as intellectuals, have incorporated these ideas into their thinking. This is how the caste system has currently become a fixture of politics. To make matters worse, the Indian government adopted this divisive British classification system and turned it into law; it has been used to define various rights and privileges under the Constitution of India. Finally, democracy turned these fragmented and divisive groupings into vote banks. These fault lines are rigid and not easily harmonized.

Sharma's overall perspective is that the conflict which has persisted over time is not between varnas or between genders, but between dharma and adharma. The idea of adharma is what has been consistently opposed. How this is to be done keeps changing with the circumstances and the context. When adharma is seen to be embodied in certain types of people, for example those with certain diets or lifestyles or occupations, then those people become underprivileged. Those bearing the markers of adharma, whatever they happen to be at a particular time and place, become the target of discrimination. It is not that certain people by virtue of race, blood, birth, etc., are inherently inferior and that this is a permanent, long-term, fixed, artefact of Hinduism.

Diverse voices in the traditional texts

Different traditional texts have interpreted varna in diverse ways. This is an important point worth discussing.

Let me start by citing numerous examples of the egalitarianism view in texts. Yudhishthira in the Mahabharata says the following:

> The marks of the shudra are found in a brahmin; but a shudra is not necessarily a shudra nor a brahmin a brahmin. In whomever a brahmin's marks are found, he is known as a brahmin and in whomever they are not found, him we designate as a shudra.[37]

It is clear from this that as per the Mahabharata, it is the behavioural marks or characteristics of persons that determine their varna and not anything else. Swami Prabhupada of ISKCON followed this principle and let each individual have a varna based solely on accomplishments. There was no birth-based assignment of varna or duties.[38]

Bhavishya Purana (1.41, 1.45–1.46) says as follows:

> A father has four sons. All the sons, naturally, must belong to the same caste. God is the father of all people. Then wherein lies the difference of caste? The fruit of a tree are akin in color and shape and alike to touch and taste. Human beings are fruits that grow in God's tree. How then can we make distinctions as between the fruit and the same tree?[39]

A similar idea is expressed by Thirukkural (verse 972): 'All men are born equal. The differences among them are entirely due to occupations.'[40]

And *Yoga Vashishtha* (5.18.61) says:

> The idea that this one is my brother and that one is not is entertained only by petty-minded people. How can one be said to be a brother and another not, when the same Self equally pervades all? All classes of creatures, O Rama, are your brothers. There is none here who is absolutely unrelated to you.[41]

Similarly, the Bhagavadgita (9.29) declares: 'I am equal to all beings, there is none hateful or dear to me. But those who worship me with devotion, they are in me and I am in them.' This indicates that at least from the point of view of the Lord, all of us are equal. A similar view is expressed in the Upanishads in the famous statements 'tat tvam asi' or 'thou art that' and the statement 'aham brahmasmi' or 'I am Brahman'.

P.V. Kane quotes Yudhishthira in the Mahabharata to make the point that the intermingling of castes makes it difficult to determine varna based on birth:

> It appears to me that it is very difficult to ascertain the caste of human beings on account of the confusion of all varnas; all sorts of men are always begetting offspring from all sorts of women; speech, sexual intercourse, being born, and death – these are common to all human beings and there is scriptural authority for this view in the word.[42]

This goes to show that the different categories for varna were intermixing even at the time of the Mahabharata leading Yudhishthira to say that it is impossible to ascertain their caste.

However, *Manusmriti* is the text that has been over-quoted to make the opposite case, i.e., in support of discrimination. Here, Sharma observes that Manu places more emphasis upon the *duties* of the various varnas than upon their *rights and privileges*. Duties, being a kind of work or labour, are what he is classifying into different categories. Hence, one may see varnas as a way to think of different types of professions.

Kane's interpretation of *Manusmriti* shows that a brahmin was required to live very simply. Accumulation of wealth by him would be seen negatively. Though entitled to receive gifts, he could only receive them from worthy donors; he had to be learned to be worthy of receiving gifts. He was not supposed to be a ruler and he could not drink liquor.[43]

Nor were brahmins entitled to collect taxes from the people for their own benefit. Sharma contrasts this with the practices of the Roman Catholic Church where the clergy were not under the laws of the land, and they paid no taxes to the state. The Holy See (which was the Roman Chancery) collected taxes from the people. Sharma cites numerous ways in which money was collected, extorted and accumulated by the priests acting on behalf of the church: a practice that was never carried out by brahmins. Similarly, he says, the brahmins never took it upon themselves to have the authority to depose a king or to hand over vast territories to somebody. Contrast this with Pope Alexander VI who issued a bull (similar to a fatwa in Islam) in 1493. All the new lands of the Americas, and other places that were being supposedly 'discovered' by the Christian conquerors, were made the property of the kings and queens of Europe. This type of act done by churchmen, is very different from any action carried out by brahmins.[44]

In fact, there were distinct benefits assigned to a shudra. In particular, a shudra could pursue any profession except for those few that were reserved specifically for brahmins or kshatriyas. Also, the shudra was not obligated to perform the countless daily rituals and activities that the brahmins were compelled to do; he was not compelled to undergo any sanskar except marriage; he could indulge in any kind of food, and drink wine; he had to undergo no penances for lapses from the rules of the shastras; he had to observe no restrictions of gotra in marriage.[45]

Furthermore, *Manusmriti*, 2.238, says that one can learn paramdharma (highest dharma) even from a shudra, thereby indicating that a shudra could also be a guru.[46]

Sharma also spends many pages giving details of the negative treatment of shudras advocated in *Manusmriti*. However, he echoes what several historians have maintained, namely, that there is no evidence that the harsh provisions as per Manu's recommendation were actually carried out. Sharma also cites that in case of theft, in *Manusmriti* the punishment increases with the status of the varna, i.e., brahmin gets the highest penalty and shudra the lowest. Overall, one may conclude that in *Manusmriti*, discrimination was highly contextual and changed from one situation to another.

Sharma proposes a difference between the notion of equality and that of equitability. He suggests that while *Manusmriti* does not advocate the same social characteristics and treatment for the various varnas, it does treat them with a sense of equitability. By this he means that those with higher status should also shoulder greater responsibility. This is a different approach to justice than one where everyone has equal status and responsibility.

Finally, it is worth mentioning that *Manusmriti*, 4.176, advocates flexibility in its own implementation: One should give up dharma (or a practice of contextual dharma) if it is denounced by the public (loka). This implies that if some provision of dharma (including a provision made by Manu himself) is considered unworthy by the public (such as caste discrimination, which is widely denounced today), such a dharma practice should be given up. This implies a fluidity in the application of varna.

Sharma shows contradictions and divergences between important texts on the matter of varna. For instance, he says the Mahabharata completely disassociates itself from birth-based varna. It attributes the birth-based varna thesis to *Manusmriti* and repudiates *Manusmriti* in this regard. On the basis of the evidence provided by Sharma, it appears that the Mahabharata cites verses attributed to Manu, which in some cases are not even found in *Manusmriti*.[47]

The fact that the different texts differ in their treatment of the varnas can also be illustrated by comparing the *Arthashastra* and *Dharmashastra*. Clearly, the specific text being used in a given situation would influence the outcome. Even though the *Dharmashastra* tradition of *Manusmriti* often dominated the discourse, the *Arthashastra* tradition always existed alongside it. The point being made is that the *Arthashastra* tradition, which is a better reflection of the actual policies being carried out, is much more muted and nuanced on varna. *Arthashastra*, 9.2, even mentions armies of shudras and refers to shudras becoming kings.

Sharma assertively disagrees with the fundamental premise that the shudras did not have access to the Vedas in an absolute sense. In his numerous works, he has marshalled several pieces of textual and historical evidence to indicate that the shudras *did* have access to the Vedas at some time and that the restrictions were contested and not absolute.[48]

Krishna Shastry on widespread access to oral Sanskrit

Many traditional scholars often disagree with Pollock's claims about Sanskrit and its grammar's alleged elitism. For example, Chamu Krishna

Shastry, head of the very successful organization called Samskrita Bharati, has compiled textual evidence showing that Sanskrit was spoken by common people in early times. Hence, it was not a brahmin monopoly as alleged by Pollock. The rest of this section paraphrases many of the points from Shastry's book.[49]

Panini, the celebrated grammarian, did not *create* the rules of grammar; he studied the actual usage of language and codified it. When discussing words in current usage, he does so under distinct headings: those that occur in Vedic rituals and those that occur in ordinary spoken language. He refers to these categories as 'chhanda' (Vedic language) and 'bhasha' (spoken language), respectively. The latter was used for worldly (laukika or vyavaharika) purposes. The root of the word 'bhasha' means 'to speak manifestly' or 'to speak aloud', implying the language was used orally.

The very term 'vyakarana' (grammar) means the analytical presentation of words and sentences that *are being used*. Hence, Sanskrit grammar is descriptive of the way the language is actually in use at a given time. This is significant, because if the grammar mentions words that pertain to ordinary vyavaharika or laukika activities, it would falsify Pollock's claim that Sanskrit was used only for Vedic rituals and not for ordinary speech. Furthermore, as we shall see shortly, if certain Sanskrit words in common use refer to the activities of farmers, labourers and other common folks, it would disprove the claim that only brahmin elites had the right to use it.

In the first chapter of his *Mahabhashya*, Patanjali says that Sanskrit in his time is in active use across all regions of India with certain words enjoying higher currency in some respects in certain regions. He gives concrete examples of how different regions use distinct words to say the same thing. This implies widespread usage across a vast geography, with local variations as one would expect when a language has informal usage as well. He uses the phrase 'is spoken' (bhashito bhavati) and not the phrase 'is written' to describe the usages.

As a communication technique, Patanjali presents a dialogue between a grammarian and the driver of a chariot over the correct usage of words;

the implication is that Sanskrit was also used by common persons for ordinary purposes. Patanjali's *Mahabhashya* gives examples of ordinary usage on almost every page.

Sanskrit's richness in idioms is clearly an indicator that its vocabulary emerged from daily usage by ordinary people. For example, there is a specific vocabulary of Sanskrit words pertaining to agriculture and various kinds of physical labour, realms where brahmin scholars were not active. There is a substantial Sanskrit vocabulary meant specifically for use in agriculture, indicating usage by common folks to discuss farming. Panini also designates certain words as being used by ruffians, gamblers and tricksters. Krishna Shastry cites several words that elitists would not consider appropriate for their own usage.

A more complex form of evidence is offered by the way in which certain words with clear and specific referents in the world of everyday life lost their initial restricted applications and became more general. In fact, many words first gained currency among common folks for ordinary purposes before grammarians introduced novel suffixes to incorporate them and their derivatives. These were clearly spoken informally before becoming formal.[50]

Many concerns of the grammarians reflect the problem of trying to formulate laws and rules in the activities that comprise worldly transactions, not only farming, but joking, teasing and so forth. It is clear throughout his grammar that Patanjali is frequently drawing these rules inductively from everyday speech and not from literary or liturgical usage.

Re-evaluating the Buddhist impact

Ashok Aklujkar disagrees with Pollock's claim that Buddhism toppled restrictions that were built into the Vedas. He says that brahmins were competing with Buddhists and Jains in Sanskrit knowledge production. The social restrictions, he feels, may have been a competitive strategy to assimilate all social groups and the texts being produced. By way of analogy, one may think of norms and rituals within fraternities and clubs today as mechanisms for strengthening group identity. This is not theologically driven but a competitive strategy to promote group cohesiveness for the sake of gaining market share.[51] Hence, it is pragmatic and not metaphysical in origin.

Pollock repeatedly claims that in the pre-Buddhist era Sanskrit could be used solely for sacred rituals and not for laukika/vyavaharika (worldly) purposes. He says it was Buddhist intervention that led to Sanskrit entering 'the world of men' in the sense of laukika uses.[52]

Many Sanskrit exponents disagree with this idea of a radical discontinuity in Sanskrit being caused by Buddhism. They feel that Sanskrit was *always* used both in mundane matters and for Vedic chanting. Panini's *Ashtadhyayi* was written for both domains and was partly based on using previous (pre-Buddhist) grammarians as well.

Is it fair to blame Sanskrit grammar?

Pollock's real agenda in these intellectual gymnastics is to prove a causal link between grammar and social oppression. He writes: 'The order of Sanskrit poetry, and the grammar and literary sciences that underpin it, are somehow thought to recapitulate the order of the social and political world.'[53] In another place, he uses similar logic, saying: 'The "preservation of language sounds" and the "preservation of social orders" are expressed by the same words, *varṇa-sthiti,* and so are ontologically linked.'[54] However, the use of the word 'varna' in two different ways does not imply a causal or ontological link. Such an epochal claim by him requires identifying the *specific structures* of Sanskrit grammar that cause social oppression. Chapter 7 will discuss this further.

A king's obligation, he says, was the stability and regulation of social orders and life stages, and these depended on ensuring the stability of the language through its grammar.[55] He explains the top-down political influence in promoting grammar:

> Only in a language dignified and stabilized by grammar – not in a lawless vernacular, unconstrained by predictable and universal grammatical norms and therefore in constant danger of degeneration – could the fame of the ruler receive permanent, even eternal expression:

> It is the Sanskrit poet who, according to the old trope, produces the 'glory body' of the king, which remains on earth even after his mortal body has disappeared. The perfect language of textuality functions as a stainless mirror continuing to reflect his glory image even when he himself is gone.[56]

K.S. Kannan comments that Pollock's statement quoted above is a mix-up when he refers to 'a stainless mirror continuing to reflect his glory image even when he himself is gone'. Pollock is conflating different statements.[57] A more balanced view would be that Sanskrit as a pan-Indian language was considered better at spreading a king's fame. This would be like saying today that in order to be famous one must publish in high-class English.

User-friendly access to Vedic knowledge for everyone

A balanced discussion on the subject must consider that many other aspects of the Vedic tradition offered access to the same knowledge for *all persons*. For example, itihasa and various arts and crafts provide paths to advancement, and these were universally accessible to all varnas. Itihasas were composed specifically to transmit knowledge from the Vedas, and *Natya Shastra* facilitated the entertaining presentation of complex narratives from the itihasas to the entire population.

Written in Sanskrit, *Natya Shastra* is sometimes known as 'the fifth Veda' within the tradition, even in the text itself; it is seen by Hindus as being meant for use by all varnas. It provides the structure for composing performances that would make the knowledge of the Vedas more easily accessible. *Natya Shastra*'s own introduction shows the capacity of Hindu traditions for adapting to diverse types of psychologies and circumstances. Here is one account of its background:

- In a certain era, when humans with rajas guna (passion) as their dominant quality were prompted by selfish desires and emotions, placing them on the right path could not be achieved through direct Vedic instruction. Their cognitive faculties lacked the sattvic guna (purity) that is required for acting on Vedic knowledge.

- The devatas wanted indirect methods of access to Vedic knowledge for those varnas that lacked the sattvic guna. This method had to be different from the style of instructions provided in the Vedas. It could not be achieved by providing rules/injunctions and had instead to be delightfully experiential.
- The devatas requested Brahma to create itihasas which could be performed in a way that was pleasing to the various senses, and lead people automatically to follow the path of dharma. The itihasas and their performance were thus designed to bring Vedic knowledge to those whose lifestyle was dominated by rajas. Dramas based on itihasas are intended for the diversion of the mind towards enjoyment.
- Such performances do not demand rigour and they gradually lead to the inner transformation of people using pleasant sights and sounds. They mix the bitter medicine of Vedic instruction with the sweet milk of dance and music.
- These were the circumstances, which led to the creation of 'the fifth Veda' by Brahma at the request of the devatas. It was created for those who were recalcitrant about following the Vedic path.

Hence, according to this traditional view, rather than denying common people access to Vedic knowledge, user-friendly methods were developed for helping those whose cognitive capacities prefer or require such methods. *Natya Shastra* is seen as having been designed for those whose desire for play and pleasure does not allow for focussed, disciplined learning of analytical texts. Hence, such individuals learn from the itihasa by enacting natyas. In the high-tech world today, such methods are called 'infotainment' (information + entertainment) or 'edutainment' (education + entertainment). A common person unable to access a complex system is provided user-friendly ways to benefit from it.

Dramas enacting the itihasas for the general public were based on *Natya Shastra,* and these texts were written in Sanskrit. In addition to *Natya Shastra* and itihasa, there are many other shastras, such as Ayurveda and Vastu, which are also in Sanskrit and available to all varnas. The same was true in the case of all the Puranas. Pollock's claim that Sanskrit was banned to certain people is debatable.

Karma is free choice that shapes varna

Another serious red flag among many Indologists today is their claim that one's varna is not under one's own control but is the result of 'fatalism'. However, from the traditional perspective, a shudra is anyone whose lifestyle choices are not compatible with the pursuit of Vedic knowledge; this incompatibility is a reflection of individual guna, and ultimately of one's karma. The Bhagavadgita verses 4.12–13 explain this point. The guna–karma combination of an individual determines the varna in accordance with the patterns of personal karma and character. Individuals can and do change their guna composition through their own efforts.

Empirical evidence differs from 'theory'

One can cite empirical data that contradicts the assumption that prejudices against shudras have been built into sanskriti. Dharampal, the noted Gandhian, used British data during the colonial period to show that in the nineteenth century, the shudras comprised a larger student body than any other community did.[58] For example, in the British collectors' reports for the Madras Presidency for 1822–25, the shudras constituted 50 per cent and brahmins, 20 per cent of the student population. Besides the large number of schools at that time, there were also approximately a hundred institutions of higher learning in each district of Bengal and Bihar. Unfortunately, these numbers rapidly dwindled all across India during the nineteenth century under British rule. The British also noted that Sanskrit books were being widely used to teach grammar, lexicology, mathematics, medical science, logic, law and philosophy.

Furthermore, in the early British period in India, British officials noted that education for the masses was more advanced and widespread in India than it was in England. In England, at the end of the seventeenth century, there were Charity Schools, the purpose of which was to ensure that every child would be able to read the Bible. However, by 1802, reports said a 'new system' had been introduced that was borrowed from India. Colonial reports also stated that the Indian villages had more schools in proportion to the population than the English villages did. Indian villages educated their children in ways that were practical for local needs. According to Dharampal, the British later replaced this Sanskrit-based system with their own English-based one, the goal being to produce low-level clerks for the British administration.[59]

According to ancient practice, about one-third of the revenue from agriculture and seaports was assigned for the social and cultural infrastructure. The British overturned it all. They centralized revenue collection in order to be able to siphon it off more efficiently for themselves. There was hardly any budget left for local expenses towards social and cultural infrastructure. The killing of the indigenous education system caused a rapid decline in practical knowledge for the masses. The social balance among various communities was disrupted and the economic system suffered immensely. All of which caused many communities to become what we now refer to as 'backward classes'. Pollock ignores all such evidence.

Moreover, many of Pollock's examples refer to a very old era, the circumstances of which do not apply today in an absolute sense. If one wants to go back in time, one also needs to acknowledge that there were dynasties of shudra kings that lasted for several centuries.

Many communities that the texts considered as shudras did not see themselves as shudras. The Indologist A.L. Basham said: 'There is good evidence that shudras engaged in manufacture and commerce and by the Mauryan times many shudras were free peasants.'[60] He also explained:

> As the rigidity of brahminic observances increased, groups which refused to accept orthodox custom or cling to old practices which were no longer respectable, fell to the ranks of shudras. There are today castes which themselves claim to be kshatriyas but which are branded by the brahmins as shudras because they adhere to customs which have long become objectionable, such as meat eating or the re-marrying of widows. Persons born illegitimately, even when of pure high class blood were officially counted as shudras.[61]

The point that Basham is making is that the reclassification of people into different varnas was an ongoing process based on their behaviour in terms of their compliance or non-compliance with various norms, and had less and less to do with their birth or their actual work. Many positive qualities and privileges attributed to the shudras are mentioned in a variety of smriti texts.

A concrete example of an anomaly is that the temple where Sri Ramakrishna (guru of Vivekananda) served as priest was funded by a rich widow from a shudra family. This involves multiple transgressions, if we are to go by the normative theories that Indologists have asserted: She was a woman, a widow, and a shudra by birth. Each of these three conditions is said to be a disqualifier, as per many social theorists, but this was not so in her case. Would such a person's temple become an important place of worship among Hindus today? Stereotypes about Hinduism would suggest not. Also, her shraddha for establishing such a temple runs counter to the image that shudras felt alienated and belittled. That she was rich adds further complexity to fit this into the normative theories.

My (speculative) reinterpretation of varna for today

The meaning of varna has been contested since early times and continues to be such. Hence, it is a dynamic concept that has periodically been renegotiated. The relationship between varna and jati has also been debated intensely. Clearly, we are free to interpret it for our times in ways that benefit dharma and society today.

In my article 'Varna as a form of capital', I have offered a creative interpretation that varna may be seen as a form of social capital.[62] Modern societies often think in terms of their financial capital (vaishya), political capital (kshatriya), intellectual capital (brahmin) and skilled labour (shudra). The *Purusha Sukta* is the primary text that is commonly used to interpret varna; I feel it lends itself to varna being both individual as well as a collective quality. Given the allegorical or symbolic nature of the verses, I see the description of each varna as being applicable also to a nation or humanity at large, and not merely to individuals. Each of the four varnas represents a function or type of effort that society needs, and each is shown to emanate from the corresponding part of Purusha's own body.

Note that *Purusha Sukta* does not give any reason as such for this fourfold division; it merely states this as the nature of things. However, *Manusmriti*, 1.87, does give the criteria that the protection of the universe is the purpose of this system. It is reasonable to assume that the protection of the universe must include the general well-being of all people. Therefore, a legitimate interpretation of varna must be such that it shall optimize the general well-being of everyone and not just some select people. If an approach to varna oppresses some segments of society, it cannot be a legitimate interpretation, as this would violate the criteria of overall well-being.

In view of this, when a king is asked to uphold the varnas, under my interpretation he is to optimize these diverse forms of social capital in order to have a healthy society. When he intends to protect and maximize one form of capital, it is not meant to be achieved by oppressing another. Seen in this manner, there could be a notion of 'varna capitalism' as a free market system in which individuals can participate with their portfolio of competences. Varna would not be transmitted genealogically by birth but flow freely based on merit and competition.

Another novelty I wish to speculate upon is that I do not see these four kinds of capital as being mutually exclusive even at the individual level. Most persons I know today combine multiple varnas. When I do the dishes or do data entry, I could be considered performing shudra work. When I negotiate a financial transaction or balance my bank passbook, I am a vaishya. When I do research or deliver a lecture, I am being a brahmin. When I face opponents in intense encounters that could turn political, I am a kshatriya.

In olden times, formal institutions as we know them today had not emerged. Therefore, each form of capital was personal and not institutional. Therefore, these capabilities tended to be seen only in terms of an individual's characteristics. Nevertheless, perhaps we should now explore social theories where these varnas could be forms of capital stored at various levels: from one individual, to small groups, to a nation, to humanity at large.

Given how our tradition evolves and new interpretations emerge for each era, I see nothing wrong with such speculations and experiments in the evolution of dharmic social theory.

Discrimination is unfortunately prevalent worldwide and requires active opposition, but does it make sense to single out a particular language or civilization as the culprit? I definitely agree that we must revisit any restrictions whatsoever on access to knowledge and social capital. We must make amends wherever there are bottlenecks. To the best of my knowledge, access to Sanskrit and its texts is available to all strata of society today. In fact, Samskrita Bharati is spreading spoken Sanskrit without any social restrictions whatsoever. On the other hand, the critique of elitism should be applied to point out that Pollock's camp is creating a new breed of elitists by infusing the English language with complex Western theories. I will return to this issue in a later chapter.

Widespread support for Sanskrit until recent times

I wish to also point out that Dr Ambedkar, the pioneering Dalit leader, had worked zealously to promote Sanskrit. A dispatch of the Press Trust of India dated 10 September 1949 states that he was among those who sponsored an amendment making Sanskrit, instead of Hindi, the official language of the Indian Union. Most newspapers carried the news on 11 September of that year.[63] The proposed amendment read:

1. The official language of the Union shall be Sanskrit.
2. Notwithstanding anything contained in Clause 1 of this article, for a period of fifteen years from the commencement of this constitution, the English language shall continue to be used for the official purposes of the Union for which it was being used at such commencement: provided that the president may, during the said period, by order authorize for any of the official purposes of the Union the use of Sanskrit in addition to the English language.

Unfortunately, this amendment failed to pass by one vote, and yet this action demonstrates the level of support enjoyed by Sanskrit even among Dalits as well as many prominent Muslim leaders.[64]

Comparisons with the West

In order to understand that varna was not normative, one must appreciate the nature of religious dissent in India. One must point out that there were no beheadings or burnings at the stake of dissenting Hindus as there often were in Europe. Nor did India follow the Christian chronology of epochs changing radically and violently with the destruction of prior texts and sacred places. Christianity wanted to crush completely the previous world view held by people, as for example when the Church crushed the pagans.

P.V. Kane draws comparisons between the treatment of brahmins in *Manusmriti* with the treatment of the Christian clergy in the church. He avers that in many ways, the clergy in the Christian church enjoyed far greater superiority over the rest of the population than the corresponding privileges enjoyed by the brahmins in Hinduism. He points out that up until the early twentieth century, there was a lot of positive discrimination enjoyed by people of European origin in places like India. The criminal code in India was very discriminatory in favour of Europeans. Hence, in evaluating the legal discriminations in ancient India, one should keep in mind what was prevalent in other parts of the world until very recently.

Blaming Sanskrit for European atrocities

Saving colonial Indology

As already mentioned, Pollock wants to establish that the social and political abuses by Europeans, although commonly associated with colonialism, actually originated long before. He says the initial source should be attributed not to Western Indology but to Sanskrit texts.[65] His thesis is that Sanskrit has Orientalism embedded deep in its structure, which then manifests itself in texts and social structures.

However, I submit that if this thesis were valid, the following issues would arise: Why did the so-called Sanskrit Orientalism not lead to genocide in any foreign country where the Hindus went for trading, export of knowledge and settlement? Hindus ventured outside of India and traded with and influenced cultures across South-east Asia. This was especially true during the first millennium BCE (the Kalingas) and the first millennium CE (the Sangam era and the Chola Empire), but nowhere did they colonize or set about banning the local languages or customs. A similar case can be made for Indian influences in China, Mongolia and Central Asia, where there are no local histories or other evidence accusing Indian knowledge of transmitting oppression and mayhem.

Cambodia was a Hindu kingdom starting around the first century CE and this continued up to the fourteenth century CE. And again, there is no known evidence of Hindus either orientalizing the Khmers or exploiting them through economic or cultural colonization over those 1,400 years. The same is true of Bali and parts of the Philippines, which saw considerable Hindu cultural influence over approximately the same period.

Sanskrit was learned and used in these countries through the Hindus' cultural and economic influence, but this did not translate into the oppressive structures that Pollock insists were embedded in it. He does not ask why, if the Vedas are so poisonous, the Hindus themselves never engaged in external colonialism, like the British did, or perpetrated an internal holocaust like the Germans did.

Furthermore, in evaluating the origins of European Orientalism, Pollock does not pursue the influences that came from within European culture. For the British had *already* practised 'othering' in America against the Native Americans by committing genocide against them, against the African-Americans by enslaving them and subsequently against the Irish by colonizing them. British intellectual and popular literature had become infused with such racist projections of others, that this racism was clearly influencing their Orientalist project in India. In fact, several Western scholars have written about the blatant racism, gender and other biases among the leaders of the European Enlightenment movement.

I submit that neither the mercantile nor the evangelical aspects of colonialism originated in India. These were well developed, tried and tested in America, Africa and Ireland by the time the Indologists entered India.[66]

Blaming Sanskrit for Nazism

Pollock takes the blame game against Sanskrit to new heights when he argues that German Indologists of the early twentieth century borrowed ideas of racial purity and ethnic violence from their study of Sanskrit. This influence, he charges, contributed to the ideology that prompted the Nazi holocaust against the Jews.

Hence the flow of influence of Orientalism, according to him, was:

> *Sanskrit's internal Orientalism ==> Colonial Orientalism ==> German Nazism.*

He quotes one source as saying: 'Whatever act the *aryas* who know the Vedas claim to be *dharma*, is *dharma*; whatever they reject is said to be *adharma*.'[67] Then he explains who the aryas are: 'The binary pair *arya/anarya* is one of several discursive definitions by which the Sanskrit cultural order constitutes itself. It overarches the world of traditional Indian inequality.'[68] But he ignores that the Indian tradition sees 'arya' as refering to noble qualities and the term has nothing to do with birth-based social hierarchy.[69]

Pollock then provides an extensive list of such injustices by aryas (i.e., speakers of Sanskrit) against anaryas (non-aryans or shudras, whom he characterizes as non-Sanskrit speaking). He considers this racist and calls for the construction of a 'biogenetic map of inequality'. He concludes that, '*it may seem warranted to speak about a "pre-form of racism" in early India*.'[70] Pollock is misleading some people to believe that 'arya' refers to a member of a race, with the binary of arya/non-arya becoming a projection of white/non-white races.

He gives many examples of Nazi Indologists who cited Vedic literature and Sanskrit to construct their own 'Aryan' past and then used this for their racist agenda. Alongside this analysis of what he sees as Sanskrit racism, Pollock does a detailed comparison of discrimination found in Sanskrit texts with that found in the Nazi state's doctrines. By looking for similar kinds of prejudices in both, he wants the reader to see a causal link from Sanskrit to Nazism.

Pollock conflates the alleged ban on shudras accessing Sanskrit with Hitler's ban on Jews learning German in the 1930s. This appears at best to be a forced comparison and a case of guilt by association. The fact is that German Indology included many misinterpretations and this topic itself deserves a whole discussion. Pollock, unfortunately, over-emphasizes one text written by a brahmin named Bhatta Lakshmidhara from the twelfth century, and compares it with the National Socialist texts of the 1930s, which led to Nazi fascism.

According to Pollock, 'high Brahminism', as represented by the Purva-mimamsa school, contributed to the 'ideological formations of precolonial India', and Nazism borrowed this and implemented it 'at home' in Germany. Pollock argues that it was this Sanskrit influence that ultimately contributed to the 'legitimation of genocide'. Wilhelm Halbfass, the late Indologist at the University of Pennsylvania, took such ridiculous statements into strange, speculative areas and wrote:

> Would it not be equally permissible to identify this underlying structure as 'deep Nazism' or 'deep Mimamsa'? And what will prevent us from calling Kumarila and William Jones 'deep Nazis' and Adolf Hitler a 'deep Mimamsaka'?[71]

Response: European Enlightenment as origin of biases

We can see the implications of American Orientalists continuing to use the idea of the Aryan in the Indian context, with references to 'Aryan invasions' and so forth. I have written elsewhere that European racial ideas made their way into India, where they were reframed in terms of light-skinned 'Aryans' and dark-skinned 'Dravidians'. These distinctions were first promoted in colonial times but remain powerful to this day in the study of India.

Pollock's attempt to connect Sanskrit Vedas with Hitler's fascism ignores a significant part of the history of German Indology. He avoids considering the influences of various sources on Nazi ideology, including that of Hegel and Max Müller's Aryan invasion theory. Had he examined a more thorough history of Indology, he would have realized that early Indologists distorted Sanskrit literature for their *own* Eurocentric projects, and that it was this distortion, not Sanskrit literature itself, that had led to the Germans' conception of an 'Aryan' identity.

A study of this would show the biases originating in German/British/French rivalries (as I explored briefly in my book *Breaking India*). Hegel, a key early nineteenth-century German philosopher, explicitly supported the 'othering' and elimination of Native Americans (who were seen by him as beyond the possibility of civilization) and the active slavery of African-Americans in America. Hegel had these views well before British scholars had begun expressing their Orientalist views on India. None of this is taken into account by Pollock. I also provide more details on these historical trends in *Being Different*.[72]

Response: Critiques by European scholars

Pollock's claim that the National Socialists (Hitler's political party) funded Indology has been refuted by European scholar Reinhold Grünendahl, who shows that Indology was not funded by the German state even in the 1930s.[73] Grünendahl offers a trenchant criticism of Pollock's approach to research on Orientalism.

He says Pollock's narrative 'is not an evidence-based study of Orientalism or Indology in Germany, but a sophisticated charge of anti-Semitism based largely on trumped-up "evidence"'.[74] He further states:

> Pollock's post-Orientalist messianism would have us believe that only late twentieth-century (and now twenty-first century) America is intellectually equipped to reject and finally overcome 'Eurocentrism' and 'European epistemological hegemony' that is 'a pre-emptive European conceptual framework of analysis [that] has disabled us from probing central features of South Asian life, from pre-western forms of "national" (or feminist, or communalist, or ethnic) identity or consciousness, premodern forms of cultural "modernism," precolonial forms of colonialism'. (Pollock 1993: 115) The path from the 'Deep Orientalism' of old to a new 'Indology beyond the Raj and Auschwitz' leads to the 'New Raj' across the deep blue sea.[75]

Thus, Grünendahl has noted Pollock's tendency to develop broad narratives without any supporting evidence. Moreover, he draws attention to Pollock's messianism in promoting American scholarship in the late twentieth (and now twenty-first) century, casting doubt on Pollock's attempt to analyse Sanskrit objectively. He raises the pertinent question as to whether Pollock is providing the intellectual foundations for America's 'New Raj', to replace the dead British Raj – i.e., whether American imperialism is replacing the dead British imperialism.

Grünendahl goes on to make the point that Hitler had many European sources from which he learned discrimination against the Jews. He takes up the question of Pollock's attempt to associate Indology with Paul Lagarde (1827–91), a noted German scholar who focussed his analysis on Greek, Arabic and Hebrew texts using tools of comparative philology. Grünendahl says there is no evidence that Lagarde was influenced by Indology or had any association with it.[76] Lagarde's *The Current Tasks of German Politics* is supposed to have deeply influenced Hitler. In it, he called for (a) unification of the German peoples, and (b) relocation of Polish and Austrian Jews to Palestine. During his lifetime, he was seen and celebrated for his knowledge of classical Greek and Hebrew – not anything remotely connected with Sanskrit. Interestingly, the 1906 *Jewish Encyclopedia* has a detailed entry on Lagarde with no mention of his association, in any way, to Sanskrit, Indology or India.[77]

Response: Ignoring how Sanskrit benefited the West

Pollock's one-sided view also completely ignores the *positive* impact of Sanskrit on the West through the appropriation of various shastras. When, in the late eighteenth century, Sir William Jones of the East India Company announced that Sanskrit was close to many European languages, a frenzy of intellectual activity started. In the half-century that followed, almost every premier European university had started a Sanskrit and Indology department. It became important for intellectuals to learn this language, or at least be familiar with the contents of its texts. Western thought was transformed forever as a result of this encounter.

It is unfortunate that when the European intellectual movement known as the Enlightenment is taught, the Indian influences are ignored or else reduced to mere footnotes. The European Enlightenment is made to look like an entirely internal development by Europeans, without any contribution from elsewhere. Nonetheless, during the time of that movement, there was great enthusiasm for appropriating Sanskrit ideas, digesting them into Western languages and frameworks, and using them in intellectually innovative ways. The benefits of this knowledge were felt in several modern fields, including philosophy, botany, psychology, linguistics, anthropology, ethics, mathematics, Christian theology and comparative religion.

The process of digesting Sanskrit-based knowledge did not end after colonialism; in fact, it went on to reach new heights. It is now being done in a more sophisticated and subtle way so that the digestion is not discernible. To understand and explain this inter-civilizational flow of knowledge from India to the West, I have spent the past twenty years researching what I call the 'U-Turn Theory' and the process of digestion that results from it.

Pollock's call to action to politicize Sanskrit studies

Pollock argues that the study of Sanskrit and its ancient texts holds clues to understanding oppression in Indian society today. The domination built into Sanskrit is not gone, he says, but has morphed and lives on. It is implicitly built into the linguistic structures of Sanskrit, such that both the oppressors and the oppressed rationalize the status quo by citing texts. Pollock wants to liberate Indians from their own shastras.

In other words, what I call the non-translatable aspects of Sanskrit (the Crown jewels of the civilization) are precisely what he would *not* like to see being used as a means for producing new knowledge; according to him, such categories lead to oppression. To encourage spoken Sanskrit would simply transmit the old structures of violence and mystification built into it, he implies. Rather, he wants to make it a 'classical language' to be studied at arm's-length by English-speaking scholars. He wants such a project to be carried out with an explicit political agenda to bring power to the downtrodden of India and free them from the upper-caste elites.

As part of Pollock's project to get rid of hierarchies and biases, he finds it necessary to highlight aspects of Sanskrit as implicated in this oppression. He wants people to pursue what he calls 'morally sensitive scholarship' and this entails learning about the asymmetries of power along with the abusive political 'products' of Sanskrit culture.

His very clear demonization of Sanskrit was quoted earlier, but is worth repeating in greater detail below:

> Domination did not enter India with European colonialism. Quite the contrary, gross asymmetries of power – the systematic exclusion from access to material and nonmaterial resources of large sectors of the population – appear to have characterized India in particular times and places over the last three millennia and have formed the background against which ideological power, intellectual and spiritual resistance, and many forms of physical and psychological violence crystallized.
>
> This violence is the great absent center of classical Indian studies, the subject over which a deafening silence is maintained. *One task of post-orientalist Indology has to be to exhume, isolate, analyze, theorize, and at the very least talk about the different modalities of domination in traditional India* ... but can we forget that most of the traditions and cultures in question have been empires of oppression in their own right – against women, above all, but also other domestic communities?[78]

He goes on to say that 'the Western Sanskritist feels this most acutely', implying it is the white man's burden to civilize the Indians. He emphasizes the need for activism in helping the victims of Sanskrit today: 'This critique of domination should be coupled ... with an awareness of forms of traditional social and cultural violence sedimented in contemporary India – which in turn should entail solidarity with its contemporary victims.'[79]

The goal, he says, is to save Sanskrit from 'the criminal attempt at its appropriation by the alphabet soup of indigenist forces (RSS, BJP, VHP ...)'.[80] He announces his goal going forward: 'One way to begin to neutralize those forces is through analysis of the construction and function of such a meaning system, and of its contemporary redeployment.'[81] He adds that 'such a project remains for me compelling'.[82]

He finds the entire corpus of Sanskrit texts to be tainted with oppression, including all the shastras. He explains:

> When, for example, we are told by a contemporary Indian woman that she submits to the economic, social, and emotional violence of Indian widowhood because, in her words, 'According to the shastras I had to do it'; when we read in a recent dalit manifesto that '*The first and foremost object of this [cultural revolution] should be to free every man and woman from the thraldom of the Shastras,*' we catch a glimpse not only of the actualization in consciousness of Sanskrit discourses of power, but of their continued vigor.[83]

This is a clear attempt by Pollock to justify his anti-shastra stand which runs through most of his works over several decades. He stresses the importance of studying the history of Sanskrit prior to colonialism: 'How is it possible, then, to survey the constructions of colonial domination without a detailed topography of pre-colonial domination?'[84] Only by constructing this topography of pre-colonial Sanskrit can we understand the Hindu origins of oppression, he feels. In most current scholarship, according to him, 'this topography, charted throughout the expanse of Sanskrit cultural production, does not really yet exist'.[85] Therefore, he wants to remedy this deficiency in Sanskrit studies:

> The failure to trace with any adequacy a historical map of social power in traditional India, which alone can anchor our estimations of the impact of colonialism, is all the more surprising considering what appear to be the extraordinary density, longevity, and effectivity of authoritative power – or at least of its normative claims, though the two are not easily distinguishable – in the high culture of early India.[86]

In other words, it is vital for his collaborators to embark on the project to chart the Sanskrit cultural abuses that existed long before the colonial period. This would be the lens through which to see contemporary Indian society. Pollock wants Indologists to do social engineering in radical ways. They should open up new perspectives that would give priority to what has hitherto been 'marginal, invisible, and unheard'.[87] This would counteract the 'radical silencing and screening out of communities effected by "classical" culture'.[88] The result would be 'disembedding the discursive structures by which such censorship and occulation were effected'.[89]

Pollock says he is developing a new kind of social theory because the eighteenth and nineteenth century European theories do not explain the social systems to which Sanskrit gave rise and which continue to exert oppression. The Indian left has, in his eyes, failed to explain India adequately, owing to its dependence on Western theories that are based on European experience. His project is to deconstruct Indian intellectual history using Indian texts processed through his own brand of political philology. This would explain India to Indians better than they have been taught previously. The irony is that Pollock is blind to his own dependence on Western thought and his radical distortion of Indian traditions by deleting the sacredness.

How will he develop this new social theory? He answers: 'If we are to reach a different theory of the theory for the *future*, one that grounds a different future practice, we need a *new past* and better ways to make sense of it.'[90] In other words, Pollock is focussed on inventing a 'new past' for Sanskrit history, i.e., a project of blatant revision of history. This new theory (based on an invented past) would then help him chart the future of India.

Response: Problems with American Orientalist social engineering projects

I wish to give Pollock the benefit of doubt regarding his good intentions. Also, I acknowledge that Indian society, like all others, has injustices and abuses that must be addressed. Indeed, I have materially supported numerous causes aimed at addressing some of these ills. Furthermore, I am well aware that there are world views, both religious and secular, that sometimes even promote injustice, and I agree these need to be identified and eradicated.

However, we cannot throw the baby out with the bathwater. My issue is with his determination to cut out from Hinduism the very internal resources that have always sustained it and that provide the basis for its ability to move forward on social and other fronts. I also object to his frequent lack of transparency and his failure to reflect on his own position and its implications. In my view, whatever his intentions, the effect of his work is *not* to empower Dalits, women, oppressed Muslims, etc., but ultimately to disempower Indians by subverting their sacred traditions. His work is being used by many to advocate marginalizing the sacred and disenfranchising those who wish to work on solutions from within those traditions.

This form of American Orientalism diverts the focus away from Western (especially American) hegemony by spotlighting something Pollock considers far worse: Sanskrit Orientalism. He exhorts his fellow Western academics and Indian subalternist scholars to suspend their critique of Western Orientalism and instead shift their attention to the social toxins spewing forth from the Vedas. He finds this Vedic toxicity a lived reality for hundreds of millions of Indians today.

Such a plan is based on a strategic template which Western scholarship has used since the beginning of the nineteenth century in its subjugation of India. It is a twofold process: first, acknowledge a fault in the West and claim it has been corrected, and second, recognize the same fault in India and start a Western intervention in order to correct *that*. This process repeats itself as the correction discovers a new fault in the West, requiring a new correction, followed by a search for that fault in India, and a continuation of Western intervention.

Historically, these phases have unfolded as follows:

- In the first phase, the Western problem of paganism was corrected by converting European heathens to Christianity. Corresponding to this there was intervention in India to rescue India from its 'false gods'.
- Then Christian religion itself was found to be too narrow and unscientific, and the West corrected itself by science. Western intervention in India was deemed necessary to rescue it from Indian religions in the same manner.

- Now even science is seen by many postmodernists as a hegemonic discourse and is being studied as an aspect of the nexus between knowledge and power. The West has corrected itself by exposing the nexus between knowledge and power evident in Orientalism. It is now time to repeat this feat in India – to discover, expose and challenge the so-called Sanskrit Orientalism. This is what Pollock's Sanskrit revival project is all about.

Pollock's proposal would hand over the authority of Sanskrit studies to westernized scholars using his political philology and not Sanskrit's own literary theories or Indian socio-political resources. Persons who are outsiders to the Indian traditions would call the shots, and even become the proxies to represent the downtrodden.

He puts Western style academia at the helm of the study of ancient and modern India, even when it is being carried out by Indians in India. The West would become a 'visva-guru' so to speak. Western methods and criteria would select the problems, define them, and recommend projects and programmes to address them. This would disempower the traditional adhikari and marginalize Sanskrit shastras that deal with such issues from within the tradition. Rather than liberation, it would lead to a new form of domination: a recolonization of India.

In other words, the Western gaze at India remains unscathed, merely updated. In many ways, Orientalism 2.0 (i.e., American Orientalism) is even more dangerous than Orientalism 1.0. (i.e., European Orientalism).

I have so far explained how Pollock *removes the sacred* and *looks for social oppression* to frame Sanskrit and sanskriti. In a later chapter, I will explain how his lens also sees India's cultural history in terms of political domination by brahmins and Hindu kings. This 'political' qualifier in his political philology is what separates him from previous philologists of Sanskrit. In summary, he removes one quality from sanskriti and inserts two qualities in its place: *He removes the sacred and adds social oppression and political hegemony.*

5

Ramayana Framed as Socially Irresponsible

Pollock's view of Ramayana as a project for propagating Vedic social oppression

In 1984, Sheldon Pollock began fashioning some of the building blocks for his study of Sanskrit texts by publishing an important work on Valmiki's Ramayana. He does not see the Ramayana reflecting historical events but as a myth potentially inspired by a Buddhist Jataka tale about a man named Rama. One argument he cites for this hypothesis is that the metrical verse form of the Jatakas was imitated by Valmiki in writing the epic:

> However, although the 'Ramáyana' must represent the culmination of a long bardic tradition of heroic song, and although the monumental poet must have adopted certain motifs from folk literature as we find it represented, for example, in the Buddhist játakas, the poem is more

> easily considered as the first chapter in a new volume of Indian literary history than as the last of an old one.[1]

Here Pollock appears to sideline the traditional view that the Ramayana is a reflection of actual events; he does not even discuss the issue of historical evidence. It is presented by him as a poem from 'a long bardic tradition' constructed out of motifs drawn from 'folk literature' that the clever Valmiki tied together into a heroic story. Pollock is superimposing the model of European bards on to Valmiki. In pre-Christian British culture, a bard was a professional poet or travelling singer employed by a wealthy patron, such as a monarch or nobleman, to commemorate the patron's ancestors. Later on, this bardic tradition disappeared and the term came to mean an epic author/singer/narrator who mythologizes, and is therefore an unreliable source of history.

According to him, the Vedic brahmins co-opted the new literary Sanskrit developed by the Buddhists in order to write the Ramayana as their first kavya. Doing so enabled them to propagate Vedic principles in popular poetic form. To fit this chronology, Pollock places the date of Valmiki's Ramayana at about 150 BCE, in the period when he says Buddhist writings had become well established. Other scholars propose a much older date for the Ramayana. However, such a date is important for Pollock because it enables him to claim that the Ramayana was written in part as a response to the Buddhist assault on the Vedas.

He asserts that the primary purpose of the king's rule in the Ramayana is to protect the Vedic social hierarchy with the brahmins on top. An important duty of the king as part of protecting his society is to fight external threats. This requires that the public must see their king as endowed with divine powers and the enemies as demonic. Therefore, he argues, the Ramayana provides a two fold divine/demonic construct as follows:

- The *divinization* of the king is a Vedic process by which a human is 'magically' infused with powerful divine qualities. Once divinized in this way, the king becomes authoritarian and despotic. In the Ramayana, divinization is used to infuse divine qualities into

Rama, who is then able to overcome great odds and win victories that would be impossible for mere mortals to achieve. The source of this principle of divinization, he claims, is the Vedas.

- The *demonization* of some outside group is the process that complements this. It entails branding a certain group of outsiders as enemies who have such extraordinary powers that no ordinary human can defeat them. Only a divine king can protect the public from such an evil force, and this requires that the king must exercise violence to kill the demon. Ravana personifies this demon. Pollock says that this Vedic principle enabled Hindu kings to demonize all those who did not toe the line, so that they could consolidate their power.

Valmiki is the supplier of the narrative whose purpose, according to Pollock, is to show how this divine/demonic dichotomy functions. He claims that ever since the Ramayana this dichotomy has become the basis for the idea of 'raj dharma', the Hindu ideal for governance. Since the sanatana dharma is eternal and changeless, he says, the raj dharma must also continue forever. Therefore, he says, Hindu society even today can be interpreted using the framework of an authority (i.e., the modern state) performing the role of a divine king fighting external enemies.

Another important aspect of Pollock's framework is that he considers the major characters in the Ramayana lacking in free will. In other words, they are bound to act fatalistically. He alleges that the epic was used by Hindu kings to supress their subjects and marginalize women, excluding them from power. In this respect, he says:

- Rama is depicted as completely obedient and subservient to Dasharatha, and as such, is an exemplar of fatalistic thinking for Hindus.
- Kaikeyi is shown as cunning and manipulative for attempting to exercise her free will in her dealings with her husband (Dasharatha), while Kaushalya and Sita are portrayed as exemplars of blind subservience to husbands, even when they are wronged.

He argues that the Ramayana was used to arouse Hindus and demonize Muslim invaders from the twelfth to sixteenth centuries. The Hindu rulers projected themselves as divine kings who were protecting the public, and projected the Muslim enemies as demons who had to be killed. He then says that the Bharatiya Janata Party/Vishwa Hindu Parishad (BJP/VHP) have used the Ramayana in modern times to present themselves as similar to the Hindu kings who must kill the Muslims by demonizing them. He suggests that the Ramayana has *intrinsically* lent itself to such co-opting. This is Pollock's way of blaming the epic.

I will now trace Pollock's explanation of how these constructs start in the Vedas, then become popularized in the Ramayana, finally becoming an essential aspect of Hindu chauvinism and aggressiveness to this day.

The divinization construct

Pollock says there are numerous examples of the divinization–demonization construct in the Vedas, wherein one social group is shown as possessing an elevated, divine status while another group is depicted as demonic.[2] The Vedas show how Vishnu overcame the asuras (translated by Pollock as demons), confiscated their material possessions and gave these to the devatas (translated by him as gods). For Pollock, Vishnu here represents a divine force, and the brahmins performed yajnas to invest this divine force in the king. As a result of this divinization process carried out by the brahmins, the king is no longer an ordinary human and is elevated above all humans. Thus, according to this 'myth' as Pollock would call it, the king gets a mandate for absolute power.

Having located the source of divinization in the Vedas, Pollock steps back to explain his idea of what a myth means:

> When I speak of 'myth' here, I am referring to a patterned representation of the world, with continuing and vital relevance to the culture, which furnishes a sort of invariable conceptual grid upon which variable and multifarious experience can be plotted and comprehended. It is this essential power imaginatively to interpret and explain reality,

> social no less than other aspects of reality, that seems to have gone unappreciated in previous treatments of the *Rāmāyaṇa* from the point of view of myth.[3]

By being explicit about the social aspect of this myth, which according to him is a 'conceptual grid' that can be applied based on one's imagination, Pollock signals his political approach to these texts.

He then argues that the Vedas are based on a deep pattern in which ordinary humans are seen as weak. Because of 'man's natural incapacity', he says the public depends on a king, and not just an ordinary human king. He must be 'infused' with Vishnu's power to be able to protect his subjects.[4] He refers to such a king as a 'second-order being'. The Ramayana was the first vehicle, he says, through which this Vedic 'ancient motif' became a part of everyday life in traditional India. He explains this as follows:

> What makes the adaptation of the ancient motif particularly suggestive, complex, and powerful in the *Rāmāyaṇa* is the fact that this second-order being, this divine human or mortal god, is here coupled with a socio-political representation of everyday life in traditional India: Such intermediate beings, gods who walk the earth in the form of men, are kings.[5]

He says that the brahmin's importance stems from the fact that he performs the yajna to infuse the king with Vishnu's power. In return, the king must protect the brahmins so that they are able to continue this critical role which nobody else can perform. Hence, the kshatriya king as well as the brahmins who help him achieve his divine status are both indispensable to the well-being of society. For Pollock this is the core of the raj dharma doctrine.

Pollock also connects raj dharma to the Mahabharata, saying, 'I wish simply to single out one representative epic text from our most important source of traditional Indian political theology, the *Rajadharma* section of the *Mahābhārata*.' He cites the following:

> A man who acts in opposition to the king never gains happiness [cf. *Rām*. III.38.20], neither he himself nor anyone close to him – son,

> brother, friend ... All that the king owns is to be preserved as his; keep your distance from it. Taking something of his should be seen to be as fraught with terror as death itself; touch it and you perish ... The king is the very heart of hearts of his subjects, their foundation, refuge, and ultimate happiness. Putting their reliance in their king people without question win this world, and the world to come (*M Bh*. XII.68.37-59).[6]

He then connects this view back to Valmiki, thus: 'Reading Vālmīki's poem, one gets the distinct impression that the doctrine [of raj dharma] is one in the making, and that its consolidation is a principal objective of the poem.'[7] Notice that in support of his argument here, he refers to only one verse in the Mahabharata, a verse that represents only one of many voices in the epic. He does not explain the particular context in the narrative whence this verse arose. He simply assumes it is representative of a normative raj dharma and then says his reading of Valmiki confirms this view.

Pollock acknowledges that there were dharmashastras that were either silent about interpreting raj dharma in this way or else were actively opposed to doing so. He dismisses these as irrelevant to the understanding he wants to promote.[8] Interestingly, Pollock admits he is on thin ice and acknowledges that there were indeed discussions and opposing viewpoints among intellectuals about the role of the king. He then frankly admits his intention to pick and choose what best supports his thematic understanding of Valmiki's Ramayana.[9]

According to Pollock, such a divine king does not have to abide by the rules of dharmashastras because those apply only to mortal rulers. Every subject of a divine king has to follow his wishes and commands as absolutes; therefore, the divinization of a king in the Vedic tradition makes him a despot. Pollock's textual evidence for reading Valmiki's Rama in the negative light he does consists simply of quoting one verse uttered by Rama.[10]

Why does Pollock want to focus on divine kingship in the Ramayana in the first place? He claims 'oriental absolutism' is not 'constrained by a legal code of sovereign responsibility, allegiance to which was divinely ordained'. This position opens the door for him to show that the divine king in India has a licence to oppress people in a manner that is not constrained by any law or responsibility. Such an interpretation says that none of the dharmic constraints on kings in various shastras applies to the *divine* king, because a divine king does not get his power from the dharma-based institution of kingship, which would have some limitations. The divine king's power comes from Vishnu himself, by virtue of a Vedic yajna performed by brahmins.

Pollock observes that 'the dichotomy between king and kingship finds little support in Indian epic texts. The notion itself is a juristic concept belonging primarily to the European medieval period ...' Despite this disclaimer in which he expresses sensitivity to the differences between Western and Indian models of kingship, Pollock continues to superimpose the European model on to the Indian situation; he is differentiating to reach a negative conclusion for India. In European medieval history, the formal separation between the king and the institution of kingship is often seen as a wedge that allows challenges to and constraints on kingship itself. It is the beginning of the end of the infamous 'divine right of kings'. This move is thought by scholars to have been crucial to Western political progress. Pollock is implying that by contrast, in India, where no such distinction is made, the result is to enable oriental despotism. So India and the West are different, he says, but in a way that allowed the West to progress out of the 'divine right of kings' whereas India cannot do so.

Pollock's analysis is flawed. In the West, divine kingship was based on Abrahamic revelation, which means it depended on the will of God, which operates notoriously independently of any preordained constraint. In the Indian context, divine kingship is based on the dharmic order, which has *built-in constraints to which even Vishnu is subject.* As a result, the lack of separation between king and kingship in the Sanskrit epics does not inherently elevate the king above all limits, contrary to what Pollock claims.

To prove his point about the Hindu divine king being invested with totalitarian power, Pollock cites the *Taittiriya Brahmana.* This text describes how in the royal consecration ceremony, when the king 'takes the [three] strides of Viṣṇu, he becomes Viṣṇu himself and thereby triumphs over all these worlds'.[11] Pollock's 'proof' is unconvincing: How does this ritual prove that 'becoming Viṣṇu' is a matter of personal power? Could it not be a symbolic enactment of the principle that kingship is constructed and constrained by a *higher* power? Pollock does not consider this alternative. Instead, he emphasizes that the political duty of a consecrated king is to protect the power of brahmins. He writes: 'Once created, the king vows righteousness, promises to protect "the earthly brahmans" and preserve the brahmanical social order.'[12] In other words, for Pollock, the king's primary duty is to preserve brahmin supremacy.[13]

This duty, and this duty alone, is for Pollock the core of raj dharma. He selectively picks phrases from the Mahabharata to say that dharma itself is rooted only in the king, that the king's dharma consists of protection, and that it is this protection that 'maintains the world itself'. All beings depend on dharma and the dharma depends on the king. But what precisely is it that the king must dutifully protect? Pollock answers by saying:

> The king provides security, to brahmans and ascetics in particular ... This is a 'gift of life' equal to no other, and by means of it alone the entire brahmanical order and the sacrificial cult by which it sustains the universe are preserved.[14]

To sum up, Pollock repeatedly makes the following allegations about raj dharma in the itihasas:

a. The king's core function is protection of the brahmins;
b. The well-being of the brahmins is necessary so that they may perform Vedic yajnas in order to maintain balance in the cosmic order; and
c. The supposed unlimited power of the king is thus implicitly justified, no matter how oppressive it may be.

While it is true that great emphasis is placed on protecting the domains of sacredness (associated with brahmins) and governance (associated with kshatriyas), Pollock is silent about the *other duties* of raj dharma. He simply ignores other shastras, such as the *Arthashastra,* which explicitly lays down the reasons for the king to maintain the welfare of all subjects and which offers specific injunctions on how to go about doing so. Ensuring economic welfare and ecological balance are, for instance, two key principles of raj dharma as laid out in the *Arthashastra.*

K.S. Kannan (via private communication) offers a rejoinder to Pollock by citing the following compilation of evidence concerning the responsibilities of the king as per the Ramayana:[15]

- At the coronation of Rama, Dasharatha consults his assembly which consisted not just of brahmins but also of city leaders and village leaders. This clearly implies a form of rule where the people participate rather than a despotic rule (Ramayana 2.2).
- The king never ruled as per his whims and fancies. He was to adhere to the dharmashastras, and was also guided by the assembly and council. An erratic king could be exiled. There is the instance of the banishment of Asamanja, the son of King Sagara, for his misbehaviour (Ramayana 1.38.21).
- Ramayana 2.67 details the perils of anarchy, which imply the important role the king must play for his people beyond simply protecting the interests of brahmins.[16]
- As the king, so the citizens. Hence, he must lead them by example of his own conduct (Ramayana 2.109.9).
- Even when attacking an enemy, a king had to follow certain norms, such as not attacking anyone who was asleep, drunk, unarmed or in the company of women (Ramayana 4.11.36).
- Rama used to confer with the ministers regularly, and then decide the course of action (Ramayana 6.41.58).
- Citizens, all abiding by dharma, had Rama as their ideal (Ramayana 6.131.98).

All this contradicts Pollock's view that the divine king could behave like an absolute despot without constraints.

The demonization construct

I have shown how Pollock develops the divinization side of the two-sided construct of divinization–demonization and sees it as the foundation of raj dharma. He then takes up the other pole of the dichotomy and discusses the politics behind what he calls demonization. He says the problem Western Sanskritists have had in grappling with the figure of Rama, who is both human and divine, may be resolved if we consider Ravana, who represents the demonic side of the same coin. He writes:

> The problem of the divine status of the hero of the *Rāmāyaṇa*, which fundamentally conditions our understanding of this crucial text, has rightly, if inconclusively, preoccupied Western scholarship. The limitations of both text-critical and purely impressionistic studies may be avoided by an intensive analysis of some larger narrative features of the poem. One such is the theme of Rāvaṇa's boon, an integral component of the tale.[17]

Pollock says the demonization of Ravana begins with his gaining a boon that makes him more powerful than the divinized king. He writes:

> The boon, to recall its specifics, was granted to Rāvaṇa by Brahmā in response to the intense asceticism the rākṣasa had performed over thousands of years, and it provided that he could never be slain 'by gods, *dānavas, gandharvas, piśācas,* birds, or serpents'. It is virtually formulaic in epic and puranic literature that the performance of *tapah* compels the divine regents of the universe, however unwilling, to give free play to the forces of evil. Quite mechanistically 'holy' ascetic self-mortification can oblige the gods to cede the power by which alone they can maintain their supremacy: that deriving from immortality, won by them at such great cost at the churning of the empyreal ocean, and laid up in heaven where it is jealously guarded. But the very formulation of these boons always works to ensure their subversion.[18]

In the above quote, Pollock mistranslates tapasya and tyaga as 'self-mortification', a projection of Judeo-Christian asceticism. Furthermore,

Hindus are taught that (1) bad conduct after getting the boon is what makes Ravana an enemy, and nothing else, and (2) being a brahmin (and son of a great rishi) does not exempt him from being considered wicked. Pollock ignores this significance, perhaps because it would undermine his depiction that brahmins were always considered good.

Ravana is a human who has extraordinary powers, and only the divinized king, in this case Rama, can destroy him and thereby protect his subjects. Pollock claims that this combination is a standard formula in the Vedas – a magical 'morpheme' that dates back to the earliest history of myths, produced, in Pollock's view, by foreign Indo-Aryans:

> [The] formulation of the boon itself, a 'morpheme' of Indian myth reverting, it seems, to the earliest stratum of Indo-Aryan mythopoesis, inherently entails the counteraction of the boon by some previously nonexistent creature or phenomenon, either one purely deceptive or else – and this is more frequent – one entirely outside the catalogue of natural possibility.[19]

So Pollock is now asking scholars to search the myths made up by Aryans in order to interpret Ravana's boon as well as the divine king. The origin of the divine king myth, he says, lies in some archaic 'nonexistent creature or phenomenon' that could be 'outside the catalogue of natural possibility'. In other words, these constructs that are central in the Ramayana are, as per Pollock, myths from the earliest stratum of primitive man's imagination.

Sociological criticism of the Ramayana

I will now examine Pollock's contention that the Ramayana is 'readily available to reactionary politics'. He asserts that poets of this period were professionally employed in royal courts and wrote for kshatriya audiences. He correctly notes that the key characters of the Ramayana are kshatriyas; the plots revolve around kshatriya characters, with brahmins such as Vashishtha playing minor roles; and other jatis play even smaller roles.

Pollock then insists that the ideological discourse at the centre of the Ramayana is as follows: 'Social subordination and political domination now become "the eternal way of righteousness".'[20] In other words, righteousness – sanatana dharma – takes the form of the king's domination and the public's passive subjection.[21]

One of Pollock's fundamental views is that all the important sacred figures of the tradition lack individuality and free will. He holds that Rama's feelings are quite irrelevant to the poem's purposes. Indeed, he says, we cannot know what any of the characters in the Ramayana feels or why they choose to do something, because *no one in the Ramayana believes himself or herself to have any freedom of action.* In general, he sees the characters in Valmiki's Ramayana as lacking agency and freedom of choice and therefore having no control over what happens to them. This acceptance of suffering means there is no justice. He writes:

> The characters of the 'Ramáyana' believe themselves to be denied all freedom of choice; what happens to them may be the result of 'their' own doing, but they do not understand how this is so and consequently can exercise no control ... The fate of Rama and others is prepared for them, at some plane beyond their intervention or even comprehension. 'Justice' never enters the picture.[22]

He contrasts this view with the ancient Greek system, saying:

> Since in the archaic Greek world fate has both a cosmic dimension and an aspect of justice, the gods can guarantee the whole process as guardians of a just and moral order ... Significantly, gods play no role whatever in 'Ayódhya'. There is a mechanical quality to the course of human affairs.[23]

When he says 'gods play no role', he is ignoring Valmiki's own testimony that the rishis appealed to Vishnu about being oppressed by the rakshasas. He continues:

> In the *Ayodhyākāṇḍa* man is prohibited from making his destiny, and cannot truly comprehend the cause of his suffering. Fate – *daiva*, 'what comes from the gods;' *kāla*, 'time;' *adṛṣta*, 'the unforeseeable;' *kṛtānta*, 'doom' or 'destiny' – is something one cannot understand and against

> which one cannot struggle. *Rama has no choice; no one does. Choice is replaced by chance, and action is nothing more than reaction.*[24]

He refers to karma as a form of fatalism; but equating karma with the Western concept of mechanistic fate is based on a profound misunderstanding. The one has nothing to do with the other. Karma is the result of prior actions and its future can be altered by new ones. It is better to see it as a system of causation in which a portion of the effect is time-delayed.

Pollock says Rama is shackled by his culture, thus ensuring that he is unable to act even though he knows that what is being done to him is unjust. Rama's behaviour is shown to be inferior compared to the heroes in Greek mythology, according to Pollock:

> In some respects it may be erroneous for us to think of the protagonist of the *Rāmáyaṇa* as a hero. Properly understood, heroes are those who do great things in the face of certain defeat, such as Achilles, Siegfried, Roland, Cuchulain. They far transcend us and are not figures we are supposed to emulate. Rāma emphatically is; and the various types of behavior that he exemplifies – filial devotion, for example, or obedience – we have already observed.[25]

In other words, he says that Rama's filial devotion renders him devoid of free will, unlike the Greek heroes.

Pollock also wishes to show that the Ramayana is sexist, which he does by examining the women characters in the volume known as the Ayodhyakanda. He begins by stating: 'Like the Ramáyana as a whole, the *Ayodhyākāṇḍa* is as interested in the domain of sexual relations as in socio-political life in general.'[26] Then he presents a series of verses that highlight the inequality of women in Valmiki's time, and without any reference to the same problem as it existed in other cultures across the world almost three millennia ago.[27] He ties all these gender-related quotes to *Manusmriti*:[28]

> In childhood a woman must bow to the will of her father, in adulthood, to the will of the man who marries her, and when her husband is dead, to the will of her sons. She must never have independence.[29]

Pollock says the locus for these views is found in the law book of Manu, which recasts the idea of women's subjugation unambiguously and appends the logical conclusion that she must never have independence.[30] Shrinivas Tilak rejoinders that Pollock is distorting Manu by turning his descriptive statements (on the prevailing situation in his time) into prescriptive statements (on how things *ought* to be).[31]

I do not doubt that, using modern criteria, the Ramayana at times manifests a view of women and gender relationships that needs to be adapted for today, but to judge this narrative by completely anachronistic standards is misleading. Furthermore, when these verses are isolated from their context and presented as being representative of the Ramayana's ethic, the epic's true meanings, which have to do with a relationship to dharma that goes beyond gender, become obscure.

Claiming Ramayana was popularized to demonize Muslims since the eleventh century

Latent in the Ramayana, according to Pollock's thesis, is the self/other dichotomy whereby the established Hindu rulers saw themselves and their subjects as members of a divinely ordained political power structure while their opponents were vilified as demons. Hindu kings had to use this ideology when they were challenged by the Muslim invaders from Central Asia, he says. The king demonized the Muslims by having brahmins write kavya showing the king to be the earthly representative of heroic Rama. The king was thus depicted as defending his subjects against the invading Muslims, who were shown to be demonic. Pollock cites Prithviraj and Vikramaditya VI of the Vijayanagara Empire as examples which illustrate his theory.

In this manner, he asserts, the violence built into the divine/demonic dichotomy became unleashed when the Ramayana was deployed as a weapon against the Muslim Turks, who were depicted as the new rakshasas. He offers a range of evidence to argue that the epic was used to fuel the Hindu–Muslim conflict that began in the eleventh century. As a matter of fact, he generalizes far beyond what the data shows. He writes:

> Rāmāyaṇa has served for 1,000 years as a code in which protocommunalist relations could be activated and theocratic legitimization could be rendered ... it makes sense that it would be through this mytheme par excellence that reactionary politics in India today would find expression in the interests of a theocratization of the state and the creation of an internal enemy as necessary antithesis.[32]

As I have noted earlier, Pollock says this politics of violence is rooted in Valmiki's Ramayana. For him the Ramayana had already been important as an elitist text sponsored by kings, but he argues that something very different happened during the Islamic invasion period. At this time, he says, 'The tale comes alive in the political sphere and for the first time.' It is now that kings *become* Rama. As he puts it, 'The tradition of invention – of inventing the king as Rama – begins in the twelfth century.'[33] From then onwards, the Ramayana became a 'language in which the political imagination expresses itself'.

He claims: 'The Rāma cult in South Asia is almost totally non-existent until at the earliest the eleventh, or more likely the twelfth, century, and the growth of this cult took place in virtual synchrony with a set of particular historical events.' Prior to this, he says, 'the cultic practice devoted to Rāma is sparse' and 'the evidence prior to the twelfth century that Rāma may have been the object of worship is scanty indeed.'[34]

Pollock cites a few 'minor exceptions' which show that Rama was important in earlier periods, but he downplays them. His goal is to trace the rise of Rama's popularity as contemporaneous with the arrival of Muslims from Central Asia, and to make the case that the Ramayana was deployed for the purpose of supporting anti-Muslim violence. He lists many scattered places where prior to the Muslims, parts of Ramayana get displayed in temples across India but concludes that 'nothing in all this indicates dedication to or a cultic significance of Rāma.'[35]

He asserts that he can be specific and accurate about when the Ramayana began being used as political symbology by Hindu kings:

> It is possible to specify with some accuracy the particular historical circumstances under which the Rāmāyaṇa was first deployed as a central organizing trope in the political imagination of India.[36]

> I suggest … that the Rāmāyaṇa came alive in the realm of public political discourse in western and central India in the eleventh to fourteenth centuries in a dramatic and unparalleled way.[37]

He presents data to show that between the mid-eleventh century and end of the twelfth century, local kings began to develop Ayodhya into a major Vaishnava centre, including a substantial temple-building programme. At the end of the thirteenth century and the beginning of the fourteenth, several major cultic centres devoted to Rama were created or reinvigorated. The growth of 'the Rama cult' reached its peak in the fourteenth century with the founding of the Vijayanagara Empire, according to him:

> At first extraordinarily restricted in time and space, it [the 'cult of Rama'] exhibits striking efflorescence and assumes a prominent place within the context of a political theology from the end of the twelfth century onward, achieving in some instances a centrality by the middle of the fourteenth.[38]

He devotes many pages to interpreting a single poem from the twelfth century that refers to the Muslim invaders as a demonic force, and it is on this one poem that he bases his case. Pollock is implying that Ayodhya began to be built only after Mahmud Ghaznavi invaded and destroyed temples in India.[39]

However, contrary to his claim, one must examine the fact that Ayodhya had already been the capital of kings in the pre-Mauryan era for hundreds of years.[40]

Although Pollock presents considerable scattered evidence to make his case, there are historical data that give extensive counter-evidence about the worship of Rama across India and South-east Asia before the eleventh century. Appendix B presents some of these data. It would be interesting to have both sides on this issue of Ramayana's history debate the evidence.

As we have seen, Pollock depicts the Ramayana as a framework that has been used for demonizing Muslims by using the notion of rakshasa. Ramayana, he says, represents the outsiders as deviant in multiple ways.

He then goes a step further and briefly imposes a Freudian reading on the text, a reading outdated and crude even in the current Western context of cultural criticism. He says the depiction of 'the other' in Ramayana can be understood as a projection of the unfulfilled sexual desires of traditional Indians:

> One productive way to think of them is from a psychosexual perspective, as representing all that certain traditional Indians – within a Sanskrit cultural formation – might most desire and most fear, concretized both together in a single symbolic form.[41]

In other words, the 'othering', conveyed through the rakshasa imagery, is really a projection by Hindus of the dark psychosexual side of their own selves, that is, the desires and fears which they repress.

Pollock notes that while earlier newcomers to India became assimilated within a generation or two, the Central Asians in the medieval period (i.e., the Muslims) had so secure and assertive an identity that they did not assimilate in linguistic or religious ways. To deal with this threat, he says, 'Rāmāyana was repeatedly instrumentalized by the ruling Indian elites of the middle period to provide a theology of politics and a symbology of otherness.'[42]

The image of the Hindu by the end of the second millennium CE is now more or less complete for Pollock: Hindu men who are in power are reckless and lustful, they use mythic stories as a means to divert the attention of the masses away from their despotism; those not in power are abjectly obedient and incapable of reasoned inquiry and argument; women are nothing more than victims of oppression; and those who are considered outsiders are demonized through projection of the suppressed sexual deviance lurking in the Hindu mind.

He sums it up by connecting this entire picture to the Ramayana:

> The Rāmāyaṇa is profoundly and fundamentally a text of 'othering' ... Outsiders are made other by being represented as deviant – sexually, dietetically, politically deviant ... the Rāmāyaṇa, with its demonizing imagery, provides, as does no other Indian text, a conceptual instrument for the utter dichotomization of the enemy.[43]

As mentioned earlier, a lopsided picture is presented when one examines the Hindu society in isolation at a given time in history, without bringing in the state of other cultures of that era. The motive of applying a totally alien framework, viz., the Freudian one, to a traditional Hindu text is something that is questionable, as I have discussed elsewhere. These claims need to be countered in greater detail than I have done here, and debated by scholars.

Ramayana considered secular

Pollock implies the Ramayana is a purely laukika (this-worldly) text because it is not used for performing Vedic yajnas. However, this is a critical error in his assumption that only fire rituals concern paramarthika, and everything else is strictly laukika. This error is what leads him to think of itihasas, including the Ramayana, as being laukika with solely political purposes.

Hindus would argue differently and assert that the traditions of bhakti, tantra, katha, meditation, etc., are considered among the numerous approaches to Brahman, parama-Shiva, moksha, purusha, and so forth. Hence, the itihasa, based as it is on the knowledge from the Vedas, may lead to paramarthika. *The Ramayana is a this-worldly (vyavaharika) text that provides a bridge to the paramarthika realm.* The Ramayana was and is seen by its adherents as itihasa, that is, as presenting the teachings of the Vedas in a manner accessible by most people who are inclined towards pleasure and play, rather than with introspective tendencies as are required by jnana. Contradicting this, Pollock says kavyas are laukika and concerned primarily with the aesthetic expression of socio-political power. Chapter 6 explains this further.

Claiming Valmiki Ramayana came after Buddhist influence

Pollock has modified the historical chronology of the Valmiki Ramayana by manipulating the evidence. I will use arguments from within the tradition as well as the work of Western academicians such as Robert

Goldman to compare and contrast a traditional point of view with Pollock's politically driven one.[44]

Pollock dates Valmiki to 150 BCE rather than 800 BCE or prior, as has been argued by many Indian and Western scholars alike.[45] This dating enables Pollock to suggest that Valmiki had learned the Rama story from Buddhist Jataka writings.[46] Robert Goldman disputes Pollock's assertion of a Buddhist influence on the Valmiki Ramayana, an assertion which he traces back to Max Weber in the nineteenth century and which he critically and categorically argues and rebuts as follows:

> The suggestion that the story of the *Rāmāyaṇa* could be traced to Buddhist sources was put forward by Weber who saw it as growing, under the influence of the Greek epics, to its present form out of the Buddhist legend of Prince Rāma; the point of which was a glorification of the virtue of indifference to events in the real world. Weber then saw the *Daśaratha Jātaka* as the original of the *Rāmāyaṇa,* which was, he felt, a poetic expression of, among other things, brahmanical hostility, to the Buddhists. This theory was cogently refuted shortly after it was promulgated ... There can be no doubt, however, that on the basis of the best historical and literary evidence available to us, the *Daśaratha Jātaka* is substantially later than the *Vālmīki Rāmāyaṇa* and that it is both inspired by and derived from it.[47]

Goldman is one of the few scholars to have openly challenged Pollock's scholarship in this regard.

Summary: Ramayana interpreted as atrocity literature

Pollock argues that since the dichotomy between divine and demonic was part of sanatana (eternal) dharma, it could be and was regarded as eternal and changeless. He concludes that Hindus viewed, and continue to view today, this raj dharma as the core set of principles with which to govern the state. The implications of setting up the construct of a divinized king and his demonic enemies, according to Pollock, are summarized as follows:

1. With the support of the brahmins, the king can declare some individuals or groups as being demonic enemies. Those that are potential threats to the king's position are branded as such. The subjects are roused into using the Ramayana to go to war against these enemies and kill them.
2. The divine king can demand complete obedience from his subjects. This form of rule is what colonial Indologists have labelled 'oriental despotism'. It characterizes Hindu kings in terms of the horrific, abusive treatment that the public was allegedly subjected to purely on their whim.
3. A social system built on such blind obedience, then, makes Indians incapable of questioning or having any semblance of individuality or free will. The Hindu, therefore, lacks agency to think for himself or to question authority.
4. The king, according to this view of raj dharma, has unconstrained divine power, and can be sexually deviant and abusive towards women without hindrance. Pollock alleges that Dasharatha is an example of such a king.
5. The BJP/VHP is currently using this construct against Muslims and other minorities because it inherently authorizes violence against them.

According to Pollock, since the late 1980s, political events in India are consistent with the theme of the demonization of Muslims. He notes that in order to arouse the public to demolish the Babri Masjid in Ayodhya in 1992, the VHP/BJP leaders had projected themselves as being Rama while depicting the Muslims as enemies. The point he is making is that because the cult of Rama had long been employed for this purpose, this latest deployment was easy to do. He says this is what the Sangh Parivar movement is doing even now: demonizing Muslims by using the Ramayana to rabble-rouse the Hindus.

Ramayana is only one of the texts which American Orientalists have analysed in a manner that goes contrary to the traditional understanding;

also the 'new history' that this reasoning creates goes contrary to the lived experience of the Indian masses. As discussed earlier, it is necessary to critique Pollock's stands, methods and reasoning by turning the traditional lens towards his work. I am only raising red flags for other scholars of the home team to investigate.

Ramayana-based political action plan of intervening in Indian politics

Pollock is calling for the English-speaking elites of India who follow him to reinterpret Sanskrit texts politically in order to neutralize the dangers of the Ramayana. His position seems to be that:

- The communalist tendency in India has been present for a thousand years, due in part to such developments as the use of Valmiki's Ramayana for theocratic vilification of outsiders.
- This communalist tendency has nothing to do with the British divide-and-rule policy.
- Nor can Muslim invasions be seen to play any role in it.
- Sanskrit texts are at the root of the Sangh Parivar's actions and their threat must be neutralized by reinterpreting these texts in political terms.

Pollock's goal of political intervention in India today is apparent in his 'Ramayana and Political Imagination in India', written very soon after the demolition of the Babri Masjid in 1992.[48] Even a dozen years later, the intensity of his involvement remains with him, and he gives an interview in 2005 to explain the reasons for writing that earlier article:

> When I was traveling in India early in 1992 and arrived in Hyderabad, there were atrocities against the Muslim community and the *Ramayana* was everywhere, and I thought: I have been working on the *Ramayana* for so long, I have got to say something about the role of this text in Indian political life. And my need to understand what enabled it to function as an instrument of violence became even more desperate after

> the Babri Masjid was destroyed – actually twelve years ago today. So I decided to look at the long history of *Ramayana* discourse and what I saw was very upsetting. But how are you supposed to suppress that sort of information? My feeling was that it was crucial to bring that material out and to critique and defang it. ... When you are on the frontline of struggle I understand you have to do certain things, like denouncing the Vishwa Hindu Parishad for its 'political abuse' of history. [...]
>
> The *Ramayana* article was meant as a contribution to the critique of *Hindutva*, to the critique of the *Ramayana* as an instrument of political manipulation and to the critique of domination. And if the historical record looks bad for some people, if the pre-British past is not entirely utopian, well, that's unfortunate. But the only way you get out of the past is by confronting it.[49]

He sees himself on the front line of the movement to critique the Ramayana as an instrument of violation and political manipulation. The article itself begins as follows:

> From December 1992 through January 1993, more than 3,000 people were killed in 'communal' rioting across India, from Surat to Calcutta, from Kanpur to Bangalore. The likes of this rioting had not been seen for generations; in Bombay, for example, more than 600 people died, and the city was brought to a standstill for a week and a half.[50]

He then explains that his goal is to explain the *causal nexus* of this antagonism between Hindu and Muslim communities. He starts off by stating that the nexus had announced its intentions earlier when the BJP decided to perform the rathyatra (chariot procession) from Somnath to Ayodhya. He writes:

> It was this *yātra* that led, with the force of logic, to the event that inaugurated the most recent riots, the actual demolition of the mosque on December 6, 1992, not by a mob but by what appears to have been a trained group of Hindu militants.[51]

He states that his goal is to examine the 'Hindu theocratic politics against the Muslim population', which his article claims was achieved by 'the invocation of a specific set of symbols: the figure of the warrior-god Rāma, his birthplace Ayodyhā, and the liberation of this sacred site'.

He then clarifies once more his agenda going forward: 'One way to begin to neutralize those forces is through analysis of the construction and function of such a meaning system, and of its contemporary redeployment.'[52] And he adds, 'Such a project remains for me compelling.'

As I have said before, dragging the BJP/VHP into arguments over the interpretation of an entire tradition introduces a huge red herring which only draws attention away from the real issues. Such distractions work against the construction of sane and effective political responses from within the tradition to oppose violence and oppression. It is my view, and the view of many who defend sanskriti on indigenous terms, that the way to a more just and free society lies in a fuller understanding of sanatana dharma. This requires that we ground ourselves in the sacred, transcendental (paramarthika) realm, as well as the secular, immanent (vyavaharika) one.

To drag in the spectres of communalism, fascism and violence as ways to frighten people from exploring their tradition's potential on their own terms amounts to a serious threat to rich and poor, male and female, elite and common alike.

In effect, Pollock is developing ways of demonizing opponents like me who want to defend a traditional approach, while granting himself and his cohorts a kind of divine right to propagate their own reductive Charvaka interpretations.

6

Politicizing Indian Literature

This chapter along with the following one will examine the lens through which Pollock views such issues as the development of the genres of kavya, shastra and itihasa, the birth of a literary Sanskrit culture, the rise of the vernaculars and the response of the tradition to these changes. I will summarize his account of the *history* of Indian languages and culture. He has some very original and interesting theories on the processes at work that shape the cultural history of India.

To reiterate, his approach is to consider all the important historical developments strictly from the point of view of politics and social domination. He ignores that any legitimate quest for spiritual wisdom could have driven these cultural developments. Seen through his lens, the Vedas were the pre-rational liturgical discourse of brahmins; they are relevant only as an ancient mythic cosmology perpetuating social hierarchy and oppression. His project is a typical Marxist approach to the history of culture, although his work is much more based on studying Sanskrit and other Indian texts than any previous Marxist scholar has been able to do. His primary concern is to trace the politicization of languages and culture in India. The motive of the Hindu leaders is alleged to be hunger for power over others.

Kavya is for him the primary field of cultural production on which this politicization plays out. Shastra, while he is fascinated by its elaborate and intricate texts, is hampered by what he sees as blind reproduction of Vedic constraints. He finds the Vedic metaphysics to be problematic and unable to produce science, political liberation or cultural progress. Therefore, he holds up kavya as the playground of political innovation and sidelines shastra as a socially regressive, outdated and fossilized form of pseudo-knowledge. In doing this, Pollock is breaking with the Indology of the past and drawing on a number of modern and postmodern Western theories of culture.

The purpose of this chapter is to provide a general introduction to these theories while raising a number of red flags. My goal is to educate the traditional interlocutors on his views and highlight some issues for their attention. I reiterate at the outset that these theories are not problematic merely because they are Western. In fact, they do raise important questions and present useful challenges to an insider's point of view. Among other things, they draw attention to issues of power and social justice in ways that the defenders of Sanskrit and Hinduism must take note of and respond.

I am especially interested in highlighting Pollock's distinction between literacy and what he calls 'literarity', his concept of the 'aestheticization of power', and his interest in bracketing off the transcendent dimension so we can better see what is going on at the merely human level. All of these deserve our close attention.

It is important for traditional scholars to examine these theories and their applications carefully to see where and when they have merit and where they distort and weaken the tradition. It is my view that they often have negative consequences, and that Pollock and his school are blind to the tradition's potential for stimulating progress. In particular, the branding of all Vedic wisdom as pre-rational, primitive and childlike, the dismissing of all forms of ritual as regressive, and the view that any talk of transcendence or sacred practice is simply mystifying and scientifically invalid, cannot be accepted at face value and are worth debating.

If the Ramayana, for instance, is read through his lens, there would be no reason to perform natyas (dance) or kathas (storytelling) as a way to transmit certain cultural values to the young; in fact doing so would be dangerous. Only when safely contained in the academy and in the hands of trained specialists would such toxic materials be appropriate to engage. As for the chanting of mantras, or the belief that certain things can best be said only in non-translatable terms, or indeed that Sanskrit has any special properties not shared by other human languages, he would see this as a quaint, dated and even a dangerous form of chauvinism.

A dramatic break from earlier Orientalism

Pollock's secular and political approach to Sanskrit is clearly visible when he turns his attention to kavya, a distinctive genre in which much of the Sanskrit literature of the past was written. This chapter will address the two parts to his reinterpretation of kavya:

- **Removing the sacred dimension:** He does not regard kavya as valuable for transmitting ethics and knowledge of the sacred, because he would regard those ethics as based on outdated and oppressive structures and the sacred as unknowable at best and a dangerous illusion at worst. He emphasizes the separation (and tension) between kavya and the Vedas.
- **Adding the political frame:** Instead of showing its sacredness, he frames kavya as having developed into political literature used by kings for their own selfish purposes. For this, he adapts the Marxist theory of the aestheticization of power, a theory that emerged in the West as a way of analysing how totalitarian regimes use culture as a political tool.

In developing this approach, Pollock broke ranks with the principles and methods of his major precursor and mentor in Sanskrit studies, Donald Ingalls of Harvard University, one of the most influential Western Indologists of the twentieth century and a pioneer in the study of Sanskrit kavya in the West.[1]

Ingalls had insisted that Indologists like him must use the Sanskrit tradition's own lens in studying kavya, at least to the extent westerners were capable. His approach to mahakavya, the great and most prestigious kavya/poetry, emphasizes the importance of the tradition's own perspective. He notes that such a text is meant to take its subject matter from a *sacred* source such as the Ramayana or the Mahabharata. Its content must address the challenges contained in the four pursuits of life as per dharma: righteousness (dharma), material wealth (artha), pleasure (kama) and liberation (moksha). These abstract philosophical ideas have to be presented in an attractive way in the kavya so as to capture the average person's attention. This is how the vyavaharika (mundane) lives of people were infused with the tenets of paramarthika (transcendence).[2] Ingalls was emphatic about the traditional guidelines laid out for writing such a poem:

> These are not random suggestions but specific requirements. Every complete mahakavya that has come down to us from the time of Kālidāsa contains the whole list, which, if one considers it carefully, will be seen to contain the basic repertory of Sanskrit poetry. Contained in it are the essential elements of nature, love, society, and war which a poet should be able to describe. The great kāvya tested a poet by his power of rendering *content*, which is a better test at least than the Persian diwan, which tested a poet by his skill at rhyme.[3]

Ingalls taught that scholars must appreciate such poems as a narration of sacred stories meant to show common people how to live a dharmic life within a given individual's circumstances. *Ingalls wanted nothing to do with examining the Sanskrit texts through an externally imposed political lens looking to find exploitation.* A kavya's purpose, he insists, must be respected and this purpose was to communicate the dharma to the lay public in a friendly and aesthetically pleasing manner.

Unfortunately, many of Ingalls's students departed from his approach. Chief among them was Pollock, whose departure from the tradition was driven by his desire to develop his own political approach to Sanskrit kavya based on Western critical theories. To make his political frame logical and consistent, he had to remove the sacred aspect as that would interfere with his focus on power. This manoeuvre was a defining moment in the rise of American Orientalism.

The first part of this chapter addresses Pollock's removal of the sacred from kavya, and the second part deals with his politicization of kavya.

Sacredness removed from rasa and kavya

Pollock says that while Sanskrit kavya appeared with Valmiki's Ramayana in the second century BCE, the tradition lacked a developed theory of kavya until the seventh century CE, about 900 years later. He writes: 'Sanskrit literary theory is a tardy development, remarkably tardy.'[4]

Traditional scholars give great importance to rasa as a central element in kavya from the very beginning. (Rasa, as explained earlier, means the feeling evoked in an individual combined with the emotional theme embedded in a work of art.) Rasa's importance to my analysis stems from its spiritual significance as a kavya's bridge to transcendence. However, Pollock seems to think that rasa was something that evolved only fairly recently.

The table below summarizes the important milestones in the history of kavya theory, comparing the way tradition sees this with how Pollock saw it earlier and how he sees it now. I have picked four major historical milestones to highlight how Pollock's views differ from those of the tradition.

It becomes clear that his views have shifted recently after remaining fixed for nearly thirty years. But he still cannot afford to revise them adequately as that would call into question his entire life work.

The main point I wish to bring out in the table is that he has tried to erase or minimize the spiritual dimension of kavya by trying to disconnect the Vedas, *Natya Shastra* and the subsequent writers of kavya theory. This way he can claim to show that kavya was originally a secular development and thereby situate it as a political tool. Only recently has he acknowledged the spiritual aspect of rasa, and even now he sidelines its relevance in the earlier periods of history. I will explain these points in greater detail below.

Kavya Theory Milestone	Tradition's Position	Pollock's Position for the First Thirty Years	Pollock's Most Recent Position
Vedas	Vedas provide insights into paramarthika and vyavaharika, and supply principles to build bridges from vyavaharika to paramarthika.	Sees Vedas as expressions of primitive people who consider natural phenomena as gods with magical significance.	Unchanged.
Natya Shastra	Vedic insights used in *Natya Shasta* to give the general public paths starting from vyavaharika and leading to paramarthika.	Largely ignores *Natya Shastra* or finds it insignificant in the development of kavya theory.	Acknowledges role of *Natya Shastra* as source of kavya theory, but claims it was influenced by Buddhist writings, hence secular.
Abhinavagupta	He extended *Natya Shastra* and articulated the role of bhava-rasa in the practices of the Shaiva tradition.	Sidelines Abhinavagupta's bhava-rasa development.	Acknowledges Abhinavagupta for extending *Natya Shastra*, but sees it as secular.
Rupa Goswami	He articulated how bhava-rasa concept can be used in bhakti practice in Vaishnava tradition.	Ignores Rupa Goswami.	Says Rupa Goswami introduced spirituality into kavya tradition for the first time in the fourteenth century, which had been secular until then.

Tradition's position on the history of kavya theory

The tradition sees kavya from the perspective of an integrated vyavaharika-paramarthika unity. The origin of kavya is seen in the Vedas. The metrical forms (chhandas) used in the Vedas continue to be used to this day in kavya compositions. The core subject matter of the Vedas was to articulate insights of paramarthika and vyavaharika, as well as practices to connect them. This was expressed in kavya form. Kavya is a way to evoke certain bhavas (emotions) in the individual reader/listener. The emotions evoked lead to rasa (including sublime, transcendent or subtle emotions triggered by the bhava).

The *Natya Shastra* extended insights and practices from the Vedas to make them available to *all* individuals in a user-friendly manner. It described how modalities of poetry, music, dramatics, dance, sculpture and paintings can be used to engage ordinary people in communicative participation and enable them to get knowledge from the Vedas. It incorporates the musical expression of the Sama Veda and key themes from Puranas and itihasas.

Abhinavagupta (tenth century) and later on Rupa Goswami (fifteenth to sixteenth centuries) are among those who extended *Natya Shastra* into their distinct and sophisticated rasa theories. Abhinavagupta used the formulations of *Natya Shastra* to develop his bhava-rasa theory in the framework of the Shaiva tradition. He put a spotlight on kavya's ability to create a connection between the vyavaharika and paramarthika. Rupa Goswami articulated his theory of bhava-rasa in the Vaishnava bhakti context. He too developed kavya concepts based on *Natya Shastra* and incorporated elements of rasa in the kavya tradition as a way of deepening one's devotional relationship with the divine.

Pollock's position on the history of kavya theory

For several decades of his academic career, Pollock saw the Vedas as poetic utterances of primitive people who were fearful of natural phenomena such as thunderstorms and eclipses. They attributed such phenomena to supernatural beings with magical powers. He also believed, as we have seen, that the Vedic chants were used primarily as hymnology – the ritual magic practised by brahmins to perpetuate an abusive social hierarchy.

Pollock argues that Vedas are not kavya, because the Veda 'exists forever in beginningless time and was composed by no author, human or divine'. Also, he says, the Vedas are not anyone's voice, and hence 'there is no one to have desired in the first place'. The wording of the Vedas is so precise, he claims, because it 'reflects an archaic conviction about the magical efficacy of its purely phonic dimension'.[5]

Pollock takes this distinction between Veda and kavya to a level beyond what the traditionalist today sees. Even though Pollock admits some overlaps between Vedas and kavya, he insists they are completely separate domains. Any overlaps, he says, are 'unintentional and therefore entirely irrelevant' because traditional audiences would not even be able to understand them.[6] He has also sidelined and/or downplayed the role of *Natya Shastra* in bringing access to Vedic ideas to the common people through kavya.

He does write that Abhinavagupta's tenth-century theory of bhava-rasa is 'philosophical-religious', but fails to provide any further 'religious' perspective on this; he quickly moves on, avoiding any links between the transcendent and worldly realms in the kavya tradition.[7]

In his latest works, Pollock's knowledge and acknowledgement of the spiritual dimension have moved in the right direction. He now admits that kavya theory originated much earlier than he had previously claimed. He also acknowledges the influences of *Natya Shastra* and subsequent developments in kavya theory.[8] However, he continues to highlight discontinuity and conflict within the Indian traditions. He claims that it was only suddenly after 1500 CE that the sacred aspect enters Indian literature:

> The rise of a new style of religious devotionalism in the early modern era (from around 1500) opened a remarkable final chapter in the history of the idea of rasa. Indian aesthetics had always shown a certain awkwardness in dealing with religious 'literature,' the scare quotes signaling that sacred writings were expressly excluded from what our

> thinkers classified as *kāvya. The fact that* kāvya *itself had its origin, or one of its origins, in Buddhist religious literature had long been forgotten; as for Vedic or even puranic works, Sanskrit poeticians never cite them when discussing rasa or rhetoric or any of the other features of kāvya.*[9]

Not only does he appear to claim that the devotional dimension was recently added; he is also adamant that kavya started only after Buddhism. Therefore, he forces a late date for *Natya Shastra* to make sure that there was plenty of time for Buddhism to have caused kavya to emerge.

Although he *now* gives a broader perspective of the kavya tradition, he continues to deny the paramarthika/Vedic roots of kavya. He now acknowledges Abhinavagupta's work, but claims it was based on secular *Natya Shastra* and is hence devoid of the sacred. He writes: 'Unsurprisingly, secular poetry is the exclusive concern of Abhinavagupta in his aesthetic works.'[10]

He has also recently started to acknowledge Rupa Goswami's extension of the *Natya Shastra* concepts of kavya for use in bhakti. Nevertheless, he says the sacred use of kavya did not exist before this happened.[11]

In summary, for Pollock, kavya has been devoid of the sacred element for most of its history, and only recently was 'religion' (as he calls it) added to kavya. My issue with him is that he excludes the sacred dimension of rasa and kavya as something inherent from the very beginning. By doing this he is undermining the integral unity of kavya with the rest of the Vedic tradition. His agenda compels him to do this because he wants to argue that kavya was strictly political (and hence *not* spiritual) in nature. As we shall see later in this chapter, his entire theory of the history of Indian culture hinges on this secularization and politicization of kavya.

The theory of the aestheticization of power

Pollock uses three words extensively throughout his work: power, politics and prashasti. These terms play a significant role in framing his approach:

- **Power:** The word 'power' occurs approximately 600 times in his book.[12] One of his key interests in studying Sanskrit is in showing it as an instrument of power used by brahmins and kings.
- **Politics:** Whereas power can be of many kinds – ritual, political, economic, etc. – his predominant emphasis is on political power, specifically the political power exerted by kings. The words 'political' and 'politics' occur almost 900 times in his book.
- **Prashasti:** As the linchpin and key to his analysis, Pollock focusses on royal prashastis (poems of praise), which he believes hold clues to an understanding of the history of Sanskrit and other languages. Prashasti is a specific form of writing whose purpose is to praise the king.[13] Such writings are common on coins, rocks carvings and other kinds of inscriptions in all parts of the world. Since these prashastis were made on hard, durable materials like copper or stone, they tended to survive, unlike perishable texts written on palm leaves. He has curated a select set of prashastis and relies heavily on the evidence provided by them to reach his conclusions about the role Sanskrit played in the lives of people. The word 'prashasti' occurs more than 120 times in his book.[14]

In order for the reader to understand Pollock's thesis on how kavya is linked to political power and was an instrument in the hands of Hindu kings, it is important to appreciate *the theory of the aestheticization of power*, because Pollock's work uses it extensively.

This theory was first formulated by Walter Benjamin, a prominent Western Marxist who made an enduring contribution to the theory of aesthetics.[15] His work was an attempt to understand the appeal of modern art and literature and provide an explanation for the rise of Nazism. Traditional Marxist theory had relied on class struggle to explain all major historical changes, but this theory was unable to account for the rise of twentieth-century capitalism and Nazism, nor for the importance of culture, literature and art as support for (and resistance against) that rise. Benjamin was associated with the Marxist group that later became known as the Frankfurt School. This school set the agenda for postmodern philosophy in the academia and continues to be influential.

The key point in Benjamin's theory is captured in Pollock's frequently used phrase 'aestheticization of the political' or 'aestheticization of power'. The basic idea here is that power, in order to be extended over a wide territory, must harness cultural forms. These forms help to romanticize that power and disguise its uglier aspects. A sophisticated and mystified cultural aesthetic is developed and gains such a lock on the popular mind that ordinary people themselves adapt to it and begin to think in its terms. They are thus blinded both to the brute reality of domination and to its vulnerability. The arts, and in particular the language arts, are then a veneer or mask behind which lurks the real mechanisms of power.

This Marxist theory of the aesthetics of power says that politics drives the artistic lifestyles that influence people. In turn, politics must be viewed like an art form. Therefore, there is a nexus between art and politics. This two-way relationship is what is referred to as 'the aestheticization of politics'. Benjamin says that artistic expression is emotionally gratifying to the lower faculties of the masses; it gives them a mode of expression and glamour. This camouflages the manipulation that is taking place.[16]

Benjamin explains his thesis using the analogy of a puppet master hidden behind the curtain and the performing puppet in the forefront of the stage. The theologian (representing religion) is the puppet master pulling the strings of the puppet from behind the curtain. The puppet is the aesthetically pleasing culture being projected. Put another way, theology is in the background manipulating the strings of some artistic production that the audience sees as benign. Benjamin speaks about this eloquently:

> It is well-known that an automaton once existed, which was so constructed that it could counter any move of a chess-player with a counter-move, and thereby assure itself of victory in the match. A puppet in Turkish attire, water-pipe in mouth, sat before the chessboard, which rested on a broad table. Through a system of mirrors, the illusion was created that this table was transparent from all sides. In truth, a hunchbacked dwarf who was a master chess-player

> sat inside, controlling the hands of the puppet with strings. One can envision a corresponding object to this apparatus in philosophy. The puppet called 'historical materialism' is always supposed to win. It can do this with no further ado against any opponent, *so long as it employs the services of theology, which as everyone knows is small and ugly and must be kept out of sight.*[17]

For Benjamin, religion (or theology) is 'ugly' because it creates a false consciousness and is in collusion with oppression, and so it must be kept hidden behind the curtain. Religious theology is the puppet master pulling the strings, and the puppet is the benign, aestheticized face that performs the required actions in order to influence.[18]

Benjamin used his ideas of art to theorize the links between artistic expression and the aesthetics of political life in Nazi Germany:

> Fascism sees its salvation in giving these masses not their right, but instead a chance to express themselves. The masses have a right to change property relations; Fascism seeks to give them an expression while preserving property. The logical result of Fascism is the introduction of aesthetics into political life.[19]

So, the Nazis' political strategy was to give people the means to express themselves aesthetically, such that they achieve satisfaction merely by expressing themselves. The underlying power structure remains unchanged. On the surface, this aesthetic expression seems to benefit people by letting them vent their feelings, but in fact it helps preserve the status quo; hence it is a tool of political oppression. The expression by people is at the superficial level only; it does not disrupt the underlying power structure. It is a sort of diversion in so far as it gives people an opportunity to express themselves.

In India, Pollock claims this same dynamic worked through what he calls 'literarization' (with an extra 'ar'), a neologism he has created to mean the development of language arts in such a way that they become formalized and have a powerful impact. Formal Sanskrit grammar was infused with structures to produce a sophisticated platform that could be used for emotive and manipulative purposes, as in an epic or a drama.

Writing is the precondition for achieving this power through literature; the process is completed by introducing grammars and rules of rhetoric.[20] 'Literarization' is thus different from 'literization'. Pollock uses the term 'literarization' approximately thirty times in his book *The Language of the Gods* ... in order to emphasize that it is not the same thing as the act of writing but refers instead to the development of a large arsenal of structures, knowledge and texts used for political domination.

His cultural history of India is based on the claim that each language must go through the following three distinct stages of evolution:

- **Orality** is when the local language is expressed only in oral terms, and there is no written communication in it.
- **Literization** is when the language is written down, but only for mundane transactions such as land deeds and accounting. It is not yet ready for producing sophisticated shastras and kavyas.
- **Literarization** is when the process of formalizing happens. This is when (a) the codified grammars and literary forms are added that enable complex and sophisticated usage, and (b) the written language begins to be used to produce imaginative works of poetry and drama.

All this development of literarization is claimed to have been sponsored by the king in order to support the production of political literature. The result is to make the public feel as though they have agency to express themselves politically, when in fact this is a mirage. This is a deception since there is no intention to dilute the king's political power in any real sense. Politics decides who gets to write literature and what the content and purpose of the literature are. These works, in turn, serve the political interests of the elites.[21]

It seems obvious that Pollock is committed to the Marxist theory linking literary works and political power. He wants to deploy it as his lens for analysing how the aesthetic use of languages in India became interwoven into the fabric of politics. At a deeper level, beyond the aesthetic and political usage of Sanskrit, he finds that old Marxist demon: theology. For him, as for most Marxist-oriented scholars, all forms of spirituality/transcendence are, in effect, irrational, deformed and mystified ways of thinking. They are designed to stop critical inquiry and creativity; they also mask or disguise power structures and resist change.

Before he can adopt his aestheticization theory, he has to modify it in part.[22] He believes that the aestheticization of power drives the politics of oppressing the low-caste and other people in India. The oppression in India that interests him is often non-violent and in the form of the negative branding of a community. The aesthetics at work is empowering the elites by legitimizing their actions. Thus, Pollock extends Benjamin's idea to make it applicable to Indian society, where there is a difference in degree, not in kind. In both contexts, a glorified elite group uses art to further its hegemony, be it violent or non-violent.

The diagram below shows Pollock's model of how kings use Sanskrit (and other languages later on) to maintain their power structure in an appealing, aesthetic manner. This amounts to duping the public in such a way that they feel the stirring of cultural pride and other positive emotions. The diagram is to be read from top downwards, following the arrows.

Using some of Benjamin's ideas with Pollock's own enhancements, Pollock interprets Sanskrit's historical development as follows: Its trajectory should be interpreted 'less as a departure from the sacral discursive domain than as an extension of that domain to include such new concerns as the aestheticization of actually existing political power'.[23] Pollock calls this extension 'post-liturgical' in the sense that Sanskrit is no longer just shoring up the mystifications of religious power but is now directly in the service of kings.

In Pollock's theory, formal Sanskrit literary expression did not *create* the royal political power structure of any given location. It merely had the capability to aestheticize and therefore legitimize the *existing* royal power structure, which is why it became useful for political purposes. Pollock uses many examples to show how Sanskrit kavya was used for the purpose of political aestheticization. He gives the example of Kalidasa's composition *Raghuvamsha*, 'in itself a notable instance of the aestheticization of the political'. He claims that 'the works of this great poet were assiduously studied across the [Sanskrit] Cosmopolis, from

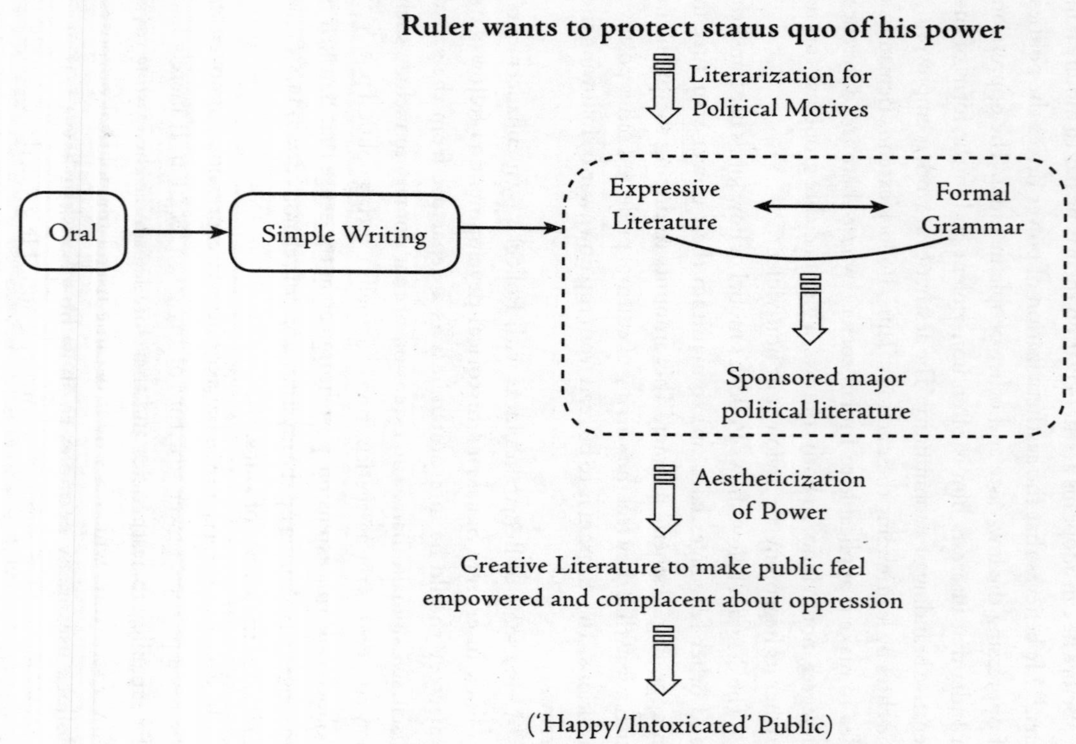
Ruler wants to protect status quo of his power
Literarization for Political Motives
Oral
Simple Writing
Expressive Literature
Formal Grammar
Sponsored major political literature
Aestheticization of Power
Creative Literature to make public feel empowered and complacent about oppression
('Happy/Intoxicated' Public)

Kashmir to Angkor and Java, and none more so than *Raghuvaṃśa*'. The intense study of Kalidasa across Asia was 'no accident but rather a consequence and a sign of the political impulse that lay at the core of cosmopolitan Sanskrit culture'.[24] He summarizes his point by saying that, 'the cosmopolitan cultural gestalt generated by these transregional developments consisted of not just a shared language but a set of shared expressive practices and political representations, which points towards something like an aestheticization of power.'[25]

Therefore, according to Pollock, by studying Kalidasa's *Raghuvamsha*, the royal courts across South and South-east Asia learned how to express and represent their political power in terms of the 'qualification to rule in consequence of history, identity, piety'.[26] Things like the king's piety were part of this aesthetic that Sanskrit brought and this piety became part of his public identity. (It is interesting to note that he does not consider that a king's piety might have been a genuine spiritual quest rather than being politically motivated.)

Pollock is convinced that 'culture was centrally important to power both during the period of the Sanskrit cosmopolitan order and during the vernacular millennium. All the critical innovations in the aestheticization of language and its philologization came from the stimulus offered by court patronage.'[27] He says that Sanskrit kavya was infused with politics and was the foundation of the cosmopolis that dominated South and South-east Asia in the first millennium CE.

Kavya characterized as primarily political

In this section, I will further describe how Pollock deconstructs kavya with a singular view to interpret it as an expression of the aesthetics of power. He makes the following claims in support of his proposition that kavya is entirely a political function:

- The theory of kavya was immature and became robust only at the time of King Bhoja in the eleventh century.
- Political kavya was infused into all other genres of Sanskrit texts.

- Kavya was primarily produced in the royal courts and in support of royal mandates, by resident royal poets.[28]
- Kavya content was complicit with the socio-political stratifications and oppression of Dalits and women.
- Kavya motifs highlighted the expansion of geographical space in order to support the kings' expansive ambitions.

Pollock is clear about saying that his project is to link political rule (rajya) and kavya. He says: 'How *rājya and kāvya* interacted, how the one underwrote or did not underwrite the other, how the one did or did not presuppose, condition, foster the other – these are the problems of "power" central to this book.'[29]

Pollock goes on to assert that politicized kavya became embedded in all the significant genres of Sanskrit texts. He writes that for two thousand years 'such an astonishingly broad and long-lasting consensus among readers and writers about how *kāvya* should be written and interpreted produced literature of ever greater refinement, and reading of ever greater sophistication'.[30] The implication is that Sanskrit kavya was widely accepted as a separate genre, and that it went through much refinement to become more sophisticated, all in the cause of serving politics.[31]

He says that owing to kavya's heavy dependency on a particular power structure, there was 'a consensus that arose in and made sense for *a particular world, a particular sociality and polity*; and when these changed, Sanskrit literary culture was unable to change with it'.[32] The 'particular sociality and polity' in this quotation refer to domination by the brahmins and kings. Chapter 7 will show Pollock making use of this assumption. He notes that kavya was produced and performed in Hindu royal courts and that it must therefore reflect the politics of the courts:

> ... its [kavya's] primary site, the main source of patronage and of the glory ... conferred by the approbation of the learned, undoubtedly always remained the royal court. And it is *kavya* as courtly practice that we need to understand if we are to understand the heart of Sanskrit literary culture.[33]

To support this assertion that the primary site was the royal court, he relies on one eleventh century text describing the nature of a king's actions.[34] He describes in detail how the text assumes the king to be not only a patron of literary arts but also a connoisseur of kavya. He concludes:

> The practice of Sanskrit literary culture was, in the first instance, an intellectual endeavor. It consisted of theoretically informed reflection on normativity and thus presupposed active knowledge of all the categories of literary understanding. ... Kāvya was above all a component, and perhaps the supreme component, of royal competence and distinction, of royal pleasure and civility.[35]

As an example, he notes that the Ramayana was 'recited before the hero of the tale, and in this moment much that characterizes the entire history of the culture is encapsulated. The location of the performance is the royal court, whose fortunes were by and large to be the fortunes of *kāvya*.'[36]

As a counterpoint to this, a traditional scholar would point out that kavya was *also* performed in private homes, public squares, universities and schools such as Nalanda, and numerous pathashalas (traditional schools) across India, as well as at mathas and temples. Many counter-examples could be cited to refute the theory that it was politics that drove all kavya. For instance, Abhinavagupta was explicit about not composing or performing in royal courts. He composed and performed in homes and temples.

Furthermore, many important kavyas are about topics entirely unrelated to politics. For instance, while he selectively quotes from one chapter of one work of Kalidasa as an example of political kavya, Kalidasa's *Shakuntala* is widely appreciated for its aesthetics independent of any political framework. Similarly, Pollock talks about Bilhana's *Vikramankadevacarita*, in the eleventh century, as another example of political kavya. He does not mention Bilhana's *Caurapancasika* (The Love Thief), which is appreciated for its romantic aesthetic.

One should also consider the reproduction of the Ramayana in Tamil (twelfth century, by Kamban) and in Avadhi (sixteenth century, by Tulsidas) as non-political kavya expressions of bhakti. Goldman points out the twelfth-century retelling of the Ramayana in Tamil, *Ramavataram* by Kamban, under patronage of the Chola kings. This is literary evidence of the Ramayana having been used as kavya without political purposes. Goldman also points out Tulsidas's *Ramcharitmanas* in the sixteenth century which was done without the sponsorship of royal patrons and was used as an integral part of the mobilization of Hindu culture through bhakti.[37] Clearly, one ought to question Pollock's fundamental assumption that kavya predominantly reflected the king's political interests. That was only one out of many kinds of kavya.[38]

Pollock further claims that spatial references in Sanskrit literature imply a bias about geographies. Some places are shown as rustic and others as sophisticated. Naive rustic maidens are, he says, differentiated from the cultured, beautiful ladies of a city. He wants to imply a moral and social hierarchy descending from the urban to the rural, from the north to the south.[39] He explains how the Ramayana and the Mahabharata give detailed descriptions of the various places where the journeys and episodes take place and sees this as evidence of the 'vision of culture and power'.[40] All this suggests to him that it was the politics pertaining to various geographies that played out in the literary descriptions of those geographies.

In response, however, tradition says that the vivid description of geographies was one of the requirements of the mahakavya tradition, the purpose being to hold the audience's attention through reference to concrete things. Thus, kavyas tend to have detailed descriptions of the space being traversed; there was no socio-political hegemony necessarily implied over these spaces.

Pollock seeks to show the impact of the itihasa on political developments by claiming that the Vijayanagara Empire was to some degree imagined to be located in the geography of the Ramayana. Similarly, he claims: '*Mahābhārata* space is recreated in later inscriptional accounts of royal conquest, which in turn find their way back into *kāvya*.'[41] He says, 'historical agents' sought to emulate 'the literary geography of power in Sanskrit culture' and that, at the same time, 'these aspirations themselves often seem to have been shaped by literature.' The evidence cited by Pollock correctly indicates that several important rulers were inspired by the Ramayana and the Mahabharata in the foundation and development of their kingdoms. However, reversing the gaze, one would say that the *purpose* of this geographical reference was different from what Pollock insists. Tradition says that understanding the epics would help a king rule wisely for the benefit of his subjects. They were not meant to foster any expansionist political ambitions.

This chapter was a summary of Pollock's seminal theory of kavya. He sees its main purpose as being a tool used by the kings to reinforce and perpetuate their power. The spiritual dimensions are ignored as that would show a non-political motive at work. The next chapter will use the foundations laid down in the present chapter; it will explain his equally important theory on the rise of Sanskrit, followed by its decline and the rise of the vernaculars.

7

Politicizing the History of Sanskrit and the Vernaculars

Overview of Pollock's account of history of how power shaped languages

There are for Pollock two key constants throughout the history of Indian culture:

- One is that the social oppressiveness of Sanskrit and sanskriti remains entrenched no matter what.
- The second is that the brahmin–kshatriya hierarchy drives history, by combining the power of kings with the support of brahmins.

I have explained both these elements in previous chapters. This chapter will show how these assumptions are being used to develop a certain account of the history of Indian languages. The following chapter will offer some ideas as a rejoinder.

The compact table on pages 227–28 summarizes and characterizes Pollock's grand narrative of Indian intellectual history. The driving force of his account of history is: (A) the hegemony of brahmins and rulers, and (B) the aestheticization of power (explained in the previous chapter) as a strategy to spread this hegemony.

The table is my simplified presentation of a large corpus of his work. I do this for the purpose of introducing his theory to the traditionalists who have not otherwise had access to it. I am cognizant that in doing so, I run the risk of oversimplification or inaccuracy, but the intention is to open the conversation and refine it as we proceed.

The rows of the table describe the eras as per Pollock's claims of chronology.

Pre-Buddha Vedic era (Pre–400 BCE)

In Pollock's view, Sanskrit was monopolized by brahmins and there was no writing in this era. This gave them exclusive control over the performance of rituals. They defined the ritual hierarchy, assigning the rights and privileges of different social groups in the performance of the rituals. They explicitly banned shudras and women from ritual performances. Since ritual performances were central to social life, this hierarchy translated into social hierarchy, with kings and brahmins on top. The first section in the first chapter of Pollock's book *Language of the God's...*, 'Precosmopolitan Sanskrit: Monopolization and Ritualization', deals with this.

Buddhists adopt Sanskrit and change it forever (200 BCE–200 CE)

Foreigners who had earlier migrated from Central Asia became kings and adopted Buddhism. They discovered that Buddhist monks across India used multiple languages, so they sponsored the use of Sanskrit to unify their works. It was already an advanced language with Panini's *Ashtadhyayi* and Patanjali's *Mahabhashya*. This adoption by the Buddhists is, according to Pollock, how the brahmin monopoly over

Sanskrit was broken. It became a public language.[1] The Vedic use of Sanskrit continued to have the social structures inherited from the Vedas; but the Buddhists adapted Sanskrit so as to not transmit its oppressiveness because they abandoned the Vedas, the very origin of the toxicity.

Sanskrit started its amazing ascent soon after the birth of Jesus because of support from 'imperial polity'. This changed it from 'a sacred language restricted to religious practice', and it was 'reinvented as a code for literary and political expression'.[2] This is how, says Pollock, the 'language of the gods' entered 'the world of men'. In other words, Sanskrit became separated from paramarthika (the realm of the gods) and turned into mainly vyavaharika (the world of men). It was 'desacralized' to use Pollock's term. It became a written language.

Valmiki's Ramayana (200 BCE–200 CE)

Brahmins responded to the Buddhists by publicly using Sanskrit for non-Vedic purposes. This is how the genre of kavya got started, Pollock claims. The first kavya was the Ramayana written by Valmiki: sponsored by kings, its main theme was the Vedic-based political theology of raj dharma. It promoted the divinization of kings and the demonization of all those who opposed the kings. It laid the foundations for oriental despotism in India as the core of raj dharma. The Ramayana borrowed from the Buddhist Jataka tales and hence gets dated after them. Embedded within it were the hierarchical structures of social bias from the Vedas.

Shastra (200 BCE–200 CE)

In parallel with producing kavya texts, brahmins also produced shastras. These are texts of structured knowledge based on Vedic metaphysics. Because of this Vedic foundation, Pollock finds them problematic. The shastras, also sponsored by kings, were developed by accomplished brahmins who were accorded privileged positions of authority (for example, Chanakya, who wrote *Arthashastra*). Once promulgated, the shastras could not be changed, and this ensured that the status quo of the established Vedic hierarchy was maintained. Therefore, according to him, shastras are instruments of oppression.

Sanskrit cosmopolis (200 BCE–1100 CE)

The combination of Sanskrit kavya and shastra made for a powerful and sophisticated platform for the aestheticization of power, Pollock theorizes. This platform became the basis for establishing kingly franchises across South and South-east Asia, with the brahmins implementing the ritual framework for the divinization of the king, wherever they went. This collaboration between brahmins and kings succeeded in fooling people into thinking that kavya gave them knowledge and control over their own lives, when in fact it was the basis for implementing and maintaining the Vedic social hierarchy.

Rise of vernaculars (1000 CE–1400 CE)

Kings in South and South-east Asia replaced Sanskrit with local languages for use in their jurisdictions beginning early in the second millennium CE. Pollock cites numerous sporadic examples to show this. The kings sponsored brahmins to infuse Sanskrit grammar and rules of kavya into the local languages (a process Pollock calls 'literarization' of the vernaculars), along with translations of important Sanskrit works, such as the Ramayana and the Mahabharata. Thus, Vedic hierarchies and structured codes of conduct permeated the local languages and ensured continuity, even though Sanskrit itself no longer played the central role in the royal courts. Sanskrit became dead, he claims.

He theorizes that this vernacularization was done perhaps in response to challenges coming from growth in international trade, a sharp increase in agricultural production, and/or Islamic invasions. However, no definite theory of the causes emerge despite Pollock spending considerable energy presenting a large quantity of data.

Mughal and British periods (1500 CE–1947 CE)

Sanskrit's role, which had already diminished in the first half of the second millennium, was further reduced to ritualistic chanting of hymns by the brahmins. Pollock says that the Mughals and the British tried in their own ways to support the wider learning and usage of Sanskrit. The British efforts to study and research Sanskrit resulted in two negative consequences: British colonialists fell into what is known as oriental despotism to rule India, using the structures that had already been in existence in India. The other thing that happened was that Germans learned Sanskrit and its abusive methods of 'othering': they used it to give support to fascism which resulted in the holocaust.

Present and future goals

Pollock's view is that Sanskrit needs to be studied with a focus on its unjust social structures which have infiltrated the Indian vernaculars. Change can be brought to India by exposing Sanskrit's culpability especially in oppressing India's Dalits and women. His strategy is to co-opt the Indian left, the government and the private sector to fund such Sanskrit studies; these studies would be carried out mostly by Indian scholars trained in the lens of American Orientalism.

The table that follows is my understanding of Pollock's views on the flow of events. It attempts to present a simple overview of several hundreds of pages of his scholarship.

Introducing the 'Sanskrit Cosmopolis' and sidelining sanskriti

The epoch that Pollock calls the 'Sanskrit Cosmopolis' is the crucial period in the 'desacralizing' of Sanskrit; this brings it out of the confines of ritual and into the real world. By the end of the first millennium CE, according to him, Sanskrit had 'become the premier vehicle for the expression of royal will, displacing all other codes, ... [and] Sanskrit learning itself became an essential component of power'.[3] By the fifth century CE, it had become the sole language of the royal courts throughout India, replacing various Prakrits. The latter were still in use, but only for mundane, day-to-day business.[4] Royal courts became linguistically homogeneous, using a standardized form of Sanskrit. He explains: 'Power in India now had a Sanskrit voice. And by a kind

Pollock's Chronology of the History of Languages				
Epoch	**Role and Status of Sanskrit**	**Role of King**	**Role of Brahmin**	**Nature of Embedded Toxins**
Pre-Buddha Vedic era (Pre-400 BCE)	Language of Vedic rituals only. Strictly oral	None explicitly defined	Exclusive control of Sanskrit and performance of rituals	Shudras, women excluded from learning Sanskrit or participating in rituals. This creates social hierarchy which must be preserved
Buddhists adopt Sanskrit (200 BCE–200 CE)	Language used by ordinary men, for worldly communications	Foreign-origin Shakas, Kushans sponsor works in Sanskrit	Many are serving Buddhist kings	None within Buddhist sangha, but Vedic society unchanged
Valmiki's Ramayana (200 BCE–200 CE)	First kavya. First Hindu writing	Sponsored by kings; boosts king's power as divine and demonizes his enemies	Divinizes the king by performing rituals	Despotic Orientalism in the form of divine king, who commits atrocities against women, shudras and enemies
Shastras (200 BCE–200 CE)	Encodes Vedic metaphysics and spreads it into all domains of knowledge	Sponsorship	Authors of works and privileged position of power	Fatalism, social hierarchy, cripples artistic creativity

Pollock's Chronology of the History of Languages

Epoch	Role and Status of Sanskrit	Role of King	Role of Brahmin	Nature of Embedded Toxins
Sanskrit cosmopolis (200 CE–1100 CE)	Provides structure, sophistication and platform for aestheticization of power	Collaboration of kings and brahmins to spread the franchise		Using aesthetics, public deluded into believing they have agency to participate in power
Rise of vernaculars (1000 CE–1400 CE)	Sanskrit is 'dead' and replaced by the vernaculars	Localization initiated by kings; Brahmins serve to 'literarize' the vernacular to replace Sanskrit		Vedic structures permeate vernaculars, especially through shastras and old narratives
Mughal and British periods (1500 CE–1947 CE)	Used only for arcane, obscure rituals	Muslim and British rulers try to revive Sanskrit but brahmins did not cooperate	Unproductive	Social oppression in India and export to European Orientalism and Nazism
Present: American Orientalist goals	Revive study of Sanskrit in English using Western framework	Co-opt the government to support American Orientalism	Co-opt the academics and media	Goal: to detoxify the tradition by infusing with English

of premodern globalization – even Westernization – it would have a Sanskrit voice in much of the world to the east.'[5]

The objective of this sweeping historical narrative is to explain how and why Sanskrit and this kind of literature spread so successfully across India, South-east Asia and East Asia. Its royal usage in 'the world of men' is what led Sanskrit to spread, he says. Pollock develops an entirely political theory to account for this dissemination, and in doing so, completely ignores the ways in which Sanskrit and its texts also played positive humanistic roles such as providing spiritual fulfilment and creativity in people's lives, quite independently of kings and elites.

Nevertheless, the real debate I would like to see between his view and that of traditional scholars has to do with his notion of Sanskrit cosmopolis, which he uses to replace the term sanskriti. Here we have two competing models:

- The **sanskriti** model I support says there was already a kind of widespread social–cultural ecosystem in which languages spread in multiple ways that included grass-roots processes as well as the top-down role of the elites. The next chapter will elaborate on this decentralized model.
- The **Sanskrit cosmopolis** model insists that Sanskrit was driven by kings and brahmins primarily from above.

Pollock is clear from the start that he does not want to use the term 'sanskriti' for Indian culture and civilization, because he finds these notions to be modern inventions. He claims: 'Even the word *saṁskṛti*, the classicizing term adopted for translating "culture" in many modern South Asian languages, is itself unattested in premodern Sanskrit in this sense.' Sanskrit discourse, he says, lacked 'an adequate self-generated descriptor' of its own political or cultural sphere. In other words, he is saying that Sanskrit has no vocabulary to describe its own socio-political culture. So he feels obliged to invent his own terms to replace the notion of sanskriti, because 'Sanskrit never sought to theorize its own universality'.[6]

It is to fill this perceived gap in Sanskrit vocabulary, and control the definition of what a Sanskrit-based culture has been that he coins the term 'Sanskrit Cosmopolis'. The 'polis' part of the term is intended to give prominence to the political dimension. A cosmopolis in the Greek sense is a city defined by people from many different countries. Therefore, the Sanskrit cosmopolis was an extended physical area, in this case much of Asia, in which people from many countries shared Sanskrit as a common meta-language, along with the cultures based on it.

In Pollock's view, this extended area was governed by a vast culture-power configuration in which the rule by various disparate kings was based on the structures embedded in Sanskrit and its cultural artefacts. For this configuration to come about, he argues that Sanskrit had to be brought down from its earlier status as the language of the gods, where it had been restricted to brahmins and used only for ritual purposes. To Pollock, Sanskrit entering the 'world of men' means that it came down from the unreality and mystification of transcendental discourse and became the primary mode of political expression in the 'real' world.

Pollock is startled that so soon after literary (i.e., written) Sanskrit became publicly available as per his chronology, it had spread from Kandahar to Sri Lanka in the south and to Java in the east.[7] He describes this rapid and unprecedented dissemination as follows:

> The Sanskrit cosmopolis was characterized by a largely homogeneous language of political poetry along with a range of comparable cultural-political practices. Constituted by no imperial state or church and consisting to a large degree in the communicative system itself and its political aesthetic, this order was characterized by a transregional consensus about the presuppositions, nature, and practices of a common culture, as well as a shared set of assumptions about the elements of power – or at least about the ways in which power is reproduced at the level of representation in language. For a millennium or more, it constituted the most compelling model of culture-power for a quarter or more of the inhabitants of the globe. And it only ended, at various times and places in the course of the first five centuries of the second millennium, under pressure from a new model.[8]

The expansion of Sanskrit is especially surprising to him given that it occurred in an era that predates any modern forms of transportation or communication. To explain how Sanskrit spread, he makes a key assumption that the spread of Sanskrit across a vast geography took place in a vacuum and that it happened suddenly. By eliminating the notion of *a pre-existing sanskriti,* he can claim that the vacuum was filled by the Sanskrit cosmopolis.

Although he sees this process as politically driven, Pollock does acknowledge there were no conquering Sanskrit legions that caused Sanskritization, unlike the coercive Romanization which followed Roman military legions. Nor was there a central church-like religious institution and hence no evangelism that could have Sanskritized through religious conversion. He admits that the notion of the Sanskrit cosmopolis does not fit the Western notion of an empire. Nor is it a civilization in the Hellenistic sense, for Hellenistic civilizations had considerable homogeneity, unlike the diversity that characterized the Sanskrit cosmopolis.

Thus, he makes it abundantly clear that he conceives of this cosmopolis as a system of intellectual-cultural control wherein the subjects were victims of a clever form of manipulation. It was not a physical, militaristic control. What he thinks happened was 'some impulse towards transculturation that made it sensible, even desirable, to adopt the new Sanskrit cultural-political style as an act of pure free will' by the elites.[9] The elites opted in because this served their interests. Note that he does not consider the free will of common people, but only of the elites. This is a serious red flag for me to highlight.

Although Sanskrit was adopted voluntarily by the receiving kingdoms, for Pollock such a system stifled innovation and freedom as soon as it had become entrenched. He asserts that as a consequence of Sanskrit's elite role in royal courts, it retarded and even arrested local literary traditions.[10] This brought benefit to a small minority of Sanskrit-based cultural producers at the top, he claims; the rest of the population had no recourse to such cultural development owing to their lack of access to Sanskrit. In this sense, Pollock is insinuating that the arrival of Sanskrit was tantamount to an act of cultural violence against the local languages and cultures.

The royal elites across this Sanskrit cosmopolis shared more than the language. They shared the criteria which qualified them to rule, namely, their 'identity, piety, valor, intelligence, culture, civility, beauty and an account of what that rule meant in terms of good works and heroic deeds'.[11] In other words, his notion of the Sanskrit cosmopolis indicates a sort of 'virtual empire' (my term for Pollock's notion) in which one's position in the power structure was determined by one's relationship to Sanskrit.

Pollock develops a very original theory as to how this came about without military conquest or homogeneity. It is clear early in his analysis that his explanation is headed in a political direction:

> The single available explanation of the social function of Sanskrit cosmopolitan culture is legitimation theory and its logic of instrumental reason: elites in command of new forms of social power are understood to have deployed the mystifying symbols and codes of Sanskrit to secure popular consent.[12]

He insists that, 'the scholarly cultivation of language in premodern India ... should not be seen – as it typically is seen – as a purely abstract intellectual discipline ... [but in terms of] its relationship to political power'.[13] Sanskrit philology, he explains,

> was inextricably tied to the practices of power. Overlords were keen to ensure the cultivation of the language through patronage awarded to grammarians, lexicographers, metricians, and other custodians of purity, and through endowments to schools for the purpose of grammatical studies. They were also responsible for commissioning many of the most important grammars. For a polity to possess a grammar of its own was to ensure the proper functioning and even completeness.[14]

Pollock, in effect, argues that Sanskrit contained resources for a king's assertion of power and that is why kings and princes all over Asia quickly adopted it. Brahmins colluded in this use of Sanskrit in return for receiving royal patronage. In the process, Sanskrit became the exclusive language of high culture across a whole cosmopolis. To explain its dramatic spread and control on literary expression, he draws attention to 'the new conception of power and its supraregional domain of projection that made the cosmopolitan language the only possible language for its self-expression'.[15]

I do not contest that this top-down instrumental use for pure politics was being made to *some* degree; but to reduce the entire process of cultural evolution to a matter of politics betrays a profound misunderstanding. This view disregards the intrinsic appeal of the Sanskrit tradition, including for non-elites, and the various roles it played in the cultures it touched. In particular, to dismiss the entire symbolic discourse of Sanskrit as 'mystifying' is to apply a reductive Marxism that cannot account for sacredness in the lives of people. I feel that although many discourses in all cultures can and often do encode a primitive will to power, that is not always the case. They also function, in many instances, to guide and instruct both kings and commoners alike in genuine spiritual quests. However, Pollock dismisses all transcendental values as primitive magic and/or as political manipulation by rulers.

He assumes that wherever culture and power intersect, power always trumps culture. Power is the driver of cultural events and their cause, and not the other way around, he feels. In my hypothesis (to be explained in the next chapter), these two realms of culture and power have a much more complex and bidirectional relationship. Sometimes culture can also drive power – or at least shape it. There are instances when a spiritual awakening transforms a royal person and his rule. There are also many instances when a king has bowed to the spiritual advice of a sage. Sanskrit can thus be the vehicle for a truly dharmic kingship.

My purpose here is not to suggest that kings never used Sanskrit and its literary expression as tools of exploitation; nor do I deny that many of the concepts about society, hierarchy and authority in Sanskrit literature were bolstered by the power of kings. But certainly not *all kings all of the time* used Sanskrit in this way. Such support of power was not the only function of Sanskrit. Thanks to a number of internal properties of the language and of the arts it generated, Sanskrit was always more than a mere social instrument; it was also a vehicle for understanding the cosmos and a process of transformation that was holistic and profoundly inspired.

These internal properties were well understood. Traditional scholars were not always naive about the elite and their potential for control. Nor were they reductive about such things. Also, they did not underestimate the power and agency of Sanskrit to benefit those it touched.

Grammar as a form of political power

Pollock applies the theory of the aestheticization of power, according to which the formalization of Sanskrit grammar and the use of Sanskrit kayva in the form of itihasas deepened the hold of royal power. He sees the development of a formal grammar as a crucial feature in its use as a hegemonic device. It increased the prestige of Sanskrit and regularized it for use in various situations, allowing the political will of the king to prevail. He says:

> The elite's adoption of Sanskrit literary culture for the expression of political will shows [that] rulership and Sanskrit grammaticality and learning were more than merely associated; they were to some degree mutually constitutive. This is demonstrated by, among other things, the celebration of grammatical learning especially in kings, the royal patronage of such learning, and the competitive zeal among rulers everywhere to encourage grammatical creativity and adorn their courts with scholars who could exemplify it.[16]

He provides a long and detailed list of instances across the Sanskrit cosmopolis in which kings learned the formal rules of Sanskrit grammar and encouraged the production of kavya in their courts. He ends by saying:

> Further amassing of data would only be redundant; the main point should be clear: that power's concern with grammar, and to a comparable degree grammar's concern with power, comprised a constitutive feature of the Sanskrit cosmopolitan order.[17]

Here is a summary of his theory on the nexus between grammar and kingly power:

1. For a king to be credible, it was essential that he display excellence in Sanskrit.[18]

2. To gain such excellence, kings were required to learn Sanskrit grammar from authoritative teachers and therefore patronize these texts.[19]
3. To show their excellence in Sanskrit, kings had to display 'grammatical correctness', which Pollock claims led to 'political correctness'.
4. Panini and Patanjali were working under the direction of kings to produce their grammatical works.[20]

He gives many examples of prashastis in honour of kings who had attained expertise in grammar, and lists some books on Sanskrit grammar which included praise for the patron monarch. He presents details of who patronized whom among kings and grammarians, and then gives a list of grants endowed by kings for the promotion of grammatical knowledge.

However, I am unconvinced by his argument of guilt by association. It is a banal point that the royal students would patronize their teachers. Yet, Pollock regards this as a crucial piece of evidence to allege that grammar served the purpose of political power. Such reasoning is analogous to listing all the grants received by Pollock and reaching a sweeping conclusion that the purpose of his entire work was to serve his sponsors. Certainly, grammar received royal patronage, but the king also carried out other aspects of raj dharma, including the development and teaching of other shastras, artistic performances and various other projects of value to society.

Pollock's theory is far more applicable to the top-down Mughal imposition of Persian as the official language of the court and to the British patronage of English language and literature in India. Both these were direct political interventions achieved through the manipulation of aesthetics. However, he does not wish to dwell on these examples much; his target is Sanskrit.

I feel it is important for scholars to explore *how* exactly grammar and politics worked together to achieve the kind of tight 'constitutive relationship' he claims. My red flags are intended to start debates.

An example of Pollock's statement that cannot simply be taken at face value and needs to be debated is the following:

> Grammar is a veritable weapon in the hands of a king, but one that works best when it is also in the hands of the *prajā*, the people of the realm. And what grammar preserves is not just language but sociality as such ... the social and grammatical orders are related by their very nature.[21]

But I wonder in what way is giving the public ('praja') use of grammar considered to be a weapon for the king? He compounds the confusion by saying that the king's 'philological judgment' was an index of 'correct political judgment'. This was so, he says, because of the 'ontological linkage' between 'the order of language and the order of society ... The political was thoroughly pervaded by the poetical and the philological – and above all by the grammatical.'[22] By philological judgement, Pollock means 'grammatical correctness, rhetorical propriety, and literary good taste'.[23] I agree that these features are the hallmarks of high culture in many societies; but to claim that there is some ontological link that joins them to power is a leap that is questionable.

Pollock then produces one concrete example to support his thesis: The word 'varna' is used both in grammar (to mean a range of language sounds) and as a social term (referring to individuals and groups with certain capabilities), and he conflates these to claim they are *causally* linked:

> The implications of the association between grammatical and political correctness are far-reaching. If the preservation of language sounds (*varṇa*) that grammar achieves was linked essentially to the preservation of the social orders (*varṇa*), and so to that of the polity at large, the obligation to maintain the order of language was no less than, and perhaps no different from, the obligation to maintain the political and spiritual order.[24]

I am dumbfounded by this alleged link between grammar and social order. His statement does not explain *how* the use of varna as language sounds can be causally linked to the preservation of social orders. An analogous example in the English language will help explain the farcical implication of his reasoning. The word 'yard' means a measurement of length. It also means a place in front of or behind a house (as in 'front yard' or 'backyard'). Such words with more than one meaning but which are spelled the same are called 'homographs'. Could visiting scholars into America, who do not have complete knowledge of English, conclude that those who own houses with yards (as opposed to apartments) control the unit of measurement, the 'yard', and therefore have power over how lengths are measured in America? If the example seems ridiculous, the same may be said of Pollock's analysis of 'varna', a Sanskrit homograph, used in two unrelated contexts.

Pollock gives evidence that an Indian king produced a Sanskrit grammar text and then funded its wide distribution across South and South-east Asia. His example is from Gujarat, a thousand years later than the period which he is trying to explain. He says that after an important work of grammar was completed, the king had it copied and circulated as far north as Nepal and as far south as what is now Tamil Nadu.[25] But so what, I must ask? He must prove that such actions had a *causal* political impact in those regions. However, no such evidence is offered. He merely repeats his assertion that grammar, language, literature, society and polity were all symbiotically joined as soon as Sanskrit entered any kingdom.[26]

He does proffer another 'proof' of Sanskrit culture's implication with power. In the royal Hindu courts there was emphasis on the correct use of language to invoke the Vedic deity. Pollock claims that reciting a poem as part of a court event was a tool of political power. There is no question, he says, that such poetry was

> a far more potent shaping force of culture and power. And its human makers participated fully in this force by creating new shapes of word and meaning: new shapes of words called meters, new shapes of meanings called tropes, new structures of signification called aesthetic feelings. What is most important, however, was preserving inviolate the literary deity's most vulnerable spots by correct use of language.[27]

Having failed to give hard proof of what he set out to establish, Pollock hedges his bets. He says: 'Again, this equivalence comes about not through any simple instrumental application of philology but by some broader process of self-discipline and self-constraint.'[28] In other words, he now wants to give up on the 'instrumental application of philology', because he cannot prove a direct cause and effect relationship between a king's use of grammar and its political outcome.

Finally, he brings in the history of medieval Europe as his reference point, remarking that one of the purposes of grammar in Europe was to help impose imperial law and seek 'a more cohesive political unity by means of a more cohesive linguistic unity'.[29] He refers to laws being imposed in Europe that oppressed the speakers of certain languages. However, I claim that this European experience is not applicable to India. No Hindu king banned any language. Therefore, Pollock seems to be presuming that grammar is connected with power just because it was so in Europe.[30]

The role of itihasas in spreading the Sanskrit cosmopolis

One of his key insights is that the itihasas became the carriers of raj dharma across royal courts, where they were installed and interpreted by brahmin pandits. These brahmins also carried and reproduced Sanskrit grammar texts, as well as their own interpretations of dharmashastras.

The same template of the Ramayana, for instance, could get adapted to include many local fables, local places, characters and actors. Pollock explains that the core Sanskrit principles and Vedic metaphysics got exported from one place to another by travelling brahmins who convinced the rulers to accept their system and give them patronage. These structures got adapted into localized dharmashastras and localized itihasas. By implication, the metaphysical structures installed in his kingdom gave the king the benefit of absolute dictatorial power and the licence to oppress his subjects. The brahmins, in turn, became powerful as the developers and implementers of the elaborate structures across numerous kingdoms. Pollock calls this the culture–power connection through which Vedic systems proliferated and dominated across vast territories.

He explains that the social structure of the Vedas was being spread among the populace throughout the Sanskrit cosmopolis by making public performances that had a strong political dimension. Yajnas became a public spectacle that made the kings seem divine. Itihasas were adapted for local use and their performances became a political platform to justify the king's rule. Grammars were reproduced and learned, and the correct use of language became the signature quality that enabled brahmins and kshatriyas to claim elite status.

Pollock says that the deepening of Sanskrit Power would not have been possible without the spread of itihasas and Puranas, particularly the Ramayana and the Mahabharata. These travel wherever Sanskrit goes and put down deep roots locally by reproducing a sacred geography and corresponding narratives. The process begins with the production of multiple editions and multiple copies of the Mahabharata. Again, Pollock claims that we should interpret these texts and their geographical dissemination primarily in terms of power. His evidence consists of showing that there was royal patronage in popular oral performances of the Mahabharata. Oral performance was 'the final component of the epic's supraregional diffusion' and was

> perhaps more effective and vital than any other in ensuring that the transregional narrative achieved transregional impact. Endowments or other forms of support for public recitation and exegesis of the Mahabharata were provided by the ruling elite over a long period of premodern history.[31]

In response, one must point out that royal patronage of the arts is not necessarily a tool for self-aggrandizement and naked oppressive power over others. Most governments, even today, like to patronize the arts.

Another important factor he mentions as a cause for Sanskrit's success was its ability to express narratives that went beyond the region. Pollock lists many instances in which the places mentioned in itihasa get substituted by local places. Sanskrit was also trans-ethnic, he says; hence its views did not seem limited to any particular place and were applicable everywhere. This ability to localize the message was important.[32] However, I find it unfortunate that he sees this as a projection of royal power for the purpose of controlling people. Tradition sees this as an important way for a mahakavya to serve the masses.

For Pollock, the fact that traditional local writers have written about Ayodhya, Mount Meru, Ganga, etc., in multiple locations is dumbfounding and irrational. He characterizes this as part of India's peculiarly 'different, plural, premodern logic of space'.[33] He stresses that the unified views of India's geography are a modern construct that did not exist previously. He writes that the 'premodern space' of Indians was mythic and differs from notions like 'Akhaṇḍ Bhārat' (undivided India), which are modern creations, and which he describes as 'one of the deadly weapons of nationalism and a source of the misery of modernity'.[34]

I propose a different interpretation of the same data. As per our tradition, the conceptual space of Hindus can be replicated and localized easily. The Hindu metaphysics of immanence leads to the decentralization of sacred geography. The Vedic principle of 'ṛtam' is about recreating a universal structure in one's own particular locale, desh. This is why such localized references to the sacred geography of India are prevalent, and are perfectly fine. In fact, in the Vedic yajna, the mantras define the local space of the yajna as a replica or representation of the cosmos, and the universal deity is invoked to be present locally. Pollock ignores the Vedic bandhuta principles that made it easy to find local equivalences and adaptation rather than impose a homogeneity from a central template. This is why people in south India substitute their local rivers for Ganga for ritualistic purposes; there is a town called Ayodhya in Thailand; the cognitive landscape of people in Java started to include Mount Meru as a local place, and so on. Besides the mountains and rivers, the Mahabharata's regions and kingdoms were also mapped on to local substitutes.

Unlike in Islam where the Kaaba is the *universally exclusive* spot one must point towards for prayers (and Kaaba cannot be replicated in one's local mosque or substituted by anything else), in Hindu cosmology the cosmos is present in every part of it. This is to be seen as a distinguishing quality of Hinduism rather than as some royal conspiracy to exert power.

It is this ability of Hinduism to decentralize its sacred spaces that has helped it spread *without* centralized power. People separated by thousands of miles felt a common bond as participants in the cosmic narrative and yajna. None of this has to do with any top-down royal power. In fact, I would use Pollock's data to argue in the opposite direction: when they patronized Sanskrit grammar, itihasa, and other forms of Vedic culture, kings were merely performing their role as per the cosmic yajna and the dharma.

Summary of issues with the grammar-itihasa-power theory

I would like to pause and summarize the red flags that traditional scholars might raise concerning many of Pollock's sweeping statements. A few points of contention that ought to be debated are listed below:

1. He ignores the positive role of itihasa, arts and culture in which people of all strata and communities participated for their benefit and general well-being. In his mind, the primary purpose of Sanskrit culture was to support power regimes.
2. He does not explain in concrete terms how the brahmins managed to spread the Veda-based Sanskrit culture to royal courts throughout India and South-east Asia. An implication in his theory is that the cunning brahmins were able to root themselves wherever they went by replicating a common vested interest they had with local kings. But this is speculation at best.
3. He does not explain how it is that the social structures in South-east Asia did not change to 'caste oppression', as he claims to have happened in different parts of India. How did the Veda-based structures manifest themselves in those societies without replicating the caste abuses he finds in India?
4. He says the translation of itihasas into various native languages along with their local enactments are what led to the acceptance

and justification of the Veda-based royal culture. But he has no data to show that oppression increased in those countries after the introduction of Sanskrit and this Vedic culture. Nor does he examine whether social oppression decreased later on when Sanskrit was displaced by vernaculars as the royal court language.

5. He cites the brahmins' production of Sanskrit dharma nibandhas in the royal courts as evidence of elitist segregation of royal culture from the populace. But these dharma nibandhas were specifically written by brahmins for their own communities. The British colonial administration collected and translated them with a view to understanding how to administer in India. Later the colonialists realized that each of these documents was specific to a given community. They concluded that the nibandhas could not be used as normative in the way Europeans were accustomed.

Pollock fails to make good on his promise to prove his thesis with hard data, so he constantly hedges his assertions. On the one hand, he says, 'Royal power seems to have provided the essential precondition for the flourishing of the postliturgical philological tradition;' but he is aware that this is difficult to verify, especially with respect to the early period. As he notes, 'For the earliest period of Sanskrit grammar the historical data are too thin to allow us to demonstrate the mutually constitutive relationship of grammar and power with much cogency.'[35]

Even for the later periods, the closest he comes to 'proving' such a nexus is that he supplies a list of kings sponsoring grammarians. That does not prove that grammar and politics had a tight and exclusive relationship to the extent he claims. He alternates between claims of normative causal relationships that are established by his data, and statements like: 'We remain to some degree in the realm of legend and conjecture.'[36] But again he flips back into the mode of claiming that 'This long list makes it obvious that Sanskrit literary culture was seriously nourished by the courtly elite, but it also suggests how far that elite felt called upon, perhaps even compelled, to provide such nourishment.'[37]

Pollock is silent on the fact that royal patronage for grammarians was small compared to the patronage given by them for many other forms of learning and culture. Kings also patronized astrologers, ayurvedic specialists, mathematicians, musicians, chefs and so forth. To magnify his case, Pollock provides data about grammarians while excluding data about other patronage. There is no quantitative analysis or comparative analysis and hence his data are entirely anecdotal.[38]

I am unconvinced that his massive compilation of examples proves that kings exerted political control over the *substance* of the grammars produced. His data merely shows the following links:

- Royals wanted to be seen as learned in grammar.
- Grammarians and poets wanted to acknowledge their royal sponsors using writings of praise called prashasti.
- Royals sponsored forums for the display of knowledge and other forms of intellectual delight.

He compiles and enumerates a massive number of factoids, many of which are trivial or not adequately explained as to their significance. There is no meaningful pattern, at least none that is discernible to me. By merely repeating his case, he expects the reader to conclude there must have been some concrete elitist power structure that caused all these instances. His own data show considerable political tension among regions at various times and certainly no homogeneity in political systems or processes. This makes the single-cosmopolis idea appear strange.

After 250 pages, he finally raises some key questions and doubts concerning his own hypothesis and yet refuses to concede that these are fundamental flaws. Rather, he regards them as minor issues, writing: 'Admittedly, to speak of aesthetic practice may be thought only to restate the question of the political in premodern South Asia, not to answer it.'[39]

The rise of the vernaculars

The rise of the vernacular languages across the Sanskrit cosmopolis between the eighth and fifteenth centuries presents a challenge to Pollock's model. If his model is right and the widespread adoption of Sanskrit by royal courts was indeed a way to consolidate elite power, then why did the kings not just continue with Sanskrit? Nothing in his model presented earlier in this chapter suggests an expiration date when it would stop working.

If they did switch over from Sanskrit to the vernaculars, how and why did this happen? In order to be consistent with his model that all linguistic and cultural processes are fundamentally driven by politics, his challenge is to establish that this switch from Sanskrit to vernaculars was sponsored by rulers to help them politically. He must explain why the elites made the switch for their own self-interests. He also needs to prove his claim that the vernaculars *replaced* Sanskrit as a tool of power rather than coexisted with it.

He addresses this problem by arguing that the rise of the vernaculars was caused by a shift in which political power became more localized than it previously was. In Pollock's view, Sanskrit became a kind of antiquated and fossilized remnant of the high culture of the past. He rejects the possibility that Sanskrit remained alive as part of a bilingual system, with people using both it and the vernaculars and often combining them.

After considerable analysis, Pollock eventually acknowledges that he is unable to identify any convincing *causal mechanism* that would have driven this switch to the vernaculars that displaced Sanskrit. He tries various hypotheses but accepts that these are not really valid explanations.

I believe there *are* better explanations for the rise of the vernaculars – not *instead* of Sanskrit but *parallel* with it, in a relationship of mutual nurturing and understanding. I would argue that the vernaculars did not triumph over or *displace* Sanskrit in some supposed clash of languages, but that they had a dual and reciprocal relationship with each other. Indeed, it is at least plausible that the rise of the vernaculars was *also* driven from below and that this rise had nothing to do with any power struggle between elites and 'the people'. It is also plausible that there might have been different reasons for adoption of the vernacular in different places, as opposed to a one-size-fits-all explanation, which is what Pollock proposes. My hypothesis is that the causes were not merely a matter of material forces and that they also have to do with the human spiritual quest for the transcendental realm, a motivation that, as we have seen, Pollock has ruled out a priori. I will elaborate on my hypothesis in the next chapter.

Vernacularization and the kings

The standard definition for vernacular in socio-linguistics is 'native language of a speech community'. This conventional definition would cover written as well as oral texts. However, as we shall see in a moment, Pollock explicitly rejects oral expression for the purpose of his study, and even in terms of written language, he makes qualifications.[40] He wants to distinguish what he calls 'vernacularization' from the simple use of language for everyday affairs.

In his system, although writing is a necessary condition for vernacularization, it is not sufficient. When writing first started, the written language tended to be used only for simple things like inscriptions or factual documentation such as land deeds or gifts.

The vernacularization of a language occurred at a much later stage – when 'people began to produce texts that were local rather than translocal in body and spirit'.[41] Not only was the language itself local; the content was too. Thus 'desh', or local place, becomes more important, as does 'desi', or local people. For example, in many places Sanskrit epics such as the Ramayana are retold in the local language and in local terms. The forest in which Hanuman is described as living is not some distant place in the imagination but the forest near the desi village, and Mount Meru is their local mountain.

Pollock places the rise of the vernaculars at a given moment in time, and for political, cultural and social reasons that he thinks he can explain. The choice of switching to a local language was, in Pollock's view, made by the cultural elites, both in terms of the formal development of the language and in terms of its new localized content.[42] He outlines the following specific executive decisions that the king and his coterie of writers made in order to bring about the vernacularization:

1. The kings knew they were leaving behind 'the spatial matrices at work in Sanskrit culture'. The writers involved in helping the kings were projecting their writings on to 'new culture-power places'.[43]

2. This shift was based on a new vision of power that was locally focussed.[44]
3. It was the king who made the conscious decision to vernacularize, and thereby de-Sanskritize the discourse.[45]
4. Sanskrit begins to live inside the vernacular as a sort of 'engine' driving it. This Sanskrit engine or linguistic technology consists of grammar, itihasa and socio-political ideas of hierarchy and oppression. In other words, vernacularization requires that Sanskrit's built-in concepts, which in turn have Vedic principles buried in them, get infused (grafted) into the heart of the vernacular.
5. The king and the writers he sponsored knew they were creating a new vernacularization process that had not existed before in the kingdom.[46]
6. Driven by the royal courts, vernacularization was a watershed event in the way power was projected.[47]

The timing of this Sanskrit infusion into the local languages differed in each case, according to him. Nevertheless, in all cases, he insists, the site of such an infusion (of Sanskrit structures being embedded into the local language) was always a royal court; hence it was commissioned by a king. This infusion happened when the local king decided the time had come to provide his subjects with a means for expressing their imagination in writing. This would keep them happy and dissuade them from disrupting the king's power.

As soon as this process of vernacularization starts for a given vernacular language, it too, like Sanskrit, develops a body of formal grammars, kayva and itihasa. In terms of grammar, there is what Pollock calls 'a powerful imperative towards standardization, often accompanied by formal grammaticization'.[48] As he explained in the case of Sanskrit, the grammars get codified, rules of rhetoric and genre are established, and the vernacularized language that results becomes fit as a vehicle for literary arts. This is how a local language gets standardized and begins to be used for exchanging creative ideas. It is no longer limited to just documentation of facts and practical exchanges. The content gradually becomes more expressive and imaginative as the language proceeds on this trajectory.

Finally, over time, Pollock says a literary corpus emerges, which also embodies the king's vision of power. Now it can be used to support the king's authority and give people an imaginative way to participate in it – but it is not a genuine participation since it does not challenge or disrupt the structures of power. The public is bamboozled into imagining they have agency in the power structure when in fact it serves the rulers, allowing them to perpetuate the same old hierarchical structures.

In one fell swoop, Pollock connects the process of vernacularization of each of the Indian languages to the agency of various royal courts and to the replacement of Sanskrit. The aestheticization of power (explained in the previous chapter) continued as before; only now it was performed in the common languages of the people.

Superimposition: Sanskrit infused into local languages

As we have seen, Pollock says that before the rise of the vernaculars, Sanskrit had already developed a sophisticated literary culture involving the extensive aestheticization of power. In his model, the sophisticated structure of Sanskrit got 'infused' into the local language by wholesale adaptations. This, he says, was done 'during the crystallizing moments of many vernacular literary cultures and formed a core component in the creation of what is here named the "cosmopolitan vernacular"'. The objective was 'to localize the full spectrum of literary qualities of the superposed cosmopolitan code' – in other words, make the local language and literature the beneficiary and successor of all the resources and templates of the Sanskrit Cosmopolis.[49]

The rise of the vernacular thus depended on the established presence of 'the notion of literary language that Sanskrit had defined'. Sanskrit had become the 'dominant transregional cultural formation' and this in turn enabled the 'alternative cultural world produced by vernacular literature'.[50] Pollock calls this process the 'superposition' (or 'superimposition') of Sanskrit on to local languages. He writes that 'only by appropriating the signs of superposition in everything from vocabulary to aesthetics could it [i.e., the vernacular] become a world, a self-adequate literary culture according to the prevailing scale'.[51]

Sanskrit itself disappears from usage in literary works, but its structure lives on within the local vernacular and transforms it.[52] The Sanskrit literary content is also reproduced in each local language, such as in the itihasas and Puranas. *Pollock explains that this is how, for instance, the idiom of domination in the Ramayana became infused into the vernacular.*[53]

The problem I see with Pollock's model is that he assumes a dominant–subservient relationship between Sanskrit and the vernaculars. He compares the situation with what happened in the Latin adaptations of Homer's Greek epics.[54] He claims that (1) Valmiki's Ramayana in Sanskrit played the same role as Homer's compositions in Greek, and that (2) translations of the Ramayana into Indian vernaculars mirrored the translations of Homer's works into Latin by the Romans.[55] However, the fact is, the literary movements in India and Europe were only superficially similar. Latin was not a vernacular; the translations of Homer into Latin never achieved wide currency; and Hindu kings did not resemble the Romans in their kingship style or their metaphysics.

To refute Pollock, Srinivas Reddy writes that it would be difficult to make bhakti fit into Pollock's model, because bhakti was not court-centred and it tended to harmonize the dichotomies Pollock highlights. In fact, bhakti poets accomplished a return to orality whereas in Pollock's model only written texts could bring about such a change. Furthermore, the bhakti poets avoided the need for funding by the royal courts and the need to carry out any political agenda through their poetry.[56]

Pollock would turn this argument around to point out that bhakti poems diverted people's attention from socio-political issues. Such devotional poems are examples of precisely how the aestheticization of power works, he would say. After all, religious literature is 'the opium of the people', as Marx had said. Pollock's thesis would argue that kings sponsor bhakti poetry because it allows them to maintain their power behind the fake mask of promoting popular culture. Nevertheless, in support of Reddy's position, we should remember that bhakti poets were usually not sponsored by kings.

Vernacularization disconnects from Vedic traditions

While the power structure remains the same as before, Pollock says, something does change: vernacularization disconnects 'people of the place' (desis) from Sanskrit. In other words, Sanskrit becomes seen as alien to the common people. Localized versions of itihasas and Puranas are developed; the stories told are restricted to locales where the language is prevalent. He writes:

> In vernacular narratives, the boundless universalizing Sanskrit tale was refitted onto the perceptible, traversable, indeed governable world of regional political practice ... cultures of Place were intended to at once replicate and replace the global order of Sanskrit.[57]

In the case of Kannada, according to Pollock's analysis, this 'disconnect' from Sanskrit happened in the tenth century, a hundred years after the local king had initiated the vernacularization process using Sanskrit grammar and kavya as the basis. The authority for the rules of correct usage and grammar of Kannada increasingly came to be local. He writes:

> ... local language[s] were hereby being empowered to authorize correct usage; it was not correct language itself – the perfect language of the gods forever preexisting human practice – that authorized their usage, as had been the case for earlier [Sanskrit] cosmopolitan writers.[58]

He is saying the writers no longer had to consult Panini's grammar as the authority on correct usage.

His idea of the transition from Sanskrit to vernacular implies that there was *disconnect* from the Vedas. Sanskrit as the 'language of the gods' was sidelined in this new context. This desacralization of literature as part of the de-Sanskritization is very important in Pollock's overall agenda.

As an example of this movement from a sacred to a mundane usage, he describes how the meaning of the Sanskrit word 'akshara' changed:

In Sanskrit, akshara originally meant 'a-kshara', or that which does not decay, such as in the sound 'Om'. However, in Kannada it was used to mean ordinary letters of the written alphabet.[59] Pollock shows how the deep, philosophical significance of the word 'akshara' in Sanskrit, was lost in Kannada. He says: 'By the tenth century in Karnataka, however, the term had come to predominantly signify written letters, the knowledge of writing, and literacy-based knowledge in general.'[60]

What he is telling us is that the impact of vernacularization was to separate the people from Sanskrit, and hence from the Vedas.

On the other hand, he also says that writers felt they were producing vernacular literature under divine command of some sort:

> In South Asia the felt need for the direct command of a god to underwrite vernacular literature persisted long into the second millennium; we saw this to be so in Maharashtra and Andhra even in the fifteenth, sixteenth, and seventeenth centuries, when Tukarām, Śrīnātha, Kṛṣṇadevarāyā – Shudra, Brahman, and even [the] king – all needed to receive a divine commandment in a dream to be able to write in the vernacular ... [61]

Here he is trying to show that some 'god' controlled the writings from the background, because authors would express themselves only after being instructed do so in their dream by 'divine commandment'.

What led so many kings to vernacularize?

The question remains as to *why* the kings wanted to vernacularize in the first place? After all, according to his theory of the aestheticization of power, Sanskrit had become well established as a weapon for protecting the power of kings across a vast and diverse region. Why would they want to disrupt a successful model? And why would all the kings, independently of one another, choose to do this during a particular time?

He offers many possible answers to these questions. But right away, he summarily dismisses the following three explanations for the rise of vernacularization:

1. **Possible explanation:** Bilingual people could have all along used their skills in Sanskrit to express themselves in a local language. Therefore, the vernaculars would have been developing side by side with Sanskrit, and there would be no such things as two separate Sanskrit/vernacular epochs.

   Pollock rejects this explanation, saying, '[it] cannot withstand serious scrutiny'. However, he does not explain why bilingual scholars could not have used both languages all along.[62]

2. **Possible explanation:** Religion could have been the trigger, as proposed by some leading political Indian subalternists in the 1990s.[63]

   Pollock rejects this notion, saying vernacularization was driven neither by brahmins nor by a revolt against them. He finds such explanations dubious because the 'presumed concomitance between Sanskrit and Brahmanism on the one hand and vernacularity and non-Brahmanism on the other does not hold for much of the period under discussion'.[64] He says that vernacularization in India was not the result of some uprising of the people against the kings and the religious elite, as is often said about vernacularization in Europe. In other words, these texts were other-worldly, unlike the Protestant texts produced in local languages in Europe, and therefore they had no 'consequences for the structure and functioning of polity'.[65] His position is that religion does not *cause* the vernacularization but benefits from it in so far as the status quo is maintained.[66]

3. **Possible explanation:** Vernacularization might have resulted from an attachment to one's mother tongue or ethnicity.[67]

   Pollock rejects this explanation, noting that there was no 'discourse that links language, identity and polity'.[68] Such ethnicity, he feels, did underlie the rise of the vernacular in Europe but was not found in India. He says no Indian text before British colonization, 'whether political or grammatical, even acknowledges any conjuncture of these two [ethnicity/kinship and language] elements'.[69]

After quickly eliminating these three possible explanations for vernacularization, Pollock returns to the vital question that remains unanswered: What motivated the kings to want to vernacularize? He then lists four possible drivers and correlates the timing of vernacularization with four corresponding political upheavals:

- A sharp increase in international trade between the eighth and fourteenth centuries, in parallel with the Arab occupation of Sindh.
- The rise and establishment of major agrarian regions on the subcontinent between the mid-fifth century and the end of the thirteenth century.
- The Islamic invasions from the north beginning with the nomadic Turkish tribes in the eleventh century and consolidating with the Mughals in the fourteenth century.
- The influence of the British.

After positing all these nebulous explanations and writing in great detail about hundreds of factoids scattered across geography and time, Pollock ends his book with some sobering reservations and concessions concerning his thesis on vernacularization. Vernacularization cannot have a single cause, he admits. It is not something mechanical or deliberate like the designing and manufacture of a watch. Nor is it purely random. There cannot be a single strong cause, for 'its complexity cannot be accounted for by any monocausal model'. He does however claim to have come up with 'some other principle' of causation, one for which he makes global claims, by saying that 'such evidence as this goes some distance in helping us decide among the various hypotheses seeking to account for large-scale language change'.[70]

In essence, the principle at work in vernacularization, according to Pollock, is that these kinds of linguistic changes are driven by a purely pragmatic will to entrench power:

> What we are seeing here is not an unwilled, blind, predetermined development of language, which branches out into vernacular diversity

> [...] not the blind watchmaker, [...] but, on the contrary, the sighted handyman, who knowledgeably puts things together *in order to achieve immediate pragmatic ends.*[71]

All he can say in the end is that it is the history of 'people making choices about the use of phonemes, lexemes, registers, themes, genres, whole languages [...] *to achieve specific expressive and political ends*'.[72] There remains, he admits, a telling gap between his theory and the evidence he can cite:

> It is one thing to recognize that literary-language diversity is willed and quite another to specify the historical factors that go to shape the exercise of this will. If we examine the theoretical frameworks on offer that do try to provide such specification, moreover, we soon find that none of them is entirely adequate to the evidence of premodern South Asia.[73]

He sees his own theory as providing such a framework, but in effect there is nothing there except pure ideology. His writings are filled with tacit assumptions about human nature and the mundane and transcendental cosmologies, but he never explicitly states or defends them.

We need to deliberate further on these points before we can be sure, but I get the impression that Pollock has checkmated himself here. He admits that none of his theories for the rise of the vernaculars can be indisputably supported by facts. Yet he refuses to let go of his presuppositions, or even reconsider them.

The mysterious and unexplained cause for vernacularization is not an isolated challenge for Pollock. Indeed, an inability to explain vernacularization would be fatal for his overall model. This threatens to unravel his entire theory that the politics of elitism drives the history of literature and languages.

Claiming parallels between European and Indian vernacularization

Towards the end of his lengthy analysis, Pollock offers a few European examples that he regards as parallels to the situation in India. Once again, he draws on the work of Benjamin, Gramsci and Vico to explain how and why all across Europe the vernaculars emerged from Latin. This is where he 'goes global' with his analysis and presents a sweeping thesis.

Just how viable is this 'big picture' extension of Pollock's work on India? I would say it is debatable for it ignores some crucial differences between Europe and India.

Pollock claims that the same process was going on all over the world. All he has to do is show what he has learned about Europe and assume we can apply it to India as well:

> A sketch of some key moments in the historical transformation of literary culture and power in western Europe should suffice to point up some of the extraordinary parallels with contemporaneous developments in southern Asia. The great innovation that was to enduringly change these two worlds occurred during the first five centuries of the second millennium, and it shows a remarkably consistent morphology.[74]

His first claim is that the rise of Latin paralleled the rise of Sanskrit in the first millennium.[75] He then points out how Latin literacy was determined by the Christian church, just as Sanskrit literacy in South Asia was controlled and expanded by the brahmin–kshatriya nexus.[76]

Just as Latin literacy spread with Christianity, but took a long time to transform into local vernacular literacy, so also, he says, Sanskrit literacy spread to Cambodia and Java by about the fifth century CE, but the vernacularization did not arise until about the fifteenth century CE. He says:

> there is no doubt that the early centuries of the second millennium witnessed in Europe what can only be described as a vernacular revolution, one that followed a timeline closely approximating the analogous process in South Asia.[77]

Another parallel he points out is that the rise of local languages in Europe was due to a clear impetus from the royal courts. In fact, 'The vernacular revolution in Europe was unthinkable without the central stimulus provided by the increasingly powerful royal courts of the later Middle Ages and Renaissance.'[78]

From this, he generalizes the time frames in which the Latin order dissolved in the second millennium and the European vernaculars arose. 'The gradual dissolution of the universalist Latin order' is what had led to 'a concomitant creation of new, self-consciously regionalized forms of literary production and political communication.'[79] Thus, Europe's process began to regionalize (or 'balkanize' in today's jargon).

One of the early formations of this regionalized identity was in England: 'Alfred's England at the end of the ninth century was a model early instance of the creation of a vernacular literature and the beginnings of a vernacular documentary state under the direct guidance of the royal court.'[80] He is describing a process that is almost congruent with what he has described with respect to India, i.e., Kannada's rise in the ninth century under direct guidance of the royal court. In India, this process emerged out of a prior substratum of Sanskrit whereas in England it was based on Latin. He confirms this parallel, saying:

> Many of the processes at work there [i.e., in Europe] – translation, adaptation, philologization, documentation – remind us strongly of what was occurring at precisely the same epoch in the Kannada-speaking areas of the Deccan.[81]

The vernacularization of Kannada with the use of Sanskrit grammar was followed by similar vernacularizations of Telugu, Tamil, Oriya, Bengali, Nepali, Khmer and Javanese from the tenth to the fifteenth century. In tandem, the wave started by the vernacularization of English swept across Europe by the sixteenth century.[82]

I am unconvinced that these purported 'parallels' between Europe and India can prove anything. None of these coincidences of timing has causal links between Europe and India. The so-called parallels are in many cases quite a stretch, and there are a good number of counter-examples Pollock ignores in his filtering.[83]

8

The Sanskriti Web as an Alternative Hypothesis

Pollock's model of how and why languages rise is definitely original and highly ambitious. Few recent scholars have studied the history of the relationships between Sanskrit and the vernacular languages with the same rigour as he has. Therefore, there is no alternative work of comparable scope that could independently corroborate or refute his assumptions. Most readers have formed opinions of his work based on small, isolated portions of it; certainly, the general public has an insufficient overall understanding of his arguments. His own admission, that in many respects he has failed to fully prove what he claims, gets lost in his voluminous works in the absence of serious critique.

In dealing with the relationship between Sanskrit and the vernaculars, he:

- sees all changes as being the result of top-down actions by kings and ignores the flow of knowledge and influence at the grass root that is independent of kings;

- frames history in terms of separate 'Sanskrit millennium' and 'vernacular millennium', in a way that exaggerates the tension between Sanskrit and the vernaculars;
- highlights the gaps between being desi (belonging to the local place) and being Vedic in outlook.

In general, his approach is to sideline many domains of knowledge and pick out those texts that serve his purpose. This amputation of the crucial limbs of the Sanskrit tradition leads to a flawed view of history. Like many American Orientalists, he is obsessed with discovering (and exaggerating) conflicts and disharmony among aspects of the Sanskrit tradition rather than seeing harmony, flux and integration. I have shown this already in the case of issues he raises with regard to oral vs written, paramarthika vs vyavaharika and shastra vs kavya.

In order to stimulate debate, I wish to speculate on an alternative model to explain the history of Indian languages. My hypothesis is that there has been an organic process that respects the sacred dimension in people's lives and their agency in bringing historical changes. Hence, one cannot presume top-down politics as the sole cause for change.

I propose that Sanskrit in its earlier forms (especially oral) could have been *already* prevalent across these large territories long before Buddhism. Besides being a language Sanskrit had also been encoded into the culture we call sanskriti. In fact, the language could be considered as one representation of the culture, and vice versa. In other words, centuries before Pollock's dates for the arrival of Sanskrit in various kingdoms, it is plausible that the common public practised a 'Hindu-like' faith, regardless of the name by which they referred to it. Such a scenario would open up explanations for the spread of Sanskrit that would differ from Pollock's theory.

The Mahabharata contains detailed accounts of people communicating with each other across long distances, from Kandahar (the ancient Gandhara) to Assam and to the south of India. Since the Mahabharata is much earlier than the Buddha, it could be that Sanskrit thrived as a link language across a vast territory.[1] It may be that the Buddhists switched from Pali to Sanskrit because they could benefit from Sanskrit having already been established with a ubiquitous cosmopolitan presence. They had to debate with the Vedic brahmins who had developed technical competence in Sanskrit for nuanced and intricate discourse; Pali was perhaps not adequate for this.

We know that there was a flow of knowledge that connected places far away. The ancient Silk Route, by land, and the sea routes in the Indian Ocean are well documented. These links and journeys transported not only material goods but also ideas, languages, literatures, philosophies, scholars and more; hence there was an ancient 'sanskriti Internet' or a very slow worldwide web of sorts.

Obviously, my metaphor of the worldwide web is not to be taken literally. Sanskrit did not spread either as fast or with as much sophistication as, say, the Java computer language has. Nonetheless, the metaphor does point to the way in which sanskriti and Sanskrit became trans-regional – through a decentralized network where ideas flowed freely in all directions.

There are multiple reasons and causes as to why a given technology is adopted across a large geographical area. There is no need to conjure up conspiracy theories or sinister intentions (such as Pollock's theory of political power wanting to oppress people) in every locale. There are various ways in which any new technology negotiates with local economies, cultures and politics, and there need not be only one theory of adoption that is applicable everywhere. Why not regard Sanskrit's widespread presence in a similar light, as a communication technology that had competitive advantages over other available methods?

I prefer to speculate that Sanskrit spread and took root on its own merit. Political patronage might have been only one factor in its dissemination, but it was not necessarily the primary one in every case. *My hypothesis is that long before the transmission of Sanskrit through political kayva, there had existed a thriving sanskriti web based on some of the same structures as the Sanskrit language.* If we were to develop this idea further, it could conceivably serve as a viable alternative to Pollock's theory according to which the power of monarchy was at the helm of all cultural history.

Vedic metaphysics, the sanskriti cultural web and the Sanskrit language were all replicated in different places because they enjoyed a deep place of respect in the hearts and lives of ordinary people. Sanskrit and its texts expresses the fabric of cosmic reality, and it is natural for people to be drawn to explore, discover, share and celebrate the manifestation of this reality in their personal and social lives. Therefore, individuals in different capacities – be they kings, brahmins, merchants, or farmers – have performed their roles as part of the Vedic social yajna.

The mode of transportation for Sanskrit and sanskriti was the human body. Individuals carried these ideas in their person and engaged in formal and informal discussions, lectures, arguments, seminars and training academies. Therefore, the changes that were put forward in one locale travelled elsewhere within a few generations. What we may think of as the 'applications' of Sanskrit had 'market pull' that created demand for Sanskrit as the development platform.

One can use other ways to illustrate how sanskriti and Sanskrit might have travelled. Songs, for example, travel today across a whole generation of fans in faraway places without any top-down political agency making this happen. They travel by word of mouth, just as the wind spreads seeds and a species of plants travels long distances. Similarly, ideas can 'go viral' on the Internet today with no central authority promoting it. It is interesting that Pollock's study of communities is fixated only on those that remained entirely local because of the nature of their occupation (e.g., agriculture), but he does not adequately examine the communities that travelled (as traders, for instance).[2]

Pollock does note in passing that a trans-regional Sanskrit pre-existed across much of Asia before the era he calls cosmopolitan: '... long before the onset of the cosmopolitan era it [Sanskrit] had become transregional – though not yet cosmopolitan – through the spread of Vedic culture.'[3] He is essentially correct when he refers to Sanskrit's uniqueness among world systems of language and thought:

> The study of language was more highly developed in South Asia than anywhere else in the premodern world. From the archaic invocation to the Goddess of Speech (Vāk) in the Ṛgveda to the etymological

> speculation that lies at the heart of the sacerdotal thought of the brāhmaṇas to the grand synthesis of Pāniṇi and the sophisticated tradition of exegesis that it stimulated, and in the many rival systems that sought to displace and surpass this tradition, premodern Indian thinkers were consumed by the desire to understand the mystery of human communication.[4]

This statement contradicts his own stand that prior to the Buddhist revolution in Sanskrit, the brahmins had monopolized Sanskrit and used it *exclusively* for ritual purposes. He is also incorrect in saying that the use of Sanskrit before Buddhism lacked innovation and creativity. In the above quote he indicates that there was *continuity:* from the Rig Veda's invocation to Vak, the Goddess of speech, to the sacred thoughts of the brahmins, to Paṇini's consolidation of prior works into his masterpiece of grammar, and to many rival systems that emerged from the same source. In other words, the above quote indicates a great continuity in Sanskrit language, etymology, speculation and grammar long before the Buddhists. He admits that the Vedic brahmins were consumed by the desire to understand the mysteries of human communication.

Unfortunately, after acknowledging this just for the record, he then heads off in the opposite direction, arguing that before the Buddha came, the brahmins were frozen in the uncreative pursuit of performing rituals mechanically. He coins the terms 'liturgical era' and 'postliturgical era' to describe two distinct eras of Indian history. The 'liturgical era' was when Sanskrit was used solely for liturgy, i.e., brahmins chanting Vedic hymns for ritual purposes. This was replaced by the 'postliturgical era' in which Sanskrit usage changed from hymns to political kavya due to the human rights interventions by the Buddhists. I do not accept his separation of ritual and non-ritual uses of Sanskrit into two separate eras. Both uses coexisted in parallel, before and after the Buddha.

The features that differentiate my web model from Pollock's top-down political one, are highlighted in the following table:

My Sanskriti Web Model	Pollock's Sanskrit Cosmopolis Model
Decentralized ecosystem with no central power or agency driving it.	Driven by the royal courts of kings, hence centralized in a given country.
Knowledge flows in all directions.	Knowledge flows exclusively from centre to the periphery.
Knowledge workers travelled long distances for conversations, debates, lectures and education. These and various travelling merchants and bhakti groups spread Sanskrit.	Domination/subordination relations existed, with the kings and brahmins driving the discourse to rule over others.
Sanskrit was a spoken language by ordinary people.	Prior to the Buddha, Sanskrit usage was restricted and used only for ritual purposes.
Vedic metaphysics had a deep place in the lives of people; hence it was replicated in different places, with local geographies and kingdoms substituted in place of those mentioned in the source texts.	Projecting the epic space on the local geography was driven by motivation to gain credibility for sustaining political power.
Sanskrit spread through its cultural applications – such as Ayurveda, astrology, philosophy, mathematics, performing arts, etc.	Sanskrit spread as an aesthetic device that kings used to assert their power.
Sanskrit and vernacular languages have always had a bi-directional flow of information and influences.	Sanskrit and vernaculars had asymmetry and separate domains of usage. This tension led to a Sanskrit-dominated era, followed by the death of Sanskrit and the rise of the vernacular era.

Diglossia versus hyperglossia models

Pollock cannot, I think, *disprove* the possibility that Sanskrit and the local languages had long existed side by side as a single linguistic family. According to this alternative hypothesis I wish to explore, they could have been in relative parity with bilingual writers and speakers moving back and forth between them, allowing each to enrich the other. The term used in linguistics for this type of relationship is 'diglossia', and Pollock explicitly and assertively rejects this notion. He writes:

> The split in standards between Sanskrit and local language was such that 'diglossia' seems an entirely inadequate category to describe it. For what we encounter is not an internal split (di-) in registers and norms, typically between literary and colloquial usage, in what local actors conceived of as a single language, but a relationship of extreme superposition (hyper-) between two languages that local actors knew to be entirely different ... derived ultimately from the *discursive restrictions and social monopolization, the extreme compartmentalization of usage as well as the difference in cultural opportunity.*[5]

The diglossia model is consistent with the view that many people were bilingual. Here Sanskrit would indeed provide the requisite grammar, rich vocabulary and complex structures, along with a large and respected body of literature learned by formal education and used for writing and speaking. The vernaculars would be more community-specific and used for ordinary conversation.[6] What is significant is that the two would flow into each other and mutually inform each other, leading to new developments. Diglossia represents a dynamic equilibrium in a family of languages in which top-down politics is not the key driver.

Pollock wants a model that is based on the assumption that Sanskrit caused the segregation of social groups through compartmentalization and monopolization. He calls his model 'hyperglossia', which denotes a relationship of language *domination* by one group over another. In other words, it is not the kind of reciprocity I propose above, but rather the superimposition of one language over another (i.e., Sanskrit superimposed on to the vernaculars).

The insider's view

Indian tradition sees Sanskrit and local languages as partners. There was a process of interdependent exchange between them without any hegemonic connotation. Panini's concept of the lists of 'open-ended' words, for instance, is illustrative of the reciprocal exchange and mutual reinforcement between Sanskrit and Prakrit. From popular speech patterns, Sanskrit picked the usages in specific instances and abstracted them into syntactical relationships. Once information about local or regional cultural traits is recorded and encoded in Sanskrit, it becomes part of the pan-Indian sanskriti. On the other hand, when elements of Sanskrit are given local flavour, they acquire a distinctly regional identity. Long before the time of Kalidasa, Sanskrit had become a pan-Indian language that was studied and mastered consciously by the literati for the dual purposes for which it was intended.

Sanskrit has also been a vehicle of reciprocal communication among the regional languages. It has served as a foundation for India's unified identity while Prakrit has provided diversity by spontaneously blossoming into a variety of regional languages. These languages are informal in the way they are learned and used by the wider populace.

The great grammarian Bhartrihari recognized that Sanskrit and vernaculars are felt to be related – something overlooked by Pollock. Kamasutra (1:4) observes that a person could become highly esteemed in the world by having conversations in the assemblies that are neither too much in Sanskrit nor too much in the local languages. The relation between Sanskrit and Prakrit is discernible in the works of the Kashmiri poet Bilhana (twelfth century CE), who affirmed that everywhere in his native Himalayan area, the women spoke both Sanskrit and Prakrit with native fluency.[7]

Srinivas Reddy also supports the view that bilingualism was common. He cites many 'polyglot writers who composed in several languages'.[8] This is more accurate than the view of dominance/subordination between Sanskrit and vernaculars. In some cases, he says, a vernacular's similarities with Sanskrit were 'the natural evolution of meaningful modes of expression ... rather than superposed sources'.[9] There was no dramatic shift in politics that created a sharp divide between any such thing as the Sanskrit epoch and a vernacular one.

Reddy also takes Pollock to task for saying that the cultures of 'folk' and 'desh' are alienated from Sanskrit. He says the

> development [of Sanskrit] as a language was intimately connected to the regions of diverse languages through which it so pervasively spread, and therefore, any holistic understanding of its literary historiography must be based in part, or at the very least, set in opposition to, modalities of production outside the cosmopolitan sphere.[10]

Reddy says Pollock and others incorrectly disregard the influence of vernaculars on Sanskrit: 'The process of language development is always a two-way process, a dialogue if you will, rather than a hegemonic superimposition by a so-perceived dominant linguistic/cultural formation upon a subdominant one.'[11] Reddy supports the bidirectional flow of influence, not merely between languages but between the world of gods (paramarthika) and the world of men (vyavaharika), writing:

> The elevation of kings to god-like status was part of an evolving process that was paralleled by the domestication or rather humanization of the gods. This bidirectional movement worked in relation to and in conjunction with other pan-Indic processes such as vernacularization and the spread of *bhakti* ideals. ... This makes a pointed comment on the modeling of deities (especially Viṣṇu) on the image of kings, their domains, actions and so forth, thus creating a cyclically influencing dynamic whereby the mythic and the historical, the philosophical and the political, were readily constituting each other.[12]

Hans H. Hock is another scholar who has noted that the interaction between language groups in India seems to involve more convergence than subversion. Subversion would be any one-directional transfer of structural features from one language family to the target language. Convergence, on the other hand, involves a reciprocal or bidirectional influence through which languages that are in long-term contact become more similar in structure while retaining distinct vocabularies. In contrast to subversion, convergence leads to bilingualism and indicates social equality among the users of the languages.[13]

Approaches suggested by T.S. Satyanath

The writings of Professor T.S. Satyanath of the University of Delhi offer an alternative approach and thus a valuable stimulus for further discussion. Satyanath finds it incorrect to frame Indian traditions into separate compartments as separate disciplines, or in a linear sequence of discontinuous epochs.[14] He sees the entire tradition from prehistoric to modern times as a continuum. The various systems of knowledge are seen as interwoven even though they apply to different domains. He finds Indian systems to represent 'a knowledge involving continuity and change, a system that suggests mutual absorptions across time and space and at the same time, also suggests them to be continually evolving systems'.[15]

He says that the knowledge systems tend to become encyclopedic in nature, incorporating the details cumulatively whether it is represented through architectural practice, or architectural texts, or literary representations. Thus, different representational formats of traditional knowledge systems are in a continuous dialogue, cutting across time, space and society, and thereby making themselves available for reinterpretations. For example, he explains in detail how the archaeological sites of old cities correspond precisely to the structures described in the *Arthashastra* architecture texts:

> Despite being far removed in their temporal, spatial and linguistic dimensions there is surprisingly a high degree of agreement among the findings of the archeological excavations of early cities, the canonical texts and the literary descriptions available in the *mahakavya*s [epic poems].[16]

Another tight relationship is between kavya and shastra. While acknowledging that the kavya and shastra are distinct types of works, Satyanath sees their distinction as only a heuristic device and not a clear-cut or absolute boundary. Indeed, many kavyas incorporate knowledge of various types of shastras and over time have increasingly become knowledge-based documents. Similarly, shastras are often expressed in a poetic format and are of excellent literary quality. Scientific treatises in Sanskrit sometimes have the fragrance of poetry. Mathematical problems discussed in Bhaskara's *Lilavati* are equally admired for their lyrical charm. Felicitous plays on words, lovely similes, novel metaphors, and touches of humour enliven many a book on medicine, music or metaphysics. This is not found in any other language in the world!

To illustrate the correspondences across these knowledge domains, Satyanath analyses the 'description of a city' in detail as per the requirements of a mahakavya, to show how closely it corresponds to actual human habitat systems over a long period.[17]

He comments on how the Western ideas of literacy were shaped by colonialism's alleged preoccupation with teaching morality and how this in turn was embedded in the West's history. This reduction of expression to written literature, and within that, to morality, does violence to the Indian way of expressing which, he maintains, 'is first of all oral, collective, and narrative in nature and often existed only in performance. In this sense it was neither available in print nor in manuscript format.'[18]

As an example of Indian plurality of different kinds of systems, Satyanath notes that the Virashaiva bhakti poets in Karnataka (twelfth century) opted for the popular oral tradition, while in parallel the Jain kings and authors established writing as their mode of choice. Vachana, the term used by the Virashaiva poets for their works, suggests the importance given to oral over writing. The early Virashaiva poets were from the artisan and service jatis. Their own bodies constituted the repository of their specialized professional knowledge. They were highly mobile and their spiritual tradition emphasized hard work. Satyanath notes that 'their knowledge systems always remained with their body and moved wherever they went. The knowledge systems were not transferable to others, nor could be dominated and confiscated by others'.[19]

He observes that Indian knowledge is often represented in terms of the human body. One may think of a threefold typology of how knowledge is represented: phonetic/oral, script/writing, and body. These three are not isolated from one another but entangled in a complex system of exchanges and transactions.

India's body-centric knowledge systems have a tendency to codify knowledge in terms representing parts of the body. This can be found in representations of human habitat, architecture and the construction of a temple or house. Bhakti poetry provides ample examples of the body being conceptualized as a temple. Also, the blacksmith's furnace, used in smelting iron for making steel, has been considered as the form of the mother goddess. Elaborate narratives, rituals and beliefs surround the technological process of transforming the ore into the metal, which is done during the night. Indeed, it is believed that the ore smelts in the womb of the goddess. It is not only the furnace but also the ore and the finished product (iron in the form of a ball) that have all been considered as representing the goddess. Similarly, the loom in textiles has been perceived as a body with head, eyes, nose, mouth, ears, shoulders, hands, legs and so on. All these are examples where a non-written representation system is the primary one used for storage, application and transmission.

Satyanath takes exception to Pollock's position on how the cosmopolitan Sanskrit world became replaced by vernaculars starting from the ninth century CE. That is when Kannada and Telugu became the languages of literary and political expression in the courts of the Rashtrakutas and the Chalukyas. Satyanath disagrees with Pollock's model of using a 'unidirectional path of change' for such a transformation. Instead, he prefers using the pluralistic approach of a network of multiple causes and effects, because the changes were far more complex than Pollock's reductionism suggests. Many different dynamics coexisted. Satyanath says there was 'sometimes [movement] from cosmopolitan to vernacular as Pollock has stipulated, but more often [it was a matter of] mutual absorption within the scripto-centric, phono-centric and body-centric traditions and also through a reversing [of] the direction of flow, from vernacular to cosmopolitan'.[20]

Satyanath uses data from the same ninth-century period and the same Rashtrakuta kings as Pollock does. However, he reaches a different conclusion: 'The codification of knowledge during the Rashtrakuta period actually witnessed all the three processes mentioned above – writing, oral and body-centric.'[21]

Despite the court-sponsored projects to transfer oral and body-centric knowledge into writing, the oral and body-centric systems not only survived in their original formats but also coexisted side by side with their written counterparts. One of the reasons was that specialized knowledge was often protected by religious or jati communities. This is why even today, when printed and institutionally transmitted knowledge sources are available, several indigenous trades in Kannada-speaking regions, such as carpentry and masonry, still function as inherited body-based knowledge systems.

He also gives examples of the most important Hindu Kannada literature texts. Although these were available in manuscript form, only their oral representations existed in a practical sense through dramatic recitation performance.[22] He cites many other examples of mutually enriching relationships between written, oral and body-based knowledge systems, concluding:

> The lack of distinctions between scripto-centric (written) and phono-centric (oral) texts on the one hand and the crucial role of body-centric performing traditions in shaping and determining the texts on the other have played an important role, both at conceptual and performing levels, eventually shaping the construction, composition, maintenance and transmission of textual, oral and performing traditions of Karnataka.[23]

The flow of oral and written literary works between Hindus and Jains, between Sanskrit, Prakrit and Kannada, between various specialized fields of knowledge, between different communities marked by jati or religious identities, and across various geographical regions – all these have been open, fluid and responsive to changing environment. Pollock's attempt to collapse all this complexity and pigeonhole it into rigid normative categories is too reductive.

Many body-based performance genres emerged in Kannada, including recitation and enactments of kavyas from the itihasas and other literature.[24] Satyanath goes on to explain how the multimedia form varies based on the location of an enactment. At home a text might be read as a ritual. In the temple or courtyard of aristocrat families, the same literature might be recited in an open-air space for the public to enjoy. Many different styles and permutations in the use of music, visual dimensions and various meters for recitation were combined, often in the same performance.

As the text moves from home to temple to open public space, there is a gradual increase in scope and diversity. It moves from the written manuscript format to a recitation format and to folk play and pictorial formats. In the process, the audience gradually increases and the text becomes accessible in a more diversified manner. Satyanath says that such a process also expands the message across communities and 'assumes a trans-linguistic, trans-sectarian, trans-religious and trans-social dimension'. For example, 'the sculptural representations of episodes from the *kavyas*, located on the exterior walls and pillars of the temple and depicted at a human vision level, provide certain key narrative visual elements that are representative of the episode on which the viewers could rebuild the story for themselves', without needing a written or verbal text and 'which is closer to Indian aesthetic experience'.[25] Satyanath says such pluralistic epistemologies and their survival are 'a time-tested phenomenon in India and are highly relevant to us even today ... '[26]

Another example of non-written knowledge representation is the tradition of rangoli (ritualistic floor drawings). This is a complex mathematical computing activity involving intuitive and strategic understanding of spatial reasoning. It is traditionally practised by women. Culturally sensitive aesthetics of patterns and colours are learned through body-centric transmission without the use of written texts or instructions.

The implications of this interpretation of Indian culture also compel us to re-examine views on jati/caste fixations. Satyanath suggests that caste boundaries were not so rigid in blocking the flow of knowledge. He points out that 'medieval Indian performing traditions ... provided opportunities for the participation and involvement of all the communities in them, suggesting [that these communities served] as sites of pluralistic epistemologies and cooperative systems'.[27]

He is critical of Western-inspired tendencies to use binary categories in a hierarchy of high/low, primitive/modern, marga/desi, etc. This is a colonial mindset many Indians have adopted in their approach to Indian culture. He rejects the basic premise that Sanskrit/non-Sanskrit and brahmin/non-brahmin have been mutually exclusive camps and proposes that we 'escape from dominance of binary oppositions and substitute them with pluralistic epistemologies of equal significance'.

Satyanath sees Pollock's fundamental logic of marga versus desi as flawed, and writes:

> We must note that *marga* and *desi* do not oppose each other the way their Western counterparts do. Whereas the first etymologically suggests a well-established path, the latter refers to a regional world. In this sense they are neither mutually exclusive terms nor do they stand in opposition to each other. Apart from this, they always stand in multiple relationships with different aspects of performing traditions and are primarily an attempt intended to capture stylistic variations. At least for the grammarians in regional languages the two were not in binary opposition.[28]

Integral unity, open architecture and sanskriti web

My thinking is aligned with Satyanath that Indian representations are repositories of knowledge that are best appreciated in pluralistic epistemologies across multiple domains, and not separable epistemologies, of the kind found in Western 'synthetic' knowledge systems. I have used the term 'integral unity' to refer to this pluralistic epistemology across disciplines, social groups, geographical locations and epochs.[29]

India's diversity shows a replication of structural patterns throughout the country such that each regional culture may be seen as a microcosm of the full system. Sanskriti encompasses a broad repository of human sciences, art, architecture, music, theatre, literature and pilgrimage.[30]

In modern times, the state operates broadcasting agencies and publishes school textbooks while the film and pop culture industries act as agents for the spread of culture. Similarly, in earlier times, there was a vast ecosystem in which rulers, pilgrim centres and temple complexes were among the agents of Sanskritization. This was a profound and multidirectional cultural process – not a top-down, one-way process controlled by kings, as Pollock claims.

An entirely different and more authentic picture emerges when we see diverse groups not as constituting an absolute hierarchy but as peers. A better view is one in which there are multiple hierarchies for different domains: vaishyas dominating in economy, shudras dominating in embodied expertise, kshatriyas dominating in politics and administration, and brahmins dominating in ritual processes. Someone higher up in one respect tends to be lower down in other respects, and vice versa. The communities which populate these functional hierarchies have also been known to move from one function to another over time: thus shudra communities have been known to move to the kshatriya functional hierarchy and vice versa.

India's complex formations were in dynamic mutual exchange. Their equilibrium was never permanently fixed but rather continually renegotiated by the very nature of the integral unity of knowledge. Indian knowledge systems undergo mutual absorptions across time and space as encyclopaedic mechanisms of knowledge storage and transmission.

The following table summarizes the main differences between Pollock's fundamental assumptions and claims, and the alternative views I support:

Pollock's Assumptions	My Alternative Hypothesis
Either Sanskrit or vernacular used for literary production, but not both.	Indians were bilingual, often multilingual.
Asymmetry of power between Sanskrit and vernacular: • Dominant/subordinate relation • Flow of influence: Sanskrit → Vernacular	Peer relationship: • Not a power play • Bidirectional flow of influence
Sanskrit = foreign brought by Aryans Prakrit = indigenous Each evolved separately.	Both Sanskrit and Prakrit indigenous, with interactions right from ancient times.
Linear chronology: Sanskrit millennium → Vernacular millennium	No hard separation of epochs. Both co-existed in parallel.
Marga (a path) versus desi (people of a geography) tension. Desi became alienated from Vedas.	No marga–desi tension. Desi not alienated from Vedas.
Caste, gender separate language zones.	Fluidity. No separate polity.
Shastra vs kavya hard separation. Separate knowledge domains.	Integral unity based on common metaphysics across multiple domains: architecture, physiology, yajna, cosmology, etc. Kavya and shastra interwoven.
Quest for single model of causation of vernacularization driven by political power of kings.	Many causes for vernacularization, not just kings. Multiple hierarchies, no single power structure.

9

Declaring Sanskrit Dead and Sanskriti Non-existent

Agenda in declaring the death of Sanskrit

Pollock begins his important paper, 'The Death of Sanskrit' (2001), by announcing his political agenda:

> In the age of Hindu identity politics (Hindutva) inaugurated in the 1990s by the ascendancy of the Indian People's Party (Bharatiya Janata Party) and its ideological auxiliary, the World Hindu Council (Vishwa Hindu Parishad), Indian cultural and religious nationalism has been promulgating ever more distorted images of India's past. Few things are as central to this revisionism as Sanskrit, the dominant culture language of precolonial southern Asia outside the Persianate order.[1]

Right from the start, Pollock condemns India's latest attempts to re-popularize Sanskrit as political 'revisionism' in the service of nationalism. As I have pointed out earlier, his writings constantly exploit dichotomies within India – Sanskrit versus the vernaculars, Buddhists versus Hindus, Hindus versus Muslims, men versus women, and Dalits versus brahmins, to name a few. He now adds a new dichotomy: Hindu nationalist attempts at reviving Sanskrit versus his own liberation philology approach that would detoxify it. He is using Hindu identity politics as an effigy to make a sweeping case against the efforts to promote Sanskrit's viability as a spoken language.

It seems he does not want Sanskrit to regain its role as a viable medium of expression for sacred and analytical knowledge. Pollock's treatment of Sanskrit, its origins, its history, its way of working, and its relationship to vernacular languages and to social power is governed by a political agenda. For instance, he promotes the idea that Sanskrit was brought to India by foreign Aryan invaders and blames 'Hindutva propagandists' for claiming that Sanskrit is native to India:

> Hindutva propagandists have sought to show, for example, that Sanskrit was indigenous to India, and they purport to decipher Indus Valley seals to prove its presence two millennia before it actually came into existence.[2]

Besides denying its Indian origin, in the above quote Pollock says Sanskrit began about two millennia *after* the Indus Valley Civilization. By implication, if Sanskrit did not exist until that time, then the Vedas, being in Sanskrit, could not have existed then. His work is based on this assumption of foreign origins, as if there is no legitimate debate about this issue. At the very least, he should acknowledge the existence of a very old script of the Indus Valley Civilization even though it has not been decoded and its relationship to the Vedas and Sanskrit remains actively debated. Regardless of whether it was the same language as Sanskrit, one cannot accept his claim that Indians did not know how to write until after the time of the Buddha.

The following paragraph from 'The Death of Sanskrit' offers some scathing remarks concerning its revival:

> In a farcical repetition of Romantic myths of primevality, Sanskrit is considered – according to the characteristic hyperbole of the VHP [Vishwa Hindu Parishad] – the source and sole preserver of world culture. The state's anxiety both about Sanskrit's role in shaping the historical identity of the Hindu nation and about its contemporary vitality has manifested itself in substantial new funding for Sanskrit education, and in the declaration of 1999–2000 as the 'Year of Sanskrit', with plans for conversation camps, debate and essay competitions, drama festivals, and the like.[3]

In mainstream media, when he wants to impress traditional Indians and their government, he projects great love for Sanskrit. Yet in his academic writings as illustrated above, he says that praising Sanskrit as a great source of world culture amounts to 'a farcical repetition of Romantic myths of primevality'. He sees India's plans to revive education in spoken Sanskrit and its use in cultural expression as nothing more than 'the characteristic hyperbole of the VHP'. He seems upset at plans for Sanskrit camps, debates, essay competitions, dramas and festivals.

This chapter will show that Pollock's main agenda is to establish the following points:

- Sanskrit became a dead language many centuries ago. The structures that are built into Sanskrit grammar and literature from Vedic times were a serious cause of India's social oppression and decadence. This is why it died.
- The British and the Muslims played no role in its death.
- In fact, both the Muslims and the British were often good to Sanskrit and tried to rescue it from its demise.
- The fault for killing Sanskrit lies with Hindu kings, whose drive for political power led them to abandon it and turn to the vernaculars.
- The degraded Hindu kings, in turn, were the product of social decay due to inequality and the unjust structures of ritual and hierarchy.

Claiming Sanskrit has been dead for many centuries

In attempting to explain 'the death of Sanskrit literary culture as a historical process', Pollock examines four separate regions of India: Kashmir, Vijayanagara, Mughal Delhi and Bengal. He describes these regional declines:

> Kashmir, a premier center of literary creativity, after the thirteenth century; its diminished power in sixteenth century Vijayanagara, the last great imperial formation of southern India; its short-lived moment of modernity at the Mughal court in mid-seventeenth-century Delhi; and its ghostly existence in Bengal on the eve of colonialism.[4]

He then presents anecdotal factoids from these four regions to illustrate that Sanskrit had died.[5] His conclusion (for Kashmir as an example) is succinct:

> There can be no doubt about the fact that profoundly debilitating changes did take place: in Kashmir after the thirteenth century, Sanskrit literature ceased almost entirely to be produced; in Vijayanagara, not a single Sanskrit literary work entered into transregional circulation, an achievement that signaled excellence in earlier periods; in seventeenth-century Delhi, remarkable innovations found no continuation, leaving nineteenth century Sanskrit literary culture utterly unable to perpetuate itself into modernity.[6]

He bases his declaration of the death of Sanskrit on his own survey of selected kavya texts sponsored by certain rulers between the twelfth and the twentieth centuries. Sanskrit's death is attributed chiefly to corrupt Hindu kings but also to the emergence of vernacular languages and to the inability to resist the effects of the Islamic invasions. He concludes by eulogizing Indian intellectual life as something that has died. In sum, according to him, *it was shattered as a result of its own internal flaws, including lack of critical thought, isolation from (and misunderstanding of) the political sphere, and a chronic inability to recognize change.* He writes:

> No idiom was developed in which to articulate a new relationship to the past, let alone a critique; no new forms of knowledge – no new theory of religious identity, for example, let alone of the political – were produced in which the changed conditions of political and religious life could be conceptualized.[7]

He says, Sanskrit ceased to be a language of reflection and knowledge production and hence, for all practical purposes, became dead. He argues that this death was also brought on by the weakness and cultural defection of Hindu kings.

His assumption is incorrect about the centralized nature of power in Indian society. He fails to consider the multiple hierarchies of power in India through which Sanskrit was sustained and developed. Although the kshatriya king held political sway, the brahmins held their own domain of ritual and intellectual power. And vaishyas had wealth and economic power that neither kings nor brahmins had the right to control. Shudras controlled many thriving professions and many of its members knew Sanskrit well enough to participate in cultural events. Hence, contrary to European rulers who wielded absolute power over all domains, Indian kings did not entirely control the production and dissemination of knowledge.

In fact, several major Sanskrit texts were written independently of kings during the same period in which Sanskrit was allegedly dead. The following examples illustrate this:

- Abhinavagupta (tenth to eleventh century CE) of Kashmir, was a prolific Sanskrit writer of spiritual literature and kavya theory. He is known to have disdained kings and yet was very influential.[8] His voluminous writings on Kashmir Shaivism were further extended by Jayaratha in the thirteenth century, Lalleshwari in the fourteenth century and by such twentieth-century figures as Bhagwan Gopinath and Lakshman Joo.
- Gangesha's 'Navya Nyaya' ('new logic') darshana of Indian logic was started in the thirteenth century and remained active until the eighteenth century.[9]

- Jagannatha Pandit Raja contributed to Sanskrit kavya at the time of the Mughal prince Dara Shikoh, who was his friend.
- Varanasi was a period of great literary productivity in Sanskrit scholarship, even in the seventeenth century when the Mughals ruled over it. Scholars produced influential works on a wide array of subjects, from Ramayana to grammar to *Dharmashastra* to aesthetics to astronomy.
- One also sees the creation of fresh magisterial works in this era. At the same time, fusions were produced between previously disparate intellectual currents. One example is the blending of intellectual forms such as Advaita philosophy with popular forms such as bhakti. There is also a widespread fusion of tantra practice with various devotional and philosophical spiritualties.
- Rupa Goswami, in Vrindavan of the fourteenth to the fifteenth centuries, wrote on the theory of kavya as applied to the bhakti process. These influential Sanskrit writings were done independently, i.e., without the support of kings.
- Nilakantha of Kerala wrote *Tantra-samgraha*, a treatise on astronomy, in the year 1500.
- Appaya Dikshita's prodigious contributions to alankara shastra in the sixteenth century were not only widely patronized in the south of India but also adopted and celebrated in the seventeenth century.[10]

There is ample evidence that Sanskrit texts covering both kavya and other genres flourished, with and without the support of Hindu kings.

Space does not permit me to elaborate on the vast bibliography of Sanskrit productions in this era and the important impact these new works had. One example will suffice to illustrate such innovations. Nilakantha Caturdhara, a Marathi-speaking scholar in the era of Aurangzeb (seventeenth century), flourished in Varanasi where he studied a wide range of texts with various teachers. A great example of bilingualism, he wrote Sanskrit works that have had a lasting impact. He is known for his Sanskrit commentary on the Mahabharata, which became the standard companion to the great epic, eclipsing many other commentaries. One passage includes a celebrated verse in which he describes how he had assembled many manuscripts from different regions and then settled on the best reading of the text.[11]

Nilakantha often mixed Sanskrit and Prakrit words. He said he wanted to interpret the Ramayaṇa and the Mahabharata in a way that no previous commentator had done, so as to reveal their hidden sense and essence. His interpretations consisted of adhyatmika and yajna perspectives on the Ramayana and the *Bhagavata,* respectively. He included verses from the Rig Veda that might appear unrelated and used them to interpret the stories of the Ramayana and *Bhagavata.* He showed (1) how the verses reveal the story of Rama as the great manifestation of the deeds of the Supreme Being in human form, and (2) how these same verses reveal an underlying Vedantic meaning about the gaining of enlightenment through knowledge of the Self as Brahman. He explained that the Rig Veda verses are not just about deities and rituals but have a deeper truth.

Nilakantha's innovations have been dismissed by many Western Indologists, who maintain he has violated their idea of a canonized book based on a critical edition and standard schools of thought.[12] As against this scepticism of Western scholars, Hindu scholars find Nilakantha innovative, especially in the way he combines multiple techniques across the disciplinary boundaries. Using Sanskrit and Vedanta philosophy, he rationalized the popular expressions of devotion that were in the vernacular. This technique bridged the divide between Vedic philosophical thought and popular culture. Pollock would claim this as an attempt to infuse the popular vernacular discourse with 'elitist' values; in fact, the opposite is the case.[13]

Pollock's history of Sanskrit relies so much on what the kings were doing that he fails to grasp that the production and dissemination of knowledge in India were, for the most part, decentralized. The difference between top-down flow of knowledge (as in the Western case) and decentralized, bottom-up flow (as in the case of India) is explained in my book *Being Different.* The Western process is the result of relying on history-centric prophets, ecclesiastical authorities and instrumental reason. Indian traditions rely rather on the empirical experience of the rishis and the replication of that experience through intuitive and embodied knowing. Ground-breaking knowledge in India has typically emerged from remote corners and from individuals who were not necessarily pedigreed by rulers until they became famous in their own right.

Claiming Hindu kings killed Sanskrit, and Muslim rulers tried to save it

It is important for Pollock that Muslims not be blamed for the decline of Sanskrit. He writes that any theory 'can be dismissed at once' if it 'traces the decline of Sanskrit culture to the coming of Muslim power'. As he puts it:

> The evidence adduced here shows this [Muslim culpability in the death of Sanskrit] to be historically untenable. It was not 'alien rule unsympathetic to *kāvya*' and a 'desperate struggle with barbarous invaders' that sapped the strength of Sanskrit literature.[14]

Hence the invaders cannot be at fault. On the contrary, he believes Mughals patronized Sanskrit and that the collapse of the Mughal Empire could have debilitated Sanskrit in so far as it lost its Mughal patronage:

> It is conceivable that the breakup of certain kinds of patronage structures after the collapse of the Mughal Empire was a factor in the erosion of Sanskrit knowledge, as the coming of the Mughal peace two centuries earlier was a factor in its efflorescence.[15]

A key cause of the decline, he says, 'was the internal debilitation of the political institutions that had previously underwritten Sanskrit, pre-eminently the court.' He offers this analysis:

> ... a large part of any explanation [for the decline of Sanskrit] is almost certain to lie in the transformation that occurred in the social-political sphere. What we might identify as the courtly-civic ethos of Kashmir came undone with accelerating intensity during the first centuries of

> the second millennium, and this ethos, it becomes clear, was crucial to sustaining the vitality of Sanskrit literary culture. The events of the twelfth century are themselves to some degree prefigured a few centuries earlier.[16]

In discussing Kashmir as an example of a locale where Sanskrit had died, he attacks the Hindu kings who presided over that death. His focus is on the two centuries before the Turks established their power in the Kashmir Valley. Trying to prove the timing of Sanskrit's decline prior to the Turkish invasions enables him to absolve these invasions of any blame. It was under Hindu rule, he insists, and not as a result of Turkish invasion, that 'the social-political sphere imploded, and took the creative Sanskrit literary culture with it'.

He offers references to one 'degenerate king' and to a 'deranged Khaśa princess', and based on these references, he lays the blame for Sanskrit's decline on the 'new extremes of royal dissolution and criminality for which it is hard to find precedents'. Hindu Kashmir, as he sees it, was a world 'shaken by unprecedented acts of royal depravity and irreligiosity, by the madness and suicide of kings'. India went through what he calls a long period of 'impiety, violence, and treachery', highlighted by the 'atrocities of King Harsha' whom he accuses of having destroyed Hindu temples, deities, etc.[17] I am willing to give his analysis the benefit of doubt but it is a red flag that ought to be closely examined and debated.

After pronouncing the Hindu kings guilty, he endeavours to delve deeper to find the causes within Indian society that resulted in such a catastrophe. The blame goes to 'longer-term tensions within the social order' – which is code language for the oppression of Dalits and women. This opens the door to further projects by American Orientalists, the goal being to compile and interpret texts in a manner that provides more atrocity literature against Indian civilization. This seals the case that Sanskrit died prior to the Islamic invasions as a result of the cruelty of its Hindu sponsors and the elitist values contained within it.

In sharp contrast to his treatment of Hindu kings, he depicts Zain-ul-abidin, the Turkish sultan, as a great hero. In fact, Pollock calls him 'a pious devotee' of the Hindu goddess, and writes:

> The Sultan Zain-ul-abidin ... established civic peace after decades of anarchy and violence, while at the same time reinstituting courtly patronage of Sanskrit learning. This represents a fascinating experiment in cross-cultural communication, which has yet to receive the scholarly attention it merits.[18]

The Turkish sultan is presented as a good ruler who tried to help sustain Sanskrit literature. However, Pollock claims that the Hindus were too corrupt and degenerate, so the sultan's best efforts could not reverse the demise of Sanskrit.

We might note that when Sultan Zain-ul-abidin wanted to have an epiphany of Sharada Devi in his dream, but failed, according to one account he destroyed her murti! Pollock cites a source explaining the destruction of the murti as having been dictated by the goddess herself: 'The goddess "made him smash to pieces her own image".'[19] The sultan, following her express command, pulverized her murti! He leaves the reader wondering whether this behaviour was caused by 'the general evils of the Kali age' or by 'the new ruling lineage'.[20] Either way, he picks his historical sources and plucks out juicy quotes from them.

With these anecdotes of the sultans and the Mughal court, Pollock exonerates the Muslim kings of any role in the decay of the genre of Sanskrit kavya produced under royal patronage. However, all he has really shown is the relative absence of political kavya that depended upon kings, and nothing more; but he projects this as the death of all of Sanskrit.

Hindus, he says, were unable to produce an intellectual response to the Islamic invasions, because these invasions brought new identities and social and political structures. Here Pollock stands in a long line of Western scholars who accuse the victims of conquest of being intellectually too weak to resist. After destroying the Native American culture, white Americans had written in a similar manner to denigrate their victims – arguing that the Native American cultures were to be blamed because they were not strong enough to respond. In the case of African Americans, whose cultures, identities and kinship groups were shredded apart through slavery, the accusation is often made that they have failed to establish resilient families. The allegation is Pollock's own unconscious projection of the white American experience of justifying its oppressiveness by blaming the victims. It is the ghost of Pollock's American Orientalism gleaming through. This is the oppressor's habit of blaming the victims' inferiority for their plight.

I get the impression that Pollock does not want to dwell on whether Muslim invasions had debilitated the Hindu political and intellectual institutions in the first place. He does not examine the devastation suffered by Hindu rulers that made it difficult to have large-scale wealthy and politically powerful institutions to match the power of the Muslims. Throughout Pollock's analysis, hardly any Muslim ruler gets blamed for the destruction of Indian culture. *He simply avoids discussing the issue of Muslim invasions and their destructive influence on Hindu institutions!*

Among other things, he gives too little weight to the way in which Sanskrit knowledge production and creativity suffered as a result of the destruction of the Nalanda University complex in the late twelfth century during the Muslim Mamluk dynasty. The university hosted as many as 10,000 students, not only from India but other countries as well, including faraway places like China. Its destruction would be proportionate (in terms of the total population of India then and now) to more than the destruction of all the Indian institutions teaching technology, medicine, law and management today. What impact would such destruction have on the current intellectual capital of India?[21]

If, as Pollock asserts, the responsibility for sponsoring knowledge systems and works of kavya had earlier belonged to the Hindu rulers and elites, then he cannot dismiss outright the responsibility of Muslim destroyers for dismantling the old learning systems and for their failure to establish any new ones in Sanskrit. He does acknowledge that the '*civic ethos* embodied in the court' had eroded dramatically but fails to correlate this with the fact that the courts were increasingly under Muslim control.

In his discussion of Kashmir, one of the foremost sites for his theory of the death of Sanskrit, he also neglects to mention the two incursions Kashmir faced at the time, one led by the Mongol Dulca from the west and the other by Rinchana from the north.[22] The impact of various invasions in Kashmir was so enormous that it cannot be ignored in any historical analysis. It destabilized the social and political structures and affected Sanskrit cultural production far more than any pre-existing Hindu weakness. The negligence of Hindu kings may have been one factor, but the other causes were probably far more serious and must not be ignored.

I will now turn to Pollock's assertion that the Mughal court under Akbar opened up to Sanskrit scholars in the late sixteenth century. In response to this claim, I submit that his statement must be seen in the broader context of the entire Mughal dynasty and not just one of its emperors:

- The brief interlude (just over two decades) for Sanskrit scholars began with Akbar's Din-e-Ilahi initiative (which provided a platform for non-Muslim religions to participate in the court) around the 1580s and went into decline after Akbar's death in 1605.
- The next emperor, Jahangir, was supposed to have continued a degree of openness to non-Persian cultures, even though Persian was *always the only official language* of Mughal India.
- His successor, Shah Jahan, was a more orthodox Muslim than his father and grandfather. Upon his accession, he adopted new policies that steadfastly reversed Akbar's relatively liberal treatment of non-Muslims. Shah Jahan imposed Sharia-based provisions against the construction or repairs of Hindu temples, and subsequently ordered the demolition of newly built Hindu temples. He celebrated Islamic festivals with great pomp and grandeur and with an enthusiasm unfamiliar to his predecessors.
- After 1658, with Aurangzeb in power, there was no doubt that Islam was the only religion and Persian the only language patronized by the Mughal court. There was no question of Sanskrit scholarship being promoted in the Mughal court.

I would like readers to bear in mind the overall fragmentation of political power in India when the Muslims started to consolidate their stranglehold. During this period, Hindu rulers were squeezed into ever smaller and isolated territories. Small and localized Hindu kingdoms meant that the production of literature sponsored by them tended to be local; hence, it was being increasingly done in local languages. And once again, foreign disruption played a significant role in the rise of what Pollock calls 'vernacular consciousness'. Thus, Pollock's stance that Sanskrit literary culture decayed and disappeared despite Mughal patronage deserves to be challenged.

Contrary to Pollock's stand on the matter, the destabilization of the social and the political domains due to Muslim invasions from the north of India must be considered as a cause for the stagnation and decay of Sanskrit literary culture. There is further evidence to support this: In the south of India, in the sixteenth century and beyond, there continued to be an effervescence of Sanskrit literary production. The impact of the Muslim invasions on the geographical regions that are now Kerala, Tamil Nadu and south-eastern Andhra was relatively minimal. Pollock does not adequately consider the social and political stability in the south of India, which was distant from the most destructive Muslim invasions being experienced in the north and east of India. For example, the sixteenth-century flourishing of Appaya Dikshita's kavya and further development of the theory of kavya in the south is documented by Yigal Bronner.[23] This fermentation and cross-pollination of kavya theory and practice across regions of India from the twelfth to the seventeenth centuries are further proof that Sanskrit was vibrantly alive at the time.

There is a serious contradiction in the way Pollock accounts for the role of Muslims in India. On the one hand, in his paper on 'Ramayana and the Indian Imagination', he claims that prior to the twelfth century there had been no 'cult of Rama' and that the popularity of the Ramayana in the social and political imagination took hold from the twelfth to the fourteenth centuries, specifically as a *reaction against Muslims from Central Asia*. Contradicting this, in his thesis on the death of Sanskrit, he claims that during the same period there was no impact of Muslims.

This contradiction between his two accounts, published separately, is serious: Muslim invasions created a traumatic enough shockwave to cause

Hindu kings to mobilize the 'cult of Rama' and therefore the Hindus funded the production of extensive Ramayana texts for this agenda. And yet, the death of Sanskrit taking place at the same time had little relation to the arrival of Muslims. When Hindus are to be blamed for their alleged hatred towards Muslims, the Muslims are shown to have an important presence; but when Muslims are to be protected from being assigned any responsibility for destruction, they are mysteriously made to disappear from the scene.

Accusing other Indian languages of killing Sanskrit

Pollock cites another factor that he feels led to the death of Sanskrit: 'heightened competition among a new range of languages seeking literary-cultural dignity'. He writes:

> Sanskrit, the idiom of a cosmopolitan literature, gradually died, in part because cosmopolitan talk made less and less sense in an increasingly regionalized world. In addition to the weakening of the political framework that had traditionally sustained Sanskrit, and the growing dominance of vernacular cultural consciousness, the failure of what appear to be new forms of sociality to achieve institutional embodiment or to attain clear conceptualization may have played a role.[24]

In other words, according to him, because a certain political framework (i.e., cosmopolitan Sanskrit-based Hindu kingship) was weakened, Sanskrit itself was weakened. When Hindu kings became localized, it made no sense for them to patronize cosmopolitan Sanskrit. Additionally he sees that there was a growth of 'vernacular consciousness' and various other changes, but that Sanskrit did not reinvent itself in the face of these; hence it died.

Sparing British colonialism and Nehruvianism

Pollock also turns his gaze to the twentieth century, specifically post-1947. He makes a sweeping statement that Sanskrit is long dead. He says that if Sanskrit is showing any sign at all of 'quasi-animation', it is only because of artificial life support supplied by the Government of India. He mocks Sanskrit as a dying patient being kept artificially alive:

> Its cultivation [post-1947] constitutes largely an exercise in nostalgia for those directly involved, and, for outsiders, a source of bemusement that such communication takes place at all. Government feeding tubes and oxygen tanks may try to preserve the language in a state of quasi-animation, but most observers would agree that, in some crucial way, Sanskrit is dead.[25]

Pollock is thus bemused that Indians are using Sanskrit to remind themselves of their supposedly glorious past.

He also subtly insinuates that the decay of Sanskrit prior to 1947 had nothing to do with the British. An important part of Pollock's style is to casually mention statements from the opposing view, ostensibly to cover himself, but then to abandon them and return to the argument he wants to prove. For instance, he does acknowledge the following, tucked away in an obscure place in his writings:

> The two centuries before European colonialism decisively established itself in the subcontinent around 1750 constitute one of the most innovative epochs of Sanskrit systematic thought (in language analysis, logic, hermeneutics, moral-legal philosophy, and the rest). Thinkers produced new formulations of old problems, in entirely new discursive idioms, in what were often new scholarly genres employing often a new historicist framework; some even called themselves (or, more often, their enemies) 'the new' scholars (*navya*). Concurrently with the spread of European power, however, this dynamism diminished so much that by 1800, the capacity of Sanskrit thought to make history had vanished.[26]

Here he appears to be suggesting that Europeans are to blame for disrupting Sanskrit, but this is not what he is actually saying at all. A closer reading of the entire paper reveals a subtlety: although 'the spread of European power' was happening 'concurrently' with Sanskrit's decline, it was not, in his view, the cause of the decline. His argument is that just because X and Y occurred concurrently, it does not mean X caused Y. That is what he says here and elsewhere concerning whether the British had any role to play in this disruption.

In his treatment of the British period, at times he depicts the British as the heroes of Sanskrit. He remarks that Europe became the centre of Sanskrit studies in the eighteenth and nineteenth centuries, and goes on to cite sporadic attempts by the British to revive Sanskrit in India. He attributes the Hindus' failure to revive Sanskrit to their lack of having 'the structures for collective action'. He is hinting at social injustice that prevents the collective action needed to make progress. His arguments as to what caused the death of Sanskrit are elaborate and support his position that the Hindus are to blame and for reasons internal to Sanskrit and its culture.

The Sanskrit Commission established by the Indian government soon after Independence produced a report in 1957 that gives a different account from Pollock's view concerning the role of British rule in undermining Sanskrit. This report shows the systematic undermining of Sanskrit as a deliberate policy of the colonialists, starting in the nineteenth century. (I shall hereinafter refer to this report as the 'Sanskrit Commission Report', noting that there is currently a second Sanskrit Commission that was established in 2013 whose report has not become public as of this writing.)

There were many controversies and arguments amongst the British rulers concerning what was best for Indians. The most famous debate was between the British camps known as the Orientalists and the Anglicists, respectively. The backdrop was that a large number of British people regarded their language, literature and culture as distinctly superior to those of the Indians and hence wanted these imposed upon the Indians in their own best interest. However, what eventually helped this view to prevail was the growing section of newly westernized Indians who sincerely believed in the necessity for Indians to study in the English medium. They felt the indigenous schools of higher learning (pathashalas) were unable to compete. The prestige of the English language opened up superior job opportunities under British rule.

The Orientalists (as 'good cops') wanted to introduce English but alongside Sanskrit, based on the Orientalist writings on Sanskrit. Eventually, the Anglicists won in their call for imposing English-medium education for Indians. This manifested in the form of the Hindu College of Calcutta. It was meant to teach Hindu boys primarily English language and some modern subjects; Sanskrit also was introduced into its curriculum several years later.

The earlier influence of the Orientalists as 'good cops' quickly faded away. English-medium education rapidly gained popularity. This culminated in Lord Macaulay's famous Minute of 1835, which sought to produce 'a class of persons, Indians in blood and colour, but English in taste, in opinions, in morals and in intellect'. Macaulay called an immediate stop to all printing of Arabic and Sanskrit books, abolition of the madrasas and the Sanskrit College in Calcutta, and solid support for the English-medium in Banaras.

In 1844, the British government passed a resolution declaring for the first time that employment preference would be given to those educated in the British system. The educational policy of the East India Company became aligned with the new ideal of 'Western knowledge through English'.

There was eventually a countermovement in favour of Sanskrit by Indian nationalists, including Balgangadhar Tilak, Madan Mohan Malaviya and Mohandas Gandhi. Although several Indian maharajas organized libraries of manuscripts and set up Sanskrit colleges alongside, by then irreparable damage had been done.

Despite many attempts and announcements of the death of Sanskrit over the previous hundred years, one finds substantial evidence to the contrary. As K.M. Panikkar notes, we see new Sanskrit works in many places, such as rebuttals in the form of *Satyagraha Gita* by Pandita Kshama Row. The Purva and Uttara volumes of *Satyagraha Gita* were published in 1944. Both were composed in the arsha meter of Anushtubh chhanda, in which the mahakavyas were largely composed. In the foreword, to the *Uttara Satyagraha Gita*, K.M. Panikkar wrote an extended discussion of this issue:

In Sanskrit more than in any other language women poets have at all times been held in high honour. Apart from quotations in well-known anthologies, many notable works by women poets of earlier times have come down to us. Among them may be mentioned the well-known political drama *Kaumudi Mahotsava*, Queen Ganga Devi's *Kavya* entitled *Madhura Vijaya* and the *Champu Varadambika Parinaya*. Pandita Ksama Row, who is undoubtedly our most eminent Sanskrit poetess, is therefore the inheritor of a great tradition which she has upheld and enriched with great distinction. Her earlier publications, especially *Katha Panchakam* and *Mīra Lahrī*, have earned for her an honoured place not only among poets writing in Sanskrit, but in the modern Indian literary world. The *Purva Satyagraha Gita* brought her deserved fame as an epic poet, for in that volume she had, in the manner of Valmiki and Vyas, dealt with the story of Gandhiji's life up to the Gandhi-Irwin Pact. ... *It may seem strange that such a poem should be written today in Sanskrit which is held by some to be a dead language. It is necessary to emphasize that it is only out of ignorance that people call Sanskrit a dead language. It is the one language that unites India culturally, which is the repository of our living traditions, which unites our regional languages in a community of thought and form.* Can it not be legitimately claimed that the National Government of India should recognize this fact and give to Sanskrit the importance it deserves in our education? *Satyagraha Gita has shown that Sanskrit, in spite of neglect of the last hundred years, still holds an important place in the cultural life of India.*[27]

Pandita Kshama Row was the daughter of Shankar Pandurang Pandit, who was a noted Sanskrit scholar in the late nineteenth century.[28] Pandita Kshama Row's daughter, Smt. Leela Rao Dayal, continued the tradition of Sanskrit composition; her work includes an acclaimed Sanskrit play, *Jayantu Kumauniyah*, in 1967. There are other examples of family lineages which have produced Sanskrit literature in the twentieth century across multiple generations.

Besides Sanskrit kavya and natya production in the twentieth century, there was active development in the late nineteenth and early twentieth century of Sanskrit literary theory. This was in response to the encounter with Western philology, especially in Kerala. The following was written as a historical overview of Sanskrit literature published by the Sahitya Akademi in 1959:

> The historical study of Sanskrit language and its literature was made part of the courses of study; it was included in the curricula of studies even in the traditional Sanskrit Pathashalas. It was all the more necessary to inculcate the historical and critical perspective in the Pandit. Thus there arose the Sanskrit prose accounts on the modern science of Comparative Philology, with special reference to the Indo-European, and the history of Sanskrit literature. Rajaraja Varma included in his *Laghupaninya* a supplement on Indo-European linguistics.[29]

There are dozens of other twentieth-century works: kavyas and advanced texts on alankara and many other disciplines. Pollock's research has not adequately considered these extensive Sanskrit works of the nineteenth and twentieth centuries. He expresses perplexity and contempt for what he sees as the vain efforts of Indians to keep a comatose culture alive.

Contrary to Pollock's views that the decline of Sanskrit was inevitable due to its own social oppressiveness, the Sanskrit Commission in the 1950s concluded otherwise. While Pollock's views are largely developed sitting in a library, the Commission conducted extensive field surveys across India to document the state of Sanskrit in all segments of society. Its report concludes that 'untenable is the attitude which becomes evident in the unfortunate propaganda that Sanskrit is the language of a particular community'. The fact that Sanskrit was, even as late as the 1950s, held in high regard by numerous non-brahmin communities across India is worth quoting in detail:

> That Sanskrit does not belong to any particular community is proved by Andhra and Kerala where the entire non-Brahman classes are imbued with Sanskrit and speak a language highly saturated with Sanskrit. In Kerala, even Izhavas, Thiyas, Moplas and Christians read

> Sanskrit. In Madhya Pradesh, we were told, a paper in Sanskrit was compulsory at the School Final Examination and even Muslims took it. In a Lucknow Intermediate College, there are Muslim girls studying Sanskrit; in Gujarat, Parsis study it; in Panjab, there are several Sikhs among Sanskrit students and teachers, and Sastris and research scholars in Sanskrit. The Director of Public Instruction of Madhya Pradesh, who is a Christian, told us that he advised the Anglo-Indian students also to read Sanskrit. ... In the course of our tours in South India, we interviewed several non-Brahmans in high position and active in public life, business, etc., and we found them all favourable to Sanskrit.
>
> It was again the non-Brahmans, particularly the great benefactors belonging to the Chettiar community, who had, in the recent past, endowed many Pathashalas for Veda and Sanskrit. As we moved among the people, in the temples and the streets, in public and private meetings, we found that, in Tamil Nadu, the antipathy towards Sanskrit was confined to a section trying to make political capital out of it, and that it was strongly organised and effectively expressed.[30]

Having presented arguments against Pollock's position, I do agree with him that there has been a deterioration of Sanskrit in India in the Nehruvian period after Independence. However, he is silent about the fact that the revival and renewed attention given to Sanskrit have been routinely attacked as 'Hindu chauvinism' by his leftist collaborators who perceive it as a threat to diversity, to Muslims, to Dalits, and to 'the oppressed masses' in general.

He sidesteps the rise in the funding of Persian and Arabic by the secular Indian government and by foreign sponsors, and the concurrent dramatic decline in Sanskrit funding. He does not expose the downsizing and dismantling of the institutions, both formal and informal, on which Sanskrit and sanskriti have traditionally thrived. Pollock is careful not to implicate the non-Hindu forces that have wreaked havoc against Sanskrit.

Silence on the extraction and digestion of Sanskrit shastras into the West

As we saw in Chapter 3, Pollock differentiates between Sanskrit shastra (knowledge systems) and Sanskrit kavya (literature). He translates kavya as 'fiction' and shastra as 'nonfiction normative texts'. By reducing shastras to the level of normative texts, he is suggesting they are driven by religious and moral concerns, not by the quest for creative and critical knowledge. We saw that he sidelines Sanskrit-based knowledge systems; had these been included, Sanskrit would be far from dead in terms of knowledge production.

Many of the Crown jewels of Indian heritage come from shastras – in mathematics, biology, medicine, linguistics, astronomy, philosophy, adhyatma-vidya, physics, political thought, etc. These large domains that he excludes from his analysis are precisely where many Indians today are bringing about revivals. His omissions and silences have not yet been noticed and problematized adequately. When he does mention shastras, it is to assert that they are prescriptive constraints, rather than platforms for innovation.

In his description of the state of Sanskrit in the British colonial period, Pollock acknowledges and deplores the impact of the transfer of Sanskrit studies to European universities and their comparative neglect in India, where the policy was to spread English. However, he does not give full weight to the way in which Sanskrit was ensconced at the heart of the intellectual life of Europe for over a hundred years.

Pollock also does not explain that the oldest copies of core Sanskrit texts (i.e., those that had survived Islamic destruction) were taken from India to European research centres. These manuscripts are still in Western hands and there has been no movement by scholars like Pollock (or anyone else) to get them back to India. Chamu Krishna Shastry has told me that approximately 500,000 Sanskrit manuscripts are lying outside India today, and most of them are still unpublished.

Pollock is also silent on the fact that considerable mining of Sanskrit knowledge systems is now under way, and in the very same academic system where he works.

Chamu Krishna Shastry responds on behalf of the tradition

A far superior explanation for the decline of Sanskrit has been offered by Chamu Krishna Shastry, head of Samskrita Bharati . Contrary to Pollock's view that spoken Sanskrit for ordinary laukika purposes was non-existent, Krishna Shastry maintains the exact opposite: that spoken Sanskrit was what gave Sanskrit its strength, and that the decline of Sanskrit was correlated in large part with its decline in usage for common speech.

His explanations for the decline covers historical, social and individual factors. They include a frank acknowledgement of the social problems upon which the American Orientalists also ruminate. In a paragraph worth citing in full, he writes:

> How then did such a language cease to be encountered in common usage? Many may be the causes ... Historical reasons could be ones such as the blossoming of regional languages; resorting to languages other than Samskrita by the propounders of new schools of thought; shrinkage of royal patronage; the invasion of foreigners; the destruction of the mathas and mandiras; and so on. Social reasons could be ones such as – lack of Samskrita education for women; the growth of social evils; the transformation of the varna-system into the jati-system; the creation of schisms such as high and low, and touchable and untouchable, etc.; cultural imperialism; the rule of mere convention, and so forth. And among individual causes are: not taking up desirable and adequate measures for the protection of the language commensurate with the changed times or changing times; non-understanding of the etiology of the ailment; and so on.[31]

Krishna Shastry goes on to note that when such a decline took place, a certain formal convention emerged to protect the essence of the language, but at the cost of the willingness of the common folk to speak it for fear of breaking the rules. Gradually, even scholars gave up the use of Sanskrit for daily transactions and it was used only for technical discussions among scholars and for writing books. This led to an increase in rules, which protected it for rigour and high standards, but also made it tougher for casual speakers who were not so sophisticated.

Unlike Pollock, Krishna Shastry gives considerable weight to the devastation dealt to Sanskrit under the British. The closing of all traditional Sanskrit schools (pathashalas) and the self-serving propaganda that Sanskrit was dead were powerful and decisive blows by colonialism. According to Krishna Shastry, the pivot for undermining Sanskrit was the method of teaching that was forcibly changed by the British. This was extremely damaging. He writes:

> In the past, Samskrita was being taught in the Samskrita medium. The language and lexicon used to be taught first, and grammar was taught only thereafter. But the British did not use this method. The method of teaching via grammar and translation, a 200-year-old method, was brought to India by them. The consequence was that students were able to comprehend Samskrita literature, and were able to translate, but they did not get the ability to *use* Samskrita. The currency of the language was completely lost.[32]

The British imposition was to reverse the traditional system in which oral fluency was taught first and grammar later. As a result, students trained in the British system learned grammar to be able to comprehend and even translate, but could not speak the language. Over time, the British took control over the publication of written works. Indians became mere consumers of Sanskrit and no longer producers of its texts.

The 'grammar method' introduced by the British was already being used by them to teach Greek and Latin, both seen as dead languages. The traditional Indian way had been to teach vyakarana (grammar) through the language itself. However, under the colonial Orientalists, 'Bhandarkar Readers' were produced in Pune to change the system such that vyakarana (grammar) was taught in English, not in Sanskrit.

Previously, all commentaries on Sanskrit and its texts were written in Sanskrit. About 80 per cent of the surviving 4.5 million traditional manuscripts dealing with Sanskrit were written in Sanskrit language using various scripts; this implies that Sanskrit discourse was self-sufficient. However, the British changed this by making English the medium of teaching Sanskrit and the medium for discussing and analysing it. As a result, almost every commentary or interpretation concerning Sanskrit is now written in English.

In fact, Krishna Shastry explains that Sanskrit grammar was *rewritten to match the style of English grammar*. It is unfortunate that most books about Sanskrit (including, unfortunately, my own) are now being written in English and not in Sanskrit. Consequently, Sanskrit is now an *object* of study from the outsider perspective and has lost its own voice.

In explaining the importance of the traditional method of learning, Krishna Shastry discusses the importance of the transmission of a mother tongue from parent to child. He stresses here the primacy of sound in human cognition, a factor that American Orientalism and postmodern scholarship in general tend to dismiss. The natural stages of a child's relationship to the mother tongue are: 1) hearing, 2) speaking, 3) reading, and 4) writing. Unfortunately, today this is taught in reverse sequence, which is artificial.

He says that only the knowledge that is backed by usage truly conveys the dharma. Even in purely practical terms, the encouragement of spoken Sanskrit is the only way to convey ideas to the common people and to those who are not specialists. Hearing and speaking are not extra features added on to the transmission of a language through time; they are key elements. As Krishna Shastry says, 'The royal way, the easy way, and the short way for the acquisition of any language is conversation through that language.'[33] 'Teaching the language itself, not teaching *about* the language' is a key principle here.

Krishna Shastry then deals with three modern objections to the encouragement of spoken Sanskrit: that it is difficult, that it is lifeless and that it is the language of a particular caste. He responds that the notion of Sanskrit being difficult is largely because of the way it is taught, and of the bombastic and pretentious way in which many scholars and pandits use it. This makes it intimidating. On the other hand, when it is conveyed through speaking, there are bodily supports, hand gestures and facial expressions that make it easier to grasp the meaning.

He says that we must accept the importance of speech competence for daily use, and not simply for scholarly lecturing. If we are 'bereft of conversation', he notes, and mere lectures are delivered, this would be an actual *disservice* to Sanskrit. Furthermore, if Sanskrit speakers resolutely engage as many people as possible in speech, without regard to caste or gender or religion, then the allegation that Sanskrit is just the language of a brahmin elite will no longer be sustainable.

Krishna Shastry then goes on to discuss aspects of Sanskrit that a secular philologist would simply dismiss as mystification. He speaks of a certain 'force' in the spoken word, and a 'spirit' that is not mentioned in the written form. That force awakens an enthusiasm which begins itself to bring the language alive.[34] A certain taste develops along with a sense of pride and mastery. He also argues, in a way that most Orientalists of any stripe would simply reject, that Sanskrit has certain unique qualities that have made India the 'jagad-guru', the preceptor of the world; and he finds the traces of this pride in the way that certain phrases dear to the Indian consciousness are almost always cited in Sanskrit.

Krishna Shastry cherishes a positive vision for the future of Sanskrit. Contrary to the view that it harbours social oppression, he finds in it a serious potential for uniting many schisms in society, even splits between castes, genders and religions. It can raise not just the social status but also the self-understanding and self-presentation of all socio-economic classes and genders. He notes that some of the most successful programmes for teaching spoken Sanskrit have been those in the slums.[35]

However, the potential benefits of Sanskrit cannot take place as long as it is relegated to the level of a classical, rather than a modern, language. I am glad that he rejects the branding of Sanskrit as 'classical', and writes:

> As long as Samskrita remains adorned by the label 'classical language', and as long as Samskrita does not sit in the line of modern languages, Samskrita will not be able to get the place that other Indian languages get, or importance, or the grants, etc.[36]

To revive it, I agree with Krishna Shastry that Sanskrit must once again become a language of innovation and change, absorbing new words from elsewhere, and inventing new ones internally as and when the need arises. The ultimate goal he feels is the production of shastra, helping the growth of knowledge; and conversation is the gateway. Krishna Shastry says there is nothing to fear in the use of Sanskrit in the public sphere, in the marketplace or the on the street; nor are efforts to retain its purity necessary. The fear that one will speak it incorrectly must be overcome. Even Patanjali insisted that while adharma may accrue from improper usage, refinement will come through usage, and it will eradicate the impurities over time.

Krishna Shastry speaks passionately of the dharmic duty to use Sanskrit even in everyday speech, and of the whole process of embracing it as a yajna. He takes great pains to indicate his respect for other languages, and constantly argues that spoken Sanskrit was not intended to replace any other language. Clearly, his spirited defence of Sanskrit, his insistence that it must be transmitted orally, and his positioning of the issue of its revival in the context of the perpetuation of dharma, distinguish him from the secular approach. At the same time, he is frank and accepting of the problems of discrimination and elitism that have haunted some parts of its history.

Krishna Shastry does not like to engage the question of whether Sanskrit is living or dead, since this way of framing only perpetuates the issue and keeps the negative notion alive. He says: 'By reiterating that Sanskrit is not a dead language, we are only doing a *neti-vada* – an argument of denial – and keeping the problem alive.'[37]

Before leaving this section, I wish to point out that Krishna Shastry's views are not some recent 'saffron' ideas. Many similar views were also expressed in the Sanskrit Commission Report written under the Nehru government in the 1950s. That report declares: 'The State in ancient India, it must be specially pointed out, freely patronised educational establishments, but left them to develop on their own lines, without any interference or control.' It says that until the British disruption, the salient features of our traditional education included: 'oral instruction, insistence on moral discipline and character-building, freedom in the matter of the courses of study, absence of extraneous control ...' The report is a historical record of the era immediately after Independence; it explains just how important Sanskrit was considered by the newly independent Indian government at that time:

> After Independence, the Constituent Assembly ... [felt] that if the binding force of Sanskrit was taken away, the people of India would cease to feel that they were parts of a single culture and a single nation. ... We can never insist too strongly on this signal fact that Sanskrit has been the Great Unifying Force of India, and that India with its nearly 400 millions of people is One Country, and not half a dozen or more countries, only because of Sanskrit.

It says that India in the 1950s faces 'the growth of fissiparous tendencies ...' which I have called forces breaking India; and that Sanskrit is important to help 'build up character and the faculties of the mind and spirit in general'.

The report praised the traditional pathashala system for its 'remarkably close contact between the teacher and the pupil' in which there was a transmission from human to human whereas in the modern system it is a mass production method of teaching. In the traditional system, education was personalized and 'there was no rigidity regarding time-table and curriculum'. The report is at the same time also critical of the pathashala system because it failed to adapt to the changing times and remained static and isolated.

A noteworthy point in the report is that it praises the link between Sanskrit and religion/dharma in the traditional education, as contrasted with the secular approach in modern universities: 'For the pathasalas, education is part of a living religious tradition. In the University, education is carried on in a secular atmosphere.' The report is critical of the Western-style university approach and in particular the 'historical method' that Pollock also uses:

> In a good many cases, the knowledge obtained by the [westernized] University student is second hand. The very historical method, which is claimed to be a characteristic feature of University Sanskrit Education, is liable to degenerate into a superficial antiquarian attitude; religious and philosophical texts come to be studied as relics of the past. ... Thus the University student is apt to become estranged from his heritage, an uneasy sojourner in the domain of his own native culture. ... The relation of Sanskrit to Indian Languages and to Indian culture

> is not that of a past historical antecedent to its successor; it is that of a continuing perennial source to its tributary streams. Sanskrit has been supplying the literary and cultural norms down the ages. An intimate knowledge of Sanskrit is essential for understanding the systems of philosophy and religion which constitute the pride of Indian achievement.

The report cites the advice that was given to Western Indologists by Louis Renou, the prominent French Indologist. I feel that today this advice applies to Pollock and other American Orientalists. Renou wrote:

> What the Western Indologist needs to do is to renounce his Aristotelian norms of thought which have become so natural to him that he finds it difficult to believe they are not valid for everybody. He must resolutely unlearn a part of what European humanism has bequeathed to him – the heritage of the Mediterranean World which he gloriously translated into universal terms.

Western academic critiques of Pollock

Pollock's positions have also been criticized by some Western scholars. One such critic is J. Hanneder, who finds him reaching conclusions by using evidence that is 'often arbitrary'.[38] Hanneder is sympathetic to Pollock's goal of 'expose(ing) pseudo-scientific propaganda' emanating from 'modern Indian nationalism with its distorting reconstructions of India's past'. No one can say Hanneder is a friend of Hindu nationalist politics; yet he disagrees with Pollock on matters of intellectual rigour. He finds Pollock taking too many liberties with the evidence.

Hanneder cites several examples to demonstrate that Pollock has interpreted the evidence to fit his thesis 'without considering other options' and often with the use of exaggerated, misleading or outright false data. He says, 'Pollock has over interpreted the evidence to support his theory.' Hanneder even grasps the underlying political motivation here, as I do, saying that Pollock is perhaps driven by 'his understandable anger over current nationalistic statements about Sanskrit and indeed new attempts at resanskritization'.[39]

Hanneder writes that he can easily disprove a number of Pollock's statements, most notably his statement that in Kashmir, 'Sanskrit literary writing of any sort from the period after Zain-ul-abidin is rare.' One has only to refer to the works of the Kashmiri writer Sahib Kaul (seventeenth century) and his followers, Hanneder points out. These works encapsulate religious developments in Kashmir, contradicting Pollock's declaration that Sanskrit in Kashmir is 'culture reduced to reinscription and restatement'. There are also other major innovations in that period such as an indigenous grammatical tradition with its own uniqueness.[40]

Hanneder also notes that even though Pollock rests his argument solely on kavya, he overextends the scope of his conclusions to include the whole Sanskrit tradition. One cannot so easily dismiss developments in logic, tantra, mathematics and other domains during that period. For instance, Hanneder notes the massive output of Sanskrit works in tantra in that period. He takes Pollock to task for using data selectively and not accurately:

> I fear that his argument loses much of its force. If there really was a break in activity, it is strange that many genres of Sanskrit literature not only recovered in the next generations, but sprang, from our perspective, into an unprecedented activity. Furthermore I doubt that our catalogues of datable works are really complete enough to exclude that anything of poetical worth was written during the tenth century. [...] The present state of research does not permit conclusions from supposedly negative evidence.[41]

Hanneder also faults Pollock for asserting that in the Vijayanagara kingdom the learned Sanskrit scholars merely reproduced old works and did not produce anything new or original. He cites counter-examples of intellectual giants like Vidyaranya and Sayana, whose original works came to be considered among the fundamental Hindu tenets. He dismisses Pollock's assertion as a 'surprising statement produced by the necessities of argumentation, rather than through evidence'.[42]

Hanneder also challenges Pollock's declaration that 'most observers would agree that, in some crucial way, Sanskrit is dead'. He considers this misleading for popular usage and ambiguous for academic usage. As he points out:

> Sanskrit is quite obviously not as dead as other dead languages and the fact that it is spoken, written and read will probably convince most people that it cannot be a dead language in the most common usage of the term.[43]

Below is a short list of Hanneder's point-by-point criticisms of Pollock's scholarship on the history of Sanskrit:

- Pollock complains about modern Hindus introducing Sanskrit in pathashalas, seeing it as Hindu nationalism at work. This allegation is wrong according to Hanneder because, 'There is no reason to assume that this everyday use of Sanskrit in *pathashalas* is a recent invention.'[44]
- The large quantity of 'low quality work' in Sanskrit to which Pollock refers could also indicate that it was being used to spread Sanskrit education at popular levels (which is in accordance with Krishna Shastry's recommendations), rather than being an indicator of scholarly incompetence in an entire period.
- Pollock's judgements on what comprises 'good quality' of Sanskrit works are arbitrary and disputable.
- Pollock arbitrarily identifies certain theories as 'core', such as hermeneutics and literary theory. He uses these as his sole barometers for evaluating the status of Sanskrit at a given time and place.
- Pollock sees the lack of activity in the production of kavya as a sign of lifelessness. Hanneder responds: 'Perhaps the parallel with the decline of Latin leads him to take the production of religious literature as less indicative of an alive Sanskrit culture, while the religious Stotra is for this reason not a valid genre for him!'[45]
- Soon after 1835, Indians were allowed to own printing machines and soon there was an enormous boost in Sanskrit and in the output of other Indian languages. Yet Pollock misses this

phenomenon completely when he claims that 'there was no sustained creation of new literature – no Sanskrit novels, personal poetry, essays – giving voice to the new subjectivity'.[46]

- Pollock is overconfident in his dating of certain texts. He comes up with dates to fit his scenario and chronology of events. Hanneder writes: 'Our dating of many a Sanskrit author of this time does not permit such detailed arguments.' He is saying that scholars today cannot date many texts so precisely as to be able to reach the broad conclusions Pollock makes.
- There is a long list of important Sanskrit works belonging to the period after Pollock's so-called 'last Sanskrit poet', but he turns a blind eye to them. Furthermore, there are more writers of that period who were studied in India but who 'were almost completely ignored by Western Indology'. There are many examples of Sanskrit being alive in the period when Pollock declares it to be dead.

Hanneder lists the following among the innovations in Sanskrit production in that era:

> The first is the development of a particular brand of Campū from the 10th century onward. The other is the recent adaptation in Sanskrit literature of new genres like that of the modern short story. One, in my view, particularly impressive synthesis of classical Sanskrit style and the modern social critical short story is found in Kṣamā Rao's (1880-1954) works. It would not be surprising to find more of this sort in the Sanskrit literature of the 19th and 20th century. One should also not forget that the transformation of Sanskrit Pandits who came in contact with or were under the influence of the British education system in India, are not only examples for the power of the 'Sanskritic culture' to adapt and interact with modernity ... [47]

The most disturbing thing Hanneder points out is Pollock's habit of exaggerating and manipulating the references in the literature being cited. Sometimes Pollock even outright misquotes these references. For example, Hanneder says Pollock misquoted Ingalls by making it seem that the latter had considered Sanskrit dead. This is false. *The statement made by Ingalls was that although court patronage had been withdrawn, the traditions of Sanskrit scholarship continued.* Pollock cites this in such a way as to suggest that Ingalls supported the death-of-Sanskrit thesis. Contrarily, what Ingalls wrote is as follows:

> The traditions of Sanskrit scholarship, however, were not broken. The brahmins living in the capital or on their tax-free grants of land saw that their sons were taught Sanskrit grammar and the traditional Sanskrit sciences, in many cases teaching their sons themselves. The tradition was especially well maintained in Śaiva philosophy and literary criticism.[48]

Hanneder also warns against assuming that Sanskrit was not a language of common usage in daily life. Such assumptions, Hanneder warns, suggest that we could be 'projecting our own suppositions without any evidence'. He feels that many times in its long history, Sanskrit has 'changed' rather than died, because it got reinvented each time.

He finds that Pollock has a 'fundamental cultural misunderstanding', owing to his being a westerner:

> To the traditional Indian mind the cyclic renewal of cultural phenomena is not necessarily viewed as problematic. One predominant modern western concept of historical change is in comparison teleologically conceived as a development that has culminated in the present achievements. But we cannot overlook the fact that just as Kalhana held that good poets revive the style of former poets, modern Indian critics of contemporary Sanskrit poetry seem to have significantly less problems with the renewal of Sanskrit than many a Western scholar. For academic purposes it is far more interesting and fruitful to understand the underlying thought structures than to prove that the idea of renewal is historically wrong, and that those who favour it are desperately attempting to resurrect a language from the dead.[49]

The history of attempts to 'kill' Sanskrit

Based on all my studies of various accounts thus far, I feel further research is needed to understand what exactly happened historically concerning the rise and decline of various Indian languages. However, provisionally, I offer the following summary of the factors causing the decline of Sanskrit. I list eight stages in this process, many of which run in parallel and feed each other:

1. Sanskrit was taught orally by listening and speaking. It was the language of choice used in courts, scholarship, popular poetry and analytical shastras.
2. State support for Sanskrit declined, replaced by foreign languages that became the official languages (first Persian, then English).
3. Sanskrit education was radically altered by imposing the method of formal grammar (and eliminating the oral method) and by using English as the medium of instruction. This gave a boost to English as the language of learning and thinking, with Sanskrit as a mere 'topic' or subject matter to be studied in English. This was the golden age of Orientalism and Western philology. While claiming to be its champions, these Orientalists had the effect of reducing Indians from being knowledge producers to being knowledge consumers.
4. There was (and continues to be) a widespread public abuse of Sanskrit-based Hindu practices such as yajna, meditation, puja, etc., because these are seen as primitive and as obstructions to 'progress'. These practices had to go underground, or they became sidelined as merely nostalgic and meant for public display. This undermined the application of Sanskrit that previously served as the mainstay for its support.
5. Many Sanskrit pandits and scholars betrayed their tradition and switched over to join the other side, because of better personal opportunities. This has accelerated after India's Independence.
6. Sanskrit was no longer studied as a linguistic and intellectual technology for composing new works. Its study became largely for the purpose of translating its old works into English, thereby enriching the English database of content and knowledge. Sanskrit

texts became irrelevant because they were increasingly available in English with greater ease of access and prestige. This has facilitated the process of digestion of sanskriti into Western universalism.

7. Sanskrit pramanas (means of knowing), siddhantas (theories and conclusions) and other intellectual systems have become replaced by Western hermeneutics and critical theories. Sanskritists in the academic world are expected to use Western theories when discussing Sanskrit texts. I have cited many examples of this occurring in Pollock's work.
8. Sanskrit texts are being studied mainly as the source material to locate abuses in Indian civilization, in the Vedas, and in modern Hinduism. This is so because we live in the age of Western human rights and liberation philology.

Pollock's theory of Indian languages includes his assertions about the rise of Sanskrit, followed by the rise of the vernaculars, accompanied by the death of Sanskrit. Each of these three significant developments was allegedly driven by political considerations in maintaining and expanding the king–brahmin hegemony over the people. (Also, curiously enough, his timing of the alleged death of Sanskrit is roughly synchronous with the death of Latin in Europe and the rise of the vernaculars there.) Contrary to his thesis, many scholars argue that Sanskrit continued to flourish, which is remarkable considering that it was downgraded by the imposition of Persian, and later, English, as the official language of India.

I have also mentioned that Pollock is opposed to the popular and oral revival of Sanskrit, because that would be diametrically opposite to his wish to make Sanskrit a classical language, like Greek and Latin, meant to be objectively studied mainly by the Western-trained elite.

It would be natural for some traditionalists to say that Pollock has a death wish for Sanskrit. He wants all Sanskrit studies to be conducted in English. This requires him to train the next generation of Indian Sanskrit scholars who will infuse the Indian discourse with his theories and those of his Western peers. The end result will be for English to get permanently established as the lingua franca of all Indians, powered by Western ideologies and idiom.

The reader is reminded that the Romans had declared Hellenistic traditions dead in order to remove them as a living threat, and digest from them whatever qualities they found useful. Similarly, the Native Americans had to be 'emptied' from the land to make the geography 'dead' in terms of human society, and this rendered it available for occupation by white settlements. In an analogous manner, it would not be entirely unreasonable to think of Pollock as a frontiersman wanting to make Sanskrit seem dead so he can champion its 'revival' in a way that would amount to the digestion of its useful elements into Western universalism.

The next section discusses a related position of Pollock that is extremely dangerous from the traditional viewpoint. While the foregoing sections of this chapter show his pronouncement that Sanskrit has been dead for a thousand years, when it comes to discussing Indian civilization and the Indian nation, his allegation is far more sinister: he claims that these never existed, and the claims of their existence are of relatively recent origins.

Rejecting Indian civilization and Indian nation

Pollock explicitly denies the notion of an Indian civilization or nation as a legitimate construct. He says that the important influences on the politics and general culture of India have always arrived from foreign places to its West. Thus, the notion of India as a civilization or nation is, in his view, an imported one.

I will show in this section that from his perspective the sense of 'Indianness', that there is an Indian nation, was itself a Western influence and that Indian civilization is an illegitimate premise constructed out of borrowings from the West.

Western influences shape so-called 'Indian civilization'

When explaining the history of the rise and fall of Sanskrit, Pollock looks for political causes that would have triggered these developments.

The speculation that intrigues him most is that the political and cultural influence could have entered India from the West. He cites many Greek and Persian influences on Sanskrit culture as evidence in support of this hypothesis.[50]

His list of claims of possible or likely Western influences on India includes the following:

- The European kings had played significant roles in the relationship between Greek and Latin in Europe. This might have influenced Indian kings to play similar roles concerning Sanskrit and vernaculars.
- Greek theatre existed in Gandhara (which is now in Afghanistan) and influenced Indian theatre. Thus, Sanskrit drama might have been an adaptation of Greek theatre.
- Greek sculpture was copied by Indian artisans in Afghanistan.
- A Sanskrit work written in India on horoscopes was translated from some lost Greek text. Thus Indian jyotish was shaped under Greek influences.
- A major Indian work on architecture was copied in almost every detail from a Greek text.
- A particular south Indian and Sri Lankan goddess was the result of a cultural transmission from Greece.
- Even the Ramayana might have been influenced by a translation of a work by Homer.

In proposing these ideas, Pollock once again gives an abundance of disparate data, though none is analysed for direct causation or for the direction in which the causation might have happened. He does not consider the possibility that the influence might have travelled in the opposite direction, i.e., from India outward into the West.

He ends the above list of 'potential causes' by nuancing his position with some uncertainty: 'Until more data becomes available to decide the matter, it remains an open question whether or not India and Rome participated at the eastern and western frontier, respectively, in the same system of literary-cultural circulation.'[51] He also lists a few key differences between the language experiences in Europe and India.[52]

Then, some 300 pages later in *The Language of the Gods*, he essentially repeats the same claims, this time with even more examples. He writes that the very notion of such a thing as 'Indianness' was not indigenous but came from the West:

> The Indianization of Southeast Asia was possible only because *Indianism in India itself was coming into being through new cultural inputs from the West*: the public display of royal inscriptions that began with Aśoka in the third century BCE, as well as his very idiom of rule, were borrowings from Achaemenid Persia; political inscription in Sanskrit began at the court of Śaka newcomers from western Asia. We have seen that an Indian called the 'Lord of the Greeks' invented Indian astrology by translating a Hellenistic horoscopy into Sanskrit in the mid-second century (the greater part of the Indian doctrine of omens and portents was likewise borrowed, from Mesopotamia), and that the author of the *Mānasāra*, a sixth-century Sanskrit work on architecture, adapted Vetruvius. Had we the eyes to see them, we might discover that Greeks and Romans left other traces of their literatures in the subcontinent as common as the *denarii* horded in Arikamedu in Tamilnadu and the shards embedded in the alluvium of the Bay of Bengal that bear 'the names of craftsmen whose kilns lay on the outskirts of Arezzo'.[53]

'Indianness', the sense that there is an Indian nation, was itself a Western influence, according to Pollock. His points in the above quote are worth restating as a simple list:

- Ashoka's royal inscriptions were an idea borrowed from Persia.
- In mid-second century CE, Indians translated Greek astrology into Sanskrit.
- The 'doctrine' of omens and portents was borrowed from Mesopotamia.
- The Greek work on architecture, *Vetruvius*, was adapted into the standard work on Hindu architecture, *The Manasara*, in the sixth century CE.

- Arikamedu, near Pondicherry (now Puducherry), was a trading place with Rome and Greece, so it is natural that archaeologists have found several ancient artefacts from those countries. Pollock does not provide any analysis to support his conclusion that Roman and Greek literature influenced Tamil works.

He surmises that westernization is more universal than is suggested merely by its influence on India. Persia, for example, is west of India and its influence may also be seen as a form of 'westernization'. He shows that the direction of civilizational influence has been from west to east even in other places: such as Germany influencing Russia, which lies to its east; England influencing France, to its east; and China influencing the western side of Japan.[54]

Such reductionist speculation would be fine if Pollock were willing to consider equally the possibility of influences flowing in the reverse direction. There is considerable evidence of Indian influence moving westward, but he chooses to ignore that.

No such thing as Indian civilization or nationhood

Pollock then debunks the notion of any such thing as an Indian civilization or an Indian nation. These are false notions, he insists. He refutes the theories of cultures and civilizations by scholars such as J.G. Herder, J.G. Fichte, Martin Heidegger, Alfred L. Kroeber, R.C. Majumdar, Alfred Foucher, O.W. Wolters, George Lakoff, Denys Lombard, Oswald Spengler, Arnold Toynbee and Samuel P. Huntington, among others. He argues:

> ... it is erroneous to think of a civilization, or a 'great tradition', as a unitary entity of whatever size. Indeed, a stable singularity called 'Indian culture', so often conjured up by Southeast Asian indigenists, never existed. What did exist was only a range of cultural and political codes and acts, many recently developed (Sanskrit *kāvya*, public inscriptions, free-standing temple buildings, quasi-universalist political imagery, land-grants to Brahmanical communities, and so on) and undoubtedly generated out of various local practices.[55]

Civilizations, he says, are processes without boundaries, and hence nothing can be considered 'indigenous'. He explains:

> All cultures participate in what are ultimately global networks of begging, borrowing, and stealing, imitating and emulating ... and it is false to claim an indigenous origin. Indian civilization or culture becomes nothing but an arbitrary moment illegitimately generalized, a freeze frame in a film taken for the whole story.[56]

Using this idea as a way to open up the topic, he sets about deconstructing the notion of an Indian nation. He uses many theories by westerners – mainly Hegel, Ernest Gellner, Benedict Anderson, Gramsci, Georg Lukacs and Mikhail Bakhtin – and uses them to argue that an Indian nation never existed.

In fact, the Pune project to develop the Critical Edition of the Sanskrit text of the Mahabharata after the First World War is seen by him as a bogus attempt at nation building. It was modelled after European nationalism, even though it claimed to be ancient. He calls it

> an instance of a powerful ideological conjuncture of philology and nationalism of the kind clearly visible a generation earlier in Europe, in the Franco-Prussian war of philology around the Frankish epos; it seems hardly accidental that the project should have been organized in the region that a few years later (1925) gave birth to the neo-Hindu rationalist movement. *The nation-state then gestating in the womb of the colonial order certainly required an ancient birth certificate in modern printed form.*[57]

He is troubled that India and China did not disintegrate into multiple states the way Europe did, but remained united politically. He would like scholars 'to explore the historical contingencies that made nation-states of France and England but not of Tamilnadu and Maharashtra'.[58]

Western theories of nation and civilization cannot be applied to India, he says, because India lacks any semblance of an indigenous theory about its own civilization and nationhood. Hence, he wants his cohorts to go back to the drawing board and develop 'a new semantics of culture-power' that would explain South Asia, because it does not neatly fit into any of the theories known to him.[59] In other words, theorizing about India cannot be done in terms of any nation or civilization at all. These constructs do not work for India and must be expunged, he says.

At the end of his book, he takes a parting shot at Hindutva, calling it

> the grotesque mutation of the toxins of postcolonial *ressentiment* and modernity known as Hindutva, or Hindu nationalism. The very names of the groups that make up the institutional complex of Hindutva – including the Bharatiya Janata Party (Indian People's Party) and its ideological wing, the Vishwa Hindu Parishad (World Hindu Council) – bespeak what had never been spoken before, postulating in the one case a single Indian 'peoplehood' (*janata*), in the other, Hinduism as an aggressive universalism. What is immediately clear from the history we have followed in the course of this book is that Hindutva is a perversion of India's great cosmopolitan past, while the many new subnational movements (as in Assam and elsewhere) represent an entirely new, militant vernacularism, indeed, a kind of Heideggerization of Indian life.[60]

It is unfortunate that he constantly conflates Hinduism with contemporary politics, rather than studying it in its own right free from politics.

My comments on the use of political philology

When I speak of Pollock's perspective, his teachings and spreading influence, a large number of Indians ask, 'So what?' They see a rapidly growing twenty-first-century globalism in which they have to raise their children to flourish. They wonder whether defending Sanskrit and sanskriti should be important. On the other hand, Hindus with a sense of sacredness turn to my work with interest. They wish to know the impact of Pollock's initiatives on their children and grandchildren being able to access paramarthika practices balanced with worldly success. It is to this latter group that I provide the following list of problems with reinterpreting Sanskrit texts using Western political philology:

1. It gives control to secularized, English-speaking Indian elites who reinterpret Sanskrit to get rid of the spirituality found in the Vedas, or what Pollock describes as a 'record of barbarism, of extraordinary inequality and other social poisons'.
2. It diverts attention away from shastras – Ayurveda (medicine), Sthapatya (architecture), Yoga Sutras, *Natya Shastra* and so forth. These texts provide vyavaharika knowledge for interacting with the material world. Such works can then continue to be digested into the western intellectual-economic machine by Westerners and sold back to Indians in new packages.
3. It teaches political philology to deconstruct Sanskrit text, cancelling any possibility of an intellectual renaissance from within Indian traditions. Although Pollock talks about dominant culture when referring to Indian sanskriti, he is speaking from behind the veil of Western universalism and thus is blind to the global dominance of Western culture. His strategy of deconstructing Sanskrit texts using political philology ensures the intellectual colonization of India. The Indian billionaires who are funding this strategy benefit by demonstrating to their Western peers that they are fully vested in Western intellectual frameworks.
4. It produces an army of Indian pseudo-pandits, trained directly or indirectly by Western Indologists. They spread the message that Vedic chants, pujas, bhakti, Vedanta teachings and homa are barbaric carry-overs from the past and are irrelevant in the twenty-first century.
5. It dissolves Sanskrit as a spoken and living language and turns it into a monument honouring something dead. The secularized, English-speaking Indian pseudo-pandits would become able to control how Sanskrit texts are to be interpreted and disseminated – much in the way selected Greek plays are taught in private elite schools and colleges in the West.

10

Is Sheldon Pollock Too Big to Be Criticized?

In order to evaluate Pollock's intellectual importance and political power, it is important to understand what has been called a hegemonic discourse. In my book, *Indra's Net,* I define this as material produced by an influential coterie of writers that continues to reiterate a given position until it becomes an accepted truth. To gain leverage for their views, the group relies on references to one another's works, as well as mutually supportive reviews and the sharing of contacts and sources of patronage. Under the guise of 'peer reviews', this process gives these academicians the aura of objectivity.

As the process unfolds, there is less and less need for them to defend their positions, and anyone who tries to assail them must bear a heavy burden of proof. Their core theses are increasingly taken for granted. This mode of thinking (or, rather, blind following) then gets adopted by other disciplines, where it is applied even more confidently. A stage is reached when, even if fresh evidence or arguments come along to challenge these positions, the hegemonic discourse continues to prevail through the power of the academic cartel.

In this chapter, I wish to point out that Pollock has developed a powerful hegemonic discourse, and that he is often less than transparent about it. In some venues, he is quite upfront about his ultimate goals and grand political project, which is to cause a major intervention in Indian culture on behalf of those declared to be the oppressed victims of tradition-based elitism. His 'liberation philology' is shaped with this intention.

In this sense, Pollock is a classic Western liberal with an agenda for India of the kind I criticize extensively in *Breaking India*. At the same time, when addressing Indians who are proud of their heritage he is not forthright in articulating this agenda explicitly. Pollock presents different aspects of himself to resonate with different types of audiences. His presentations are sophisticated and require close, objective examination.

Two goals

His underlying goals are, however, consistent, and his powerful credentials, ideological proclivities, extraordinary success in fund-raising and political agenda are all directed at promoting those goals. In academic forums, he is upfront and explains his twofold goal as follows:[1]

- **To reinterpret the past,** or, more specifically, to help Indians 'recover memories' of the distant past which today, according to him, they do not know or even wish to face. He is referring to Indians' memories about oppression and inequality inculcated by their tradition, which he says they are denying. To achieve this goal, he focusses on ancient texts, most of which are in Sanskrit, using his own particular lens of political philology. This is his way of recovering what he thinks of as the 'true history' that remains unknown concerning ancient India.
- **To transform Indian society by reframing its civilizational underpinnings in secular terms:** Pollock is explicit about his goal of using liberation philology as a tool to bring about social

> transformation.[2] He is unambiguous about wanting to challenge and dislodge the current system and scolds other Indologists for romanticizing India's past and failing to disrupt current structures of social abuse.

This goal of intervening in Indian society is worth stating at length here. He writes:

> … you transcend inequality by mastering and overmastering those discourses through study and critique. You cannot simply go around a tradition to overcome it, if that is what you wish to do; you must go through it. *You only transform a dominant culture by outsmarting it.* That, I believe, is precisely what some of India's most disruptive thinkers, such as Dr Ambedkar, sought to do, though *they were not as successful as they might have been had they had access to all the tools of a critical philology necessary to the task.*[3]

After recovering selective memories and (re)constructing narratives using political philology (his first goal), he supplies the methods of liberation philology for achieving social and political change (his second goal).

He sometimes puts a Buddhist gloss on his goals to rationalize and justify what he is doing. He says he sees dukkha (sorrow) abounding in Indian society, for which he has found an overarching cause (samudaya). He discusses the question that was asked of the Buddha: How do we overcome this overarching cause of dukkha? To which the Buddha responds by teaching his famous eightfold path. This teaching applies to *individual* dukkha for which there is an *individual* cause.

However, Pollock is interested in India's social/collective dukkha which he identifies as poverty, misery and the oppression of women, shudras and Muslims. Then, he identifies the social samudaya (cause): the hierarchical and othering structures of Sanskrit and Sanskrit-based traditions such as Hinduism. The solution he offers is political philology, that is, the political deconstruction of the language, texts and culture using analytical tools developed in the West.

There are two major target audiences for his strategy: academic and mainstream. The academic strategy is to deploy his particular philological lens to build up his own academic cadre, whose function is to spread his theories. The mainstreaming strategy enables him to win over non-academicians to his views. It is a successful strategy, as witnessed by the support he has garnered from such figures as Narayana Murthy and the top officials at Sringeri Peetham, as well as the Government of India.

The academic ecosystem

Since he uses both 'political philology' and 'liberation philology' as terms for his methodology, a brief clarification will help the reader. I will briefly explain three terms based on my understanding of Pollock's writings:

- **Philology** is the general field of the study of languages and their texts, typically in a *historical* context with the use of *written* materials. Note the italicized terms: it uses these materials to interpret the history of some culture.
- **Political philology** is largely a Marxist initiative to use philology for the specific purpose of pointing at politics (i.e., power and exploitation) as the driver of culture. Pollock cites the Indian Marxist, D.D. Kosambi, as its great champion who applied this method to Sanskrit texts in order to tease out the oppression and class conflicts in ancient Indian society. Pollock regrets there has not been any Indian successor to Kosambi, and he is intent upon creating such a team of his own.
- **Liberation philology** is Pollock's recent term which he uses to describe his particular ideological lens. It includes an important emphasis on social activism to bring change today. This is the phase when there is actual intervention for social engineering.

Let me elaborate a bit more on the last point, his liberation philology. Here is a description of it, as provided by Thomas Crowley of *Kindle Magazine*:

> Pollock has described his own intellectual project as 'liberation philology', and it is precisely this philology that can help us make sense of – and combat – the Hindutva reading of Indian religion and history promoted by the Shiksha Bachao Andolan. The term, though, needs some explaining. 'Liberation philology' is clearly a play on words, a reference to the tradition of 'liberation theology', a left-wing interpretation of Catholicism that emphasised economic and political justice, and which was widely popular throughout Latin America, especially in the 1960s. With liberation philology, *Pollock is putting his own left-wing spin on the practice of philology, emphasising that the academic discipline needs to be applied critically in order to effect social change* and, in his words, to bring about an 'inclusivist, species-wide community' to replace the divided, nationalistic, economically and socially unjust world we live in now. In a speech he delivered last year in Delhi, Pollock remarked that *he could just as well have replaced 'liberation philology' with the term 'post-capitalist philology'*.[4]

The reference to 'liberation' and its equivalent 'post-capitalist' provides clear insight into the revolutionary nature of Pollock's plan. It is well appreciated within his group as a left-wing method. He wants to develop this method of textual analysis of Sanskrit which would help the masses of India move towards some kind of post-capitalist utopia.

As Crowley goes on to say: 'Like much of Pollock's scholarship, his political project is quite ambitious. He seeks to understand, and to upend, the conceptual consequences of capitalism for scholarship.'[5] Not only is he seeking to overcome the toxicity he finds in Sanskrit, but Pollock also wants to upend global capitalism which is bringing dukkha to the masses.

Many Hindus – myself among them – would quite agree that global capitalism merits serious analysis. The irony is that Pollock's work is funded by one of India's most prominent capitalist families – billionaires who made their money by labour arbitrage sold to capitalist multinationals.

Crowley quotes Pollock saying, 'There can be no such thing as an incorrect interpretation.'[6] He goes on to paraphrase Pollock by saying that the meaning of a text can be presented in several ways: as its author originally intended, or as it was interpreted by multiple commentators over time, or its interpretation in a present-day social, economic and political context. I agree that all these approaches have existed in the (re) interpretations of Indian texts. However, of special interest to Pollock (and me) is the final of these three approaches because it opens the door for radical new interpretations. This allows for great innovations and positive revolutions in the light of present-day contexts. But we must be mindful that the same flexibility also brings vulnerability to power-driven interventions from outside the tradition.

For instance, liberation philology seems to be getting positioned as a way to groom young Indian scholars by elite American universities to develop what is called atrocity literature on India. I want to be clear that it is legitimate to focus on issues like human rights, caste oppression, empowerment of women and the like. But I am concerned about the asymmetry of power at play here. Who decides what the right present-day context is? Reinterpretations for present-day contexts have in the past played into the hands of colonizers, imperial powers, and the like. Often, the context for reinterpretation that prevails is the one with the best scholarly resources, funding and strategy. It is not necessarily based on merit or objectivity.

Some aspects of his project appear quite positive: a new and critical interest in Sanskrit, a greater attention to its texts, a desire to see its rich heritage brought into our times (for the benefit of scholars), and a profound concern for social justice. The problem is that he undercuts some of the very resources within the Sanskrit tradition that might help to achieve these goals. In particular, *his attack on the spiritual roots of the culture is not only fundamentally wrong but also counterproductive.* His relentless secularism and rejection of the sacred are debilitating for the very causes he wants to further. This is a matter for ongoing debate with Pollock and his team, which cannot be fully addressed in this book.

Politicizing the Ramayana: An example of hegemonic discourse

Pollock's pioneering role in politicizing the Ramayana is an outstanding example of hegemonic discourse. He created this discourse within the academic ecosystem and then his influence was widely disseminated.

In 1951, work began on the Critical Edition in Sanskrit of all seven volumes of Ramayana at Maharaja Sayajirao (MS) University of Baroda. By 1975, the basic ground work had been laid. That is when Western academicians stepped in to dissect the English translation with their own methods and generated their English (re)interpretations. Such translations tend to be strategic projects to make the materials more readily available to large numbers of Western scholars, so they can use them for their own purposes.

In the early 1980s, Robert Goldman invited Pollock to join the US-based Ramayana translation and interpretation team. This was a large project spearheaded by the University of California, Berkeley. Pollock had just graduated from Harvard with a PhD in Sanskrit under Daniel Ingalls. He became the translator of the Balakanda volume, which was interpreted by Goldman. It was published in 1984.

In this project, Pollock disagreed with Goldman's interpretation and published a separate paper, *The Divine King in the Indian Epic*, in 1984. He was in his early thirties at that time. I showed in Chapter 6 that he also disagreed with the legendary Ingalls because Pollock (unlike Ingalls) wanted to politicize the kavya through the lens of Western cultural theories, most notably political philology. Thus began the politicization of the Ramayana in the Western academia. Pollock then took over the interpretation of the Ayodhyakanda volume, which was published in 1988.

Pollock's involvement in the Ramayana has left a lasting imprint on the way the epic is being seen. His hegemonic discourse is visible in the way the Ramayana has become tainted in several English-speaking circles. Over the past twenty-five years, academic literature and journalistic writings have been filled with assertions resembling Pollock's spin, not only of the Ramayana but also in the portrayal of Sanskrit as a carrier of social toxicity. His involvement also promoted Western idioms and theories as the proper means for thinking about the issues in Sanskrit texts.

One of the first attempts by US academics to use his politicized Ramayana in the current Indian context was made by Lloyd and Susan Rudolph, both of whom are professors of political science at the University of Chicago. (Both were awarded the Padma Bhushan at the same time Pollock was awarded the Padma Shri by the Indian government, in January 2014.) In March 1993, the Rudolphs published an article in the *New Republic* titled 'Modern Hate', which discussed how the BJP had hijacked Hinduism and the Ramayana and made Hinduism into a monotheistic cult:

> How did it happen that the Bharatiya Janata Party was able to hijack Hinduism, replacing its diversity, multivocality and generativity with a monotheistic Ram cult? An answer can be found in the history of storytelling. The ancient legend of Ram, the virtuous godking, incarnation of Vishnu, who wandered in exile for twelve years with his wife Sita before vanquishing the Southern demon Ravana, can be found all over India. It is a moral tale, exemplifying what right conduct should be between a king and his subjects and among generations, genders and relatives. Ram was an intimate deity, his representations infinitely diverse by region and locale. He was the subject of thousands of Ramayanas in many languages, of village drama cycles, of stories told by grandmothers, and today of epic comic books. In time, Ram stories became consolidated [...] In January 1987 an eighteen-month-long serial of the Ramayana based on the manas began airing at 9:30 a.m., prime time, on state-run T.V. [...] Ten months after the Ramayana megaseries, the Vishwa Hindu Parishad (World Hindu Council) called on Hindus throughout India to make holy bricks, inscribed with Rama's name, for use at Ayodhya. There, at the site of Rama's birth, and on the place of the Babri Masjid, they would build a temple to Rama.[7]

Criticism is fair and should be open to all. However, the problem is that Pollock and his school consider that the Ramayana intrinsically and inherently encodes and supports violence. (I explained this in Chapter 5.) In the above quote, the American academics, the Rudolphs, have paraphrased Pollock's divinization-demonization thesis, connected it with political symbology through the TV Ramayana series, and then highlighted its link to the VHP campaign. Such attempts at guilt-by-association subvert the average Hindu's use of the Ramayana as a positive resource for self-improvement, pluralism and social justice.

The *New Republic* is a prestigious publication in the US that reaches the political and intellectual elite. This spread of Pollock's ideas into the mainstream took only nine years after the launch of the Ramayana translation and interpretation project in the early 1980s. The publication of Pollock's paper never received a rebuttal from academicians. After his spin reached the mainstream in the US, it travelled to Europe where it influenced the 1996 publication of Christophe Jaffrelot's book on the history of the Hindu nationalist movement. Jaffrelot references Rudolph:

> The receptiveness of the public to this manipulation of the symbol of Ram had undoubtedly been heightened by the broadcasting of the Ramayana ... Thus, the broadcasting of the Ramayana and the Mahabharata, as Lloyd Rudolph has suggested, was 'playing a leading role in creating a national Hindu, a form of group consciousness that has not hitherto existed'.[8]

Jaffrelot, a prominent French political scientist, is now a regular columnist in a number of Indian newspapers and an academic advisor in Indian universities on the teaching of India. Notice how the Rudolphs and Jaffrelot, all three of whom are political scientists with no knowledge of Sanskrit and little knowledge of the Ramayana itself, can now speak authoritatively about the Ramayana and political symbology. All of this was triggered by the translation of the Ramayana's Critical Edition in Sanskrit, which was compiled painstakingly (and innocently) by MS University over some twenty-five years, ending in 1975.

Pollock's view that the Ramayana inculcates the subjugation of women without qualification has also been adopted by Professor Jasbir Jain, a professor of English, who writes:[9]

> Rama thwarts the advances of Ravana's sister, Surpanakha, resisting her attempts to seduce him. Sita, however, is charmed by a golden deer and desires to possess it, so that first Rama, and then Lakshmana, must pursue it. On the face of it, this is not very different from Eve's yielding to Satan's persuasion, but dissimilarities soon creep in. Sita's resistance to Ravana renders her a victim of oppression by both her abductor and her husband. The trial by fire signifies both subjugation and purification.
>
> The Ramayana story, in its multiple readings, reinterpretations, and retellings, defines first the limits of legitimate sexuality and the violation of those limits. The controlling figure remains male: definitions and purificatory rites are male prescriptions. Passed on through oral tradition, these two episodes – the mythical Lakshmana-rekha and agnipariksha – define Indian womanhood within Hinduism and form a part of the socialization process, working at both the conscious and unconscious levels.[10]

Even though she is not a Sanskrit expert, Jain has written an influential interpretation of the Ramayana, and this time she says the denigration of women is pervasive across all retellings of the epic, starting with Valmiki's.

Wendy Doniger uses the same terms in viewing the Ramayana as a text that encodes anti-feminist themes. She writes:

> The Valmiki Ramayana thus sowed seeds both for the oppression of women in the dharma-shastric tradition and for the resistance against that oppression in other Hindu traditions. Rama's nightmare is that Sita will be unchaste, and the sexually voracious ogresses that lurk inside every Good Woman in the Ramayana express that nightmare.[11]

Doniger's book gives a more specific interpretation to the psychosexual perspective first raised by Pollock in the context of the Ramayana. She posits that Hindu men fear women as having a sexually voracious appetite that must be controlled by them.

Here I wish to point out that the denigration of non-white men as sexually deviant has been perpetrated by European cultures in their colonization and enslavement movements. African-American men in

America have been at the receiving end of stereotyping as well. The strategy will now be increasingly used to denigrate and discriminate against Hindu men in general. Academicians such as Pollock provide the conceptual framework and then other scholars like Jaffrelot, Jain and Doniger make more specific applications to contemporary Hindu men.

This hegemonic discourse reaches its climax when its public dissemination gets franchised to Indians who are eager to impress the West. For example, Ananya Vajpeyi wrote an article in 2011 to ensure that the credit for this Ramayana interpretation in the mainstream media went to Pollock's 1993 essay on the subject. She wrote in the *Telegraph* of Kolkata:

> Towards the end of the 20th century, India returned once more to the Ramayan. In the late 1980s the epic was serialized and broadcast, bringing the cable television revolution to India. A resurgent Hindu Right demolished the Babri Masjid in Ayodhya on December 6, 1992, claiming it stood on the hallowed ground where Ram himself had been born on earth. A constitutional crisis, widespread violence between Hindus and Muslims, legal battles in India's courts on the authenticity and historicity of competing religious beliefs and claims, and the attenuation of minority rights in secular India followed throughout the mid-1990s.
>
> On the back of its virulent Ramjanmabhoomi movement (a campaign based on the idea of recapturing the so-called 'birthplace' of Ram from Muslim control), the Bharatiya Janata Party came to power and led the national government until the general elections of 2004. The Ramayan had once again captivated India's political imagination – just like it had done repeatedly in premodernity, as Sheldon Pollock, a translator of the Sanskrit *Ramayan* argued in an important 1993 essay.[12]

I want to reiterate that I do not wish to stop such reinterpretations that criticize the Ramayana. I am merely explaining the way in which hegemonic discourse gets formed and spread, when there is no competent voice on the opposing side to counterbalance it.

The views of the Ramayana I have summarized above are what one sees through a certain lens, but this is not the only lens. The lens of the bhaktas who use the Ramayana as a sacred text gives an entirely different view. This insider view should not get subverted. There needs to be a better balance between the participation of the insiders and outsiders.

Infusing vernacular writers with political philology

Pollock has been influential in establishing Kannada studies in the US and promoting Indian leftists who write in Kannada. Two examples are U.R. Ananthamurthy and Girish Karnad. The late Ananṭhamurthy, who was a close friend of Pollock's, taught him Kannada and together they developed a theory, articulated by Pollock, that Kannada was an extension of Sanskrit developed in royal courts; by implication, it carried the poison embedded in Sanskrit and the Veda.

Ananthamurthy put into effect Pollock's goal of writing new political kavya in Kannada that shows the Vedic tradition as being unjust to shudras and women. Ananthamurthy's novel, *Samskara*, was published in 1965 and subsequently made into an award-winning Hindi film of the same name. The novel was translated into English in 1978. The back-cover blurb of the translation tells us it is a 'religious novel about a decaying brahmin colony' and a 'contemporary reworking of ancient Hindu themes and myths'. It deals with the 'moral chaos' caused by the toxicity in society (of the kind Pollock never tires of discussing). The story concerns the rebirth of a man who is able to reject such a society and transform himself.[13] The English translation is now on the reading lists of many college courses on religion in the US. It is widely read for the purpose of understanding Hindu culture and is filled with negative stereotypes.

Pollock's other protégé, Girish Karnad, has been a frequent visiting professor at universities in the US. In 2007, he wrote a foreword to Pollock's book *Last Act of Rama*. Two of Karnad's writings – *The Dreams of Tipu Sultan* and *Bali: The Sacrifice* – were commissioned by BBC to commemorate India's fiftieth anniversary of Independence. In them, Karnad depicts Hindu society as violent and backward.

Clay Library

Pollock was the general editor of the Clay Sanskrit Library, funded by the wealthy investment banker John Clay. Its last publication came out in 2009. The library produced translations and interpretations of Sanskrit texts from the first millennium CE tailored to address the following themes related to India:

> From early in the common era, a vast creative literature of novels, short stories, plays and poetry began to develop. Some took their subject matter from the national epics or the Buddhist scriptures, but many other sources also provided inspiration. This new literary culture was vibrant and vivid. The dramatists wrote plays about palaces full of dancing girls, and gardens where peacocks screeched at the approach of the monsoon and elephants trumpeted in the stables, eager for combat or mating. Courtiers intrigued for influence and promotion. Merchants set off on their voyages with sadness at separation, and returned with joy and vast profits. The six seasons spun by at breakneck speed. Lovers kept their trysts in the cane groves down by the river. Holy men preached that worldly pleasures were worthless, and often were exposed as hypocrites.[14]

Notice how Pollock's focus is on highlighting the mundane and the profane in Sanskrit: of palaces full of dancing girls and elephants, as well as holy men exposed as hypocrites. This theme of sensual women on the one hand and corrupt holy men on the other resembles the way European missionaries in the seventeenth to the nineteenth centuries pitched their case to Church leaders that India was ripe for Christian conversion. At the Clay Sanskrit Library, Pollock has at times reproduced, through textual interpretation, the European stereotyping and stigmatizing of India in a supposedly post-colonial era – this time to pitch for change through liberation philology.

Grooming the sepoy army

The effect of Pollock's project on some Hindus is alienation from their roots and the development of an inferiority complex about the very civilization that might nurture human evolution. This alienation spreads quickly. Bright young Indians who are well intentioned and understandably concerned about social justice, rush to enter the university factories of this nexus and end up spreading the indoctrination to the public.

Many of these new scholars are sharp, intelligent, articulate, courageous and outspoken. Unlike the previous generation of Western-trained Indians, many of them are also Sanskrit-educated and instilled with the ideologies of professors like Pollock, Doniger, Witzel and others at elite institutions. A sizable number of such westernized 'South Asia experts' have been trained at the PhD level in the past twenty years, mostly in the USA. They have now spread widely among Indian universities and media outlets, as well as think tanks.[15]

The hegemonic discourse goes mainstream

Sheldon Pollock's impact extends well beyond the academy as a result of three main strategies, each of which will be discussed in this chapter:

1. **Spreading his framework and ideas through the media:** He has become a celebrity in the mainstream English-language media in India, thanks to connections formed through his students and other Indian left-wing intellectuals. He has used these connections to popularize his ideas about Indian civilization, bringing them into the mainstream of the Indian elite, who see him as their authority on the subject.

   His article 'Ramayana and Political Imagination', for instance, has had considerable influence on English-speaking Indian journalists and popular commentators. It provided them with the data and arguments to blame the BJP/VHP for deploying the 'cult of Rama' in the Babri Masjid demolition, as well as blaming the impact of the TV serial *Ramayana* for this act.[16] Because this is a highly litigated matter in Indian high courts, it would have been more responsible to present legal verdicts rather than purely ideologically driven sensationalism.

At the Jaipur Literature Festival (JLF), he presented his article, 'Crisis in the Classics', which served as the basis of his fund-raising from Indian billionaires. He began with a Sanskrit verse praising the court of Vijayanagara for its literary efflorescence. This flattered his English-speaking Indian audience – making them feel good that an American was saying nice things about their heritage, especially when they themselves knew little about it. What they do not realize is that, as I have shown, his academic writings reduce the very same corpus of literature from which this verse was selected as being socially oppressive.[17] His public events before Hindu audiences give no hint that some of his most powerful works seek to prove that Sanskrit and the Vedas are the original source of injustice embedded in India's collective dukkha.

He put an entirely different spin on these same points when he spoke at The New School in New York City. On that occasion, he said he was really looking at the Indian texts from within the framework of finding collective dukkha. India, he said, is at the vanguard of a significant socio-political revolution. He stressed that his liberation philology is the answer to the problem of how to restart the global leftist movement that got stalled in the post-Soviet era. In other words, India is to be the site for this revolution; his theories are to be the weapons.

While his articles and public presentations, such as the ones described above, tend to be aimed at select audiences, he also on occasion uses interviews to reach out to the broader popular audience. This chapter examines two of his interviews. One is a video interview with *Tehelka* magazine in 2011 and the other appeared in 2014 in the newspaper *India Abroad* (and was later republished on Rediff.com). Such interviews often depict him as one of the 'last living authorities on Sanskrit' and its intellectual history.

2. **Building institutions through fund-raising:** The early drafts of Pollock's article 'Crisis in the Classics' had a seminal impact on the Murthy family of Infosys. The result was the founding of the

Murty Classical Library of India at Harvard University, under Pollock's control. It is one of the most important accomplishments of Pollock's mainstreaming strategy. In the Introduction, I already discussed attempts to co-opt the legacy of Adi Shankara.

3. **Activism in political campaigns, including signing petition:** Far removed from his image as merely an erudite Sanskrit academician, Pollock has signed numerous political petitions and participated in political campaigns that oppose the mainstream trends in Hinduism. Some examples of these are discussed in Appendix C.

The collective objective of such projects is to infuse his liberation philology into the vocabulary of the one-liner wisdom of many young Indian elites. This approach is now being instilled in the way Indians think of their literary heritage.

Considered one of the last great Sanskrit pandits

A typical example of a hagiography of Pollock by one of his students reads as follows:

> Scholarship like that of Sheldon Pollock and his colleagues helps us to understand the history, the power, the circulation and the importance of Sanskrit knowledge systems in the pre-modern world, not just in India but across Asia. We learn to really read texts, to carefully unpack their meaning in complex historical contexts of production and reception, rather than merely brandish them as false tokens of identity and imagined superiority in our own times.[18]

It is no surprise that Indians have showered him with awards and other forms of recognition. A sample of his central role at a prestigious event is conveyed in the following words of Ananya Vajpeyi, one of his most loyal and politically active students. She says:

> He read out loud from Bhanudatta's *Rasamanjari* to a rapt audience that included such literary luminaries as U.R. Ananthamurthy and S.R. Farooqui, fellow-scholars and Indianists like Mukund Lath, Wendy

> Doniger and Lloyd and Susanne Rudolph, and Gurcharan Das, who is writing a new book on the *Mahabharata*. The stories of South Asia came to perch on our shoulders, riveted, like us, by the sound of the language of the gods being recited in the world of men.[19]

Vajpeyi is referring to his reading of a Sanskrit verse at the JLF in 2009. Later that same year, he received the President of India's Award for Sanskrit, signalling that his opinions on Sanskrit traditions are to be given importance. The Padma Shri Award by the president of India was given to him next, sealing the approval by the Indian establishment. He was presented with the India Abroad Friend of India Award in 2013.

Tehelka *magazine's international authority on Sanskrit*

Pollock starts a video interview with *Tehelka* by referring to Saraswati in a 'secular' rather than a sacred manner.[20] Then he finds it weird that Indians take the Ramayana seriously enough to use it as a political platform in the twenty-first century. He compares the Ramayana to the Latin poetry of Virgil and says: 'Nobody organizes political parties around Virgil's Aeneid in Rome the way, you know, the BJP and the rath yathra ... mobilized around this epic figure.'

Here he ignores the fact that the *Aeneid was* often read as a justification for Rome's imperialist designs on the nations and various peoples around it. It is true that Italians *today* do not use Virgil's hero in *Aeneid* as their rallying figure, but comparing Rama with this pre-Christian Roman hero is incorrect. There are two reasons why this is so:

- Virgil's epic is not part of the Catholic Church's *living* tradition today. A more suitable equivalent would be the hero of the New Testament, i.e., Jesus Christ. Italians *do* organize political parties around Jesus, whose name has been used even to justify pogroms and conquests.
- Hindus see the Ramayana as a spiritual authority, comparable to how Christians see the gospels. But Virgil's epic is seen as purely

secular literature by westerners today; hence, this is not an apt analogy.

In other words, he compares the Ramayana with the dead pre-Christian traditions of Europe and not with the living Christian ones.

Interestingly, my views on why Latin/Greek should not be seen as parallels to Sanskrit are the same as what one reads in the report produced by the government of Jawaharlal Nehru soon after Independence. The Sanskrit Commission of the Indian government said in its report of 1957 as follows:

> Greek and Latin did not and do not have that same sort of deep and all-inclusive influence (except in the case of some monastic scholars) which Sanskrit has still in Indian life. They are at the best academic, the concern of scholars. But Sanskrit is something more profound and more vital than that. Not only is it academic in the true sense of the term, but it is popular also.[21]

Pollock's mapping of a living Hindu text to a dead Latin one escapes the *Tehelka* interviewer's attention. The interviewer gives him a pass, unable to show knowledge of such basic points.

This emboldens Pollock further to discuss 'the 1992 attack on Babri Masjid and the consolidation of Hindutvavadi politics' as a great opportunity for his interventions. He says that due to the emergence of Hindu politics, the 'opportunities as well as obligations of classicists in India become very compelling'. Here, he is making his case for the future of Sanskrit studies as a means for political interventions in India.

He goes on to explain that the Ramayana is 'a story of othering and the political is displaced or rather the struggle for the political is displaced by the Other'. Both the Ramayana and the Mahabharata are to him 'a sedimentation of mythic forms – kind of divides along two lines'. The Mahabharata is 'a really dangerous mythic formation where the political Other is your brother'. This otherness gets projected on to fellow Indians today who are to be killed. He says, 'The Mahabharata is the most dangerous political story I think, in the world, because it is this deep meditation on the fratricide of civil war.'

A traditional scholar would disagree with him and point out that the Mahabharata is teaching the *folly* of 'othering' between cousins; its message is just the *opposite* of what Pollock is saying. Unfortunately, the *Tehelka* interviewer seems to lack the subject matter expertise to be able to raise such issues.

The other 'sedimentation of the mythic' is the Ramayana, which he says projects the 'other' upon those deemed as outsiders. He says, 'The Ramayana was a language of othering.' These others (called 'rakshasas') are, according to him, the Muslims today. This has been a consistent view throughout his academic writings.

I do not wish to dwell on contemporary politics, but refer to it only to point out Pollock's propensity for doing so and to stress that he is using his own particular lens to interpret Hindu texts as being primarily political and oppressive in nature.

He then characterizes traditional Indian Sanskrit scholars as 'enemies of history' who are producing the 'anti-history' discourse for political purposes. They 'want to pervert Sanskrit', he says. He is especially upset at the spoken Sanskrit movement, saying: '*This whole spoken Sanskrit movement fills me with a kind of nausea.*'

To appease his Indian audiences at popular events, he often praises Sanskrit for having served historically as the mode of expression for some of the most sophisticated ideas mankind has ever contemplated. And yet his academic writings argue that its structures and texts are socially toxic, for which his liberation theology provides the remedy.

Pollock mentions the name of the Western cultural theorist Walter Benjamin in this context: 'I hope you know Benjamin's very famous line about "every document of civilization is at the same time a document of barbarism".' His focus to eradicate the barbarism mentioned by Benjamin is to 'establish serious, philologically grounded, historically sensitive, theoretically self-aware, reflective scholarship on Sanskrit; to make it into an instrument of the creative preservation of the past and a creative critique of the past'. The claim is to make Sanskrit emancipatory and egalitarian by exposing and expunging what is deemed to be its latent social oppression and domination.

This sounds positive in theory, and many Indians, myself included, would endorse it as a lofty goal. However, he is like the intellectual reincarnation of Sir William Jones. His desire for 'the project of a future Sanskrit' is to tell Indians what is good for them and present himself as their hero.

India Abroad*'s celebrity: the 'Pandit' and the 'Keeper of the Classical Past'*

When *India Abroad* newspaper gave Pollock its 'Friend of India Award', it published an extensive interview with him. In it, he is portrayed not only as being learned in Sanskrit but as one of the last remaining pandits preserving Indian heritage. The banner headline for the interview reveres him not only as "The Pandit' but also the 'Keeper of India's Classical Past'.[22] There are many such monikers he has received in the mainstream media; I will attempt to show the impact of his well-orchestrated public relations campaign.

The preface to the interview in *India Abroad* expresses awe and fascination for Pollock:

> It begins in Jaipur in the tranquil gardens of Diggi Palace, where brightly-coloured parrots flit about, contributing to the chatter, and erstwhile *ranis* issue instructions in ringing imperial voices, as they go about running the hotel that is now part of their palace, like a new kingdom. Pollock and his wife Allison Busch, a Hindi scholar, have been spending a sabbatical away from Columbia [University] in Rajasthan.[23]

The elite Sanskrit pandit of the twenty-first century is ensconced in a royal court in India, much as Pollock and his students have described the way Sanskrit scholars were honoured by past royalty. Even the ranis (queens) at the Diggi Palace in Jaipur are diligently ensuring his comfort. The interviewer whisks us away from Jaipur to Mumbai, where he says the natives 'stop to stare at the hatted, eccentric-looking, bewhiskered professor'. In Mumbai, he gives a talk to a 'small group at an event organized by Columbia's Global Center in Mumbai on "What is Indian Knowledge Good for?" and entrances the audience with his sweetly-spoken Sanskrit, probably the best across two hemispheres'.[24]

What this enchanted interviewer and the Mumbai Indian audience do not know are the kinds of issues I have raised in the earlier chapters of this book. Most of the English-speaking Indian elite do not have the first inkling of their heritage. Therefore, 'entrancing' his Mumbai audience with his Sanskrit would not be too difficult; and that the interviewer thinks Pollock's spoken Sanskrit is the best across two hemispheres is telling in itself.

The interviewer then moves on to Manhattan where he continues the conversation with Pollock. Contradictions abound. In his 2001 paper on 'The Death of Sanskrit', he declared the language to have been dead for a thousand years, but now for his non-resident Indian readers he suddenly appears concerned about the shrinking number of Sanskrit speakers. And, although he has maintained that Sanskrit was never a spoken language, now, in front of the interviewer, he expresses sadness that there are not enough Sanskrit speakers:

> We carry on, where we left off, many days later, in a French café in upper Manhattan. Discussing Indian politics and the possible impending demise of Sanskrit, a few steps from Columbia, is not at all incongruous given that one [of] the best places to study Sanskrit these days is not in India, but in Columbia, or Harvard or the University of Chicago, where generous endowments allow the continuity of studies on a language that is declining in India ...[25]

Interestingly, there is no doubt in the Indian journalist's mind that the best place to study Sanskrit is the US. He seems unaware that this transfer of authority regarding Sanskrit studies to places like Columbia, Harvard and Chicago is a replay of the way Oxford and other universities in Britain took over control of such studies during British colonialism. It would not be surprising if the journalist does not know much of Sir William Jones of the East India Company in the eighteenth century or of the history of Indology.

Pollock uses the interview to 'educate' naive, mainstream Indians on his own version of Sanskrit history. It is a questionable chronology in that it assumes, for example, that Valmiki's Ramayana was written post-Ashoka.

> I have definite ideas about what the Valmiki Ramayana was about. I think it had something to do with Ashoka, post-Ashokan India. I think it had something to do with the nature of power. Something to do with the rise of a certain idiom of Sanskrit that was used for the first time for writing non-ritual text and things.[26]

He wants to be loud and clear that the Ramayana has served as a 'weapon to mobilize and militarize a large number of people, who would do very dangerous things'. His complete statement in the interview is as follows:

> The Ayodhya catastrophe was a big turning point for a lot of us. I would never have thought that a 2nd century BCE text I was working on would become deployable in the present, in some divisive way. That it would be used as a weapon to mobilize and militarize a large number of people, who would do very dangerous things. And I was interested in the history of that.
>
> I felt there was a history to the use of the Ramayana in the political imagination of traditional India. I think it had been used a lot. I was interested in why the Ramayana is seen to appear in the 12th century in Tamil Nadu and 16th century in Rajasthan and 17th century in Maharashtra, under conditions of political danger or competition...
>
> I felt that what was happening in 1992 was a repetition, with change, in – let's call it – an old cultural practice. I wanted to understand it as a historical phenomenon over a 2,000-year period. What has the Ramayana meant to political thinking in India? Why did LK Advani appear on the cover of *India Today* dressed as Kodanda Rama, with the bow. Why that? I was concerned with the history of this phenomenon – redeployment of old images in the present.[27]

Pollock recognizes there are sharp differences in the way Indians view the Ramayana and he offers to play the mediator role, much as the East India Company once did among Indians in conflict with each other. He makes a telling remark about why he is so interested in helping Indians resolve this issue:

> It [India] is not my *janambhoomi*, but it is my *karmabhoomi* ... One of the things that is troubling about the present, contemporary moment,

> for people like me ... [is that] words and concepts from the past that are part of the Sanskrit tradition, have, to some degree, been captured by political forces in the present ...[28]

By using the term 'karmabhoomi' (i.e., the site of his life's work), he legitimizes his use of India as his personal field of activity: such as the post-Soviet leftist revolution he wants India to lead, as discussed earlier in this chapter. He claims the right to intervene when he feels certain Indian political forces are 'capturing' Sanskrit words and concepts for potentially violent political reasons. The media positions him as if only he has the authority and competence to provide the right perspective because the traditional Sanskrit pandits have withered away.

He postures himself as an inheritor of the Ramayana:

> It is a perfectly rational and a reasonable extension to say what is the relevance of this text – the Ramayana, let's say, a very ancient text from South Asia – to contemporary India, both because of my own historical being as a child of the '60s and also because of this philosophical position about all history being contemporary history. It is perfectly reasonable to ask what does this material mean to me, why should I care about it, but what does it mean to the inheritors of these great traditions today ... When I talk about the inheritors of these great achievements of Indian culture, great works of literature or systems of thought, *I consider myself as much an inheritor* as my Indian friends and colleagues.[29]

The remark about his being an American 'child of the '60s' refers to the Vietnam era, when American youth rebelled against their military establishment and other traditions, prompting some of them to go to India in search of answers. (Many of them later 'U-turned' and rejected Indian traditions.) What does Pollock find so relevant in the Ramayana which he says is his inheritance? The following statement is a sample of his interest in showing that the Ramayana is anti-women:

> ... Śūrpaṇakhā becomes the *churel,* the succubus of the Indian male's nightmare world, who threatens him with death through sexual depletion and must therefore be suppressed ...[30]

The Ramayana is not alone in this, he says, and women in general are sometimes figured as female *rakshasas* in the various Indian texts. He is sending a message that the Sanskrit tradition itself is drenched in attacks against womanhood – that it authorizes Indian male violence towards women, a violence arising out of male sexual insecurities.

American and British nurturing of Indian journalists

One of my greatest concerns about his work has to do with the way it serves as support for a kind of atrocity literature, which (as discussed in Chapter 2) is a genre of horror stories about a given culture designed to justify intervention in its internal affairs.

Some of the top mainstream journalists in India have been trained either in the USA or the UK and may inadvertently fail to realize how their position is being used in this way. They are known to highlight stories about attacks by Hindus against Muslims and women. These impressions have been fashioned and given legitimacy by the approach of Western social scientists. Trained in the skills of mass communication in the West, these squads of opinion makers are embedded within Indian media. They ensure that such messages get repeated frequently through carefully curated stories, and the repetition gives rise to an accepted 'common sense view' among the Indian intelligentsia.

For the past several decades, the British government has systematically sent Indian journalists for training and career building trips to the UK. Likewise, the US consulate in India has sponsored trips to fancy destinations and invites certain types of Indian intellectuals to its prestigious events. These are some of the ways of infusing ideologies into the Indian media.

Third-party echoes: Pollock's ideas go viral

Pollock's Ramayana interpretations enter US schools

The US government's National Endowment for the Humanities, headed at the time by Lynne Cheney, wife of former vice-president Dick Cheney, gave a grant to develop course material to teach the Ramayana in US schools. This was part of a programme to encourage multiculturalism in schools across the US. Many of my Indian American friends lauded this programme in the hope that it would educate their children and inform their American friends about our great heritage. However, when I asked them about the nature of the content of the course, they drew a blank. They did not consider it important to concern themselves with such 'details'. So, I got myself a copy of the course book that was being sold to teachers on how to teach the Ramayana.[31]

The book was published in 1995 by the American Forum for Global Education, an influential developer of school course materials with the mission of educating US school students on global cultures. Susan Wadley, one of the foremost American anthropologists on India, developed the course materials, which contained some content that bears an eerie resemblance to Pollock's theories about the Ramayana's abusiveness.

The Ramayana workbook follows his interpretation and analysis by saying that Valmiki wrote the epic to portray brahmins as wise advisors solving problems of kingship that had arisen 2,500 years ago. It then goes on to say that brahmins resurrected the Ramayana in the sixteenth century to make themselves relevant under Mughal rule:

> By the 16th century, however, the north of India was under Moghul rule and the Brahmins no longer strongly influenced ruling. In re-writing the Ramayana to make it relevant to the new times the Brahmins made Rama into a flawless, absolute, all powerful God. All the characters in the new Ramayanas become the devotees of God ... The new relationship between Rama and his devotees in the Ramayana, that between master and slave, can be recognized as a model for the hierarchical and unequal relationship between Brahmins and all other lower castes and between men and women.[32]

This school text refers to the sixteenth-century *Ramcharitmanas*, a heartfelt bhakti exposition, and brands it an oppressive text for subjugating lower castes and all women. The workbook is designed to teach American schoolchildren about the Ramayana by turning Rama into an oppressor.

Students are encouraged to write about how Shabari would respond today to Lakshmana's objecting to food offered by her to Rama, even though the response is given in the Ramayana itself. Students are invited to compare this conversation in the epic with the racially hierarchical society they experience in the US. Thus, the racial hierarchy of whites over African-Americans and Native Americans is projected onto the 'Aryan Rama'.

Students are then invited to read and sing a song that is said to be written by an unnamed untouchable in north India, which in part goes like this:

> The rulers who control all knowledge,
> Claim the Ramayana to be India's history
> And called us many names – demons, low castes, untouchables.
> But we are the aborigines of this land.
> Listen to our story.
> Today we are called the dalits – the oppressed.
> Once the Aryans on their horses invaded this land.
> Then we who are the natives became the displaced.
> Oh Rama, Oh Rama, You became the God and we the demons.
> You portrayed our Hanuman as a monkey,
> Oh Rama, you representative of the Aryans.[33]

Here we see the American academia and government asking schools to adopt the Aryan invasion theory and make Rama a representative of the oppressive Aryans. The teaching material then projects what actually happened to Native Americans in America onto India's history. The song continues to the present times, and says:

> But poverty grew and to divert the poor
> From their real need, a new enemy was found.
> Muslims were targeted and 'taught a lesson.'
> To destroy Lanka, Oh Rama, you
> Formed us into a monkey army.

And today you want us,
The working majority,
To form a new monkey army
And attack Muslims.
Oh Rama, you representative of the Aryans.
Be warned, you purveyors of a self-serving religion.
We will be monkeys no more.
We will sing songs of humanity
And we will make you human as well.

The workbook then goes on to ask the students to compose their own responses to this oppressor Rama, and then perform these responses by shouting them out loud.

Even when Pollock is not being explicitly quoted, his politicized interpretation of the Ramayana is influencing the development of course materials for teaching young American about Hindus and India. This approach to educating American schoolchildren about Hinduism is creating deep psychological scars for Hindu American children who go through the US school system. Many of them come out as self-hating individuals with low self-esteem.

High school students in the US are also being taught that Hindu texts such as the Ramayana teach Hindu men to see women as objects, not human beings, something to be thrown away. This general view of Hindu men as subjugating women is another of Pollock's interpretations that has been 'mainstreamed' by Western-trained Indian academics.[34]

Film to liberate women from Ramayana: Sita Sings the Blues

Nina Paley, a thirty-four-year-old American woman, found herself in Thiruvananthapuram in 2002 and 'discovered' the Ramayana.[35] She saw Indian women as being second-class citizens, just as Pollock would want her to see them. Like most Americans, she has a pre-conceived notion not only of the Ramayana but also of how Indian women are treated.

Paley made a feature-length animated film titled *Sita Sings the Blues* which she claims is based on Valmiki's Ramayana. She was inspired to produce it when, in her words, 'my husband dumped me by e-mail' soon after she returned to New York. She then began increasingly to project herself as Sita who had been dumped by Rama upon their return to Ayodhya:

> My grief and longing for the man who rejected me increasingly resembled Sita's; my husband's withdrawal reminded me of Rama. In Manhattan I heard the music of Annette Hanshaw for the first time. A radio star of the late 1920s, Hanshaw specialized in heartfelt blues and torch songs. In my grief-addled state, her songs, my story, and the Ramayana merged into one.

Here was a privileged American woman borrowing the Ramayana story as interpreted by Pollock, using it in whatever frame of reference she liked. Her work mixes Pollock-style allegations of social abusiveness in the Ramayana with her own autobiography and turns it into a film that gets rave reviews in the mainstream. It gets promoted as a film that is true to the subject under consideration. What she has done is to take the Ramayana completely out of context and mangle it with stereotypes, while claiming it is based on Valmiki's Ramayana. Then she turns around and positions it as a way of speaking about Sita and, through it, liberating the Indian woman.

Various anglicized non-resident Indians (NRIs), including Aseem Chhabra, a member of the board of the South Asian Journalists Association, actively collaborated with Paley and provided the conversational background explaining the Ramayana as best they could – which comes across as cartoonish.[36] Chhabra's was the lead voice in the animation.

The re-colonization of Indian minds

Defining the problem he wants to solve: Decay of Sanskrit

In a 2011 article, Pollock made a pitch for the funding of Sanskrit studies, which he notes had practically disappeared from India after

Independence.[37] He proposed a programme to provide Sanskrit philological training to Indian secularists who are proficient in English. They would, in effect, 'master and overmaster' Sanskrit to detoxify its texts and thereby move Indian society towards social equality. He pitched his proposal to those he perceived were enlightened private entrepreneurs.

He defines the problem in a manner that I happen to agree with and have discussed in many forums myself. He writes:

> India is about to become the only major world culture whose literary patrimony, and indeed history, are in the custodianship of scholars outside the country: in Berkeley, Chicago, and New York; Oxford, Paris, and Vienna. This would not be healthy either for India or for the rest of the world that cares about India.[38]

I would go much further: India's intellectual legacy has already been taken over in various ways by Western academicians and businesses. It is not a question of what is 'about to become' but what has long been under way and has largely already happened. India's literary heritage and written history began to be controlled by Western academics in the eighteenth century, when Sir William Jones claimed to have 'discovered' Sanskrit. Thomas Macaulay argued for a deliberate British move to fund the study of English and Indian vernaculars while defunding Sanskrit studies in India. The study and research of Sanskrit were moved to Oxford with the specific intention of converting the 'natives' of India to Christianity.

My concern is that far from offering a *solution* to this problem, Pollock actively *contributes* to it. He wants to take over where Oxford left off and establish American universities such as Harvard and Columbia as centres for studies in Indian classics, with him in control. However, the intention this time is not to convert the 'natives' to Christianity but rather the elite Indians to an American Orientalist project of social change using his liberation philology.

Having stated the problem, he now expresses concern over potential India-based competition for his proposal. He is fearful of 'the political transformation of India in the postcolonial period, with the astonishing rise and acceptance of new and violent forms of communal irrationality and violence'.[39] Once again, he focusses on Hinduism (without necessarily naming it explicitly), and in particular the BJP, as the cause of such violence:

> From all this you will understand my impatience with the ignorant and self-crippling attack on the classics by a shallow post-Orientalism and post-colonialism on the one hand, and *the criminal attempt at its appropriation by the alphabet soup of indigenist forces* (RSS, BJP, VHP ...'[40]

This type of branding helps him make the case that American universities are safer places to locate the world headquarters of Sanskrit studies, than institutions located in India would be. He constantly puts fear in the minds of Indians that they should not be suspected of having the remotest links with anything that might be branded as 'saffron'.

Plan to counter BJP's takeover of Sanskrit

In order to prevent the takeover of Sanskrit studies by the Hindu right, Pollock wants to produce Indian Sanskritists who are leftists to counter their moves. To that end, he is specific about the kind of Indians he wants to train. Not only do they need to have knowledge of Sanskrit and other Indian languages, they must be competent in using Western philology and certain other postmodern theories for deconstructing the texts produced in those languages. The latter requirement implies not only writing competence in Western academic English but also a certain view of the world.

I too would like Sanskritists to be as fluent as possible in multiple world views, but without uncritically embracing the Western theories the way many of his Indian followers tend to do. I will describe briefly what he considers to be the skills required of a scholar of Indian literature.

Sanskritists have to be hyper-conscious of class issues

In order to see what Pollock is looking for in his new cadre, let us consider the scholars he regards as important models. Among them is the late D.D. Kosambi, whom he regards as 'one of the most interesting and influential of classical studies scholars in the immediate post-Independence period'. According to him: 'Kosambi combined strong philological skills with a richly developed theoretical approach to his subject matter.'[41]

Besides being 'an Indian mathematician, statistician, historian, and polymath', Kosambi is appreciated by his supporters for compiling critical editions of ancient Sanskrit texts. He was a Marxist historian specializing in ancient India who was often praised for employing 'the historical materialist approach in his work' and for being 'the patriarch of the Marxist school of Indian historiography'.[42]

Indeed, Kosambi is credited by Indian intellectuals for having founded modern Indian historiography, which produced such eminent historians as Irfan Habib and Romila Thapar. Another voice is Sumit Sarkar, who said:

> ... modern Indian historiography, starting with D.D. Kosambi in the 1950s, is acknowledged the world over – wherever South Asian history is taught or studied – as quite on a par with or even superior to all that is produced abroad. And that is why Irfan Habib or Romila Thapar or R.S. Sharma are figures respected even in the most diehard anti-Communist American universities. They cannot be ignored if you are studying South Asian history.[43]

Pollock wants to produce many Sanskritists similar to Kosambi in India. More specifically, he wants them to be leftists who will combine Marxism with liberation philology.

Sanskritists have to be proficient in English

Pollock's Indian Sanskritists would be expected to follow in the footsteps of Kosambi, who unlike Habib, Thapar and Sarkar, was a Sanskrit scholar as well. He adds that there is one more qualification Indian Sanskritists should have – proficiency in English:

> A counterintuitive but potentially consequential factor in the erosion of classical language skills lies in the erosion of English language skills ... the capacity to communicate in English has decayed dramatically

> among classical, and indeed most other, scholars in India since Independence. As a result, Indian classicists are almost entirely shut out of the international community of scholarship and show little substantive understanding of what is being done in classical studies outside of India, or even in India itself.[44]

Again, the problem to which Pollock points here is one I have also identified and often discussed. However, the way Pollock wants to implement it is entirely counter to the interests of building a serious, engaged and cosmopolitan set of scholars based in India. For Pollock, English proficiency is required so that these newly trained Indian Marxist Sanskritists can get continued guidance from their Western mentors. The English-centred international community of scholarship to which Pollock refers is the one certified and nurtured by Western academics. It would appear Pollock wants to turn the clock back to the colonial period.

The Murty Classical Library of India

Looking for a sponsor

Pollock explains who should fund his project to train English-speaking leftists to do critical philology on Sanskrit. His view on this matter, he claims, has changed over time. He writes:

> I am no longer so sure that the central government is the solution rather than the problem. Having had considerable experience with *sarkari* institutions [a term often used effectively to dismiss the 'government' to which the word refers], especially in the past few years, I have grown increasingly convinced that the dead hand of the state would likely wind up perverting any such initiative ... *Perhaps the enlightened private sector can offer a way forward – the founding of the Murty Classical Library of India through an endowment from an Indian family is one stellar example – or cooperative arrangements between private Indian actors and the international community of classical programs, pressed though these themselves may be for essential resources.*[45]

He has turned to India's 'enlightened private sector'. He puts India's billionaires and multimillionaires on a pedestal and calls them enlightened (in the European sense of being rational and empirical, not in the Hindu sense of moksha). One would not be amiss in positing that this is a form of prashasti (praise for the sponsors of one's work), which he himself discusses critically in his analysis of Sanskrit kavya.

Pollock's justifications and aspirations after successful fund-raising

Upon raising the funds, Pollock described the specific objectives of the Murty Classical Library of India (MCLI) and how it will go about achieving those objectives:

> The Murty Classical Library of India aims to make available the great literary works of India from the past two millennia. Many classic Indic texts have never reached a global audience, while others are becoming increasingly inaccessible even to Indian readers. The creation of a classical library of India is intended to reintroduce these works to a new generation of readers.
>
> The series will provide modern English translations of classical works, many for the first time, across a vast array of Indian languages, including Bangla, Hindi, Kannada, Marathi, Pali, Panjabi, Persian, Sanskrit, Sindhi, Tamil, Telugu, and Urdu.[46]

The objective is to provide English translations of works originally written in a range of Indian languages, one of which would be Sanskrit. Notice that when he developed his pitch for funding, it was focussed specifically on Sanskrit, which is his area of expertise. The scope of the MCLI has expanded to include a range of other Indian languages in which he includes Persian. He points out that the MCLI represents 'the single most complex and continuous multilingual tradition of literature in the world' and that 'this is what, in all its complexity and multiplicity, the MCLI seeks to present to readers'.[47]

Many Indians feel quite proud that the accomplishments of their ancestors may be finally recognized, translated and distributed throughout the world. Then again, an important facet of the project is conveyed in the following sentence:

> We also offer rich annotation to help readers wherever literary allusion or historical reference may be difficult to comprehend.

This means the texts are going to be edited and freshly interpreted. The translations will have 'rich annotations' by the editors, which means that they will expand and/or reinterpret what the original Indian author said. Thus, the selection of the texts and the translators and editors will determine the form in which Indian literature reaches the world.

Pollock also aspires that these translations and interpretations will be available forever. They will, as per the library's name, become the 'classics of India': 'MCLI books are intended to remain in circulation in perpetuity (in whatever medium future generations will favour), and such long life demands a translation style as resistant to decay as possible.' Indeed, this is an idealistic aspiration given the drastic changes the English lexicon has undergone in just the last century, not to mention idiom and context.

This process would require scholars to interpret the translations for future generations. And where would such scholars be best produced? At prestigious American universities, of course. According to the project goals, the translations of Indian texts will be about the 'vast variety of the human past'. However, the interpretation of the past might not generally resonate with the typical Indian reader's view.

In light of the ambitious aspiration of the MCLI, a critical question arises: Who will select the Indian literary texts to be translated and who will translate, interpret and edit those texts, in effect supplying the lens through which readers everywhere will see Indian literature? Since postmodernists believe that the original author is dead and could be irrelevant now, the context for interpretation may be supplied by the scholar working on it today. This opens the door to a wide range of political agendas at the discretion of those in charge.

The rise of the American-English cosmopolis

The MCLI strategy he has devised seems to mirror his own thesis on the way Sanskrit allegedly died and the Indian vernaculars rose in the second millennium CE. Pollock explains how the vernacularization process utilized the old Sanskrit texts for new political purposes. He refers to a new 'naturalization of peoples and cultures through new conceptual and discursive practices'.[48] In the same manner, the MCLI is reinterpreting these carefully selected 'classical' Indian texts into English to fit his political agenda. He has himself emphasized throughout his study of Indian languages that politics drives such changes, and hence it is fair to ask what *his* political agenda is for replacing Indian languages with English. This should be transparently and openly discussed.

His praise for Murty, pointed out above, is not unlike the prashasti he disparages as he strives to prove that a culture-power matrix brought about the transformation of languages. Indeed, the MCLI process is the Americanization of Indian literature in the same manner Pollock claims the vernacularization of literature took place by the Indian elites of that time.

He writes that in the vernacularization process 'new regional worlds were created' and in the exact same way I feel his translation team is replicating the positions of privilege of the Harvard-Columbia-type of elites. These spaces are modelled after the dominant Western culture where they are most at home. The inhabitants of these positions are not just westerners but also westernized Indian elites.

In fact, English is rapidly becoming the new substitute for Sanskrit as India's link language. Pollock is spearheading the English/anglicized cosmopolis as it becomes further entrenched in India. His study of vernacularization examines in detail how and why various Sanskrit norms were adopted and adapted and which ones were not. The same applies to his use of English idioms, vocabulary, aesthetics of power, funding sources, and so on, through the MCLI.

His history of the dramatic changes in languages in India (from Sanskrit to the vernaculars) refers to 'the old aspiration of attaining "power to the horizons" and "empire without end" ... being re-placed, literally, by a new concern'.[49] He seems here to be also unconsciously referring to the same kind of English-language 'empire without end' that he hopes to establish.

The following statement by him admits the inherent bias of scholars using what I have called 'Western Universalism'. I am concerned that this kind of bias also applies to the translations and interpretations being done by his team:

> ... all perception is admittedly theory-laden, as many sociologists and philosophers have explained. We cannot cognize the world around us without simultaneously fitting our cognitions – or prefitting or retrofitting them, whichever is the true sequence – into the linguistic and conceptual schemata that constitute our world; the formulation of empirical observations becomes possible only within some referential framework.[50]
>
> Theories of power and culture – on legitimation of political authority, epic distance in literature, and a host of other questions – have their origins in the West in capitalism and modernity and were devised to make sense of the behaviour of power and culture under Western capitalist modernity, the first political-economic and cultural order to theorize its own emergence and specificity. These are the particulars from which larger universalizations have typically been produced, in association with the universalization of Western power under colonialism and globalization.[51]

Pollock seems to be doing what he says colonialism did two centuries ago: select texts which make sense to contemporary scholars who are all from the West or who are westernized Indians. No apparent safeguards have been articulated to ensure that such interpretations using the English language lexicon, grammar and idiom will preserve the authenticity of the original texts from a different place and time. Perhaps that is because Pollock knows already that such authenticity would deny him the freedom to make the interpretations fit into his stated political goals. By their very nature, translation and interpretation require the use of a particular lens, and such a lens – originating in another culture – changes the meaning of the traditional text. This may not have been critical in the translation and interpretation of Greek or Latin texts, as their cultures of origin were largely extinguished. In the case of India, the culture is very much alive. The question that must be asked and debated is: Will the imposition of this process of translation and interpretation, as initiated by the MCLI, bring about the slow death of a living culture?

I worry that the Murty Classical Library of India is an extension of the colonial project initiated at Oxford University in 1832 with money bequeathed to the university by Lieutenant Colonel Joseph Boden, a retired soldier in the service of the East India Company. His wish was for the university to establish a Sanskrit professorship to assist in the conversion of the people of British India to Christianity. Pollock is not looking to convert people to Christianity but rather to Marxist and trendy postmodernist ideologies that are inimical to Hindu dharma.

His focus is on developing left-leaning English-speaking scholars from India, who would work with him in translating and interpreting 500 volumes in the series. This would topple the importance of Sanskrit as well as the vernaculars. When I turn the gaze back on Pollock, using his thesis of the death of Sanskrit as being due to the rise of Indian vernaculars, I find ominous parallels in his MCLI strategy.

His stated goal is to transform the study of Sanskrit by changing it from traditional approaches to his own liberation philology. If he is successful, the Sanskrit tradition will be digested into the West, just as many other civilizations and cultures have been. This will domesticate the Indian civilization as a wholly owned subsidiary of the Western intellectual establishment and its Indian proxies.

Now that MCLI is very much in place, with its strategy of digesting texts and potentially causing a slow death of Indian languages, we need to ask ourselves: Can anything be done vis-à-vis the Murty library to recover the lost ground for multiple millennia of Indian cultural inheritance? At a minimum, I would suggest that questions of transparency and academic rigour need to be raised – questions about the selection of the Indian texts and about the scholars who translate and interpret those texts, as well as questions about how the drafts will be peer-reviewed by a deep and broad bench of traditional scholars. These are important precautions given the far-reaching impact this project will have on future generations of Indians.

Reversing the gaze: Interpreting Pollock using his own concepts

In Pollock's intellectual toolkit for analysing Hindus, there are some key concepts that can easily be reversed and applied back on to him. I will explain a few of these below.

Elitist control of the discourse

As we have seen, Pollock sees in sanskriti an asymmetry of power favouring the elitist brahmin–kshatriya nexus over the rest of the population. When we apply the same kind of analysis to his work, we see that Pollock is an American Ivy League academician and among the most elitist of intellectuals. And the financial capitalists, investment bankers and industrialists are today's political power brokers shaping politics through the lobbies they control. Pollock was initially funded by John Clay, an elite Wall Street investor. Under Pollock's leadership, the Clay Library produced fifty-six volumes of Sanskrit translations. More recently, the funding source has been the Murthy family.

Pollock constantly harps on brahmin scholars supporting their sponsors by writing prashastis (praise) for their sponsors. He points to prashastis as evidence of how intellectuals worked in the interests of their patrons and as proof that the enterprise was undertaken primarily for political motives. Whether that allegation is true or not, reversing the gaze, we note that Pollock writes many prashastis for his own sponsors.[52]

Exporting the American cosmopolis to India

An important thesis of Pollock is that the brahmins sold their services to various ancient kings. Consequently, Sanskrit literature spread across South Asia and South-east Asia in a manner that was tailored to sustain and expand the political power of their patrons. Once more, whether historically true or not, there are some startling parallels in these claims with Pollock's own career. The US financial collapse in 2008, combined with the ill health of his patron John Clay, was a setback for the Clay Library project. Just as he says the brahmins did for centuries, Pollock began to look for another patron across the seas. He went to India to ply his intellectual trade as an American Sanskrit philologist, seeking sponsorship from patrons with wealth and political clout. He found support from Indian elites to start his project of the Murty Classical Library of India at Harvard.

Pollock has, in effect, expanded what we may think of as the American cosmopolis, much as he says the brahmins of the past did to spread what he calls the Sanskrit cosmopolis. As we know, the Sanskrit cosmopolis was allegedly propagated without the aid of any military, economic or evangelical power whereas the American cosmopolis flourishes with the full support of its hard and soft power.

Infusing hegemonic structures into the dominated languages

I have shown Pollock arguing that Sanskrit structures were historically infused into Indian vernaculars by transferring kavya and grammar technology into the vernaculars. But he is doing essentially the same thing by infusing Western intellectual theories, historical assumptions and ideologies into Indian English and Indian vernaculars. I have already shown how he has infused his own view of the Ramayana into the mainstream. He has infused Indian English with Western philology, its ways of interpreting texts, its political positions and its secular allegiances and interests. Just as he claims the export of Sanskrit from its home base involved injecting its poisonous ideologies through grammar and other structures, so also his work in India may be said to consist of injecting Western theories into Indian scholarship.

His strategy for English is to emulate the way Sanskrit spread and rooted itself structurally while enabling the local languages to flourish. He says there was 'Sanskrit inside' the vernaculars, as a strategy of the elites. Similarly, he wants there to be 'Western theory inside' the Indian languages and literary works. Such is his plan for bringing the American Orientalist way of thinking into India. He writes:

> Might it be possible to transcend the dichotomies of modernizing (and homogenizing) cosmopolitanism and traditionalizing (and rigidifying) vernacularism by understanding that the new must be made precisely through attachment to the old, and by recognizing that only such an attachment enables one to grasp what in the past can and must be changed?[53]

To decode his statement, one must refer back to his 'Crisis in the Classics' paper in which he emphasizes the importance of mastering English in order to do Sanskrit studies properly. He is now asking if it is possible to have American English as the cosmopolitan language throughout the globe while at the same time allowing local languages to flourish.[54] And he would seem to be answering 'yes'.

> The Sanskrit cosmopolis offers just such an instance – another apparent anomaly of India, itself the 'strangest of all possible anomalies', as Macaulay phrased the unintended compliment. Indeed, such anomalies may be precisely what is needed in a world of almost nomologically re-enacted violence between the localisms and globalism of modernity: the anomaly of a universalism that does not stand in contradiction with cultural or political particularism or preach its own necessity, that knows its limits and yet has centers everywhere and circumferences nowhere ...[55]

He is, in effect, saying that American English, the current vehicle of 'globalism of modernity' can establish itself as a form of soft power. This will allow local languages to flourish under the umbrella of the modern (i.e., American) cosmopolis.

He proceeds further in this direction, suggesting 'the possibility of making the future one of And rather than Either/Or'.[56] Put another way, it is not one or the other, but both. Both can flourish in their respective positions – American English on top and the other languages below, all one happily Americanized family. By attaching itself to the local, the globalizing cosmopolis can decide what parts of the local must change so as to be in alignment with the new American cosmopolis. Elsewhere, I have described such processes as part of the 'digestion' of one civilization into another.

Aestheticization of power

What Pollock is essentially doing is taking Western conceptual categories and infusing them into Indian minds while at the same time claiming to be reviving Sanskrit. This makes Indians 'feel good' about their heritage, especially considering that all this attention is coming from an American. This is a ruse of aestheticization to camouflage the political colonization by American ideas; such performances are common before Indian elites and in media interviews and conversations.

At his appearances before secular audiences, he uses a different kind of appeal. Rather than present himself as a Sanskrit pandit, he is very different when he is at the New School in New York or the Centre for the Study of Developing Societies in Delhi. There he projects himself as a Marxist hardliner spreading liberation philology in order to detoxify the Sanskrit texts.

It would be a reasonable project to interpret the works of Pollock's team as a new genre of kavya designed to aestheticize the power of the American cosmopolis including its Indian American elite members. All the necessary ingredients as per his theory of the aestheticization of power are abundantly visible:

- Sponsorship of his work by the elites in power.
- Prashastis (praise for sponsor) being recited by him at public events.
- Infusion of Indian English with American idiom, complex theories, political networking and prestige by association. (This is what he calls the 'literarization' of the language.)
- Certification of the kavya producers as the 'neo-brahmins' (i.e., those with adhikara) by virtue of direct or indirect association with the Ivy Leagues.

- Intoxicated response by the Indian public expressing a sense of pride and gratitude that he has taken over such a major responsibility for them.
- Greater power accumulating in the American cosmopolis through the digestion of Indian knowledge assets, and through the appropriation of the Indian elite.

11

Conclusion: The Way Forward

The foregoing chapters show that:

- Among the Western and Western-based Indologists there are those leading an aggressive and well-organized movement to position the study of Sanskrit as a political battleground. They claim it is infused with toxic elements supporting Vedic, brahminic and royal hegemony and that it encodes oppressive views of shudras, women, Muslims and all those who can be construed as 'others'. They see Sanskrit as a repository of Vedic knowledge (shastra) or of politically motivated literature (kayva), all to be studied as curious vestiges of an outgrown past. They regard the oral tradition as marginal. Efforts to revive Sanskrit as a living language are seen as linked to Hindu violence and as hostile to the oppressed masses.
- The centres of Sanskrit studies that were earlier shifted out of India and into Europe have subsequently moved from Europe to the US. It is from the US that most academic Sanskrit research is now being conducted and driven. Western perspectives and

theories are being used as the lens for this research, a lens I call 'American Orientalism'. Young scholars in the social sciences are being trained in this new mission which is designed to produce new prescriptions (like smritis) that are supposedly 'detoxified'.

- If these trends continue, India will remain an importer of knowledge about its own civilization rather than being at the helm of the discourse concerning itself.
- At the same time, westerners from many other disciplines and walks of life are mining ancient Sanskrit for its philosophical sophistication, spiritual guidance, and potential for expanding systematic knowledge in fields ranging from physics to mind sciences. Westerners have a stake in Sanskrit studies to extract the underlying cultural wealth accumulated by the civilization over many millennia.

In other words, the study of Sanskrit and sanskriti is being taken over by two different vested interests in the West: (a) social scientists and humanities scholars wanting to reinterpret India's past and re-engineer its future by exhuming the toxicity they perceive in Hinduism; and (b) scientists, environmentalists, spiritual seekers, self-help experts and 'new-thought gurus' intent on mining its treasury of knowledge.

In this chapter, I want to spell out a potential response to the challenges presented as a result of this.

The Sanskrit ecosystem must be revived in a holistic way

In the first place, we need to create a model for the study of Sanskrit as part of a living system being practised today. Sanskrit's revival should not be modelled after the dead 'classical' languages like Latin and Greek, which are, in effect, sitting in museums and being picked apart by scholars. Rather, Sanskrit should be seen more like Mandarin, Persian and Arabic – languages which, though ancient, are still actively used today.

There is already a thriving movement by an important organization called Samskrita Bharati to revive Sanskrit's use for ordinary conversation and reading. In my opinion, the revival should go further and also produce new literary works, plays, novels and the like. Most of all, it should be used as a tool for serious knowledge research. We need modern writings of kayva and shastra and updates of the old ones.

The revival of Sanskrit should also include the perspectives of scholars using social science lenses and critical historical tools. Debates must be organized so as to provide fresh insights into our past, diagnoses of the problems we face today, and proposals for remedying these problems. However, although all analyses and descriptions are to be welcome for discussion, prescriptions for remedy should not be divorced from the transcendental understandings and adhyatma vidya methods, as these are integral to the Sanskrit tradition. The writing of new smritis for this era must not be left in the hands of secularists who lack the required lived experience and investment in the tradition.

The battles for Sanskrit, sanskriti and dharma are interrelated. The insiders cannot accept Pollock's position that paramarthika aspects are to be sidelined and eliminated simply because they are being accused of being toxic for some mysterious reason. The use of Sanskrit must remain linked to both paramarthika and vyavaharika.

Non-translatable Sanskrit terms must enter the mainstream

There must be multiple levels and ways of revitalizing sanskriti. Those who do not become fluent speakers of Sanskrit can still become aware of important non-translatable words and concepts. I would like to see, for instance, a book called 'One hundred and eight Sanskrit non-translatable terms'. The text could be accompanied by multimedia teaching materials for popular consumption. It is important to explain and argue why the common translations (such as 'atman' translated as 'soul') are false, misleading and confusing when used in a Western context. In my book *Being Different*, I have attempted to argue for this awareness.

The goal should be to infuse the English idiom with these Sanskrit terms so that the words and unique ideas they represent become part of the English mainstream discourse. (Eventually, I would like to see the project expanded to 'One thousand and eight Sanskrit non-translatables'.) By infusing Sanskrit words and concepts into common parlance, we can, to some extent, Sanskritize English. At the present time, when our ideas are translated in the West, they are almost always plucked out of context, disconnected from the source, and reinstated as part of Western thought. Preserving the Sanskrit terms as well as the correct history and metaphysical framework should help prevent such hijacking.

Another important project worth exploring would be to re-Sanskritize Hindi, which would mean 'taking back Hindi' from the way it has been Persianized to become a hybrid Urdu-Hindi. Bollywood and pop culture have made this Urdu-Hindi fashionable. A project to infuse Sanskrit into modern Indian vernaculars would, in fact, be consistent with Pollock's own theory of how this was successfully done in the past, and it would also use the same methods as his projects that infuse English into Indian languages today.

Shastras must be seen as a platform for innovation

The shastras of the past are encyclopedias and databases containing the intellectual work that has been done to date and embedded in Sanskrit. Within the shastras, many specialized fields of knowledge are covered which include: architecture, astronomy, ceramics, chemistry, ethnics, jyotisha (which is broader than astrology), mantra, medicine, metallurgy, philosophy and psychology. All await study by experts.

This knowledge must be put into the modern context, tested scientifically where possible, updated and used as the foundation for further extensions and developments. The idea is not to parrot old verses out of chauvinistic pride but to solve contemporary problems using Sanskrit as a resource combined with new knowledge. The shastras were never frozen or sealed as final. They were always challenged by rivals and kept alive as vibrant bodies of knowledge evolving with new evidence.

Unfortunately, traditional experts are getting scarce, and those that do exist today spend most of their time reproducing old texts rather than developing new ones. Consequently, most of the research into the knowledge embedded in shastras is being done by westerners, without regard for preserving the culture from which it arose. This amounts to a loss of social and economic capital for the Sanskrit tradition.

The main domain of shastras that is vibrant today is that of Vedanta. One may think of this as moksha-shastra. One must keep in mind that the pursuit of moksha should be infused into various vyavaharika practices and not seen as something in isolation. The paramarthika and vyavaharika realms comprise one integral unity. The various shastras are a unified body of knowledge that must be approached holistically. Hence, the shastras pertaining to various vyavaharika realms must be given importance as well. Interestingly, Pollock attacks shastra precisely on the basis that these are integrally and holistically unified with Vedic cosmology. For the very reason he deprecates them, we must revive them and keep them unified.

Each of the shastras is written out of a distinct intellectual tradition. For example, Sanskrit grammarians wrote extensive treatises and restatements of what their predecessors had developed. They then gave their own interpretation of the work of their predecessors and tried to show how their views differed from other contemporary writers who were interpreting the same older texts. Only after doing this extensive historical and differentiating analysis were they able to explain their own extensions and innovations. Unfortunately, in modern times there has been a serious discontinuity in this stream of intellectual history in the shastras. This tradition of evolution with continuity needs to be rekindled.

New itihasas and smritis must be written

Sanskrit has a unique tradition of writing about social memories and incorporating the lessons learned into smritis. An important way of repositioning Sanskrit as the core of an Indian renaissance is to rejuvenate the art of writing smritis.

For instance, we need to write new itihasas describing the two long-lived traumatic events that took place over the last 1,000 years: the Islamic invasions, which peaked with Aurangzeb's rule across most of India, and British colonialism from the eighteenth and into the twentieth century. The method itself by which such itihasas are written has to be studied. We can use this genre in practical ways today. For example, the Mahabharata speaks not only of the politics but also shows the lessons to be learned from the trauma at various levels: individual, group, community, social, etc. All this has to be put in a much larger framework, that of the Veda itself. Such a development would, in effect, decolonize Indians and facilitate a greater understanding of India's past.

We also need to present the Indian history of science and technology as part of what I have called the Indian Grand Narrative project. All knowledge we have of our past, from the Indus–Sarasvati Civilization onwards, must be written both analytically in modern history format and as itihasa, and spread widely.

Itihasa-based stories used to be performed on streets across the land, entertaining and educating simultaneously. These days, the term 'infotainment' is used to denote this dual purpose. The West, lacking in itihasa, now has many epic-style movies and television shows that try to fill the vacuum. Indian itihasa was always innovative in its use of aesthetics and presentation; similarly we must now use the latest technology to develop and project the new itihasa.

The new itihasa should be produced in a grand style as dramatic performances and on multiple platforms, including giant screens in IMAX (and similar) theatres. Initially, one such theatre could be started in every state capital of India; then they could be added to smaller towns until there is at least one in each of the districts that comprise the country. (The Bible – positioned as a sort of 'Jesus itihasa' – is currently being promoted in film in India's hinterlands, a fact of which Indians in the metros are blissfully unaware.)

'Sacred philology' must compete against political/ liberation philology

As this book demonstrates in detail, Sheldon Pollock has issued a clarion call for 'liberation philology' in the study of Sanskrit, a new term by which he means constant purging of Sanskrit's supposed toxic elements and deconstruction of its mystified attachment to the paramarthika or sacred domain.

He is clearly alluding here to the movement called 'liberation theology' which started in Latin America as a way to digest Marxism into Christianity, and thereby make Christianity socially friendly. Unfortunately, Pollock's term obscures the fact that the *real* liberation theology was a social movement internal to Christianity and accepting of its fundamental principles. Indeed, it was largely a call for a *return* to Christian fundamental principles. Contrary to this, Pollock rejects the core metaphysical principles of the Sanskrit tradition and sees them as no more than relics of primitive thinking or attempts to blind people. Furthermore, I have shown ways in which his liberation philology approach seriously misrepresents the texts it purports to illuminate, and distorts the function of these texts in the lives of real people. Therefore, it is a misleading term when he applies it to sanskriti.

As an alternative to this approach, I am proposing what I call a 'sacred philology', a philology rooted in the conviction that Sanskrit cannot be divorced from its matrix in the Vedas and other sacred texts, or from its orientation towards the transcendent realm. By this sacred philology, I also indicate a stance towards these studies that is quite different from the stance of the Western, secular academy that Pollock represents.

Sacred philology involves first of all a respect for, and preferably a practice of, the kinds of sadhana that have supported the dharmic traditions for centuries, including tapasya and meditation. Much of what is valuable in Sanskrit simply cannot be understood even in a basic way without some practice such as chanting of mantras.

This commitment need not exclude anyone; Christians, westerners, members of other faiths and even those whose position is agnostic or in flux can perfectly well approach Sanskrit from the point of view of sacred philology, provided they are open to its transcendental principles and respectful of its exemplars.

Nor need sacred philology mean an uncritical acceptance of every single thing written in some famous Sanskrit text. As I have said many times, the attention to issues of social justice and historical accuracy that Pollock and others call for, can and should be pursued in the context of this approach. The works of Western academic scholars who focus heavily on history and critique can actually be valuable to us as a provocation and stimulus, provided their distortions are addressed and their interpretations are not allowed to become the lone, hegemonic, discourse.

A wholehearted embrace of sacred philology, however, would require not just that traditional scholars of Sanskrit wake up from their hibernation, but that a whole new and well-funded set of programmes be launched to support it and to develop a cadre of younger scholars. It may even require a new set of institutions, for the approach would not sit comfortably either within a modern academic context or within the kinds of traditional Sanskrit mathas and peethams that tend to be insular and closed off to engagement with the wider vyavaharika world. There is plenty of work to be done here, and much creativity is needed to absorb the attention of those with deep pockets and a desire to see Sanskrit and dharma take their due place on the world stage.

In any case, sacred philology is, in my view, a far better and more comprehensive approach to the tradition than the dubious and artificial method of liberation philology which I find to be a ringing phrase with little behind it except a set of counterproductive assumptions and self-righteous posturing that do not serve either to clarify the tradition or to move it forward.

We must try to understand contemporary issues and solutions in terms of our own intellectual framework and be willing to extend and adapt them. Again, the idea is not to parrot old solutions, or ignore real issues such as social injustice, but to innovate.

The purva-paksha tradition must be revived

It is clear to me that many present-day Hindu leaders are ineffective in understanding and engaging the world of non-Hindus. It is as though we are wearing a burqa-of-the-mind that limits our view of the world to a few small windows. We tend to either avoid the differences that arise or become defensive or, in a good many cases, tragically capitulate to the other side. What is needed is a dispassionate purva-paksha and analysis of the other side that does not slip into any of these modes.

We also need to understand why Hindus have traditionally failed to do such purva-paksha when it comes to encounters with people from outside India. Why did Hindu leaders fail to do purva-paksha of Islam, Christianity and Western secular thought? The intellectual non-engagement of Hindus was evident when Syrian Christianity arrived in Kerala between the second and fourth centuries, when Islam arrived in Sindh by way of Arab traders in the eighth century CE (about three centuries prior to the Turkish invasions in the north), and more recently in the onslaught of the Western secular/materialistic discourse on Indian civilization.

There is a common misunderstanding that all the leadership for dealing with external threats or encounters must come from kshatriyas and/or brahmins. However, there have been many exceptions to this in the past. For instance, the Vijayanagara Empire from the fourteenth to the sixteenth century and the rise of the Marathas in the seventeenth and eighteenth centuries were successful military responses to Islamic invasions, and in both cases there was important leadership and support from jatis which are now classified as 'Other Backward Castes'. They were able to mobilize, train and deploy people within a short span of time.

We must look deeper if we are to understand the capacity (or lack thereof) of Hindus for intellectual engagement with groups that have a different world view. The following pages examine the history of Hindu failure to do purva-paksha on outsiders.

Encounter with Christianity

In the case of Syrian Christian encounters, it appears that a number of brahmin families were converted to Christianity, and so there must have been *some* Hindu–Christian dialogue, although little is recorded. There seems to have been no widespread purva-paksha that would lead to a serious response from the Hindu point of view.

Conversions had happened before – to Buddhism, for example, some 700 years before Syrian Christianity arrived. However, the Buddhist conversions had been met with intellectual resistance, direct encounters and dialogue. There was debate and intense give and take through the purva-paksha and uttara-paksha process. Unfortunately, I have not come across any evidence of comparable purva-paksha in the case of Syrian Christianity.

As a result of the lack of purva-paksha, a Hindu understanding of Christianity was not incorporated into the Hindu intellectual corpus. It did not become part of the curriculum for Hindus in the same manner as debates with Buddhism has been. Historically, therefore, Hindu leadership has remained largely ignorant about Christianity. We paid a very serious price for this.

As an example of our naivete, when the Portuguese were seeking a sea route to India, it was Hindu sailors from Gujarat who showed them the way. In fact, they were invited in by the local Hindu leader, Thimmaya of Goa, the fleet admiral of the powerful Vijayanagara Empire, so that they might benefit from the thriving international trading port and naval base at Honavar, just south of Goa. By then, the Vijayanagara Empire had come under attack by the Bahamanis of Bijapur, and Goa was already lost to them. Therefore, this admiral sought help from the Portuguese general, Albuquerque. Unfortunately, he lacked any understanding of the Portuguese mentality and of the Church. Thimmaya was seeking protection from one aggressor by ushering in a much more dangerous aggressor, without carrying out any investigation or purva-paksha on the party he was inviting.

Christianity had existed in India for well over a thousand years (since the early Syrian Christians as noted above); yet nobody had done a proper purva-paksha of its theology, political structure or ambitions for world conquest. This naivety is what enabled Albuquerque's invasion and the establishment of the Portuguese garrison in Goa, which became the first step for further intrusions by several European powers. What followed as a consequence was the decimation of Hindu culture in Goa, because the Portuguese facilitated the Christian Inquisition.

This ought to be investigated as a glaring example of the failure of Hindus since the first millennium CE to engage intellectually on a global basis. Even afterwards, the Hindus neglected to do any purva-paksha of the rival European Empires, each of which owed its allegiance to one European Church or another.

Encounter with Islam

The Arabs brought Islam into Sindh in the eighth century through military force. The religious, cultural and intellectual component came along with the military. The Hindu response seems to have been limited to the military for the next three centuries, and remained entirely defensive. This was a time when India was stronger by far than the Middle East in material terms and had the resources to study the other side and develop strategies to counter it. Once again, there is little evidence of any substantive intellectual engagement by Hindus with Islam during these three centuries. For instance, although Indian traders routinely travelled to Arabia, we do not know of any Hindu intellectuals who went there to understand them, engage in dialogue, build effective responses, and bring these into the teaching curriculum or discourse in India.

In the encounter with Islam, no purva-paksha was done to understand Islam's metaphysics and social and political systems, until people like Guru Nanak and Kabir began to understand Islam and articulate it in Hindu terms. However, in the meantime, for several centuries, Hindus were intellectually confused and lacked the strategies to defend themselves against Islam. This is how the Hindu intellectuals lost control of their own traditions and their own destiny. The result was the uncontested Persianization of Indian society and its discourse. Avadhi and Braj got digested into Persian, and hence we have the twin creations of Urdu and Hindi in the north.

Encounter with Western secularism

Many years later, British colonization led to the anglicization of educated Indians. This was successful partly because the economically superior Indian side did not bother to do purva-paksha on the Europeans. The British studied us systematically (and we have been proud of this fact), but we never bothered to return the compliment and study *them*!

Mohandas Gandhi's *Hind Swaraj* (Indian Home Rule) was a partial response to anglicization, though it focussed mainly on economic and social issues. He did espouse dharma by embodying a very traditional persona in dealing with the British on his own terms. However, after him, the ideological camp of Jawaharlal Nehru took control for several defining decades. In the process, India became even more intellectually colonized. Elitist Indians were championing anglicization equating it with progress. The English could not be seen as the 'others' so easily, belying Pollock's constant refrain that the brahmins were masters at 'othering'.

The Western secular movement of the nineteenth and twentieth centuries has played a key role in recolonizing India today. Europeans in the colonial era began to denounce Hinduism as unscientific, irrational and superstitious. More recently, the tendency to see India in pejorative secular terms has begun to inhabit postmodernism as well.

Traditional Hindu thinkers have not confronted these fashionable ideologies with adequate rigour, as is achievable in any solid purva-paksha, nor given an uttara-paksha in response. Each Western wave of this secular genre was facilitated by India's leftist elites, who have come to represent a form of snobbish intellectualism disconnected from Indian roots. Given that these 'experts' in Western modernity and postmodernity are Indians operating within the pre-eminent institutions of India, we now have a sort of 'anti-home team' inside our own society. They are like Trojan horses, and truculent and sententious ones at that.

What is happening is that Indian traditions are being rapidly digested into Western frameworks while Hindus themselves are failing to use these traditions as a platform from which to do purva-paksha on the West. My book *Being Different* is an attempt to do just that, yet few Indians take the matter seriously. There still needs to be a systematic, long-term programme to do purva-paksha of not only the West, but also of China and other important civilizations.

The death of purva-paksha

Hindus have always been good at engaging in purva/uttara debates amongst themselves. The Buddhists and Jains essentially arose from within the Hindu culture, as is reflected, for example, in the commonalities of karma and reincarnation. We were able, therefore, to digest elements of Buddhism and Jainism into the Hindu discourse and revise, improve and strengthen our point of view in the process. Buddhism became divorced from its Hindu matrix only outside India and this dissociation has been exaggerated by Western scholars. However, thanks to the system of purva-paksha, there was no serious political tension internally between the various dharma traditions.

So I return to the question: Why did Hindus fail to do a similar purva-paksha on Christianity, Islam and modern secularism? By the time of Madhavacharya's writing of compendiums presenting the broad tenets of sixteen schools of thought in his *Sarva Darshana Sangraha* in the thirteenth to fourteenth century, both Christianity and Islam were known in India. Yet, unfortunately, his analysis only covered the Hindu darshanas and laid the groundwork for his own Advaita system relative to other Hindu systems. He ignored the non-Indian systems in his compendium.

What made Hindu intellectuals of the calibre of Adi Shankara (ninth century), Abhinavagupta (tenth century), Ramanuja (twelfth century) and Madhava (thirteenth to fourteenth century) focus *only inward* on doing purva-paksha? They limited themselves to systems that use Sanskrit categories. Was there resistance to learning non-Sanskrit-based epistemologies and did such a resistance result in Hindus becoming stuck in silos? Were the brahmins too arrogant in assuming that the intellectual categories of outsiders deserved to be ignored? These questions need to be better understood if we are to formulate a way forward.

The following are some of the hindrances that might still be preventing us from doing fresh purva-paksha. In *Being Different* I called this 'difference anxiety'. Each of these is a form of escapism:

1. **Materialism as escape:** Today, some of the Hindu intelligentsia are focussed solely on material well-being. Many withdraw from the type of engagement I propose, by converting to another faith, or downplaying the sacred dimension, or by sheer indifference to whatever does not conduce to the pursuit of riches or pleasures of life.
2. **World-negating interpretations of Vedanta as escape:** The Vedic side in ancient times did engage the Buddhists in extensive purva-paksha and in the process they imported many Buddhist ideas into the interpretation of the Upanishads. Some people speculate that this brought an other-worldly emphasis into India – certain Buddhist ideas got infused and digested into the Vedic interpretations. Also in the same process, some argue, sanatana dharma became less pragmatic, less capable of defending itself from invaders, and perhaps less materialistic. This moksha-shastra, while important for spiritual growth at an individual level, has in effect become the last refuge of many Hindus, who now see it as the only contribution Hinduism could make to the world. The other genres of Hinduism that did not occupy centre stage were far more practical and world-engaging. For instance, tantra affirms the body rather than negating its importance as some Advaita Vedanta thinkers have (incorrectly) tended to do. Furthermore, Chanakya was thoroughly pragmatic, although he never loses sight of the moksha view in his magnum opus. Did too much other-worldliness and separation from vyavaharika prevent us from engaging meaningfully with others?
3. **Sameness as escape:** The naive notion of 'sameness', which I critiqued extensively in *Being Different,* is taught by ill-informed

and intellectually lazy teachers who espouse a limited view of Vedanta. The sameness posture leads to harmful psychological results for Hindus both as individuals and collectively. Very few Hindus realize that for the most part, non-Hindu groups do *not* reciprocate and do *not* accept Hinduism as an equal partner in the pluralistic search for truth.

4. **Bombastic escape:** Many Hindus resort to a bombastic dismissal of the matter at hand: 'there is no problem', 'we are sanatana', 'we have been around for thousands of years and will be here for thousands more' and so on.[1] This position allows them to retreat behind a psychological 'feel good' veil. Such claims serve only to bring some short-lived consolation to the ego.
5. **Glorifying the past as escape:** In responding to challenges, the easy 'default position' is to glorify the past. I have worked hard to uncover distortions of our past, so I appreciate its importance. Nevertheless, defending the past is simply not enough.
6. **Blaming others as escape:** Many Hindus blame their predicament on the aggressiveness inherent in Islam and Christianity. However, I would point out that China also bore the brunt of attacks from Islam and the West, as did Japan when it was under attack by Christianity. Both China and Japan were able to engage with those attacks, and yet retain their language and traditional world views. Engagement and resistance seem to be core reasons as to why China and Japan are able to flourish once again today. What lessons can Hindus learn from those cultures?
7. **Inability to see 'others' clearly:** Do Indians lack a well-defined concept of 'others', given that the prior purva-paksha encounters were with fellow Indians and not with outsiders? Could it be that we can only debate with those who use our own Sanskrit categories (as in the case of Hindus, Buddhists, Jains, et al.), and cannot engage outsiders because that requires understanding *their* categories as well?

All these are important questions to be discussed among those who are invested in the sanskriti of India. The tradition calls for such debates and the necessary intellectual resources are at hand.

Arvind Sharma (in private communication) has offered some interesting perspectives on this matter. He explains that Chinese thought is based on Confucianism in which each individual belongs to a multilevel system consisting of: parents, elder sibling, spouse, elder friend, and emperor. It is a complex system in which age and gender are factors as well. Hence, the emperor is in the *same type of relationship as the family*; the emperor is at the highest level of this hierarchy. This means that the political unity of all Chinese is built into the Confucian world view, according to Sharma.

Sharma goes on to point out that the British very successfully conscripted Indians into their armies and deployed them in multiple continents: Africa, China, Europe during the two world wars, besides, of course, India. By one account, Indians fought under British command in 111 wars against their fellow Indians! However, in China the British failed to raise a single regiment that would be loyal to them and fight for them.

Sharma speculates that a reason for India's downfall was the eclipse of the category of Chakravarti as mentioned in the *Arthashastra*. A Chakravarti's domain was from ocean to ocean; he was above all the other kings who were local. He feels that the *Arthashastra* at some point ceased to be taught for learning realpolitik. There appears to have been an attack on it by liberal passivism. It is ironic, he says, that during British rule the *Arthashastra* text had disappeared until a copy suddenly surfaced with a farmer in Kerala in the early twentieth century. Because *Arthashastra* also teaches the use of physical force in dealing with 'others', its loss in the Indian mind deprived Indians of the intellectual tools necessary to understand strategies for such encounters. Sharma recommends introducing the study of *Arthashastra* in all schools in all languages.

Some others suggest that *Panchatantra* ought to be taught at very young ages as a popular version of strategic thinking. It is interesting that the Arabs took the *Panchatantra* and translated/adapted it into their children's stories, which reached Europe as *Aesop's Fables*.

Well-qualified home team and institutions must be developed

Ideas will live and spread only through human containers and transmitters. And trained humans are needed to develop those ideas. Thus, we have a symbiotic relationship between the projects to be undertaken and the human resources required to carry them out. I have called these human resources 'the home team'. Such a team is needed to bring sanskriti back into the contemporary mainstream culture.

Doing so requires setting up training academies that are on par with the vast research and educational apparatus controlled by the opposite side. It requires academic conferences and journals, not for regurgitating old materials but for generating new ones. We must entirely revamp and re-envision the context and institutions within which Sanskrit is taught today. We also need to create institutions that are similar to modern seminaries. There, the tradition could be approached critically, using a wide range of tools, from philology and social science to metaphysics and cosmology. Yet all this would have to be approached from within the traditional cosmology and would have to be lived and practised. Theory cannot be divorced from practice.

All leaders and teachers of our traditional mathas and modern movements should have a good understanding of Christianity, Judaism, Islam and Western modern and postmodern philosophies and histories. They should also be able to successfully debate and respond to arguments from the best representatives of these European and Middle Eastern traditions.

Besides creating *new* institutions, we must infuse sanskriti into *existing* ones. Just as any leading organization has a chief technology officer, a chief marketing officer, a chief medical officer, etc., so too there should be a chief sanskriti officer. We must have training institutes that educate and certify them. Every government ministry, every successful corporation, every influential non-government agency and media firm should have such a person on hand, whose job it would be to champion the revival of Indian civilization in a modern, constructive manner that is pragmatic and useful. As soon as such a position is turned into a career, it will attract high-calibre, young professionals into the field.

Defining the hard work that is needed

This book argues that Sanskrit and sanskriti are alive, sacred and sources for liberation. However, the future will depend on what the insiders of our tradition do with this. The big breakthrough will take place only if serious Sanskrit scholars and important India-based institutions enter this Kurukshetra to directly make a difference. An old adage says: a pandit is one who is moved to act upon his conviction ('yah kriyavan sah panditah'). Change can be brought about only through action, not by armchair pandits.

I wish to propose a list of debates that will hopefully result from this book. Even if only a few of these debates take place with well-informed insiders representing the tradition, they could be game changers. This approach is also the best way to train intellectual kshatriyas who can represent the dharmic traditions confidently, based on solid knowledge and argumentation skills. Furthermore, the knowledge generated as a result of such debates would inform policymakers in education, culture, science, public health, interfaith affairs, foreign affairs and media. In each case, I state my position concisely in the list that follows.

A. Contesting the intellectual re-colonization of India

1. **Export of the adhikara for Sanskrit studies:** *The Battle for Sanskrit* is the result of my campaign to discourage the Sringeri Peetham from being shanghaied by American Orientalists. Such a hijacking is being attempted with the help of NRI funding and the support of senior administrators at Sringeri. This illustrates a tendency for adhikara to get transferred to institutions and individuals who are invested in other civilizations. I consider this very dangerous. Debates are needed to discuss the mechanisms required for reviving and developing our civilizational foundations in a manner that does not undermine the traditional adhikara. We

must develop strategies for collaboration with Western Indologists and install the safeguards needed for this.

2. **Western universalism as the privileged framework being adopted:** The present trend has been to train Indian scholars in the use of Western tools for critical thinking; this requires many years of mastering a wide range of Western theories and theorists. This threatens to marginalize the tools of critical thinking found in Indian sanskriti, siddhantas, paramparas and sampradayas. Meanwhile, Indian civilizational gems are being appropriated and turned into Western assets. I use the analogy of the US dollar serving as the world reserve currency. I propose that we position some powerful Sanskrit non-translatable categories as part of the global intellectual currency for the future.
3. **Status of Orientalism:** Although Sheldon Pollock claims we live in a post-Orientalist era, I argue that the old form of Orientalism 1.0 has mutated into the more sophisticated form of American Orientalism that may be seen as Orientalism 2.0. We ought to discuss whether Indology today is largely a newer and updated genre of Orientalism.

B. Contesting the use of Buddhism as a wedge against Hinduism

4. **Buddhism's relationship to Hinduism:** Is Buddhism truly at odds with Hinduism? Was it really anti-Vedic as commonly alleged by Western scholars? Evidence from traditional Indian sources suggests that the differences between the two have been grossly exaggerated. In fact, Hinduism, Buddhism, Jainism and Sikhism share a common matrix/womb of dharma from which they all emerged.
5. **Chronology of key Hindu texts:** In order to support their thesis that Hinduism lacked innovation due to brahmin monopoly and the oral tradition, the American Orientalists tend to explain all

the innovation in Hindu texts as being the result of Buddhist interventions against the Vedas. They adjust the chronology for the primary Sanskrit texts of grammar, Purva-mimamsa, the Ramayana, etc., to locate them after the Buddha. This is to support the claim that all these texts were Hindu reactions to Buddhism.

6. **Writing in ancient India:** Was writing in India introduced a few centuries after the Buddha, by foreign migrants and converts to Buddhism, as claimed by the American Orientalists? The entire history of Indian languages and culture as depicted by them disregards the evidence of writing available from the Indus–Sarasvati Civilization materials.

C. *Contesting the depiction of Sanskrit and the sanskriti based on it*

7. **Oral tradition:** The scholarship I critique in this book tries to undermine the importance of the Indian oral tradition. I have explained why the oral tradition was not only vital in the past evolution of Indian culture, but that it also holds great promise for the future development of mind sciences and offshoots into education and other fields.
8. **History of Indian languages:** American Orientalists assume that Sanskrit arrived from foreign migrants into India and that it was genetically and structurally different from the Indian vernaculars. They allege that Sanskrit eventually succeeded in dominating the vernaculars and established hegemonic control over them. This contestable premise has infiltrated contemporary social theories that are being used to divide Indians into conflict-ridden linguistic and social groups. It contradicts the traditional view that Sanskrit and Prakrit (from which the vernaculars evolved) are two mutually supportive linguistic streams constituting a speech system known as vac.

9. **Allegation of built-in social abusiveness:** According to a growing number of Western Indologists, Sanskrit and sanskriti have always abused and oppressed the women, Dalits and Muslims of India. This is emphasized as a structural defect as opposed to being a matter of isolated instances. It is alleged that Sanskrit grammar, Vedic texts and the shastras are the root causes; they are said to be laden with rules that preclude intellectual freedom. This is a viewpoint traditionalists might want to vigorously contest, and we must hear both sides.

10. **Allegations of lack of creativity:** It is further purported that shastras prevent genuine creativity and progress in vyavaharika (worldly) matters, because they are straitjacketed by the Vedic world view. However, there is an abundance of counter-evidence showing that Indians have been innovative in producing and applying shastras to both empirical and spiritual domains. Shastras, therefore, cannot be dismissed as lacking in practical innovations and creativity.

11. **Allegation of Sanskrit's 'death':** I have argued against the academicians who say that Sanskrit has been dead for a thousand years. I cite traditional scholars such as Krishna Shastry and K.S. Kannan who wish to debate this issue.

12. **Secularization of Sanskrit and sanskriti:** Sheldon Pollock's camp is committed to the secularization of Sanskrit because it regards spiritual practices such as yajnas, rituals, pujas, tirthas (pilgrimages), vratas (vows, promises) and various other sadhanas to be primitive, superstitious and exploitative. One of their principal agendas is to remove aspects that are linked to the paramarthika (spiritual) realm and only focus on those in the purely laukika or vyavaharika (mundane) realm. Traditionalists consider this a serious violation to the integrity of our tradition. I firmly resist this reductionist secularization.

13. **Allegation of kavya as political weapon:** The American Orientalist camp maintains that kavya (literature) was developed

specifically for the kings to be able to assert their power over their subjects. In other words, it is seen as an ancient form of a ruler's propaganda machinery. Such a reductionist view must be contested. Kavya cannot be collapsed into mere politics; it has served many positive functions for the general population both in the secular and sacred domains.

14. **Ramayana:** Is the Ramayana meant to portray an exploitative dominion by the kings, i.e., is raj dharma an abusive system of governance? My opponents see the Ramayana not in terms of a genuine spiritual quest but as a political device. They consider it a weapon that has been used to cause violence against the Muslims even to this day. However, bhaktas (devotees) maintain otherwise. They see Rama as a role model for all rulers.

D. Reclaiming and repositioning Sanskrit and sanskriti

15. **One-way flow of knowledge from Indian texts into English:** For centuries, Indian-language texts have been translated into English while a flow in the reverse direction has remained virtually non-existent. As a result, only English has become the language of research and communication for knowledge in most fields. Sanskrit must find its legitimate place alongside English as a repository of knowledge with its own way of thinking. Here we can learn from China's strategies concerning Mandarin.
16. **Other ancient languages comparable to Sanskrit:** Western scholars routinely categorize Sanskrit with Latin which they deem to be a 'dead' language, and/or with Greek which they hold as a classical language. Modern Indian scholars blindly accept such a classification of Sanskrit as a dead or classical language. This is not acceptable to traditionalists because Sanskrit and sanskriti did not evolve through outright *rejection* of the past but as a *continuity* with the past. Therefore, we need to make efforts to decouple Sanskrit studies from Latin/Greek studies and to classify it alongside Mandarin and Persian which are living and continuous with

their respective pasts. We should bring in discussants from Asian countries where languages such as Mandarin, Persian, Arabic, Hebrew and Japanese are given prominence, and recognized as both old and modern.

17. **Scope of Sanskrit studies:** Besides studying the Sanskrit language and its old texts, it is necessary to introduce and employ Sanskrit categories and methods for research in modern domains such as computational linguistics, ecology, animal rights, the aging population and family structures, neurosciences and mind sciences, education and accelerated learning, mathematics and other theoretical sciences and health sciences, just to name a few. We must dismantle the present system of intellectual apartheid in which Sanskrit is kept isolated from the knowledge disciplines where its treasures are being appropriated and reformulated into Western paradigms, and given new histories as so-called Western 'discoveries'.

18. **Exposing Hinduphobia:** If a scholar were to refute the very existence of Allah, or claim that the Quran does not represent the actual word of God, or that Muhammad was not a prophet, it would be called Islamophobia. This allegation would apply even if the scholar in question were saying 'positive' things like: Arabic has a rich treasury of poetry, the Quran holds a light for humanity, etc. None of that would satisfy the Muslim mind. An analogous situation exists in the way an attitude gets classified as anti-Semitic. Hindus should be alarmed by the existence of a double standard in Western academics, because the same sensitivity and adhikara to speak for our tradition is not granted to Hindus. This is why Sheldon Pollock was shocked when I characterized several of his stances as inimical to Hindu dharma (i.e., Hinduphobic). We need to define a level playing field for characterizing a work as Islamophobia, anti-Semitism, Hinduphobia, etc.

I am far from being the most qualified person to take on these tasks at hand. There are highly competent scholars who could take up these issues much better than I have been able to. Why, then, given my limited capabilities, did I carry out all this work? The simple answer is: *Because nobody else did.* If others were doing such work, my role would be more as an advisor, facilitator and supporter. As I have pointed out in the foregoing chapters, there are various reasons why nobody has taken up such projects. My intervention is designed to galvanize the spirit of a creative response in the Hindu intellectuals of the present day.

It is vital that the discussions and debates provoked by this book should be based on substantive arguments and not on tangential points or quibbles that serve to only distract. The scenario I dread the most is where some overemotional Hindus launch personal attacks on Sheldon Pollock or his coterie rather than join in a serious intellectual exchange with the issues. As I have said throughout the book, I have great respect for many of the scholars whose work I critique, and in particular for the seriousness of their concerns. Their voices are important, and engaging them respectfully will make us stronger.

The book no doubt has flaws, especially given the tight time constraints under which I wrote it. Nevertheless, I am convinced the main arguments are strong. At the very least, I hope the book will awaken a sizeable number of Indians who love their heritage and had no prior knowledge of the issues raised here. Among them will be those willing to lend their voices publicly to spread awareness of the issues in simple, honest language, as well as serious scholars who will start to question and doubt the hegemonic discourse that often prevails. Small successes will snowball into bigger ones. Gradually, I hope, there will emerge a 'home team' that is committed to responding to the entire corpus of Sanskrit-related academic mythology that has built up over time.

In light of my goals for this book, the purva-paksha parts are far more important than the uttara-paksha parts. The former pertain to explaining what exactly the new Orientalists are saying and what that implies. For most people, their arguments are hard to decipher because their writing is extremely technical and uses many Western theoretical and critical terms which our traditional scholars are not equipped to understand. To get that understanding would require that they depart from their core work and start to study Western religion, philosophy and literary theories for many years. A number of Indian scholars have already been lured into this game and in the process they got 'rewired' to think entirely in terms of Western categories, histories and schools of thought. They gradually became alienated from their own traditions.

Hinduism would indeed benefit if some of its bright young scholars studied Western thought. However, few are strong enough to go through this kind of intense study without irrevocably drifting away from Indian thought. Therefore, the best way to pursue such deep immersion in purva-paksha with the West is in the environment of dharmic commitment, guru guidance and regular sadhana, just as our elders always insisted. The problem is that few institutional environments exist to support such a context and still provide the learning and breadth of engagement necessary to understand the wider world.

My best-case scenario for the outcome of this book is for traditional scholars of Sanskrit and those who follow schools like Pollock's to come together in genuine public debate and dialogue about their respective positions and disagreements. I would like insiders to get out of their silos and outsiders to turn from opponents into interlocutors.

Appendix A: Pollock's Theory of Buddhist Undermining of the Vedas

According to Pollock's grand narrative of Indian history, some dramatic changes suddenly occurred 2,500 years ago in India. The decisive event was the Buddha's arrival, which set off a cascading chain of events. The Buddha challenged the yajnas performed by the brahmins. He had a better solution for the human condition, one that did not require brahmins or their rituals. Pollock says that suddenly the brahmins had competition and their monopoly was broken. Buddhism thus sought to free the lower castes from brahmin oppression by challenging Vedic authority. In the first chapter of *The Language of the Gods in the World of Men*, Pollock partitions the Vedic and Buddhist traditions as mutually opposing systems with normative doctrines.

Claim: Buddhists assaulted the Vedic tradition

Pollock claims that Buddhists challenged the authority of the Vedic tradition by means of processes he calls 'transvaluation of values' and 'normative inversion'. He explains these as follows: 'The dynamic at work here is familiar from other oppositional movements in the domain of religion and culture more generally and is well captured by the phrase "normative inversion", whereby one group turns another's obligations into abominations, and often vice versa.'[1]

He cites a few examples of such inversion, such as: whether animal sacrifices are allowed or not, the meaning of dharma, the meaning of 'arya' and so on. He obsessively looks for things he can interpret as 'norms' in both systems and then tries to put them in mutual contradiction as much as possible.

He highlights this so-called Buddhist rejection of the Vedas with the example of the Buddha insisting on using a non-Sanskrit language to propagate his teachings. Pollock makes a big deal out of one isolated incident mentioned in a text: Brahmin monks wanted to put Buddha's teachings into Sanskrit, but the Buddha rebuked this attempt and asked that his words remain in his own dialect and not Sanskrit. Pollock sees this purported Buddhist rejection of Sanskrit as a rejection of the Vedas. He wants us to believe that these were in an ideological war with each other.

Pollock writes that, 'the first explicit and systematized assaults on the *vaidika* cultural order' were 'embodied in the language theory and practices of early Buddhism, though these were in fact only part of a larger process, a transvaluation of values, that occurred in the last centuries before the Common Era.'[2] He continues:

> A simple inventory of the strategies, from basic terminology to core notions of culture and society, by which early Buddhists sought to appropriate, redefine, and transform the very elements of the late *vaidika* conceptual order shows both how profound this critique was and how much it can tell us about the nature of its target.[3]

Pollock cites many Vedic Sanskrit terms that the Buddhists appropriated and inverted into very different meanings – such as dharma, arya, karma, atman, etc. As already mentioned, he interprets this as proof that the Buddhists had conflicting cosmological views, which implies a rejection of the Vedas.

In opposition to this, Ashok Aklujkar challenges the view that the Buddha condemned the Vedas. He feels the Buddha could have meant that the Vedic brahmins had wrongly interpreted the Vedas. The claim of an absolute divide between Vedic and Buddhist/Jain use of languages is false, he says, as is the corresponding divide between Sanskrit and other languages. This is a crucial matter that Aklujkar is investigating. He writes:

> It is not the case that Sanskrit was not viewed as an Aryan language by the Jains and Buddhists or that languages like Pali and Ardha-magadhi were not viewed as parts of the same Aryan language continuum by the adherents of Brahmanism. [...] To hold that Ardha-magadhi is a language of gods, ṛsis, or Aryas is essentially similar to the view held in the Brahmanical tradition on behalf of (what we call) Sanskrit. The view, furthermore, fits naturally in the Brahmanical tradition and hence must be present in it at an earlier period and must have been taken over in the Jain tradition. Likewise, to say that Pali is a language of all living beings is a continuation of the kind of thinking which is implicit in the Brahmanical connecting of Sanskrit with the Language Principle through the language of the Veda ...[4]

He suggests that the Buddha's position on whether or not to use Sanskrit was entirely pragmatic and not ideological. He wanted to use whatever language would help bring out the meaning of his teachings. Aklujkar asserts:

> The religio-linguistic universes of the Brahmins, Buddhists and Jains were more in harmony than has been assumed, and the use of Pali and Ardha-magadhi as languages of religious communication by the Buddhists and Jains was modeled after the use of Sanskrit by the Brahmins.[5]

Following this logic, it may be said that Jains and Buddhists knew Sanskrit well. Therefore, they could model their religious communication in Ardha-magadhi and Pali just as the Hindus were doing religious communication in Sanskrit.[6]

But Pollock makes the sweeping remark that 'Buddhism sought to turn the old *vaidika* world upside down by the very levers that world provided' and claims that much of Upanishadic thought was 'cancelled' by Buddhism.[7] However, he does not bother to mention that Buddhism retained Upanishadic ideas and doctrines such as karma, rebirth and renunciation.

Pollock has to sideline the Brahmana and Upanishadic portion of the Vedas in order to claim that Buddhism grew in opposition to the Vedas, and not out of the concepts in the Brahmana sections (and more importantly in the Aranyaka sections). The notion that the Buddha may have been only reinterpreting Vedic ideas and not formulating an independent world view would not serve Pollock's purpose. He needs the presence of radical Buddhist opposition to the Vedas in order to show that there was a radical intellectual rupture. This is the basis for his theory of the Buddhist origin of kavya; then he can say the brahmins needed to 'catch up' and so they embarked on the writing of Sanskrit texts such as itihasa.

Aklujkar also disagrees with Pollock's notion that Buddhism grew in opposition to the Vedas or that brahmins viewed Buddhists as non-Aryas or shudras:

> As far as I know, there is no evidence available which would enable us to assume that the Jains and Bauddhas were Shudras or Anårya 'non-Aryan' in Brahmanical eyes. The Shramanic groups might have been avaidika 'non-Vedic' for the Brahmins but not necessarily Anårya, Mleccha, Barbara, Dasa or Dasyu. [...] There is no indication of any special empathy on the part of the Jains and Buddhists toward the Mlecchas or toward the Vaishyas and Shudras for that matter. In their surviving early literature too, the engagement witnessed is overwhelmingly with the Brahmins and Kshatriyas.[8]

Aklujkar also shows that according to Manu, a non-Arya could become Arya based on his conduct and that an Arya could lose his status based on his actions. Also, all non-Aryas were Aryas in the past but had descended due to their failure to meet the standards of thinking and conduct. Aklujkar is here refuting the views of caste divide that modern Indologists claim as a canonical assumption.

Claim: Buddhists invented writing and liberated Sanskrit

Pollock claims that for the first few centuries of its existence, Buddhism rejected Sanskrit. For one thing, he says that Buddhists reject any notion of divinity and hence the notion of any 'language of the gods'. All languages were regarded by them as human inventions, a matter of pure convention. He writes:

> What was at stake for the Mīmāṁsā in asserting the uncreated, eternal nature of language was the possibility that *vāṅmaya*, or a thing-made-of-language – that is, a text, like the Veda – could be eternal too, something the Buddhists sought fundamentally to reject.[9]

He believes that the Mimamsaka thinkers considered the eternal nature of the Veda to be dependent on the eternal, uncreated nature of Sanskrit. Hence, the Buddhist rejection of the uncreated nature of Sanskrit led to their rejection of the Vedas. He says Buddhists invented Pali as their language for writing and alleges that there was a similar rejection of Sanskrit by the Jains, who adopted Ardha-magadhi as their language. He says that Vedic thinkers criticized these new languages because they undermined the doctrinal authority of Sanskrit.[10]

A few centuries after the Buddha, the Buddhists turned towards Sanskrit as their language of choice for expressing their teachings. There is a debate among scholars as to how and why this happened. Pollock's theory is that Vedic culture became weak due to the liberating influence of Buddhism. He acknowledges that in the early centuries of the Common Era, there was an explosion in Sanskrit literature. He rejects the thesis that this was due to a revival of Vedic teachings and maintains that Buddhism had sidelined the Vedic rituals during that era. So what gave Sanskrit its boost at a time when Vedas were no longer dominant? Pollock credits Buddhism as the reforming agent that gave Sanskrit a new lease of life.

His theory of the Buddhist appropriation of Sanskrit is the linchpin in his entire approach to history. According to him, the Buddhists invented writing in India in or around 260 BCE in the Maurya courts.[11] Then they decided to adopt Sanskrit:

> Buddhists of the early period ... having decided to eschew Sanskrit for their oral scriptural texts, chose to revoke that decision around the beginning of the Common Era, under what appear to have been radically new political conditions introduced by the Kuṣāṇa empire. The very act of permitting Sanskrit to speak openly in the everyday world was itself a decision (on the part of the Śakas, among others) made against the backdrop of centuries of its public silence.[12]

This was a watershed event, according to Pollock. The moment Sanskrit became a written language, it ceased to be monopolized as the 'language of the gods' and became the 'language of men'. He calls this a 'new secularization ... of the gods' language'.[13] This change unleashed a flurry of innovation, including the new cultural form of kavya, because the tyranny of brahmin exclusivism had been broken. For the first time, Sanskrit was being used for mundane laukika purposes.

The entire credit, as per Pollock, goes to the Buddhist kings (in particular the Shakas and Kushans who entered India from Central Asia). Since they were 'newly immigrant peoples', according to Pollock, the grip of Vedic culture on them was weak, if there was a hold at all. In 78 CE, an important Kushan king, Kanishka, is supposed to have organized a council of eighteen different Buddhist lineages. They were asked to articulate their differences in order to bring them together. Since these lineages used different Prakrit languages, it became necessary to have a common 'link language'. Kanishka asked the scholars to translate their works into Sanskrit. Thus, Sanskrit became the cosmopolitan link language between the multiple Buddhist lineages. Likewise, the Shakas also needed to have some common language. Being foreign, Pollock says, they were open-minded and did not reject Sanskrit despite its previous links with yajnas.

Henceforth Buddhist ideas became restated in Sanskrit and developed even further than they did in Buddha's time.[14] As soon as these foreign Buddhists had taken control of the use of Sanskrit, a new dynamic was set into motion releasing Sanskrit from the clutches of brahmin monopoly, as per Pollock's account:

> The radical reinvention of Sanskrit culture seems to have occurred – at least, it is here that we can actually watch it occurring – precisely where one might expect it, in a social world where the presuppositions and conventions of *vaidika* culture were weakest: among newly immigrant peoples from the far northwest of the subcontinent (and ultimately from Iran and Central Asia), most importantly the Śakas (the so-called Indo-Scythians), especially a branch of the Śakas known as the Western Kṣatrapas, and the Kuṣāṇas [...] Śakas, Kuṣāṇas, and the poets and intellectuals they patronized, often Buddhist poets and intellectuals, began to expand that economy by turning Sanskrit into an instrument of polity and the mastery of Sanskrit into a source of personal charisma.[15]

In this process, Sanskrit itself changes, he says. Pollock highlights the big divide between the earlier Vedic Sanskrit and this new Buddhist variety. This is how, according to him, Sanskrit was reformed by Buddhists and changed forever. Sanskrit turns into a new kind of language that gets used for literary and political expression after the Common Era begins.

The new scholarship broadened the use of Sanskrit from its earlier limited purpose for yajna, because Buddhists were opposed to yajna. He says they turned it into a language for writing various other kinds of texts that were not related to the Vedas. They violated the oral tradition that required transmission to be strictly within the lineage of qualified persons.

However, traditionalists would not agree with this interpretation entirely. One of Pollock's blind spots is the Indus–Sarasvati Civilization that thrived two thousand years prior to Buddha and is known for its elaborate writing system. The moment this civilization and its culture are acknowledged, it becomes impossible to see the Buddhists as the inventors of writing in India. The Indus–Sarasvati script is the 'elephant in the room' in any discussion on the origins of writing in India, and yet Pollock ignores it completely.

Claim: All paths before Buddhism had social restrictions

Pollock says the Buddhist assault on yajna devastated the Hindus, forcing them to devise alternative methods in response to the Buddhists.

Reversing the gaze, I wish to point out that Hindus had methods of liberation other than the yajnas. We know that many other paths were available to all segments of society – paths such as itihasa, *natya nhastra,* yoga, tantra, and many other methods that do not involve fire rituals. These were different paths to the same goal as were achieved by the yajnas: which is to say, they were yajnas of another kind and embodied the same Vedic metaphysics.

Since these other paths did not have the social restrictions of the yajnas, it is vital for Pollock to prove that all such alternative methods were developed only *after* the Buddha and hence were the result of Buddha's reformation of Hinduism. This is why he must date the development of grammar and other linguistic techniques as having occurred after the Buddha. For this very reason, he insists that the Ramayana was based on Buddhist Jataka tales, thereby making all the non-fire-ritual paths seem post-Buddha.

Claim: Buddhist influence started Sanskrit literature and enhanced its grammar

Pollock considers the Jataka tales of Buddhism to be the first literary expression in India. The content was what we might call the 'secular' realm, i.e., devoid of any links or references to divinity or transcendence. The Vedic brahmins, he says, wanted to rise to the challenge posed by this new Buddhist trend of written works meant for mass consumption. They wanted a resurgence of Vedic thought which would be achieved by appropriating the Buddhists' style of producing Sanskrit literature. Their first major work of this new genre was the Ramayana. Pollock alleges Valmiki copied the Buddhist style and also the content of the Jataka tales (which, by the way, were in Prakrit) when he wrote the Ramayana, except he used Sanskrit.[16]

But he is wrong in two ways:

- Even his collaborator, Robert Goldman, accepts that the Jataka tales include references to the Ramayana because they were composed many centuries after Valmiki's Ramayana.[17]
- Pollock is also incorrect in saying that the Anushtubh chhanda was invented by the Buddhist Jataka authors and then copied by Valmiki as the meter used in the Ramayana. However, this claim is debatable.

Pollock says that as a further response to the Buddhist threat, the Vedic brahmins enhanced their Sanskrit etymology and grammar in such a way as to formalize it and make it more widely usable. Then they started producing texts like itihasas, *Yoga Sutras* and Jnana Yoga, all of which were based on the Veda. He dates Yaska's *Nirukta*, Panini's *Ashtadhyayi* and Patanjali's *Mahabhashya* after the Buddha in order to show these as being a response to Buddhism.

Nonetheless, the tradition disagrees with his dates and sees the grammar as having developed to a sophisticated level prior to the Buddha.[18] Vedic scholars had already been developing lexicons, etymologies and grammars on their sophisticated oral platform. From the tradition's perspective, Yaska, Panini and Patanjali all reference multiple sources which they draw on and summarize their own versions; this means lexicons and etymologies were in use centuries before the Buddha.

Another debate is over the purpose served by these texts. Tradition holds that they made the Vedic principles more accessible to the public, but Pollock sees them as a departure from the sacred domain and writes: 'What began when Sanskrit escaped the domain of the sacred was literature.'[19] In other words, this new kind of Sanskrit was decoupled from the Vedas. He calls this 'literary Sanskrit', and says it opened the floodgates for innovative literature.

Pollock's overarching motive is to make a chronology according to which all Hindu innovations came only after the Buddha, the idea being that prior to Buddhism the Hindus were incapable of innovation as a result of their oral tradition because they were stuck in a childlike world of Vedic imagination and superstitious rituals. Rationality entered Indian culture only after the Buddha came, according to him, and only *then* did it become possible to compose complex rational texts.

Issues

The following is a summary of some of the red flags related to Pollock's thesis concerning Buddhism's role:

- His ideas of history heavily depend on delaying the dates of Valmiki. For these dates, he fails to supply solid proof. The date of Valmiki's Ramayana is arbitrarily delayed by centuries because he wants it to be seen as a reaction to the new kind of literary Sanskrit and the kavya brought about by Buddhists.
- The date of Panini's work is also postponed to make it fit his chronology. For, if Sanskrit grammar similar to Panini's kind had existed earlier, at least in a preliminary form, it would contravene his claim that literary Sanskrit was something new and the result of interventions by Buddhist scholars and Kushan kings.[20]
- He claims brahmins were incapable of innovating, and cites the mechanical practice of Vedic chanting as his evidence. It took the Buddhists to unshackle the static Vedas and associated discourse, which then enabled future brahmins to become literary producers.
- The intervention by the foreign Shakas and Kushans is positioned as a great breakthrough. This would hint that the current foreign intervention being led by him should also be considered a favour to Sanskrit.

- Not only is the writing style of the Ramayana claimed to be the product of Buddhist modifications to Sanskrit, its content is also alleged to have been based on earlier Jataka tales about the life of the Buddha and related ethical lessons.
- He marginalizes the significance of mantra and dismisses it as 'hymnology', i.e., a sort of mechanical repetition of meaningless sounds. The vibrational function of chanting mantra is entirely lost on him.
- Pollock's strategy is to show that without the Buddhist and foreign Kushan interventions, Sanskrit would have remained a perfunctory oral system monopolized by brahmins who would have remained devoid of agency or capacity for progress.

Appendix B: Ramayana Evidence Prior to the Turkish Invasion

As we saw, Pollock claims that the rise of the Ramayana's popularity was due to the Hindu kings using it as a narrative against the invading Turks starting in the twelfth century. To back up such a claim, he asserts that there was almost no popular worship or celebration of the story of Rama prior to that period. Some Indian scholars see this to be false and, even though I am not an expert in archaeology, I believe this is a debate we ought to facilitate between the experts on both sides. Indian scholars cite evidence that Rama's story was already popular before the Turkish invasions. Furthermore, it was not a localized phenomenon.

Meenakshi Jain, in her book *Rama and Ayodhya* (2013), has collated considerable historical and literary evidence relating to Rama, covering a vast corpus of literature from the eighth century onwards.[1] The Pratihara dynasty, which ruled west and central India from the ninth to the thirteenth century, claimed descent from Lakshmana, the younger brother of Rama. The Pratiharas saw themselves as defenders of India from Mlechchha (barbarian) invaders and were proud of their victory over them. For four centuries, they put up an intrepid fight against invaders.

Jain's book covers the popularity of Rama in antiquity in three long chapters, citing evidence from literature, sculpture and epigraphy. She has compiled her evidence to prove Rama's pan-national popularity since ancient times. She responds to the claim that Rama became a deity only after the publication of *Ramcharitmanas* of Tulsidas in the era of the Mughal emperor Akbar. She cites Varahamihira's *Brihat Samhita* (sixth century CE), noting that it lays down the ground rules for making images of Rama. The Rama story also finds mention in three early Buddhist texts, *Dasharatha Kathanam* (between the first and second century CE), *Anamakam Jatakam*, and *Dasharatha Jataka*. The great poet-dramatist, Bhavabhuti, a native of Vidarbha, wrote two dramas based on the Ramayana, namely the *Mahaviracharita* and the *Uttararamacharita* (eighth century CE).

A Gupta-period stone panel from Mathura shows Ravana in a scene from the Ramayana. A brick temple from the same period at Bhitargaon, Kanpur (fifth century CE) has several terracotta panels, one of which depicts Rama and Lakshmana seated and engaged in conversation. M. Zaheer, in his book on the Bhitargaon temple, mentions two terracotta reliefs showing scenes from the Ramayana. One is of a woman offering alms to a gigantic man, clearly Ravana in disguise, while the other depicts a seated Rama and Sita.[2]

In many Hindu temples, Rama is depicted as an incarnation of Vishnu. Worship of Vishnu should be considered as well when it comes to matters of dating. It is known that Shiva was worshipped in early times as lingam rather than in human form. It follows that one cannot assume that Shiva worship dates only from his human representation. Likewise, the figure of Rama has ancient roots which predate his being worshipped in a specific form.

The large inscription embedded in one of the walls of Babri Masjid (certified by the leading epigraphists of the Archaeological Survey of India) says it was installed at the gate of a magnificent temple of Vishnu who killed Dashanana (ten-headed Ravana). This refers to Rama as the incarnation of Vishnu who killed Ravana.

Furthermore, the spread of the Ramayana across Asia demonstrates its massive popular appeal.

The examples below were compiled by Professor Makkhan Lal using evidence compiled with the help of the Archaeological Survey of India. He claims they prove that prior to the arrival of the Turkish invaders in the twelfth century, the Ramayana had been immortalized in literature, inscriptions, art and architecture. He would like to organize a debate where archaeologists can also participate.

1. We find mention of Rama's story in Buddhist and Jain literature right from the beginning of the fifth century BCE.
2. Rama is mentioned in the Sangam literature in Tamil, which belongs to the early second half of the first millennium BCE.
3. A terracotta plaque found at Kausambi depicts the story of Sita Haran. This plaque belongs to the second century BCE.
4. Rama's story reached China through Buddhism and the Jataka stories. The first mention is made in *Anamakam Jatakam* (251 CE) and then again in *Nidana* (472 CE).
5. In Bengal, a Khalimpur copper plate of Dharmapal of West Bengal (842 CE) mentions Lord Rama. Also, there are inscriptions on the sculptures depicting the Ramayana on the panels of an eighth-century temple at Paharpur.
6. Bhartrihari's *Bhatti Kavya* (which is no later than the sixth century CE) is the earliest known written story of Rama in Gujarat. Also, *Dutangada* is a play written by Subhata (thirteenth century BCE), narrating the story of Angad, a well-known character in the Ramayana.
7. The earliest rendering of Rama's story in Kannada language is in the *Chavundaraya Purana*, which dates back to 978 CE.
8. *Ramachandra-charita Purana*, popularly known as *Pampa*

Ramayana, is another important work, written in Karnataka by Nagachandra in the eleventh century CE.

9. In Tamil Nadu, the Kasakudi copper plate (dated to 752–753 CE) of Nandivarman mentions the Ramayana.
10. Additional evidence from Tamil Nadu is Kamban Ramayana, a highly celebrated work of literature on Rama's story composed sometime around the ninth century CE.
11. Sri Lanka has many sites and localities associated with the Ramayana stories, and *Janaki-harana* by Kumaradasa (seventh century CE) is a remarkable composition.
12. In Tibet, between the seventh and ninth centuries CE, a large number of works about the story of Rama were composed. These works were discovered by Hungarian-British archaeologist, Aurel Stein, and French explorer, Paul Pelliot. The archives are now housed in the Bibliothèque Nationale de France in Paris and the India Office Library in London.
13. The Rama story contained in *Anamakam Jatakam* reached Japan in the twelfth century CE and later became popular.
14. In Malaysia, *Hikayat Seri Rama* is Rama's story narrated in the form of a puppet show, popular in the twelfth century CE.
15. The famous temple of Angkor Wat in Cambodia is a living example of Rama's story narrated in massive carvings. Among them is a panel which depicts the story of the abduction of Sita by Ravana.
16. In Indonesia, *Ramayana Kakawin* is the earliest known composition of Rama's story. The date is not known; however, inscriptions of King Sanjaya (732 CE) compare the king with Lord Rama, and two other inscriptions, dated 824 and 928 CE, in Prambanam Temple mention Rama, Sita, Lakshmana and Ravana. There are also several panels depicting the life story of Rama, one of which shows the subduing of the sea.

17. A terracotta housed in Los Angeles County Museum includes a depiction of Rama with his legends inscribed on the left side. It belongs to the third century CE.
18. A terracotta plaque dated to the fourth century CE, found in Nachara Khera, Haryana, depicts Rama and Jatayu. The inscription is in Brahmi from the fourth century CE.
19. Another terracotta plaque with the same dates and likewise found in Nachara Khera includes a depiction of Rama, Sita and Jatayu.
20. And yet another terracotta plaque with the same dates and found in Jind, Haryana, shows Hanuman destroying Ashok Vatika in Sri Lanka. The inscription on the plaque is in Brahmi of the fourth century CE.
21. A panel in Nagarjuna Konda, Andhra Pradesh, is an illustration of the meeting of Rama and Bharata in Chitrakut. It is dated to the third century CE.
22. A panel at the temple of Nachna Kuthara, Madhya Pradesh, depicts Ravana in the guise of a sage at Panchavati when Rama and Lakshmana were not there. It is dated to the fifth century CE.
23. A panel in the Papanatha temple at Pattadakal, Karnataka, portrays the construction of Ramasetu over the sea. It is dated to between the seventh and eighth centuries CE.

Appendix C: Pollock's Political Activism

Pollock uses his academic clout as a vehicle for social and political activism. His liberation philology is intended to move his academic theories into the mainstream for the purpose of re-engineering Indian society. Besides writing papers and articles that have attacked modern Hindu politics directly, he has campaigned against the BJP and Narendra Modi for at least ten years, starting in 2004.

He has signed almost a dozen political petitions that his students or other collaborators initiated. Four of these are cited below as examples:

- **Petition to the Asian American Hotel Owners Association, February 2005:** 'We are writing to request you to withdraw your invitation to Gujarat Chief Minister Narendra Modi to speak at the AAHOA Convention in Ft. Lauderdale, Florida.'[1]
- **Petition to Chair of Asian American Studies, California State University, Long Beach, March 2005:** 'We are disturbed to learn

that you have invited Gujarat Chief Minister Narendra Modi to inaugurate the Yadunandan Center for India Studies on 22 March 2005. We believe that you may not be in possession of all the facts about Mr Modi, and urge you in the strongest possible words to withdraw his invitation.'[2]

- **Petition to the head of the Pearson Group that owns *Financial Times*, and to a member of the board of MacArthur Foundation, September 2009:** 'We are writing to inform you of what we consider a shocking action taken by one of the publications under the Pearson Group umbrella, an action that begs for your attention. The magazine FDI, of the Financial Times Group, has selected Narendra Modi, the chief minister of the Indian state of Gujarat, as its Asian Personality of the Year (2009). This award gives Mr. Modi, whose human rights reputation is most troubling, a huge boost of legitimacy where he deserves none.'[3]
- **Petition to the Government of India after Modi came to power, 2015:** 'We, the undersigned scholars and students of Indian history and other concerned citizens and friends of India, insist that the Government of India immediately clarify its position regarding the reported destruction of 150,000 files and documents of historical nature, reportedly including documents chronicling events immediately following the assassination of Mahatma Gandhi, by its Ministry of Home Affairs.'[4]

These four petitions are illustrative examples of Sheldon Pollock's interventions in Indian politics. While a number of other South Asian faculty signed some of the petitions, the three South Asian studies professors who signed all four of them are: Sheldon Pollock, Arjun Appadurai (Paulette Goddard professor of media, culture, and communication, New York University) and Vijay Prashad (professor of South Asian and international studies, Trinity College). Another academician who has been a leading petitioner is Angana Chatterjee, who signs on behalf of the Coalition against Genocide and whose major constituency is Sabrang, led by civil rights activists Teesta Setalvad and Javed Anand.

There were also six signatories on these petitions out of Pakistan. The petition against the *Financial Times* award in 2009 was promoted by Pakistani media.[5]

I see no problem with any scholar being in politics, but wish to mention this involvement only to demonstrate his political importance outside the walls of the ivory tower. Such activism may well be justified in many instances, but it should not prejudice the scholarship on Sanskrit and sanskriti.

Appendix D: Acknowledgements

As with all my work, I am indebted to a large number of individuals who have supported me in this intense project in different ways. I shall name those whose help was especially significant, and wish to apologize to anyone I might have inadvertently forgotten.

Prof. T.S. Satyanath of Delhi University and Shri Shrinivas Tilak based in Montreal supplied some important data and arguments to refute Sheldon Pollock's claims on the relationship between Sanskrit and the vernaculars. Prof. Makkhan Lal from Vivekananda International Foundation, Delhi, supplied the archaeological and historical data as counterpoints to Pollock's claim that there was virtually no public worship of Rama prior to the Turkish invasion in the twelfth century, and that the 'cult of Rama' was something started by Hindu kings as a response to the Muslims. Shri Ashay Naik was hired as a research assistant to submit his analysis on Pollock's work on kavya theory. Smt. Sujatha Reddy of Delhi University helped by investigating the history of Kannada for this project.

Prof. Cleo Kearns based in Vermont has gone through the drafts multiple times and pointed out many issues as well as ways to resolve them. Shri Kartik Mohan, Smt. Aditi Banerjee and Smt. Ragini Sharma have each edited some of the chapters to improve clarity, and their fresh voices made a positive impact. At the last minute I was able to get valuable help from Prof. K.S. Kannan in Bengaluru to go through the manuscript with his critical eye to raise issues and suggest improvements. Shri Kiran Vasudeva (in Europe) and Shri Sunil Sheoran (in Toronto) polished up my diagrams on very short notice towards the very end. Shri Thom Loree in Toronto has performed multiple iterations of minute editing which has helped clean up many errors of language. Smt. Aashrita Mangu checked the nearly 600 quotes used in this book for accuracy of citation. Ms. Allegra Lovejoy has assisted in curating the quotations I used into categories suitable for presentations. Smt. Usha Surampudi based in Visakhapatnam has put in a lot of hard work to edit every word of the manuscript with four iterations. Her word on language is final and I appreciate her dedication for perfection. Numerous other volunteers from my online discussion e-group have helped in various ways upon my requests. They are too many to list but I thank each of them profusely.

The discussions with the leaders of Sringeri Peetham in USA/ Canada were important, and I am indebted to Shri Ravi Subramanian (Canada) and Shri Srinivasa Yegnasubramanian (New Jersey) for their open-mindedness in hearing the issues. Smt. Rama Shankar based in Chicago was instrumental in organizing my visit to Sringeri Peetham in Karnataka, including a very special private meeting with H.H. the Shankaracharya of Sringeri. This was a very important meeting in crystallizing in my mind the importance of this research effort. Shri T.S. Mohan and Shri Sunil Sheoran travelled with me and organized the logistics.

At the recommendation of Prof. Shashi Tiwari, president of WAVES India, I was invited by Prof. Ramesh Bharadwaj, chairman of the Department of Sanskrit, Delhi University, to deliver the Thirteenth Prof. Narendra Nath Choudhuri Memorial Lecture, where for the first time I disclosed the research that turned into this book. My lecture was titled, 'Is Sanskrit Studies in the West becoming a New Orientalism?'

This was an important milestone in bringing awareness to Indian scholars of the serious nature of the problems this book exposes. This lecture also led to similar talks in Goa as well as in Sastra University in Tamil Nadu. The pre-launch awareness of these issues reached a new level when Prof. Amarjiva Lochan of Delhi and Krishna Shastry of Samskrita Bharati invited me to deliver an opening plenary at the World Sanskrit Congress in Thailand, in June, 2015. (This invitation became heavily political, because there were powerful voices who found my work politically incorrect, but by then the book's thesis had become widely appreciated.)

Shri Abhishek Jalan in Delhi and Shri S.N. Sudhee of Bengaluru are among the India-based volunteers who have performed a great service to organize important contacts and logistics for me. I wish to thank those who provided funding towards the payment of some of the assistants I used. The main donors include the following: Smt. Anu Bhatia of Uberoi Foundation, Shri Sashi Kejriwal, Shri Prashant Banerjee, Smt. Aditi Banerjee, Smt. Tejal Desai, Smt. Neeta Shukla, Shri Bhagwan Samyal, Shri Rakesh Bhandari, Shri Mittal Monani, Shri Sanjeev Chhibber, Shri Chetan Handa, Shri Ramnik Khurana and Shri Jatinder Bhan.

Finally, I must thank Shri Shantanu Ray Chaudhuri at HarperCollins, with whom this is my third book. His role as editor as well as the general guidance by others at HarperCollins has been very helpful. Also, I am glad to have received useful guidance from Shri Krishan Chopra at HarperCollins on the overall approach I followed. And my thanks to V. K. Karthika at HarperCollins whose sharp insights have been invaluable as always.

Appendix E: Editorial Policies Adopted

I decided not to capitalize Sanskrit words other than proper nouns. Therefore, 'itihas' is not capitalized, but the 'Ramayana' and the 'Mahabharata' are. Similarly, various varnas ('brahmin', 'kshatriya', 'shudra', etc.) and 'jati' are not capitalized because they refer to a category.

For a variety of reasons, I decided not to use diacritic marks for Sanskrit words in my own text, even though I have mixed feelings about this and wish to re-evaluate this policy for my future works. Nevertheless, when I quote other authors, the policy adopted is to use the diacritic marks as used by those authors.

When a Sanskrit term (such as 'rasa') is used extensively and needs an explanation, I give its brief meaning in one of the early appearances of that term, and might repeat its meaning later just to remind the reader.

When a given source is used very extensively, I decided not to clutter the text with too many 'scare quotes' with citations. However, to appraise the reader of the sources used, I provide pertinent endnotes (with actual quotations, where needed, as backup to the main text). In some instances,

I identify and attribute a given source only once at the beginning of a section and then freely paraphrase and/or borrow from that source within that section. In such instances, I make sure that the reader is clear as to where the material is being drawn from.

Pollock makes heavy use of certain Western theories in his philology toolbox, and of these I found it important to give the reader a simplified idea of the following three theorists: Vico, Benjamin and Gramsci. I have taken the liberty to paraphrase them in the context of this book, my purpose being to make them accessible to the traditional Indian Sanskrit scholar. I did not attempt to give extensive accounts of these theories and I am aware they are far more complex than the explanations I provide; but my approach suffices for the purpose of my target readers.

This is not intended to be an academic book, at least not in the conventional sense. The guiding principle has been to help the traditional scholars become familiar with the works of the 'outsider' camp. Once this is achieved to a sufficient extent, these traditional scholars should be able to pursue their own detailed reading and analyses of the sources that I have brought to their attention. Therefore, ease of readability by non-technical experts has been a primary concern, for which I have deliberately made reasonable compromises.

Notes

Introduction: The Story Behind the Book

1 According to a legend, when Mandana Misra was on the verge of conceding defeat, Ubhaya Bharati challenged Shankara to defeat her as well. Shankara was a sannyasin and lifelong celibate, and she challenged him on matters of personal relationships and sex with one's wife. Shankara, through his yogic powers, entered the body of a king who was about to die. Using this king's body, he experienced marital affairs with one of the king's wives, and before returning to his own body, he blessed the woman who had taught him so much. Shankara then resumed the debate with Ubhaya Bharati and was victorious. I am indebted to Aditi Banerjee for summarizing this legend for me.

2 The legend explains that when Shankara reached the site of Sringeri, he saw a cobra with its hood spread protectively over a frog that was in labour pains, in order to shield the amphibian from the hot sun. Inspired by the spiritual power of the place that could foster peace between natural enemies, Adi Shankara chose that site as the location for his first peetham.

3 The official documents introduce Sringeri Vidya Bharati Foundation (SVBF) as an international extension of the ancient Sri Sharada Peetham,

Sringeri, Karnataka State, India. It is incorporated as a non-profit organization in USA. It says the foundation is blessed and is under the direct guidance of the present Jagadguru Shankaracharya, His Holiness Sri Bharati Tirtha Mahaswamigal of the Sringeri Mutt, Sringeri Sharada Peetham. The foundation was incorporated as a non-profit religious organization in the state of New Jersey in 1993.

4 I received the following in an e-mail from the top financial donor: 'I want you to know that our discussions with Columbia have been with Professor Sheldon Pollock, the Arvind Raghunathan Professor in Sanskrit and South Asian Studies at Columbia. I have attached for your review the India Abroad coverage on Professor Pollock as a recipient of the Award as a "FRIEND OF INDIA".'

5 Summary of my private e-mail on 19 August 2014.

6 Meanwhile, at the intervention of Dr Subramanian Swamy in parallel, the US-based spiritual head had become more sensitive to my concerns. Dr Swamy wrote in an e-mail that he would proceed with the chair only after due consideration. I found him gradually becoming open to my concerns as expressed.

7 Dharma Civilization Foundation, comprising a group of NRIs in the US, has been similarly attempting to establish chairs in American universities funded by the community, but without the due diligence or adequate controls to ensure that such appointments are not used against the interests of Hinduism. I want to be clear that my criticism does not apply to Indians funding Western academics in fields where the donor has personal expertise. For instance, I know of wealthy donors funding academic work in technology, business and medicine where the given donor is an expert. This enables the donor to negotiate as an equal, participate in the activities performed and monitor continually, just as one would do for any other venture investment.

8 For adhyatmika and embodied knowing as I define them, see Malhotra 2011.

9 As will be clear later, the term American Orientalist does not apply to every American scholar of India or Sanskrit. Conversely, not every American Orientalist is necessarily an American national. The term refers to a certain lens and not to any nationality.

1: The Hijacking of Sanskrit and Sanskriti

1 The terms 'the Vedas' and 'Veda' are used in different ways in this book. 'The Vedas' refers to the four Vedas of which Rig Veda is the foremost. These are insights by rishis based on their tapasya, and provide the deepest knowledge of the cosmos available. On the other hand, 'Veda' is more generic knowledge of a broad kind, in which 'the Vedas' are only one kind of 'Veda'. There are many other kinds of 'Veda' pertaining to knowledge in mundane realms as well.

2 This, for example, is stated in the eleventh century *Kavya-prakasha*, one of the most popular and influential texts of rhetoric.

3 Pollock 1993b: 288.

4 In the end, liberation theology was largely disdained in the churches because of the alliance of some of its leaders with those who advocated revolutionary violence and class conflict, and although there are revered elder exponents today, its theological force is much diminished.

2: From European Orientalism to American Orientalism

1 Said wrote: 'Orientalism as a form of thought [by the colonizing powers] for dealing with the foreign has typically shown the altogether regrettable tendency of any knowledge based on such hard-and-fast distinctions as "East" and "West": to channel thought into a West or an East compartment. Because this tendency is right at the center of Orientalist theory, practice, and values found in the West, the sense of Western power over the Orient is taken for granted as having the status of scientific truth' (Said 2003: 47).

2 It is important to note that in his preface to the last printed edition of *Orientalism* in 2003, Edward Said clarified that he did not mean West and East in the sense of geography but as a dominating culture describing a culture being dominated.

3 For instance, John Stuart Mill became one of the titans of Western liberalism and championed workers' rights, democracy, etc., at home. However, for his entire working life he was an official at the headquarters of the British East India Company, where he masterminded strategies for colonizing India. The contradiction between egalitarianism at home and oppression abroad got turned into his theory of civilizational scales. This theory went as follows: Some

civilizations (most notably Indian ones) are like children, and need to be raised by other parental civilizations (of which the British are exemplars). Hence, what appears to be colonial oppression is merely the price paid to civilize the natives of India for their own good. The expropriation of massive amounts of wealth by the British out of India is merely a fair price for the tutoring service offered for becoming civilized.

4 Kipling 1987: 30.

5 During the same period, the English also colonized the Irish. Interestingly, the Irish, too, were demonized as a primitive people in need of civilizing influences.

6 Madhu Kishwar's blog: http://www.infinityfoundation.com/mandala/h_es/h_es_kishw_mythic_frameset.htm accessed on 16 April 2015.

7 Cited in Franklin 2011. It is also interesting that while lecturing against slavery, he made no mention of the slave plantations owned by his friend or by his brother-in-law. Also, Jones himself openly bought his servants as slaves in Calcutta. I am indebted to Franklin as a source that I have used heavily for factual information on Jones.

8 Franklin 2011.

9 Franklin 2011.

10 Franklin 2011.

11 Jones maps non-Europeans on to the three sons of Noah: Indians are the descendants of Ham, Arabs the descendants of Shem, and Tartars the descendants of Japhet.

12 Trautmann 2004.

13 Sir William Jones announced his 'discovery' of Sanskrit in a powerful tribute to that language: 'The Sanscrit language, whatever be its antiquity, is of a wonderful structure; more perfect than the Greek, more copious than the Latin, and more exquisitely refined than either, yet bearing to both of them a stronger affinity, both in the roots of verbs and in the forms of grammar, than could possibly have been produced by accident; so strong indeed, that no philologer could examine them all three, without believing them to have sprung from some common source, which, perhaps, no longer exists: there is a similar reason, though not quite so forcible, for supposing that both the Gothick and the Celtick, though blended with a very different idiom, had the same origin with the Sanscrit; and the old Persian might be added to the same family.'

14 After Sir William Jones's death, the directors of the East India Company canonized his legacy by installing his statue in St. Paul's Cathedral in Calcutta.

This colossal statue shows Jones wearing a toga, resting his hand on a book, which is his translation of Manu's works. The name of Manu on the book's spine is written in Devanagari script. The four sides of the pedestal on which the statue stands contain scenes from what Christians would consider Hindu myths. These include images of Vishnu and other deities, the famous churning of the ocean, and other scenes from Hindu texts. The overall impression conveyed is to focus on 'idolatry' as something primitive but benign, being from the pre-Christian period of the Bible and hence supporting the Biblical accounts of antiquity. The Hindu Trinity is shown to correspond with the Christian doctrine of the Trinity (Trautmann 2004: 75–80).

15 Ibid.: 60.

16 Franklin 2011. The *Bengal Annual*, a British publication, while praising Jones's 'disinterested love of literature', added that, 'he was not altogether disinterested, and that his object was fame'.

17 See: Malhotra 2009, Ramaswamy 2007 and Malhotra 2011.

18 Marriott 1990: 1.

19 As mentioned in Rotter 2000: 6.

20 Rotter 2000: 35.

21 L.M. Singhvi, 'Indology and the Future of our Past', lecture delivered at Asiatic Society, Kolkata, 2006. Accessed from http://www.sanskritimagazine.com/india/the-future-of-our-past-indology-genesis-and-evolution/ on 27 May 2015.

22 The CIA and Ford Foundation had started this process of appropriating Indian intellectuals much earlier. A white paper in the 1950s explained the need to train regional specialists 'who would be given all-out training, mainly in languages and cultures outside Western Europe, to match and complement his mastery as an analyst of one of the social or natural sciences or his expertise in tradecraft as an operational officer ... vigorously backed by intensive and semi-intensive sociological study at the intelligence school, at academic centers in the United States, and when possible in the country where the language is spoken. He would learn to know not only the geography, history, politics, economics, literature, and social institutions of the country but also the informal beliefs, traditions, and ideals which make up the psyche of the society. With this profound exposure he should in time acquire the sort of empathy which makes possible a maximum yield from dealings with a people. He should come to penetrate their culture.' Accessed from https://www.cia.gov/library/center-for-the-study-of-intelligence/kent-csi/vol4no4/html/v04i4a06p_0001.htm

on 31 December 2014. The Title VI National Defense Education Act was passed in 1958. It 'aimed to insure trained expertise of sufficient quality and quantity to meet U.S. national security needs'. The Ford Foundation emerged to be the biggest single funding source for Area Studies under NDEA (source: Ellen Condliffe Lagemann, *The Politics of Knowledge: The Carnegie Corporation, Philanthropy, and Public Policy*, Chicago: University of Chicago Press, 1992, p. 178). In 2012, the Ford Foundation signalled the move away from Area Studies/Nation-oriented 'methodological nationalism' towards an 'opportunity to create a truly global social science'. (See: https://globalhighered.wordpress.com/tag/ford-foundation/ accessed 31 December 2014.) That would resonate with what Pollock says: '... by decivilizing and denationalizing the Indian past where they were once lived realities, is something that might be achieved by a seriously historical account of Sanskrit in the world, one seeking not a return to roots but a "coming-to-terms with our 'routes'", an unsentimental and nondefensive history ... ' (Pollock 2006: 580). In other words, Pollock wants to remove a sense of nation and civilization from Indians by deracinating Sanskrit, and he expects such 'taking out' to be done 'unsentimentally and nondefensively'.

23 'Shraddha' is a non-translatable word which is often equated with faith. However, faith in the Abrahamic systems connotes blind belief in something that can only be experienced after death. In Hinduism, shraddha denotes a certain trust, conviction and reverence that can be borne out through anubhava/experience during one's life by following a process. This conviction develops from one's own practice and is based on self-realization rather than belief in a historical dogma.

24 Grünendahl 2012: 227.

25 Pollock 1993a: 81.

26 To take one example, he goes through twenty-five pages of his book *The Language of the Gods* canvassing the thoughts of Westerners to make his argument that Indian civilization and nationhood are false and 'imagined'. He mentions a long line of prominent figures who invest in such views, including J.G. Herder, J.G. Fichte, Martin Heidegger, Alfred Kroeber, Alfred Foucher, O.W. Wolters, George Lakoff, Denys Lombard, Oswald Spengler, Arnold Toynbee and Samuel Huntington, amongst others.

27 Pollock 2006: 75.

28 To give but one example only, his treatment of the oral tradition suffers from his silence on the benefits that research is now discovering concerning mantra, sound and embodied learning. This research is at the cutting edge of

education, cognitive sciences, neurosciences and mind-body medicine, to name a few fields. In my view, Sanskritists should expand their field of inquiry to include the medical research under way on the impact of mantra and meditation. A field called 'accelerated learning' was started by Georgi Lozanov based on his neurological studies of Indian pandits learning Sanskrit and acquiring huge memories. Related to this is the phenomenon known as ashtavadhana, shatavadhana and sahasravadhana, that deserves investigation within the scope of Sanskrit's qualities.

29 Pollock is working on a book for the Harvard Press, titled *Liberation Philology* as a 'polemic' in defence of the field. He previewed his arguments in 'Future Philology? The Fate of a Soft Science in a Hard World.' *Critical Inquiry*, 35 (4): 931–61.

30 Pollock 2006: 2.

31 The *Barhaspatya-sutras* (dated 600 to 300 BCE) are often cited as a core text of the Charvakas.

32 Vibhishana is speaking to Ravana in *Valmiki Ramayana, VI.*

3: The Obsession with Secularizing Sanskrit

1 Malhotra 2011: 355.

2 Vatsyayan 1977: 77.

3 This is an eight-step process, also called Ashtanga Yoga, in which the practitioner spends more and more time in dharana and dhyana, leading to samadhi. The eight steps of Ashtanga Yoga begin with teaching of yama and niyama (the dos and don'ts of vyavaharika life, to free up the attention span for the ever-present paramarthika) connecting with the physical asanas, followed by pranayama, pratyahara (practising withdrawal of the senses), dharana (concentration), dhyana (meditation) and finally samadhi (becoming one with the transcendent).

4 This is based on *Brhadaranyaka Upanishad* 2.4.6 and 4.5.6.

5 See Vico in *Stanford Encyclopedia of Philosophy*: http://plato.stanford.edu/entries/vico/ accessed 14 January 2015. I have paraphrased from this source and Berlin (2013) for my analysis of Vico.

6 Berlin 2013: 157.

7 Pollock 2006: 39.

8 Ibid.: 42.

9 Sri Aurobindo uses the term 'supra rational' for this.

10 Pollock 2006: 2–3.

11 Ibid.: 3.

12 Pollock equates paramarthika with 'absolute truth of philosophical reason' and equates vyavaharika with 'certitudes people have at different stages of their history'. To unpack Pollock's use of Vico, it is important to understand the terms 'verum' and 'certum' that are used. 'Verum' refers to a priori truth which is attained only in domains that the knower himself has created. By implication, paramarthika could be seen as a fantasy domain created by the rishis. It is like the rules of a game being disconnected from any 'real' world external to it. An example of this is mathematical knowledge; the mathematicians have made mathematics as a set of rules to follow and derive conclusions based on those rules. Mathematics is not the discovery of something that objectively exists in the natural world. It is a human invention of a symbolic system through which men can logically reason. The implication is that because God made the natural world, only God can know it. Humans can understand only the human world which they have made. My response is that, in Hindu metaphysics, there is the 'rishi state' of higher consciousness, where the paramarthika reality is directly experienced. This means that 'God's mind' (to use Vico's vocabulary) is not considered inaccessible to humans in the rishi state. To deny such a state of consciousness is to deny a core tenet of Hindu cosmology. In Vico's metaphysics, the companion to verum is the 'certum' principle. This means the particular facts of history through which it is possible to discover universal truth. This 'universal truth' is social and political truth, because there is no transcendental realm for us to discover, even in principle. However, the Vedas resist this bifurcation.

13 Pollock 2006: 5.

14 *Yajnavalkya Smriti* 3.115.

15 Rig Veda 10:125.

16 In explaining Rig Veda 1:164.45 (catvāri vāc parimita padān), Yāska observes that vāc is of four types: ṛcah, yajumsi, samāni and vyāvahāriki (*Nirukta* 13:9). Of these the first three are divine (devatābhidhāna) and the last is human (manuṣyābhidhāna) (Cited in Deshpande 1971: 34–36).

17 Ibid.: 83.

18 Ken Wilber, the famous life coach and 'spiritual' guru to Americans, claimed to be the first to identify this fallacy. To remedy this fallacy in his fellow Western psychologists at the time, Wilber developed his ideas based on Sri Aurobindo's writings. However, as often happens when the Western ego

takes control, Wilber claimed that this differentiation between pre-rational and super-rational was his original discovery. Actually, he had lifted the entire idea from Sri Aurobindo's tome, *The Life Divine*, as I have pointed out on numerous occasions. Worse still, Wilber later started to accuse Sri Aurobindo as not being fully evolved to the super-rational state which Wilber claimed to have discovered as his own state. Many Westerners who appropriate Indian spiritual ideas later accuse the very same Indian tradition of being 'like a child' compared with the rational West. Hence, they argue, Indians must first evolve to be rational like the Westerners before they can truly advance further to the super-rational state. India's journey forward must go through a phase of Westernization they claim.

19 One of the leading Western disciplines developed precisely to understand this third state is called Transpersonal Psychology. It began a half-century ago by Westerners who studied yogis, rishis and meditators in India. They coined the term 'transpersonal' to refer to this state of consciousness.

20 Furthermore, I predict that given the trajectory of information technology (with 3D, virtual reality, and wearable systems), cultural productions will be less and less dependent on one-dimensional writing systems. Increasingly, they will become multi-media and embodied with the help of new technologies. More important still is that they will combine with the ancient adhyatmika technologies (inner sciences). My views run counter to prevailing Western notions that civilization 'advances' through a series of epochs in a linear chronology, from inferior to superior stages, in which literacy is superior and must leave orality behind. I disagree with the over-emphasis on literacy today. It is unfortunate that education is often being equated with literacy. The policies of governments worldwide are aligned with the philosophy of literacy. The claim is that the shift from oral to written knowledge brings radical improvements in psyche and culture, and this translates into material and social advances. One of the drivers has been that disembodied culture can be turned into 'property' that has a life of its own and hence is a commercial asset. A result of the disembodiment of human knowledge and human beings has been the atrophy of our human potential. For an example of Western linear and disconnected approaches, see: Ong 1982.

21 Pollock 2006: 4. 'Writing enables textual features far in excess of the oral; for literature it renders the discourse itself a subject for discourse for the first time, language itself an object of aestheticized awareness, the text itself an artifact to be decoded and a pretext for deciphering.'

22 Pollock claims that, 'with the exception of the Rāmāyaṇa, no remains of a nonsacral, this-worldly [i.e., laukika] Sanskrit are extant from the early epoch of literacy (from the third century BCE to, say, the first century CE)' (Pollock 2006: 48). However, there is ample evidence to the contrary in Ayurveda (medicine), Sthapathyaveda (architecture) and Rasayana (chemistry and metallurgy) and other 'this-worldly' matters in Sanskrit texts from the pre-Buddha period. The issue is whether only written texts are admissible. For Hindus, it is not relevant whether these were oral compositions or written texts. Pollock also suggests that Sanskrit was never a spoken language, i.e., never 'functioned as an everyday medium of communication' and never the language of 'a specific regional community'. It was never used for 'life experiences associated with this-worldly language use' (ibid: 49). However, again there is evidence to show otherwise. An example of the mundane described through kavya is taken up in Yaska's *Nirukta*, when a fragment of a verse from the Veda is analysed and interpreted: 'Famine is personified. On account of starvation, the sight of famine-stricken people becomes dim, therefore famine is called one-eyed. On account of insufficient nourishment, people totter on their legs, therefore famine is spoken of as having a crooked gait. Famishing people scream, and so famine is called screaming. It is called barren because there are no crops, or because people are no longer liberal in their gifts.' (Sarup 1967: Appendix, 245) Yaska, the ancient Sanskrit philologist, was familiar with how kavis of the Veda portrayed the mundane and was therefore able to interpret the kavya. It was not that the kavi thought famine was a person – Yaska knew that it was a personification employed by the poet to depict the reality experienced by mainstream Hindus more than three millennia ago. This subtlety seems to be lost on some modern philologists, who suggest that ancient Hindus believed famine was a person.

23 Pollock 2006: 49.

24 Pollock 1985: 499–519.

25 Ibid. Italics mine.

26 Ibid.

27 Ibid.

28 Ibid.

29 Ibid. Italics mine.

30 Ibid.

31 Ibid.

32 Ibid.

33 Ibid.

34 Ibid.

35 Ibid.

36 Ibid.

37 Ibid.

38 Ibid.

39 Ibid. Pollock acknowledges that there are many domains (like eating when hungry) where behaviour is not based on shastra but is based on some tacit or unconscious drive. Nevertheless, even here, he cites a text to explain that the knowledge of shastra makes the practice stronger than if the practice were uninformed by it.

40 Ibid.

41 Ibid.

42 In *Being Different* I have cited the views of Roddam Narasimha according to which the Indian discoveries in mathematics were driven largely by pragmatics.

43 Pollock 1985: 499–519.

44 Ibid.

45 Ibid. Italics mine.

46 Ibid.

47 Ibid.

48 Ibid. Italics mine.

49 Cardona, George. 'Tradition and argumentation: tensions among some early thinkers and their backgrounds,' presented at the Infinity Foundation Colloquium, 2003. See: http://www.infinityfoundation.com/indic_colloq/papers/paper_cardona2.pdf accessed on 15 April 2015.

50 I agree that many purohits today as well as in earlier times were merely parroting the Vedic hymns. Yaska's *Nirukta* ridiculed such persons long ago. However, it is unfair of Pollock to stereotype the tradition this way.

51 Coomaraswamy 1943: 45.

52 Ibid.: 45

53 Ibid.: 76

54 Ibid.: 77. Furthermore, Mrs Rhys Davids, the celebrated scholar of Buddhism, also said that the Buddha was a critic of Brahmanism only in external matters but not in the internal system of spiritual values. (See: *Indian Historical Quarterly*, Vol. 10, 1934, p. 382.) Rhys Davids and Coomaraswamy said that (in *Samyutta Nikaya* 1.169) the Buddha explains the Vedic yajna as an internal process within oneself.

55 Pollock 2006: 75–76.

56 Kannan (private communication) offers the counter argument that there were kavyas attributed to multiple authors and many anonymous ones. On the other hand, each mantra is associated with a rishi (who 'saw' it, though he or she did not 'create' it).

57 Pollock 2006: 3. Kannan offers the counter argument that Ramayana was not written down by Valmiki but was taught orally to Lava and Kusha as per the Ramayana itself. Bhagavad Gita is the song of/by the Lord, hence not a written work originally.

58 Pollock 2006: 3.

59 Ibid.: 75–76.

60 *Atharva Veda*: 10.8.32

61 Kannan (private communication) refers to the Kalachuri inscription of Gayaakarna. Source: *Corpus Inscriptionum Indicarum*. Volume 4, p. 306. Publisher: Government Epigraphist for India, Ootacamund. Editor: Mirashi, Vasudev Vishnu. 1955. The reputed *Sanskrit Worterbuch* (Sanskrit-German Dictionary of seven volumes) authored by Bohtlingk and Roth (1855-1875, published from St. Petersburg) contains fifty one attestations just from the Vedic literature alone, of the word kavya, in several senses, including art, praise (as noun), and inspired and poetical (as adjective). See also K. Krishnamoorthy's article 'Poetic Artistry in Vedic Literature' in *Annals of Bhandarkar Oriental Research Institute*, Vol. 72/73, No. 1/4, *Amṛtamahotsava* (1917–92), pp. 71–77, where he shows how Indian tradition, despite its reverence for the Veda, has also treated it as kavya: for example, Rajashekara (ninth century) discusses the issue in his *Kāvyamimāṃsa.*. Also, Vedic words for beauty in poetic language have been studied by Pischel (*Indische Studien*) and Oldenberg. Even more than these, it was Dharmasuri of the sixteenth century who discussed at length in his *Sahitya Ratnakara*, the issue of the Veda as kavya, applying the regular poetic criteria to the Vedas, and showed how the Veda was good poetry. T.G. Mainkar wrote a book called *Ṛgvedic Foundations of Classical Poetics* (1977). P.S. Sastri discussed the figures of speech in Rig Veda, and traced the subtle theories of rasa and dhvani right to the Vedic literature. Nothing is clearer than the statement of Rajashekara that the authors of shastra and kavya alike draw their inspiration from the Veda.

62 The verse actually describes what elements were drawn from each of the four Vedas. And it turns out that the elements in fact comprise the very essence of each Veda, rather than a mere jumbling of some random elements

found in them. Kannan also points out to *Yajur Veda* (30.6) where there is a clear mention of actor, along with dance and music. Even more ancient is the word 'nritu', meaning female dancer, already occurring in Rig Veda.

63 Pollock 2006: 107. Kannan rejoinders (via private communication) that Pollock is merely paraphrasing what many Indians wrote much earlier and calling it his original work. Kannan cites, as one example, that Tee Nam Srikantaiyya, one of the foremost authorities on alankara shastra, discussed the trichotomy of Veda, shastra and kavya in his book of 1953 (revised in 1961, and reprinted several times), titled, *Bharatiya Kavya Mimamse* (in Kannada). Kannan says that the only thing original in Pollock's work is that he tries to drive a wedge between genres of literature that have always had a common purpose.

64 Pollock 2006: 3. Kannan finds it strange that Pollock chooses some eleventh-century reference points rather than tracing the developments since much earlier times.

65 Pollock 2006: 3.

66 Pollock 2001b: 394.

67 I am indebted to K.S. Kannan for this rejoinder (via private communication) to Pollock: In 1.3 Kuntaka says that kavyas constitute a means for attaining the four purusharthas. Elsewhere he also discusses achieving this by the shastras. In 1.5 also the same issue is discussed again, and it is shown how the method of kavya in imparting the knowledge of the purusharthas is even superior, by way of being delightful. The auto-commentary on 1.5 says shastra is like bitter medicine for destroying ignorance whereas kavya is nectar for doing the same. See Krishnamoorthy 1977.

68 Pollock 2006: 105.

69 Pollock 2015: 24. 'Radhavallabh Tripathi shared his learning at a seminar on rasa I offered at Columbia University in autumn, 2011.' He credits Tripathi for his learning of rasa.

4: Sanskrit Considered a Source of Oppression

1 Pollock 1993a: 111.

2 Ibid.

3 Ibid.: 77. In fairness to him, he also sees similar tendencies in some of the other world cultures, but his target is Sanskrit.

4 Ibid.: 101.

5 Ibid.: 80.

6 Ibid.: 111.

7 Ibid.: 115.

8 Ibid.: 113.

9 Ibid.: 115-16. Italics mine.

10 Ibid.: 116.

11 Ibid.

12 Ibid. Italics mine.

13 Pollock 2006: 39. 'From around the beginning of the first millennium BCE, when the earliest form of Sanskrit appeared in South Asia, until around the beginning of the first millennium CE, Sanskrit functioned as a communicative medium that was restricted both in terms of who was permitted to make use of the language and which purposes the language could subserve. Access to Sanskrit was reserved for particular orders of society, and it was employed predominantly in connection with the liturgy of the Vedic ritual and associated knowledge systems such as grammar, phonetics, and metrics.'

14 Ibid.: 39. 'Its transformation, around the beginning of the first millennium CE, into a far more broadly available language, with new and unprecedented expressive purposes to execute – above all, *kāvya* and *praśasti*, courtly literature and royal praise-poetry – led to the *creation of a culture-power formation* that would exhibit an astonishing stability over the following ten or more centuries.' Italics mine.

15 Ibid.: 40

16 Pollock 1993a: 77. Pollock's use of relationships between knowledge and power – where dominant groups in power establish, sustain and deepen their power through knowledge production, has its roots in Foucault and Gramsci. See Bhatnagar 1986.

17 Malhotra 2014: 115.

18 Pollock made this statement in his CSDS (The Centre for the Study of Developing Societies) lecture; it is stated as part of the abstract as shown at: http://www.csds.in/events/sheldon-pollock-liberation-philology. (It is worth noting that Paul Hacker, the pioneer of the neo-Hinduism doctrine described in my book *Indra's Net*, had also started out as a Sanskrit philologist of considerable competence before turning his knowledge to political use.)

19 Herzfeld 1997: 351. 'The roots of Greek political philology lie in the Eurocentric models of the Enlightenment, in which Western European readings of Classical antiquity provided a meticulously calibrated yardstick of cultural

sophistication. Greek cultural scholarship – notably philology and its more obviously nationalistic offshoot, folklore – is largely formed in imitation of that tradition.'

20 'In stark contrast to the Portuguese priests' earlier intense study of the Konkani language, and its cultivation as a communication medium in their quest for converts during the previous century, under the Inquisition, xenophobic measures were adopted to isolate new converts from the non-Christian populations.' See: Prabhu 1999: 133–134.

21 http://en.wikipedia.org/wiki/Clay_Sanskrit_Library accessed on 22 December 2014.

22 Pollock 2006: 8.

23 Pollock 2011: 39.

24 Pollock 1993a: 116.

25 Ibid.: 77.

26 Ibid.: 98.

27 Ibid.: 105. 'The monopolization of "access to authoritative resources" – the most authoritative of all resources, Sanskrit (*vaidika*) learning – becomes itself a basic component in the construction and reproduction of the idea of inequality and thus in what, again, can be viewed as a process analogous to colonization in precolonial India.'

28 Pollock writes: 'Actual sociolinguistic situation was far more complex than the Mīmāṃsā theory of exclusion would lead us to believe, and the borders around the sacred sphere were far more porous. The most basic linguistic data show this unequivocally. Some have argued that the oldest stratum of the Veda shows phonological and lexical convergence between Sanskrit and non-Sanskrit languages, indicating that a significant degree of intercommunity contact, both social and discursive, occurred early on' (Pollock 2006: 41–42). However, this nuance is often deleted in the way the Indian left uses the information in its one-sided criticisms.

29 Pollock 2006: 41. 'The Mīmāṃsā discussion most pertinent to an analysis of the monopolization of Sanskrit culture occurs in the chapter "On Rights" (*adhikāra*). This addresses a person's entitlement to possess the results of an act of *dharma* – the right, in other words, to participate in the moral universe and engage in the principal modes of conduct aimed at actualizing the worldview of early Sanskritic India.' Pollock also says: 'One of the key differences of the *varṇa* ordering is first articulated: the right of access to the Sanskrit Vedic texts and thereby to the ethical realm of *dharma*. There are certain prerequisites to

the right of participation in *vaidika* practices (though these are not necessarily enunciated explicitly in the rules coded in the Veda). An individual must be in possession of the ritual instruments for performing the rite, for example, and must have the financial resources at his disposal, as well as the requisite knowledge. The mere desire to gain the results of ritual action – the various benefits the rites can confer, such as fathering a son, reaching heaven, and so on – does not suffice to qualify one for participation. Mīmāṃsā argues this out with interesting complexity' (Pollock 2006: 40).

30 Ibid.: 41, footnote 4. 'Uttaramīmāṃsā, or Vedānta, seamlessly extends the Purvamīmāṃsā from the prohibition against the Shudra's sacrificing to the prohibition against his acquiring sacred knowledge (*vidyā*) in general.' He cites *Brahmasūtra* 1.3.34 ff. However, I feel that some of the following counter-points need to be examined further for a better balanced view. (a) The Purva-mimamsa restrictions on shudras were later contested. (b) Pollock's proof that brahmins monopolized Sanskrit needs to be examined for other reasons also – for example, the assertion in the earlier Purva-mimamsa that shudras did not have the right to perform yajnas does not automatically imply that shudras were not allowed to learn Sanskrit. Pollock incorrectly claims that there were no other purposes for Sanskrit besides yajnas. He does not provide any hard evidence that Vedic Sanskrit was restricted to the domain of the sacred in the sense of not being used for ordinary purposes.

31 The following pages rely heavily upon summarizing the views of Arvind Sharma from his book, *Hindu Egalitarianism*, Rupa & Co., 2006.

32 Cited in Sharma 2006: 61.

33 Cited in Sharma 2006: 62.

34 Cited in Sharma 2006: 79.

35 Cited in Sharma 2006: 60.

36 Sharma 2006: 120–21.

37 Cited in Sharma 2006: 43.

38 Most modern Hinduism movements follow similar principles in assigning work to individuals.

39 Cited in Sharma 2006: 6.

40 Cited in Sharma 2006: 6.

41 Cited in Sharma 2006: 8.

42 Cited in Sharma 2006: 17.

43 P.V. Kane cited in Sharma 2006: 37.

44 P.V. Kane cited in Sharma 2006: 37.

45 Sharma 2006: 37–38.

46 As per Kulluka Bhatta's interpretation cited in Sharma 2006: 115.

47 Sharma 2006: 44.

48 Sharma offers the following arguments. According to *Jaiminisutra* (JS 6:1.27), it was the opinion of Badari (contested by Jaimini) that the shudras could perform Vedic yajnas. The issue is discussed in considerable detail from which it is clear that the exact status of the shudra was a contested point. According to the *Bharadvaja Srauta Sutra* (5:2.8) it is 'the opinion of some that the shudra can consecrate the three Vedic fires while recognizing that there was a controversy about this. According to *Vṛddha Gautamasmṛti* (Ch. 16), shudras of good conduct are eligible for initiation (śudro va caritravratah). According to *Yoga-Yājñavalkya* (Ch. 2), it is the opinion of some sages that the shudras may enter the stage of life called brahmacharya. Interesting evidence of the eligibility for maintaining sacrificial fire by the shudras is provided by *Apastamba Dharmasutra* (5: 14.1) which lays down that fire may be accepted from a brahmin, kshatriya, vaishya or shudra who is 'well off (bahupushta)' (Sharma 2000: 236–38).

49 Krishna Shastry 1999.

50 For instance, a word meaning 'the place where cows are tied' evolves to mean a tying-spot in general, thus losing its connection to the cow. His point is that such evolution from concrete daily usage to abstract usage indicates a close interaction between pragmatics and theory.

51 Aklujkar 2003: This was a time when brahmins 'could have had (a) a well-thought-out view of social change and (b) institutions necessary to implement that view. Without discounting the possibility that their motives could have had a selfish political-economic underbelly, one must attribute to them some decency, some vision, and some capacity for flexibility. Otherwise, how could they have achieved what they did while remaining a minority with no direct control over physical power and with no passion or egalitarianism necessary for increasing their number and without giving rise to any long class warfare? In spite of their exclusivism and emphasis on purity in diet, marital relations, etc., the Brahmins were probably not all that puritanical or lacking in diversity. Their puritanism in the period we have considered could have been highly pragmatic, probably directed more toward assimilating communities through a step-by-step process than toward excluding them.' Aklujkar is saying that the brahmins' role as experts depended on increasing their support base.

Since they did not have any state institution protecting them in the pre-Shaka period, it was strategic for them to include others, but in a systematic manner. Their systematic method of propagation without diluting their expertise was achieved by demanding a high standard of rigour and ethical behaviour; it was not based on exclusivity of language or race. Aklujkar writes: 'The Brahmins, Jains and Buddhists generally understood what constituted åryatva and shared that understanding in all important respects if not in every detail or emphasis. Åryatva was not exclusively or primarily associated with language, although some languages could have come to be associated with the groups that came to be known as Åryas as their languages and as especially valued languages. The component more important and fundamental than language in the understanding of Årya seems to have been the mode of living and thinking. This is where the evidence from all the three religious traditions I have been mentioning seems to converge. A certain kind of ethics and ethico-religious behaviour was clearly at the core of Årya, although, as with all formations of social sets, the presence of a core does not mean that every member of the set lived by it or lived uniformly and exclusively by it and although, at the surface level, a certain arrangement of individual and social life also seems to have played an important role in the understanding of åryatva.'

52 Pollock 2006: 46, 47-48. 'In the conceptual universe in which *vyākaraṇa* (grammar, or perhaps more strictly, language "analysis") arose and functioned as a foundational intellectual discipline, a strong distinction was drawn between two kinds of action: instrumental and this-worldly, and non-instrumental and other-worldly (*dṛṣṭārtha* or *laukika*, and *adṛṣṭārtha* or *alaukika*). During the epoch of its formation as a knowledge system, grammar, and with it its first and originally sole analytical object, Sanskrit, were affiliated exclusively with the latter. Like everything else in this world, the character of language analysis would gradually change, but from an early period it functioned as an auxiliary science in the service of the revealed texts, as one of the six "limbs of the Veda".' Pollock goes on to say: 'In the *Aṣṭādhyāyī*, this sacerdotal function characterizes both registers of the language: on the one hand, the idiom actually used for the Vedic texts themselves, what Panini calls *chandaḥ*, verse, or better, "the Verse" (albeit not all texts classified as Veda are versified); on the other, the rigorously normative idiolect restricted to (Vedic) pedagogical environments, which he calls *bhāṣā*, speech. That both had largely sacral associations as late as the beginning of the Common Era is shown in Patañjali's *Mahābhāṣya*, the *Great Commentary* on Pāṇini's grammar.' Pollock continues: 'For Patañjali, principal heir and final

arbiter of the *vaidika* grammatical tradition, the purposes of Sanskrit language analysis were more or less exclusively tied to sacred performance and to the pedagogical practices, both social and discursive, pertaining to knowledge of the sacred. The same conception is shared by Kātyāyana, the major exegete of grammar who lived between the time of Pāṇini and Patañjali, and whose additions to and criticisms of Pāṇini are minutely scrutinized in the *Mahābhāṣya*. For Kātyāyana, the Sanskrit language is not something invented by humans but rather is *lokasiddha*, always already pre-existent in the world. ... For Patañjali, the communicative world within which Sanskrit and its grammar function is not simply coextensive with the lifeworld in general, as experience with other languages and their practices would lead us naturally to assume. The sphere of Sanskrit is markedly narrower: it is in essence the sphere of sacred textual knowledge, with only the most tentative moves toward textual practices beyond the sacred.'

53 Pollock 2006: 184.

54 Ibid.: 177.

55 Ibid.: 177–78.

56 Ibid.: 83. He goes on to say: 'The same order that informs the most exquisite instantiation of grammatical language – namely, *kāvya*, and its specific political form, the *praśasti* – was a model or prototype of the moral, social, and political order: a just (*sādhu*) king was one who used and promoted the use of correct language (*sādhuśabda*).' Dr K.S. Kannan points out that in all traditional systems of high learning it has been considered important to use the language correctly; hence Pollock is making a mountain out of a molehill.

57 In private communication with me, Kannan pointed out: Dandin in *Kavyadarsha* 1.5 says that the image of the reputation of the ancient kings does not go extinct even though they are no more, for it has been reflected in the mirror of literature. However, the 'glory body' phrase in Pollock's passage quoted above seems to have been copy-pasted from Bhartrihari *Nitisatakam* 1.20, where it refers to the fame of the poets themselves, not the kings.

58 Dharampal 2000.

59 Ibid.

60 Cited in Sharma 2006: 75.

61 Cited in Sharma, 2006: 75.

62 See: http://www.speakingtree.in/spiritual-blogs/masters/science-of-spirituality/varna-as-a-form-of-capital accessed on 10 September 2015.

63 See the Sanskrit monthly *Sambhashan Sandeshah*, issue of June 2003: 4–6.

64 Other dignitaries who supported Dr Ambedkar's initiative included Dr B.V. Keskar, India's deputy minister for external affairs, and professor Naziruddin Ahmed.

65 Pollock 1993a: 77: '... indigenous discourses of power – the various systematized and totalized constructions of inequality in traditional India – might be viewed as a preform of orientalism. Raising such a possibility, at all events, might encourage extending to premodern Indian cultures the problematics of power and domination necessary to help us interpret their products.'

66 Pollock does want to 'isolate the morphology of domination that many such discourses share'. In plain language, this means that Sanskrit knowledge needs to be analysed alongside other oppressive systems in different parts of the world. However, the goal in Pollock's own work seems to be to specifically prove how Sanskrit is '*creating the idea of race and concurrently legislating racial exclusivity, asserting linguistic hierarchy and claiming superiority for the language of the masters*' (Pollock 1993a: 78).

67 Pollock 1993a: 107.

68 Ibid.: 107.

69 He notes that the term arya has not always had a literal application to race or ethnicity but he claims that it was overwhelmingly used in this way as the tradition evolved.

70 Pollock 1993a: 107. Italics mine.

71 Halbfass 2007: 17.

72 Malhotra 2011. See Chapter 6 of that book.

73 Grünendahl writes: 'Pollock does not specify "the German state" (1993: 82) or the particulars of educational governance and administration he sees at work between 1800 and 1945. As for the crucial "years around 1933" (118n5), he illustrates the supposedly substantial investment of "the German state" in Indology with an unspecified reference to "the *Minerva Jahrbuch*" (118n5), a directory of higher education worldwide. However, my examination of the *Minerva* yearbook for the year 1934, a volume of 1,978 pages, yielded no evidence of the kind Pollock ascribes to it. The only pertinent information *Minerva* supplies are sixteen (not Pollock's ominous thirteen) bare-bone references to German university institutes (and chairs) with Indological

curricula. In most cases, Indology was not even "substantial" enough to feature in the name of the institute. More often than not, Sanskrit was taught at institutes of Indo-European comparative linguistics ("Indogermanistik"), not always by Indologists in the sense of scholars primarily concerned with Indian languages and literatures (including Prakrit, Pali, etc.), as distinguished from comparative linguists whose interest in Sanskrit focuses on language, with little concern for literary content or other aspects of Indian culture. For a comparative assessment of the supposedly prominent position of "German Indology" around 1933 I also consulted earlier and later *Minerva* volumes. Assuming that the purported "substantial increase in the investment on the part of the NS state" (Pollock 1993: 95) in Indology (and Indogermanistik) would have become increasingly manifest during the course of the NS regime, I checked *Minerva* 31 (1934) against 33 (1938). In doing so, I discovered that within this period two Indological chairs fell vacant, while the overall position of Indology remained as peripheral as it always had been in German academia, contrary to what Pollock would have us believe' (Grünendahl 2012).

74 Ibid.

75 Ibid.

76 Ibid.

77 http://www.jewishencyclopedia.com/articles/9582-lagarde-paul-anton-de accessed on 22 December 2014.

78 Pollock 1993a: 115–16. Italics mine.

79 Ibid.: 116.

80 Ibid.: 40.

81 Ibid.: 293.

82 Ibid.

83 Ibid.: 116–17

84 Ibid.: 104.

85 Ibid.

86 Ibid.

87 Ibid.: 114.

88 Ibid.

89 Ibid.

90 Pollock 2006: 565. Italics mine.

5: Ramayana Framed as Socially Irresponsible

1 Pollock 2005: 23.

2 Pollock cites the *Maitrayani Samhita* version of the Yajurveda to illustrate the Vedic roots of the divinization-demonization dichotomy. He cites the following passage here: '[The gods wanted to recover their realm from the demons.] They turned Viṣṇu into a dwarf and brought him [to the demons]. "Whatever he might cover in three strides shall belong to us [the rest to you]." He strode first over this, then this, then that [= earth, sky, heaven].' (*Maitrayani Samhita* III.7.9) (Pollock 1984: 519–20)

3 Pollock 1984: 521.

4 Ibid.: 522. '... man's natural incapacity is emphatically demonstrated by the need for the infusion in him of Viṣṇu's power (*nārāyaṇa tejaḥ*, 9.69, M Bh. III.195.18). Filled with the divine potency, this extraordinary new creature, the earthly king – and only he, no god or man – can protect the brahmanical world order (represented by Uttaṅka) by destroying evil.'

5 Pollock 1984: 522.

6 Ibid.: 523.

7 Ibid.

8 Ibid. Explaining them away, Pollock says: 'While the important passage cited from the *Mahābhārata* seems representative for much of the epic period, it has often been noted that stony silence if not outright contradiction with respect to the king's divinity can be found elsewhere; many of the early law-books, for example, seem thoroughly indifferent or sometimes even hostile to the notion. Now, it is not in the least clear that the silence encountered in the early *dharmaśāstras* should be interpreted negatively, nor that the outright denials we do meet are necessarily applicable to the period with which we are dealing.'

9 Ibid. 'Even if these denials are contemporaneous with our text, the fact that they at the same time imply a widespread belief is something we should not ignore ... Yet determining as cogently as possible the stance of the *Rāmāyaṇa* on this issue will prove essential to support the interpretation proposed of the thematic significance of the work.'

10 Ibid.: 524. 'It is kings – make no mistake of it – who confer righteous merit, something so hard to acquire, and precious life itself. One must never harm them, never criticize, insult or oppose them. Kings are gods who walk the earth in the form of men.'

11 Ibid.: 525.

12 Ibid.

13 Pollock refers to a Vedic yajna, the Rajya Abhisheka, during which, according to tradition, the king takes an oath to serve his people and work for their welfare. Pollock, however, says this yajna boosts the king as divine, whom the subjects have to obey without question: a hallmark of oriental despotism. He wants Vedic culture to look like some kind of black magic that gives the king divine powers without any responsibilities towards the people. But Pollock does not supply any analysis showing whether kings who go through the Rajya Abhisheka yajna and are surrounded by Vedic culture are more likely to become despots as a result of this yajna. The fact is that there are many despotic rulers in history who never went through the Vedic yajna. On the other hand, Rama is shown to be open to the wishes of his subjects after he is crowned king with Vedic yajnas. As a divinized king he is shown to give priority to the welfare of his subjects over his personal and family well-being. For instance, a washer-man asks Rama if he is following dharma, and whether his priorities lie in making his people happy or keeping his wife with him. Rama agrees that if by having Sita with him he is violating dharma and adversely affecting the welfare of his people, he will separate from Sita.

14 Pollock 1984: 525.

15 All the references to the *Ramayana* cited by Kannan here are based on the edition published by N. Ramaratnam, 1958, M.L.J. Press, Mylapore, Madras. (The references are to kanda, sarga and shloka numbers.)

16 These perils include the following: In a kingless country, traders going on long journeys with abundant merchandise do not feel safe on the roads (verse 22); no man can call anything his own because the law of the jungle (might is right) will prevail (verse 31); the king is the guardian of truth and protector of dharma, the father and mother of his citizens (verse 34). The good king is not despised by subjects for undue strictness in collecting dues. It is the duty of the king to protect all citizens by righteous means. A good king does not seek artha (material wealth) by sacrificing the dharma, or vice versa, nor both by kama (pleasure). A good king must have mastery over his senses. The king of high intellect who rules as per dharma attains svarga (Ramayana 2.100, verses 27, 48, 62, 69, 76).

17 Pollock 1984: 505.

18 Ibid.: 516.

19 Ibid.: 517.

20 Ibid.: 22.

21 Ibid.: 23. Pollock compares Ashoka's rock edicts about raj dharma with select verses from Valmiki to prove the connection between the Ramayana and the theo-political ideology of raj dharma.

22 Pollock 2005: 26.

23 Ibid.: 26-27.

24 Ibid.: 27. Emphasis added.

25 Pollock 1986: 64.

26 Ibid.: 53.

27 Ibid.: 53-56.

28 *Manusmriti* 5.148.

29 Pollock 1986: 53.

30 Ibid.

31 Private communications.

32 Pollock 1993b: 288.

33 Ibid.: 263.

34 Ibid.: 265.

35 Pollock 1993b: 265. Admittedly, he is aware that Rama references were in the form of devotion to Vishnu. Traditional scholars feel that Vishnu bhakti is also evidence of Rama bhakti.

36 Ibid.: 263.

37 Pollock 1993b: 264

38 Pollock 1993b: 269

39 Pollock 1993b: 277. 'Whereas the Ramayana may certainly have played a substantial role, in some instances a central role, in the political imagination of earlier India, it comes to be deployed with a fuller and more referentially direct expression – in royal cultic, documentary, and textual representations – from the twelfth century onward ... it was in reaction to the transformative encounter with the polities of Central Asia – with Ghaznavids, Ghurids, Khaljis ... and the resultant new social and political order instituted by the establishment of the Sultanate that the Ramayaaa lived anew in royal discourse. ... Although Mahmud died in 1030, Ghaznavid military campaigns continued, and within half a century or so of the death of Mahmud, the Gahadavalas began to transform Ayodhya into a major Vaishnava center, a building program that was to continue for a century.'

40 Pillai 1997: 17. While the Mauryas shifted the capital to Pataliputra, Samudragupta made Ayodhya his capital once again, beginning about 350 CE.

41 Pollock 1993b: 283.

42 Ibid.: 286.

43 Ibid.: 282–83.

44 Robert P. Goldman, at the University of California, Berkeley, led the Ramayana translation and interpretation project, of which Sheldon Pollock was a team member. The project used, as its Sanskrit source, the Critical Edition of the Ramayana constructed from multiple manuscripts at the MS University of Baroda between 1951 and 1975 with funding from the University Grants Commission of the Government of India.

45 Pollock 2006: 78, 81. 'The monumental text by Vālmīki shares too much of the Ashokan spirit to push it back earlier.' He cites his own work, Pollock 1986: 23 ff. He further asserts: 'No convincing evidence has been offered for a pre-Ashokan date of the *Rāmāyaṇa* in its monumental form (the common denominator of all our manuscripts), let alone a date before the Buddha (c. 400 BCE).' Pollock is unwilling to entertain any astronomical evidence contained in the Ramayana as an indicator of its date. Numerous scholars have used this to prove dates that are many centuries earlier.

46 Pollock claims we cannot rule out the idea that Valmiki was familiar with these writings and appropriated them from Buddhist Jataka writers. He even goes so far as to suggest that, in the story of Rama's exile, Valmiki may be creating a fictional parallel to Buddha's renunciation. He leaves these as suggestions without any specific conclusion(s) for others to pursue. Despite so many challenges to this chronology, certain eminent Indian historians, Romila Thapar for example, assume his views are factual. Thapar uses Sheldon Pollock's positioning of the date of Valmiki's Ramayana to dilute its uniqueness and reduce it to being a fantasy. See, for example, Thapar, 'Fallacies of Hindutva Historiography', *Economic and Political Weekly*, 3 January 2015: 'Composition over a period of time means diverse authors, so we need to ask who they were and what were their frameworks of reference? The Valmiki Ramayana, in the period between 400 BCE and 400 CE, had at least two contenders – the Buddhist version, the Dasaratha Jataka, and the Jaina version, Vimalasuri's Paumachariyam – both contradicting the Valmiki version. In the Buddhist version Rama and Sita are siblings, and in the Jaina version Ravana is not a rakshasa but a respectable member of the Meghavahana lineage and the fantasies of the other Ramayana are given rational explanations.' Accessed from http://www.epw.in/discussion/fallacies-hindutva-historiography.html on 28 January 2015.

47 Goldman 1984: 32.

48 Pollock 1993b.

49 Pollock quoted in Kruijtzer 2005.

50 Pollock 1993b: 261.

51 Ibid.

52 Ibid.: 293.

6: Politicizing Indian Literature

1 See: http://www.amphilsoc.org/sites/default/files/proceedings/Ingalls.pdf accessed on 09 January 2015. As I have already mentioned, Daniel Ingalls was Pollock's mentor in Sanskrit at Harvard, and was known as a pioneer in the study of Sanskrit kavya (literature) in the West. Ingalls guided numerous important Ph.D graduates at Harvard, many of whom became famous Indologists playing important roles in American Indology in the past half-century. Many of their works, and those of *their* students, have been controversial, and challenged from within the Hindu tradition.

2 Ingalls 1945: 33–35. 'The mahakavya must take its subject matter from the epics (Ramayana or Mahabharata), or from history. It must help further the four goals of man (purusharthas). It must contain descriptions of cities, seas, mountains, moonrise and sunrise, and "accounts of merrymaking in gardens, of bathing parties, drinking bouts, and love-making. It should tell the sorrow of separated lovers and should describe a wedding and the birth of a son. It should describe a king's council, an embassy, the marching forth of an army, a battle, and the victory of a hero" ... Explanations, in the form of questions and answers between the narrator and the listener of the mahakavya, were expected to be integrated to show how the fructification of the four purusharthas [goals of life as per dharma] [is] exemplified in that brief narrative segment.'

3 Ingalls 1945: 33–35.

4 Pollock 2003: 42.

5 Ibid.: 49.

6 Ibid.: 50.

7 Pollock 2006: 105.

8 Earlier he traced kavya shastra's beginnings only from the sixth-century CE, ending in consolidation in the eleventh century. But now, he implicitly acknowledges that the sixth-century writers Bhamaha and Dandin were building

on Bharata's *Natya Shastra*. Hence his chronology of kavya shastra development now goes back to an earlier period.

9 Pollock 2015: 71. Italics mine.

10 Ibid.: 71, 77, 77 note 84. He contradicts himself when he acknowledged earlier that the idea of rasa experience goes as far back as the Upanishads. He appeared to give it a spiritual meaning, when he referred to the 'Upanishadic idiom' described as: '"a state of pure blissful consciousness", "the bliss that is the self", where "the self-other distinction vanishes", a hallmark concept of monistic metaphysics.' However, despite touching upon this opening into the sacred realm, he does not want to dwell on this point at all. He adds a footnote and simply moves away from the subject: 'I pass over utterances such as *Taittirīya Upaniṣad* 27.2 *raso vai saḥ*, though cited by later thinkers like Jagannatha.'

11 Ibid.: 71, 76.

12 The book being referenced here is Pollock (2006) *The Language of the Gods*....

13 Pollock 2006: 75. 'The *praśasti* [poetry praising the kings] itself was intimately related to, even a subset of, a new form of language use that was coming into being in the same period and would eventually be given the name *kāvya*. It was only when the language of the gods entered the world of men that literature in India began.'

14 Ibid.: 114. 'When the language of the gods entered the world of men, Sanskrit literati invented two closely related cultural forms, *kāvya* and *praśasti*. From the beginning, the languages in which *kāvya* could be composed were delimited in practice ... The ideas of language and literature that *kāvya* embodied, and the unbounded sociotextual community to which it spoke and among which it circulated, differed radically from those of the world in a state of vernacularization; indeed, they were the ideas and the community against which that world would eventually define itself. Much the same is true of *praśasti*. ... Once Sanskrit became available for the enunciation of political will, it swiftly displaced every other code for the execution of this task.'

15 Walter Bendix Schönflies Benjamin (1892 to 1940) was an eclectic thinker, combining elements of German idealism, romanticism, historical materialism and Jewish mysticism.

16 Benjamin notes an early stage in which art and culture have an 'aura' of the sacred, stemming first from primitive magic and then from the more sophisticated use of the arts in religious life: 'The uniqueness of a work of art is inseparable from its being imbedded in the fabric of tradition. This tradition

itself is thoroughly alive and extremely changeable. An ancient statue of Venus, for example, stood in a different traditional context with the Greeks, who made it an object of veneration, than with the clerics of the Middle Ages, who viewed it as an ominous idol. Both of them, however, were equally confronted with its uniqueness, that is, its aura. Originally the contextual integration of art in tradition found its expression in the cult. We know that the earliest art works originated in the service of a ritual – first the magical, then the religious kind.' But then these art works moved out of that sacred context, lost their aura, and became systematic tools of politics. (Sourced from https://www.marxists.org/reference/subject/philosophy/works/ge/benjamin.htm accessed on 24 March 2015. I have used this source heavily to present Benjamin's ideas as they apply to this book.) See also Benjamin 1936.

17 Sourced from https://www.marxists.org/reference/archive/benjamin/1940/history.htm accessed on 24 March 2015. Italics mine.

18 Interestingly, Benjamin uses a Turkish puppet, as opposed to a white man as the puppet, as his mascot of untrustworthiness, i.e., someone who lacks agency and is merely a front man whose strings are manipulated from above.

19 Benjamin 1936, sourced from https://www.marxists.org/reference/subject/philosophy/works/ge/benjamin.htm accessed on 24 March 2015.

20 The word 'literarization' was first used by Brecht, a contemporary of Benjamin, as part of an analysis of fascism. Benjamin picked up the term and integrated it into his theory. See: http://www.colorado.edu/humanities/ferris/Content/Texts/Excerpt-Ferris_WB-CUP-Intro.pdf accessed 15 August 2015.

21 Pollock 2006: 4. The political importance of literarization to Pollock comes through when he says: 'The authorization to write, above all to write literature, is no natural entitlement, like the ability to speak, but is typically related to social and political and even epistemological privileges.'

22 Ibid.: 258. Pollock does not apply it uncritically. He remarks that Benjamin's theory is too narrow and that is because, according to it, cultural is 'invariably linked to fascism and war'. He also cites Clifford Geertz's theory of the state as a theatrical spectacle but finds that it does not implicate political rule and merely sees the state as displaying 'the dominant themes of high culture'. Benjamin made aesthetics too much a driver of political violence. Geertz made aesthetics too little involved in actual governance and saw aesthetics as mere entertainment for the elites.

23 Ibid.: 76. I appreciate this nuance and would like to better understand how to reconcile this with his other statements opposing sacredness.

24 Ibid.: 241.

25 Ibid.: 133.

26 Ibid.: 133.

27 Ibid.: 523.

28 Ibid.: 139. 'The unique expressive capabilities of Sanskrit poetry allow the poet to make statements about political power that could be made in no other way.'

29 Ibid.: 6.

30 Ibid.: 61.

31 An equivalent situation today would be a government expanding its brutal power while on the surface promoting television sitcoms, literary festivals, theatrical entertainment, cricket and the like.

32 Pollock 2003: 61. Italics mine.

33 Ibid.: 118.

34 He cites an encyclopaedic work called *Manasollasa*, produced in Vikramaditya III's court, which includes a wide range of military and artistic activities.

35 Pollock 2003: 120.

36 Ibid.

37 Goldman: 1984.

38 I am indebted to K.S. Kannan for pointing out many of the foregoing examples. He makes the further point that if poets had been so tightly coupled with kings, scholars would not be facing so much difficulty in determining the chronology of poets. Also, he says Pollock offers no statistical proof, and this would require the analysis of thousands of poetical works. Why did Valmiki and many others like him live humbly in a forest and not in some royal accommodation?

39 Pollock 2003: 103.

40 Ibid.: 105.

41 Ibid.: 106.

7: Politicizing the history of Sanskrit and the Vernaculars

1 Pollock 2006: 40. He writes: 'The foundational text of the system, the *Mīmāṃsāsūtra* attributed to Jaimini, dates to the last centuries (most probably

third or second) B.C.E. There is good reason to believe that the reflexivity, even anxiety, about Vedic authority evinced in the work, of which the restriction on access to the corpus and its language is only one (if a decisive) component, would have been unthinkable in the absence of the broad religious and social critique that Buddhism had enunciated in the preceding two centuries and the "disenchantment of the world" that critique had signaled.' Clearly, Pollock wants us to think of the big divide between the earlier astika (Vedic) and these new nastika (Buddhist and Jaina) traditions, and the role played by the latter in reforming the former.

2 Pollock 2006: 1.

3 Ibid.: 166. Pollock further praises Sanskrit's 'ability to make reality in a way more real by making it more noticeable, more complex, more beautiful thanks to the language's arsenal of formal and rhetorical attributes – the metrics and tropology that fascinated readers across the cosmopolis as well as the presence of a literary corpus offering successful exemplars of such linguistic alchemy' (ibid.: 255).

4 Pollock claims that the last Prakrit inscriptions found in north India are from the third century CE and that those found in south India are not later than the fourth century CE.

5 Pollock 2006: 122.

6 Ibid.: 12.

7 Ibid.: 122. 'All across the subcontinent there came into existence, by a startling, nearly simultaneous set of transformations, a linguistically homogeneous and conceptually standardized form of Sanskrit political poetry. Power in India now had a Sanskrit voice. And by a kind of premodern globalization – even Westernization – it would have a Sanskrit voice in much of the world to the east. In the first centuries of the Common Era, one of the tipping points in the history of global exchange and cross-cultural contact, which saw also a dramatic expansion of trade between South Asia and the Roman empire, people in India began to develop relationships of new complexity and intensity with mainland and maritime Southeast Asia. It is unclear why such ties, comprising not only trade but also profound transculturation, did not develop in the lands to the north and west of India, where even older patterns of interaction had recently been intensified under Kuṣāṇa rule.'

8 Ibid.: 19.

9 Ibid.: 133.

10 Ibid.: 133. An 'inverse relation of cultural power' and the spread of Sanskrit 'occurred at the cost of retarding or even arresting local literary traditions'.

11 Ibid.: 133–134.

12 Ibid.: 18.

13 Ibid.: 165.

14 Ibid.: 15.

15 Ibid.: 114.

16 Ibid.: 165.

17 Ibid.: 176.

18 Ibid.: 167. 'Excellence in the command of the Sanskrit language was therefore something kings had to achieve through mastery of a theoretical body of material that already established that excellence, and all of them everywhere could achieve this to the same degree and in the same manner, assuming they were in possession of the right textual instruments. This attainment ... was one among other celebrated royal attributes and so was as essential to kingship as the martial power, political sagacity, physical beauty, fame, and glory that are repeatedly celebrated in the *praśasti* aesthetic.'

19 Ibid.: 166.

20 Ibid.: 168–69. To establish Panini's connection with a king, Pollock's testimony is based on a legend reported by a seventh-century Chinese pilgrim: 'On completing his grammar, Pāṇini offered it to his king, who "treasured it very much and ordered that all people in the country should learn the book; one who could recite it fluently by heart would be rewarded with one thousand gold coins".' If Pollock were to offer evidence from Panini's own texts that he had developed the grammar under the patronage and for the political benefit of a king, it would be more credible compared to a Chinese pilgrim writing about the event more than thirteen hundred years after Panini. Despite the evidence being flimsy, Pollock assumes he has sealed the case. He announces that this example 'shows the salience of the linkage [i.e., the mutually constitutive relationship of grammar and power] for the tradition'. Another prominent example he cites to prove the political power nexus between king and scholar is Patanjali's *Mahabhashya*. He notes that the royal connection becomes evident in a couple of sentences, just because they make reference to the king Pusyamitra and a Yavana besieging Saketa (Ayodhya). That is enough for him to claim that development of grammar was dependent on royal patronage and meant to serve royal power: 'What is relevant is that Patañjali – or the earlier grammarian he may have been

citing – was seeking, in a very subtle way that virtually all later grammarians were to adopt, to identify himself, his patron, and the place where he worked. That location was obviously courtly, whether it was the court of the Śunga overlords (the dynasty to which Puṣyamitra belonged) who succeeded the Maurya kings or another court three centuries later.' But it is *not* 'obviously courtly' – that is merely one possibility of many.

21 Ibid.: 177–78.

22 Ibid.: 180.

23 Ibid.: 179.

24 Ibid.: 183.

25 Ibid.: 189.

26 Ibid.: 189. 'In actual fact, all the components in this dense network of forces – grammar, language, literature, and culture, as well as the society and polity to which these are symbiotically joined – have an irreducible dimension of spatiality. If we are to understand anything about the relationship between culture and power in South Asia before modernity, and specifically about that relationship within the problematic of cosmopolitanism and vernacularity, it is necessary to understand something about the history of the discursive organization of South Asian space.'

27 Ibid.: 186.

28 Ibid.: 184.

29 Ibid.: 182.

30 At the same time, he occasionally states that the precise nature of this power nexus in India is different from the equivalent Western relationship between language and power. However, throughout his book, he fails to pin down the causal relationship in India.

31 Ibid.: 232. However, his data and logic are mismatched since several of his examples are from a period many centuries after the spread of Sanskrit, according to his own chronology.

32 Ibid.: 227, 237, 249.

33 Ibid.: 16.

34 Ibid.: 17.

35 Ibid.: 168.

36 Ibid.: 169.

37 Ibid.: 175.

38 Ibid.: 176.

39 Ibid.: 258.

40 Ibid.: 287.

41 Ibid.: 283.

42 Ibid.: 24–25.

43 Ibid.: 21. 'It was in conscious opposition to this larger sphere [of Sanskrit] that these intellectuals defined their regional worlds. They chose to write in a language that did not travel – and that they knew did not travel – as easily and as far as the well-travelled language of the older cosmopolitan order.'

44 Ibid.: 27: 'The historical creation of a medium of culture that was not only new in itself but appropriate to a new vision of power – a medium of Place for a political vision of Place, but fashioned according to the time-honored model of *kāvya* and *rājya* of the great Way, which had been tied to no one place but were inclusive of them all.'

45 Ibid.: 499. 'Vernacularization ... was a cultural-political decision and often a fraught one. It entailed abandoning a cosmopolitan code and radically transforming local language practices in accordance with the expressive norms of that dominant model, and it meant applying to those practices a certain technology, writing, that had never previously been applied to them.'

46 Ibid.: 24. 'When cultural actors "choose a vernacular language" for literature and so inaugurate the vernacularization process, it is important to understand that they are choosing something that doesn't exist yet as a fully formed, stable totality; instead, Language is constituted as *a language*, as a conceptual object, in part by the very production of texts.'

47 It was 'a moment of profound transition in the history of Indian culture. And since the site of so much of this cultural production was the royal court, with both inscriptional and literary discourse participating in the same dynamic of political-cultural localization, vernacularization signaled as well a moment of profound transition in the history of power' (ibid.: 295).

48 Ibid.: 24.

49 Ibid.: 26.

50 Ibid.: 329.

51 Ibid.

52 Ibid.: 323.

53 Ibid.: 295. 'Through their idiom and imagination, both political and literary texts show unequivocally that they were modeled on Sanskrit, though modeled with highly distinctive regional differences that disclose complex

negotiations with the cosmopolitan literary idiom in everything from vocabulary to thematics.'

54 Ibid.: 297.

55 Ibid.: 297.

56 Reddy 2011: 21. '*Bhakti* poets stressed a return to oral modes of circulation that were decidedly non-courtly ... The influence of *bhakti* does not fit Pollock's model of vernacularization because it is not cosmopolitan in nature, it eliminates not only the court-centered zone of literary production but an outward political agenda as well ... The *bhakti* poets were able to harmonize, and in a sense resolve, the tension created by the dyadic notions of local-translocal, cosmic-worldly and temporal-eternal ...The *bhakta* worships god as local, translocal, and fundamentally, the nexus of both.'

57 Pollock 2006: 397.

58 Ibid.: 401.

59 Ibid.: 307-08. 'This complex transformation is suggested by the history of the word *akṣara*, "phoneme" or "syllable", as it migrated from Sanskrit to Kannada ... In the Sanskrit tradition the term had long been associated with the notion that the language is both fundamentally phonocentric as well as eternal and uncreated (*autpattika*, as theorized by Mīmāṃsā), as suggested by its usual etymology: "that which does not decay" (*a-kṣara*). *Akṣara* also came to connote the Sound par excellence, the primal Sanskrit utterance *oṃ*.'

60 Ibid.: 308.

61 Ibid.: 453.

62 Ibid.: 296. 'One such assumption, endlessly repeated and never examined, is that vast amounts of literature everywhere must have preexisted the earliest surviving texts but have unaccountably vanished without a trace: five hundred years of Marathi literature, seven hundred years of Newari literature – a thousand years of Khmer literature, which George Coedès held was destroyed in "the one long series of disastrous wars" that is the history of Cambodia ... Yet most of the objections just catalogued to charting a history of vernacularization pose problems more of detail than of foundations, whereas most of the basic reservations about beginnings cannot withstand serious scrutiny.'

63 Ibid.: 423. 'A leading political theorist in contemporary South Asia can certainly be forgiven for reporting what is after all the unchallenged consensus that the "gradual separation of [the] emerging literatures [of the vernacular languages] from the high Sanskrit tradition" is to be traced to "religious developments" hostile to the Sanskrit tradition, against which the vernacular

literatures made an "undeclared revolution": "The origin of vernacular languages appears to be intimately linked to an internal conceptual rebellion within classical Brahmanical Hinduism."' Pollock cites as an example of such subalternists, Sudipta Kaviraj, professor of Indian politics and intellectual history at Columbia University. See: Kaviraj, Sudipta: 1992a, 'The Imaginary Institution of India' in *Subaltern Studies VII: Writings on South Asian History and Society*, edited by Partha Chatterjee and Gyanendra Pandey, Oxford University Press, Delhi.

64 Ibid.: 28.

65 He is referring to the disagreements among the schools of dvaita, advaita, bhakti and their combinations that blossomed. These texts were presenting various competing arguments at the popular level concerning the nature of self, rebirth, karma, etc. They explained the Hindu ethics of 'how to act in the world'. Pollock implies that all this intellectual heritage was not pragmatic concerning political and economic issues so it left those structures intact.

66 Pollock 2006: 29. 'In most cases, vernacular beginnings occurred independently of religious stimuli strictly construed, and the greater portion of the literature thereby created was produced not at the monastery but at the court. Only after vernacularization had been consolidated, and in reaction to an already-existing courtly literary and political culture, did a more demotic and often more religiously insurgent *second* vernacular revolution take place.'

67 Ibid.: 473.

68 Ibid.: 475.

69 Ibid.: 481.

70 Ibid.: 501. 'Yet the evidence available from premodern South Asia suggests that some other principle, not encompassed by a mechanistic evolutionary paradigm, was involved in the observable transformations of many features of language change – lexicon, orthography, and others – and indeed, in the constitution and development of literary cultures generally speaking.'

71 Ibid.: 503. Italics mine.

72 Ibid. Italics mine.

73 Ibid.: 504-05.

74 Ibid.: 468.

75 Ibid.: 439. 'As in South Asia, the nature, control, and dissemination of literacy crucially affected the creation of vernacular European literary cultures; and, as in South Asia, literacy in western Europe had a specific history, inflected by factors peculiar to that world. We noticed earlier how Roman imperial practices led to the near-total elimination of regional languages (Celtic, Punic,

and so on) from the inscriptional record of North Africa and western Europe (chapter 7.1); as a result, from around the beginning of the Common Era, literacy as such in the western Mediterranean always meant *Latin* literacy.'

76 Ibid.: 442, 439. 'The critical and distinctive determinant in the history of medieval literacy lies in the Church's control of literary culture for most of the first millennium after the fall of Rome and into the thirteenth century ... Decisions as to what might or might not be committed to writing, for example, were made within the shadow of the Church and its religious values [...] If literacy accompanied Christianity wherever it went (as earlier it had accompanied Romanization), the cultural and cognitive obstacles to the transition to a specifically vernacular literacy were still substantial.'

77 Ibid.: 451.

78 Ibid.: 460.

79 Ibid.: 468.

80 Ibid.

81 Ibid.: 468–69.

82 Ibid.: 469. 'It was this English vernacular literary culture that in the late eleventh century provided the model for Norman literati. Thereupon, partly in imitation of earlier vernacularizations, partly as an independent response to comparable historical forces, the production of new script vernaculars proceeded, from the early twelfth to the sixteenth centuries, in what we saw was a wave of advance across western Europe, from England to northern France, and again, from Occitania, Catalonia, and Castile to northern Italy and southern Germany.'

83 Marathi and Gujarati are two examples of languages which were within or adjacent to the Rashtrakuta domain, impacted by the same Arab/Islam global trade dynamics in the ninth century. Yet neither of these languages vernacularized until well into the fifteenth to sixteenth century, by Pollock's definition.

8: The Sanskriti Web as an Alternative Hypothesis

1 The date of the Mahabharata is estimated at 1000 BCE or prior (source: Kak, Subhash, 'Mahabharata II Dating' accessed from http://www.ece.lsu.edu/kak/MahabharataII.pdf on 12 March 2015). Also, Panini (400 BCE) mentions the Mahabharata; hence at a minimum it was prior to that time.

2 In the subsequent rise of vernaculars Pollock does include the role played by international trade. Nevertheless, he is silent on such internationally travelling jatis in the rise of Sanskrit.

3 Pollock 2006: 20.

4 Ibid.: 164.

5 Ibid.: 50. Italics mine.

6 Ferguson 1959: 336.

7 In Bilhana's *Vikramankadevacharita.*

8 Reddy 2011: 19.

9 Ibid.: 12.

10 Ibid.: 6. 'Sanskrit is not hermetically, nor even hermeneutically sealed. ... In essence it seems imperative that there be an engagement with what Pollock somewhat dismissively, and categorically, calls the Folk.'

11 Ibid.: 7 fn 17. 'It is exactly this "Folk" with the misplaced capital "F" that Pollock and others are so easy to dismiss and disregard.'

12 Ibid.: 58.

13 Furthermore, Jan Houben made an important observation that contrasts between Sanskrit and Prakrits were rarely made in traditional Indian writings, and it is only modern scholars like Pollock who are obsessed with this. See Houben 1996: 179–80 and Hock 1996: 22–23.

14 This section is my restatement of Satyanath's work in a summary form. All references to him are from his unpublished paper: Satyanath, T.S., 'Understanding Indian Knowledge Systems'. An earlier version of the paper was presented at the National Seminar on Indigenous Knowledge Systems held at Sri Shankaracharya Sanskrit University, Kalady during March 2003. He teaches Comparative Indian Literature and Kannada in the Department of Modern Indian Languages and Literary Studies, University of Delhi. Further elaboration is available in Satyanath 2004.

15 From Satyanath's unpublished paper, 'Understanding Indian Knowledge Systems'.

16 Ibid.

17 Satyanath concludes that, 'On the one hand, the description of the city in *Śuktisudharṇavam* maintains continuities with the *śastra* tradition with regard to the description of the city available in the Sanskrit canonical text *Arthaśastra;* and on the other hand it shows compatibilities and continuities with those of the artisan traditions by comparing it with the archaeological findings' (ibid.)

18 Satyanath says: 'Literature within the modernist framework is directly connected with literacy, writing system, mechanical reproduction of texts, creativity and with alleged intellectual, emotional expression and is individualistic in nature. It is also considered as moralistic because during the eighteenth and nineteenth century literature was brought into the sphere [of] education as a means to teach morality ... Early colonial attempts of documenting India's past attempted to bridge the scientific zeal of enlightenment on the one hand, and the artistic concerns of colonial romanticism on the other' (ibid.)

19 Ibid.

20 Ibid.

21 Satyanath says: 'This period is marked by codification of knowledge, particularly the compilation of encyclopedias, in Sanskrit and Kannada. Many of these encyclopedias contain knowledge of all sorts, even knowledge such as wood-glue making for example which apparently do not look like of much value for the royal court to sponsor' (ibid.)

22 These performances were called '*gamaka-vāchana*'. Satyanath observes: 'The text's musical recitation done orally without using a written text and sometimes accompanied by an oral interpretation (*vyakhyāna, ṭīkā* "commentary") in a dramatic dialogic format constitutes a typical traditional ritual vow performance. Although palm-leaf manuscripts of the two above-mentioned Brahminical texts are available in plenty, their oral transmission has continued even to the present day through *gamaka-vāchanas* and folk plays' (ibid.)

23 Ibid.

24 Satyanath says: 'The performing traditions, as body-based knowledge systems, involving music, dance and literature not only came to the forefront during the post-fifteenth century period but also remained as agencies of disseminating knowledge among the entire cross-section of the population. Thus the development of the history of Kannada literature could be perceived as a movement from the singular to pluralistic epistemologies on the one hand and from written court poetry to oral and body-centric popular and folk performances on the other. Thus medieval Kannada knowledge and information systems that were part and parcel of the *kavya* tradition were sustained and disseminated across temporal, spatial and societal categories. The salient features of medieval Kannada literature ... [were] fused into folk and other performing traditions and continued to exist till the nineteenth century, when modernism, the print media and its mechanical reproduction mode changed the paradigm

of knowledge, its construction and retrieval among the educated population of the country' (ibid.)

25 Satyanath writes: 'In the absence of a verbal text, it is the viewer's mental text(s), through a dense intertextuality, that facilitates its mental reading' (ibid.)

26 Satyanath says: 'In pre-colonial India we had multiple modes of constructing, documenting and transmitting knowledge, which were mutually complementary to each other on the one hand, and on the other hand allowed a certain degree of permeability despite insulations through monopolistic protections. Pluralistic epistemologies and their survival is a time-tested phenomenon in India and are highly relevant to us even today for its retrieval and understanding' (ibid.)

27 According to Satyanath: 'Though it appears to be completely sectarian in nature suggesting an exclusive sectarian monopolistic consumption, the very fact that they also existed in body-centric performing traditions such as performances, painting and sculpture, made them available for the non-sectarian consumption. It needs to be pointed out here that the secular nature of medieval Indian performing traditions ... provide ample scope for secularization of sectarian representations. The annual ritual fair that takes place for the popular and folk deities brings together all the communities and creates an opportunity for them to be connected with the tradition in a modular way' (ibid.)

28 Ibid.

29 Malhotra 2011.

30 This is evident in the temple complex of Minakshi, cave sculptures and paintings of Ajanta and Ellora, the giant statue of Gomatesvara of Shravanabelagola, the Gol Ghumbat of Bijapur, the stupa of Sanchi, etc.

9: Declaring Sanskrit Dead and Sanskriti Non-existent

1 Earlier on, in (Pollock 1996) he had argued that Sanskrit had slowly evolved as a political language but that by 1300 its use as a political language had come to an end. In this earlier article, he did not claim that Sanskrit itself had died but that it had merely lost its peculiar political function. The 'Death of Sanskrit' article, however, implies otherwise (Pollock 2001b: 392).

2 Ibid.

3 Ibid.

4 Ibid.: 395.

5 Ibid.: 395. The following is his analysis of Kashmir as an example. He begins with a reference in the *Srikanthacarita* of Maṇkha, a royal poet in mid-twelfth-century Kashmir, to a reading of the work attended by a galaxy of scholars. After a picturesque description of this meeting of literary giants that would warm any Indian's heart, he sadly informs us that such a star-studded gathering was the last in the history of Kashmir. The next three centuries were a period of intense turmoil in which there was no worthwhile literary production. In the fifteenth century, after Sultan Zain-ul-abidin restored order and 'reinstitut[ed] courtly patronage of Sanskrit learning' (ibid.: 396), two substantial works emerged: the genealogical *Rajatarangini* of Jonaraja (covering the period from 1150 CE, where the former *Rajatarangini* of Kalhana ends) and the gnomic anthology *Subhasitavali* of Srivara, but Pollock finds neither of them comparable to their illustrious predecessors. He concludes that Sanskrit literary culture in Kashmir had collapsed by the end of the twelfth century, 'never to be revived in anything remotely approaching its former grandeur' and offers as forensic analysis the ruin of 'the courtly-civic ethos of Kashmir' which was allegedly 'crucial to sustaining the vitality of Sanskrit literary culture' (ibid.: 398).

6 Ibid.: 414.

7 Ibid.: 417.

8 http://www.koausa.org/Glimpses/abhinava.html accessed on 15 December 2014.

9 Ganeri writes that the Navya-Naiyayikas challenged fundamental nyaya assumptions; and they were willing to abandon even their own previous theories, starting afresh when those theories were indefensible. The later scholars of this tradition moved beyond the school's founder, Gangesha Upadhyaya, in order to build a more successful defence of their epistemology (Ganeri 2014).

10 Bronner, Yigal 2002: 441–62.

11 Nilakantha was heir to the tradition of reading and interpretation that was remarkably pluralistic. Nobody in pre-modern India was disturbed that there were 300 Ramayanas. In fact, many pre-modern commentators lauded this very diversity and saw it as their duty to create yet more interpretations. A more narrow view of Sanskrit texts only came with the development of 'Indology' as a largely Western discipline, as European scholars tried to clear away all the complexity of traditional interpretations to arrive at the one 'accurate' reading of the text.

12 Christopher Minkowski, for instance, raises the following questions: 'What has Nīlakaṇṭha accomplished in writing these texts? Is his work simply an example of an excess of learning run amok? An intellectual diversion – the pedantic equivalent of a parlor game? The overly zealous display of learning of a parvenu in Banaras, overwhelmed among the long-established families of learned Dākṣiṇī paṇḍits? Or has Nīlakaṇṭha created something new? For that matter, do we as Indologists believe that in Sanskrit literature there is ever anything new under the sun?' (Minkowski Forthcoming: 24). Accessed from http://www.columbia.edu/itc/mealac/pollock/sks/papers/minkowski_nilakantha.pdf on 11 June 2015.

13 Pollock at times does acknowledge some positive and creative Sanskrit writers of that era. For instance, in seventeenth-century Kerala, a remarkable intellectual named Melpathur Narayana Bhattathiri made an incisive impact in the field of philology: in grammar, hermeneutics and poetry. One of the most remarkable works from his large corpus is an almost unknown treatise called 'Apaniniya-Prayoga-Samarthanam' (A Proof of the Validity of Nonstandard Sanskrit). This was published along with an open letter to the scholars of Tamil Nadu who were his intellectual opponents. The text contains a good deal of revolutionary thinking. However, despite mentioning such incidents, Pollock maintains his death-of-Sanskrit thesis.

14 Pollock 2001b: 416.

15 Pollock quoted in Kruijtzer 2005.

16 Pollock 2001b: 398.

17 Pollock references how King Harsha of Kashmir (1089–1111 CE) destroyed temples for their wealth, as documented by Kalhana. Actually, in Kalhana's writings, there was no differentiation between Buddhist and Shaiva temples as being different religions. Nevertheless, Pollock separates them and makes it a point to highlight the destruction of Buddhist temples by Hindu kings. (Subsequently, William Dalrymple uses this point regarding Harsha in his article in *The Guardian* of 2008. See: http://www.theguardian.com/books/2002/sep/28/featuresreviews.guardianreview4. Accessed on 22 August 2015.) More importantly, Pollock leaves out important references in Kalhana. These references show that Harsha was beholden to Turushka captains (from Central Asia) in his army and that they led him to his misbehaviour. For instance, offering women as slaves from their conquests was something he learned as a Turuhska pattern. Was King Harsha an exception in this regard as he deviated from his dharma?

18 Pollock 2001b: 396.

19 Ibid.: 400. Here Pollock is quoting from a text he says was written in the sixteenth century or earlier.

20 Ibid.

21 Sharma, Suresh 2005: 29. Nalanda was a residential school, i.e., it had dormitories for students. In its heyday, it is claimed to have accommodated more than 10,000 students and 2,000 teachers. Chinese and other foreign pilgrims wrote about their experiences as students there.

22 See Kaul 1967: 72–73.

23 Bronner, Yigal 2003: 443–44. Appaya's most popular work, *Kuvalayananda,* became a primer for budding Sanskrit kavis (writers of kavya) in the seventeenth century, according to Bronner.

24 Pollock 2001b: 417.

25 Ibid.: 393.

26 Ibid.: 393–94.

27 Row, Kshama 1944: iv–vi. Italics mine.

28 Of the sixty one publications attributed to Shankar Pandurang Pandit, thirty three are in Sanskrit, most of them published in the late nineteenth century. Information accessed from http://www.worldcat.org/identities/lccn-n82218837/ on 24 December 2014.

29 Raghavan 1959: 213.

30 Sanskrit Commission: 1957.

31 Krishna Shastry 1999: 12.

32 Ibid.: 14.

33 Ibid.: 17.

34 Ibid.: 21.

35 Ibid.: 38. He also mentioned to me that out of the 700 pathashalas in Karnataka (as an example), only 100 are run by brahmins, which goes to show that the propaganda concerning brahmin hegemony needs to be questioned.

36 Krishna Shastry 1999: 25.

37 I like his terminology, but my use of the term 'dead' in this book serves the purpose of quoting Pollock directly to challenge him.

38 Hanneder 2002: 293–310.

39 Ibid.: 293–310.

40 Ibid.: 293–310. 'Furthermore, Pollock's analysis of the court of Sultan Zain relies on a poet named Srivara, but he is inconsistent in his deployment.

Pollock calls Srivara "the most interesting intellectual at the court", but he is later presented by Pollock as being "unable to create serious original work himself". Hanneder wonders if he happens to be the only random example Pollock knows of and hence exaggerates the importance of this one poet in drawing conclusions.

41 Ibid.: 306.

42 Ibid.: 307.

43 Ibid.: 294.

44 He also accuses Pollock of mimicking a thesis by Max Müller on this history of Sanskrit that had already been refuted by Europeans.

45 Ibid.: 301.

46 Ibid.: 417.

47 Ibid.: 309.

48 Ingalls 1990: 28f.

49 Hanneder 2002: 309.

50 Pollock 2006: 264–65. 'One social factor that has seemed salient for our analysis is the presence of ruler lineages recently immigrated from western and central Asia who not only patronized a new Sanskrit literature but may themselves have been poets ... Was the new employment of written Sanskrit as a prestige language for the creation of workly texts a reaction to superposed cultural forms then manifesting themselves for the first time on the eastern frontier of the Hellenic world, just as literature written in Latin was a response to the same cultural phenomena on the western frontier? Some evidence suggests the possibility. A Greek theater was then in existence in what is today northern Afghanistan (Ai Khanoum); bilingual intellectuals translated Aśokan edicts into literary Greek in the mid-third century BCE, while interactions among Hellenic and South Asian sculptors produced the unprecedented sculpture of Gandhāra; four centuries later, in 149-50 CE – squarely in the middle of the reign of Rudradāman – a scholar with the title Yavaneśvara (Lord of the Greeks) prepared a Sanskrit prose translation of a Greek work (probably from Alexandria) on the casting of horoscopes, which with another (lost) Greek text formed the basis of the Indian developments in the art of horoscopy until the introduction of Islamic ideas a millennium later; a portion of *Mānasāraśilpaśāstra*, a work on architecture of approximately the sixth century, was adapted from Vitruvius ("a parallel almost down to every detail"); the cult of the important south Indian and Sri Lankan goddess Pattinī and that of Isis have recently been shown to be closely linked by cultural transmission. Nineteenth-century Indology sought to demonstrate just this sort of dependency, speculating for

example that the *Rāmāyaṇa* must have been translated from Homer and Sanskrit drama adapted from Athenian exemplars (comparable to Livius Andronicus's Latin adaptations, though the parallel seems never to have been drawn).'

51 Ibid.: 266.

52 Ibid.: 277. For example, he states: 'No imperial formation arising in the Sanskrit cosmopolis ever stationed troops to rule over conquered territories. No populations were ever enumerated. No uniform code of law was ever enforced anywhere across caste groupings, let alone everywhere in an imperial polity. No evidence indicates that transculturation was ever the route to imperial advancement in the bureaucracy or military. Even more dramatic differences are to be seen in the domain of political theology. Evidence for the providential character of the Roman state – the belief that it was universal and willed by the gods – is abundant in Latin literature and is a constituent of Roman thinking from the end of the third century BCE on.'

53 Ibid.: 537. Italics mine.

54 Ibid.: 538.

55 Ibid.: 535.

56 Ibid.: 539.

57 Ibid.: 558–59. Italics mine.

58 Ibid.: 563.

59 Ibid.: 565.

60 Ibid.: 575.

10: Is Sheldon Pollock Too Big to be Criticized?

1 CSDS talk by Pollock on Liberation Philology https://www.youtube.com/watch?v=C2gZKjbEoMo accessed 08 April 2015.

2 From https://www.youtube.com/watch?v=C2gZKjbEoMo accessed on 08 April 2015 (see 1:30 minutes to 3:00 minutes).

3 Pollock 2011: 39. Italics mine.

4 http://kindlemag.in/language-save-all/ accessed on 08 April 2015. Italics mine.

5 http://kindlemag.in/language-save-all/ accessed on 08 April 2015. The complete passage reads as follows: 'The political dimension of Pollock's project makes it all the more pressing. Like much of Pollock's scholarship, his political project is quite ambitious. He seeks to understand, and to upend, the conceptual

consequences of capitalism for scholarship. He argues that the age of capitalist modernity has ushered in a particular way of thinking – and a particular way of analyzing and creating texts – that is reductive in the extreme, and that cuts off other, more pluralistic forms of scholarship. Capitalism has a singularly singular logic.'

6 http://kindlemag.in/language-save-all/ accessed on 08 April 2015.

7 Rudolph 2003.

8 Jaffrelot 1996: 389.

9 Jasbir Jain is director of the Institute for Research in Interdisciplinary Studies (IRIS), Jaipur. Formerly of the University of Rajasthan, she has headed the Department of English and worked in various capacities, including as director of the Academic Staff College. Jain has travelled extensively and received several awards, among them: the Sahitya Akademi Fellowship as Writer in Residence (2009), UGC Fellow (2005–07), Emeritus Fellow (2002–04), and K.K. Birla Fellowship for Comparative Literature (1998-2000). Elected life-member of Clare Hall, Cambridge, she has also benefited from the Fulbright Fellowship and from the American Council of Learned Societies. In 2008, the South Asia Literary Association conferred on her the SALA Award for her work in feminist and South Asian studies and her distinguished scholarship.

10 Jain 2008: 236.

11 Doniger 2010: 242.

12 Accessed from http://www.telegraphindia.com/1111103/jsp/opinion/story_14698615.jsp on 03 April 2015.

13 Murthy: 1978.

14 Accessed from http://www.claysanskritlibrary.org/about.php on 27 April 2015.

15 In the original draft of this book, I had written extensive sections describing how some of his elite students, most notably Ananya Vajpeyi, have spread his ideas widely into the Indian intellectual milieu. However, I have set that material aside for now, in order to better focus.

16 Pollock has consistently held such views for many decades. As far back as 1993, he blamed Valmiki, saying: 'Vālmīki's monumental text is doubtless the starting point, to establish a hegemonic version,' and that the television serial *Ramayana* serial merely continued this Indian method of rewriting and adapting the old 'myth' to deal with new political threats. He wrote: 'Medieval codings of the Rāmāyaṇa are an instance of a mythopolitical strategy available for recurrent deployment, such as is taking place in India today' (Pollock 1993b: 289).

17 He accuses such literature of being a tool used by Hindu kings to 'aestheticize power' – a ploy, in other words, to divert people's attention away from Vedic and Sanskrit hegemony over women and shudras.

18 http://www.thehindu.com/opinion/lead/the-story-of-my-sanskrit/article6321759.ece accessed on 16 August 2015.

19 Accessed from http://www.india-seminar.com/2009/595/595_comment.htm on 14 April 2014.

20 All quotes from this Tehelka interview accessed from https://www.youtube.com/watch?v=VXhInNUVZ6U on 15 April 2015.

21 Sanskrit Commission: 1957

22 Accessed from http://im.rediff.com/news/2014/jul/09_iapoy_sheldon_pollock.pdf on 14 April 2015.

23 Ibid.

24 Ibid.

25 Ibid.

26 Ibid.

27 Ibid.

28 http://im.rediff.com/news/2014/jul/09_iapoy_sheldon_pollock.pdf on 29 June 2015.

29 Ibid. Italics mine.

30 Pollock 1985c: 277. Accessed from http://www.indologica.com/volumes/vol13/vol13_art18_POLLOCK.pdf on 14 April 2015.

31 Wadley and Ramamurthy 1995. Downloadable at: http://files.eric.ed.gov/fulltext/ED426010.pdf

32 Ibid.

33 Ibid.

34 The following school assignment (in 2013) about the Ramayana is an example of how impressionable young American high-school students are being taught to see Hindus: 'One of the women in the Ramayana that is really oppressed by this patriarchy is Sita, Rama's wife. Once Rama rescues Sita from the evil claws of Ravana, he starts doubting her loyalty towards him. He thought that since Ravana had Sita kidnapped for so long there was no physical way that he could not have had sexual intercourse with Sita. But of course Sita denies that she had sex with Ravana. She announces to Rama that she is pregnant and Rama is certain that they're not his children, but Ravana's children. He sends Sita away and says that he does not want her. During this part of the book Sita is seen as

weak because she has no way to prove her faithfulness to Rama. Her word does not prove anything ... women in the world of this book are put aside. Women are pushed down by "the system of male dominance". Women like Sita are "objectified". They are not seen as actual human beings. They are seen as things that can be thrown away or pushed aside at the snap of men's fingers.' This was written by a high school student in New York City in June 2013, and posted on the Internet. Accessed from http://youthvoices.net/discussion/how-does-text-define-femininity-and-masculinity-what-does-it-mean-be-woman-world-epic on 4 April 2015.

35 'In June 2002 I moved to Trivandrum, India, following my (American) husband who had taken a job there. Upon my arrival I was confronted with his mid-life crisis, a complete emotional withdrawal. This left me without support in a city in which women were second-class citizens, unable to walk alone at night, and not expected to have an identity separate from their husbands. It was in Trivandrum that I encountered the Indian epic, *The Ramayana*, for the first time. Like many westerners, I initially considered the Ramayana little more than misogynist propaganda.' Accessed from http://www.ninapaley.com/bio.html on 13 April 2015.

36 For more details on Aseem Chhabra, go to http://www.aseemchhabra.com/ accessed on 13 April 2015.

37 Pollock 2011.

38 Ibid.: 22.

39 Ibid.

40 Ibid.: 39–40. Italics mine.

41 Ibid.: 25.

42 http://en.wikipedia.org/wiki/Damodar_Dharmananda_Kosambi accessed 12 September 2014.

43 Sumit Sarkar in: http://www.frontline.in/static/html/fl1705/17050260.htm accessed 12 September 2014.

44 Pollock 2011: 33.

45 Ibid.: 43. Italics mine.

46 Accessed from http://www.murtylibrary.com/why-a-classical-library-of-india.php on 16 March 2015.

47 Ibid.

48 Pollock 2006: 30.

49 Ibid.: 31.

50 Ibid.: 32.

51 Ibid.: 33.

52 An example of his prashasti for John Clay and his wife Jennifer Coutts Clay is at the Clay Library web site: http://www.claysanskritlibrary.org/people.php) He also writes prashastis for the Murthy family.

53 Pollock 2006: 579.

54 Pollock 2011: 33.

55 Pollock 2006: 579.

56 Ibid.: 580.

11: Conclusion: The Way Forward

1 I have referred to this type of logic as 'moron smriti' – which means a 'theory' for being a moron.

Appendix A: Pollock's theory of Buddhist undermining of the Vedas

1 Pollock 2006: 51.

2 Ibid.

3 Ibid.

4 Aklujkar 2003.

5 Ibid.

6 Kannan (private communication) offers the following point in support: Bhattakalanka, a seventeenth century Kannada grammarian, a Jain from Karnataka, and a master of over half a dozen languages including Sanskrit, Prakrit and Magadhi, wrote that the same divine language of the Lord [Mahavira] was heard, simultaneously, by different people in different languages! This is even more explicitly stated by Devendra that the gods took the message as encoded in the divine language, men as expressed in the human language, hunters as in their own language, etc.!

7 Pollock 2006: 52.

8 Aklujkar 2003.

9 Pollock 2006: 52–53.

10 Ibid.

11 Ibid.: 81.

12 Ibid.: 499.

13 Ibid.: 89.

14 Ibid.: 39.

15 Ibid.: 67, 72–73.

16 Pollock 1986: 37–38: 'I do not think it can be questioned that the monumental poet [i.e., Valmiki] adopted certain motifs from folk literature as we find it represented in the Buddhist *jātakas*. The *Sāma Jātaka* (#540), for example, is closely related to *sargas* 57–58 and represents, as I shall argue, the prototype for that apparently rather late stratum of the text. Similarly, the tradition of *Rāmapaṇḍita*, "The Wise Rama," which is preserved in the *gāthās* of the *Dasaratha Jātaka* (#461), seems to have been adapted in *Ayodhyākāṇḍa* 98. 15ff. where it is tacked on to the narrative. By contrast, several *jātakas* presuppose the Rāma legend in broad outline, and perhaps even the *Vālmīki Rāmāyaṇa* itself. The *Jayadissa Jātaka* (#513) is a case in point. One *gāthā* found in it refers explicitly to the events – minor events after all – narrated in *sarga* 22 of *Ayodhyākāṇḍa*.'

17 Pollock's error is that he blindly repeats Weber's analysis of the *Dasaratha Jataka* in the nineteenth century, even though by the 1980s this notion had been debunked by Western academics, as per Goldman.

18 Pollock dates Yaska's *Nirukta* to a post-Buddha date of 400 BCE (though with a question mark) (Pollock 2006: 46, n. 18). This contradicts the critical edition of the *Nirukta* by Lakshman Sarup which places it between 700 and 500 BCE, i.e., before the Buddha. (Sarup 1967) *Nirukta* is a complex document, which references previous texts, on the lexicon and etymology of Sanskrit. It is important for the use of written Sanskrit. Its dating would indicate that Sanskrit texts were already being produced for some time; hence the need to write it. Pollock places Panini's *Ashtadhyayi*, the book of Sanskrit grammar, at 300 BCE. Some in the tradition place him at 500 BCE. Tradition does place Patanjali's *Mahabhashya* post-Buddha. However, given that his text is extensively based on the *Nirukta* and *Ashtadhyayi*, it is more likely a consolidation and further development that would have taken place regardless of the Buddha.

19 Ibid.: 74.

20 Likewise, the date of Purva-mimamsa scholars such as Jaimini is moved to a period centuries after the Buddha whereas tradition puts it prior to 800 BCE.

Appendix B: Ramayana Evidence Prior to the Turkish Invasion

1 Jain 2013.

2 Zaheer 1981.

Appendix C: Pollock's Political Activism

1 Accessed from http://www.coalitionagainstgenocide.org/press/support/faculty.aahoa.php on 16 April 2015.

2 Accessed from http://www.coalitionagainstgenocide.org/press/support/faculty.csulb.php on 16 April 2015.

3 Accessed from http://www.counterpunch.org/2009/09/02/hey-ram-the-things-the-financial-times-group-does/ on 16 April 2015. Alternative: http://beenasarwar.com/2009/08/31/stop-financial-times-award-to-narendra-modi/

4 Accessed from https://www.change.org/p/government-of-india-provide-clarification-on-reported-destruction-of-files-and-documents-of-historical-nature-including-those-related-to-the-assassination-of-mahatma-gandhi on 16 April 2015. The implication of this petition is that the new government of Narendra Modi (elected in mid-2014) was attempting to suppress and destroy information and documents from around the time of Mahatma Gandhi's assassination.

5 Accessed from http://beenasarwar.com/2009/09/04/hey-ram-the-things-the-financial-times-group-does/ on 13 April 2015.

Bibliography

Aklujkar, Ashok. 2003. 'A different sociolinguistics for Brahmins, Buddhists and Jains.' In *Contemporary Views on Indian Civilization.* Edited by Bhu Dev Sharma. Meerut: World Association for Vedic Studies: 54–69.

Bandopadhyaya, J. 2007. *Class and Religion in Ancient India.* Anthem Press.

Benjamin, Walter Bendix Schönflies. 1936. 'The Work of Art in the Age of Mechanical Reproduction'. Source: UCLA School of Theater, Film and Television; Translated: by Harry Zohn; Published: by Schocken/Random House, ed. by Hannah Arendt; Transcribed: by Andy Blunden 1998; proofed and corrected Feb. 2005.

Berlin, Isaiah. 2013. *Against The Current: Essays in the History of Ideas.* 2nd. Princeton: Princeton University Press.

Bhatnagar, Rashmi. 1986. 'Uses and Limits of Foucault: A Study of the Theme of Origins in Edward Said's "Orientalism"'. *Social Scientist,* 16 (7): 3–22.

Blackburn, Stuart. 2000. 'Corruption and Redemption: The Legend of Valluvar and Tamil Literary History.' *Modern Asian Studies,* 34 (2): 449–82.

Breckenridge, Carol A. and Peter van der Veer. 1993. *Orientalism and the Postcolonial Predicament.* Philadelphia: University of Pennsylvania Press.

Bronner, Yigal. 2002. 'What is New and What is Navya, Sanskrit Poetics on the Eve of Colonialism.' *Journal of Indian Philosophy* (Kluwer Academic Publishers) 30: 441–62.

Bronner, Yigal, Whitney Cox, and Lawrence McCrea. 2011. *South Asian Texts in History.* Ann Arbor: Association of Asian Studies.

Clooney, Francis X. 1992. 'Extending the Canon: Some Implications of a Hindu Argument about Scripture.' *The Harvard Theological Review,* 85 (2): 197–215.

Coomaraswamy, Ananda K. 1943. *Hinduism and Buddhism*. New York: The Philosophical Library.

Coulson, Michael. 1986. *Sanskrit: An Introduction to the Classical Language*. New York: David McKay Company Inc.

Cox, Whitney. 2011. 'Saffron in the Rasam.' In *South Asian Texts in History*. Edited by Yigal Bronner, Whitney Cox and Lawrence McCrea. Ann Arbor: Association of Asian Studies.

Deshpande, G.T. 1971. *Indological Papers*. Vol. I. Nagpur: Vidarbha Samshodhan Mandal.

Deshpande, Madhav. 1993. *Sanskrit and Prakrit: Sociolinguistic Issues*. Delhi: Motilal Banarasidass.

Dharampal. 2000. *The Beautiful Tree*. Mapusa: Other India Press.

Dimock, Edward. 1966. 'Doctrine and Practice among the Vaisnavas of Bengal.' In *Krishna: Myths, Rites, and Attitudes*. Ed. by Milton Singer. Honolulu: University of Hawaii Press.

Doniger, Wendy. 2010. *The Hindus: An Alternative History*. Delhi: Penguin Books.

Dutt, Jogesh Chunder. 1986. *Rājataraṅgiṇī of Jonarāja*. Delhi: Gian Publishing House.

Evison, Gillian. 2004. *The Orientalist, His Institute and the Empire: The rise and subsequent decline of Oxford University's Indian Institute*. December. Accessed 12 September 12 2014. http://www.bodleian.ox.ac.uk/__data/assets/pdf_file/0009/27774/indianinstitutehistory.pdf.

Ferguson, Charles A. 1959. 'Diglossia.' *Word* 15: 325–340.

Franklin, Michael J. 2011. *'Orientalist Jones': Sir William Jones, Poet, Lawyer, and Linguist, 1746–1794*. Oxford: Oxford University Press.

Frazier, Jessica. 2009. *Reality, Religion and Passion: Indian and Western Approaches in Hans-Georg Gadamer and Rupa Goswami*. Lanham: Lexington Books.

Freeman, Rich. 1998. 'Rubies and Coral: The Lapidary Crafting of Language in Kerala.' *The Journal of Asian Studies*, 57 (1): 38–65.

Ganeri, Jonardan. 2014. *The Lost Age of Reason*. Oxford: Oxford University Press.

Goldman, Robert P. 1984. *Ramayana of Valmiki, An Epic of Ancient India, Balakanda*. Translated by Robert P. Goldman. Vol. 1. Princeton: Princeton University Press.

Gould, Rebecca. 2008. 'How Newness Enters the World.' *Comparative Studies of South Asia, Africa and the Middle East*, 28 (3): 533–57.

Grünendahl, Reinhold. 2012. 'History in the Making: On Sheldon Pollock's "NS Indology" and Vishwa Adluri's "Pride and Prejudice".' *International Journal of Hindu Studies*, 16 (2): 189–257.

Halbfass, Wilhelm. 2007. *Research and Reflection: Beyond Orientalism*. Edited by Eli Franco and Ed Preisendaz. Delhi: Motilal Banarasidass.

Hanneder, J. 2002. 'On the Death of Sanskrit.' *Indo-Iranian Journal*, 45: 293–310.

Herzfield, Michael. 1997. 'Political Philology: The Everyday Consequences of Grandiose Grammars.' *Anthropological Linguistics*, 39 (3): 351–375.

Hock, Hans H. 1996. 'Pre-Ṛgvedic Convergence Between Indo-Arya (Sanskrit) and Dravidian? A Survey of the Issues and Controversies.' In *Ideology and Status of Sanskrit: Contributions to the History of the Sanskrit Language*. Edited by Jan E.M. Houben, 17–58. Leiden: E.J. Brill.

Houben, Jan E.M. 1996. 'Sociolinguistic attitudes reflected in the work of Bhartṛhari and some later grammarians.' In *Ideology and Status of Sanskrit: Contributions to the History of the Sanskrit Language*. Edited by Jan E.M. Houben, 157–193. Leiden: E.J. Brill.

Hunter, William Wilson. 1908. *Imperial Gazetteer of India*. Oxford: Clarendon Press.

Ingalls, Daniel H.H. 1945. *Sanskrit Poetry and Sanskrit Poetics, Introduction to An Anthology of Sanskrit Court Poetry: Vidyākara's Subhāṣitaratnakoṣa*. Cambridge: Harvard University Press.

—. 1976. 'Kālidāsa and the Attitudes of the Golden Age.' *Journal of the American Oriental Society*, 96 (1): 15–26.

—. 1990. *The Dhvanyaloka of Anandavardhana with the Locana of Abhinavagupta*. Cambridge: Harvard University Press.

Jaffrelot, Christophe. 1996. *The Hindu Nationalist Movement and Indian Politics: 1925 to the 1990s*. New Delhi: Penguin Books.

Jagannatha, Raja M.K. 2009. *Passages: Relationships between Tamil and Sanskrit*. Edited by M. Kannan and Jennifer Clare. Pondicherry: Institut Français de Pondichèry.

Jain, Jasbir. 2008. 'Purdah, Patriarchy, and the Tropical Sun: Womanhood in India.' In *The Veil: Woman Writers on Its History, Lore, and Politics*. Edited by Jennifer Heath. Berkeley: University of California Press.

Jain, Meenakshi. 2013. *Rama and Ayodhya*. Delhi: Aryan Books International.

Jha, Ganganath. 1920-39. *Manusmṛti with the 'Manubhāṣya' of Medhātithi*. Vol. 7. Delhi: Motilal Banarasidass.

Kaul, Srikanth. 1967. *Rājataraṅgiṇī of Jonarāja*. Hoshiarpur: Vishveshvaranand Institute.

Kaviraj, Sudipta. 1992. 'The Imaginary Institution of India'. *Subaltern Studies VII: Writings on South Asian History and Society*. Edited by Partha Chatterjee and Gyanendra Pandey, Vol. 7: 8. Delhi: Oxford University Press.

Kipling, Rudyard. 1987. 'Yoked with an Unbeliever'. *In Plain Tales from the Hills*. Oxford: Oxford University Press.

Knutson, Jesse Ross. 2014. *Into the Twilight of Sanskrit Court Poetry: The Sena Salon of Bengal and Beyond*. Berkeley: University of California Press.

Krishnamoorthy, K. 1977. *Vakrokti-Jivita of Kuntaka*. Translated/edited by Dr K. Krishnamoorthy. Dharwad: Karnatak University.

Krishnamachariar, M. 1937. *History of Classical Sanskrit Literature*. Madras: Tirumalai-Tirupati Devasthanams Press.

Krishna Shastry, Chamu. 1999. *Does Knowledge Lead to Dharma or Does Action?* Translated by K.S. Kannan. Unpublished.

Kruijtzer, Gijs. 2005. 'A Pre-colonial language in a post-colonial world.' *International Institute of Asian Studies Newsletter*, 36: 3–5.

Lidova, Natalia R. 1997. 'Review of The Vernacular Veda: Revelation, Recitation and Ritual by Vasudha Narayanan.' *Journal of the American Academy of Religion*, 65 (3): 681–84.

Lienhard, Siegfried. 1984. *A History of Classical Poetry: Sanskrit—Pali—Prakrit*. Series on *History of Indian Literature*. Edited by Jan Gonda. Vol. 3 (1). Wiesbaden: Harrassowitz.

Malhotra, Rajiv. 2009 'American Exceptionalism and the Myth of the Frontiers' in *The Challenge of Eurocentrism*. Edited by Rajani Kannepalli Kanth, Palgrave Macmillan. Downloadable at: http://www.medhajournal.com/index.php/en/geopolitics-guru/892-american-exceptionalism.

Malhotra, Rajiv and Aravindan Neelakandan. 2011. *Breaking India*. Delhi: Amaryllis.

Malhotra, Rajiv. 2011. *Being Different*. Delhi: HarperCollins.

—. 2014. *Indra's Net*. Delhi: HarperCollins.

Mani, Lata. 1987. 'Contentious Traditions: The Debate on SATI in Colonial India.' *Cultural Critique*, 119–56.

Marriott, Mckim. 1990. *India through Hindu Categories.* Edited by McKim Marriott. Delhi: Sage Publications.

Master, Alfred. 1946. 'The influence of Sir William Jones upon Sanskrit Studies.' *Bulletin of the School of Oriental and African Studies* (Cambridge University Press), 11 (4): 798–806.

Minkowski, Christopher. forthcoming. 'Nīlakaṇṭha Caturdhara and the Genre of Mantrarahasyaprakåsikå.' Edited by Y. Ikari. *In Proceedings of the Second International Vedic Workshop.* Kyoto.

—. 2001. 'The Pandit as Public Intellectual.' In *The Pandit: Traditional Scholarship in India.* Edited by Alex Michaels. Delhi: Manohar.

Mitra, Arati. 1989. *Origin and Development of Sanskrit Metrics.* Calcutta: The Asiatic Society.

Muni, Bharat. 1951. *The Natya Shastra.* Translated by Manomohan Ghosh. Kolkata: Asiatic Society of Bengal.

Murthy, U.R. Anantha. 1978. *Samskara: A Rite for a Dead Man.* Translated by A.K. Ramanujam. New York: Oxford University Press.

Nanda, Meera. 2003. *Prophets Facing Backwards.* New Brunswick: Rutgers University Press.

Ong, Walter. 1982. *Orality and Literacy.* New Brunswick: Methuen.

Oriental Institute. 1975. *The Ramayana.* Critical Edition. Baroda: M.S. University.

Orr, Leslie. 2009. 'Tamil and Sanskrit in the Medieval Epigraphical Context'. In *Passages: Relationships between Tamil and Sanskrit.* Edited by M. Kannan and Jennifer Clare. Pondicherry: Institut Français de Pondichèry.

Peterson, Indira V. 1982. 'Singing of a Place: Pilgrimage as Metaphor and Motif in the Tēvāram Songs of the Tamil Śaivite Saints.' *Journal of the American Oriental Society,* 102 (1): 69–90.

Pillai, Devdar. 1997. *Indian Sociology Through Ghurye.* Bombay: Popular Prakashan.

Pollock, Sheldon. 1984. 'The Divine King in the Indian Epic.' *The Journal of Oriental Society,* 104 (3): 505–28.

—. 1985. 'The Theory of practice and the practice of theory in Indian intellectual history.' *Journal of the American Oriental Society,* 105 (3): 499–519.

—. 1985b. 'Daniel Henry Holmes Ingalls.' *Journal of the American Oriental Society,* 105 (3): 387–89.

—. 1985c. 'Rakshasas and Others.' *Indologica Taurinensia,* 13: 263–81.

—. 1986. *Ramayana of Valmiki, Ayodhyakanda.* Translated by Sheldon Pollock. Vol. II. Berkeley: Berkeley: University of California Press.

—. 1990. 'From Discourse of Ritual to Discourse on Power in Sanskrit Culture.' *Journal of Ritual Studies*, 4 (2).

—. 1993a. 'Deep Orientalism? Notes on Sanskrit and Power beyond the Raj.' In *Orientalism and the Postcolonial Predicament.* Eedited by Carol Breckenridge and Peter van der Veer. Philadelphia: University of Pennsylvania Press.

—. 1993b. 'Ramayana and Political Imagination in India.' *The Journal of Asian Studies*, 52 (2): 261–97.

—. 1996. 'The Sanskrit Cosmopolis, 300–1300: Transculturation, Vernacularization, and the Question of Ideology.' In *Ideology and Status of Sanskrit*, edited by Jan Houben. Leiden, New York, Köln: Brill.

—. 2000. 'Cosmopolitan and Vernacular in History.' *Public Culture*, 12 (3): 591–625.

—. 2001. 'The Social Aesthetic and Sanskrit Literary Theory.' *Journal of Indian Philosophy*, 29: 197–229.

—. 2001b. 'The Death of Sanskrit.' *Comparative Studies in Society and History*, 43 (2): 392–426.

—. 2003. 'Sanskrit Literary Culture From the Inside Out.' In *Literary Cultures in History: Reconstructions from South Asia.* Edited by Sheldon Pollock. Berkeley: University of California Press.

—. 2005. *Ramayana Book Two: Ayodhya By Valmiki.* New York: New York University Press and JJC Foundation: 15–30.

—. 2009. 'Future Philology? The Fate of a Soft Science in a Hard World'. *Critical Inquiry*, 35 (4): 931–61.

—. 2006. *The Language of the Gods in the World of Men.* Berkeley : University of California Press.

—. 2011. 'Crisis in the Classics.' *Journal of Social Research*, 78 (1): 21–48.

—. 2013. 'Cosmopolitanism, Vernacularism and Postmodernity.' In *Global Intellectual History*, edited by Samuel Moyn and Andrew Sartori. Columbia University Press.

—. 2015 (Forthcoming). *An Intellectual History of Rasa.* New York: Columbia University Press.

Prabhu, Alan Machado. 1999. *Sarasvati's Children: A History of the Mangalorean Christians.* Bangalore: Indian Journalists Association Publications.

Parashar, Sadhana. 2013. *Kāvyamīmāṃsā of Rājaśekhara.* Delhi: D.K. Printworld.

Raghavan, V. 1959. 'Sanskrit Literature'. In *Contemporary Indian Literature*. Delhi: Sahitya Akademi.

Ramaswamy, Krishnan, Antonio de Nicolas and Aditi Banerjee. 2007. *Invading the Sacred*. Delhi: Rupa & Co.

Reddy, Srinivas. 2011. *The Amuktamalyada of Kṛishnadevaraya: Language, Power and Devotion in Sixteenth Century South India*. PhD Dissertation. Berkeley: University of California South and Southeastern Studies.

Renan, Ernest. 1891. *The Future of Science: Ideas of 1848*. Translated by Albert D. Vandam and C.B. Pitman. London: Chapman and Hall.

Rotter, Andrew Jon. 2000. *Comrades at Odds: The United States and India, 1947–1964*. Ithaca: Cornell University Press.

Row, Pandita Ksama. 1944. *Uttara Satyagraha Gita*. Bombay: Hind Kitabs Ltd.

Rudolph, Lloyd and Susanne. 1967. *The Modernity of Tradition: Political Development in India*. Chicago: University of Chicago.

—. 1993. 'Modern Hate'. *The New Republic*. March, 1993. Chicago: University of Chicago: pp. 24-29.

Said, Edward. 1979. *Orientalism*. New York: Vintage.

Sanskrit Commission, Government of India. 1957. *Report of the Sanskrit Commission 1956–1957*. Delhi: Ministry of Education and Culture Government of India.

Sanyal, Sanjeev. 2008. *The Indian Renaissance: India's Rise After a Thousand Years of Decline*. Singapore: World Scientific Publishing Co. Pte Ltd.

Sarup, Lakshman. 1967. *The Nighantu and The Nirukta*. New Delhi: Motilal Banarasidass.

Satyanath, T.S. 2004. 'Body as Lexicon: Understanding Body-Based Indian Knowledge Systems.' *Electronic Journal of Indian Culture and Society*.

—. 2010. 'Kavya as Knowledge System.' Presented at the National Seminar on Indigenous Knowledge Systems, Sri Shankaracharya Sanskrit University, Kalady, March 2003. Kolkata: Centre for Advanced Study in Comparative Literature, Jadavpur University. Unpublished paper.

Schopenhauer, Arthur. 2005. *The Art of always being right*. Edited by C. Grayling and T.B. Saunders. London: Gibson Square.

Sharma, Arvind. 2000. Of Sudras, Sutas and Slokas: Why Is the Mahabharata Pre-eminently in Anushtubh Metre? In *Indo-Iranian Journal*, 43, no. 3.

—. 2006. *Hindu Egalitarianism*. Delhi: Rupa & Co.

Sharma, Narendra Nath. 1994. *Paṇḍitarāja Jagannātha, the Renowned Sanskrit Poet of Medieval India*. New Delhi: Mittal Publications.

Sharma, Shashi. 2005. *Imagined Manuvād*. Delhi: Rupa & Co.

Sharma, Suresh. 2005. *Encyclopaedia of Higher Education: Historical survey - Pre-independence Period*. New Delhi: Mittal Publications.

Shastri, Shiv Narayana. 2009. *Kāvyādarśa 'Prasādinī' Hindi Vyākhyā Sahita (Bhāga 1)*. Delhi: Parimal Publications.

Shastri, Subrahmanya. 1944. *Lectures on Patanjali's Mahābhāṣya*. Vol. I. Madras: De Nobili Press, and Trichinopoly: United Printers.

Singh, Raghunath. 1972. *Jonarajakṛta Rājataraṅgiṇī*. Varanasi: Chowkhamba Sanskrit Series.

Singh, Upinder. 2011. 'The Power of a Poet.' *Indian Historical Review*, 38 (2): 177–98.

Sreedharan, E. 2000. *Textbook of Historiography 500 bc to ad 2000*. Hyderabad: Orient Longman Pvt. Ltd.

Sreekantaiyya, T.N. 2001. *Bharatiya Kavyamimamse*. Translated by N. Balasubramanya. Delhi: Sahitya Akademi.

Stein, M.A. 1979. *Kalhaṇa's Rājataraṅgiṇī*. Vol. I. Delhi: Motilal Banarasidass.

Trautmann, Thomas R. 2004. *Aryans and British India*. Delhi: Yoga Press.

Thapar, Romila. 2015. 'Fallacies of Hindutva Historiography'. *Economic and Political Weekly*, Vol - L No. 1. See: http://www.epw.in/discussion/fallacies-hindutva-historiography.html

Vajpeyi, Ananya. 2010. 'Crisis in the Classics: A Need for a Classics Survey.' *Society & Culture*. Accessed 19 September 2014. http://casi.sas.upenn.edu/iit/vajpeyi;.

—. 2011. 'The Sudra in History: From Scripture to Segregation.' In *South Asian Texts in History: Critical Engagements with Sheldon Pollock*. Edited by Bronner, McCrea and Cox. Ann Arbor: Association for Asian Studies. Accessed 4 May 2015. http://works.bepress.com/ananya_vajpei/53.

—. 2012. *Righteous Republic*. Harvard University Press.

Vatsyayan, Kapila. 1977. *Classical Indian Dance in Literature and the Arts*. New Delhi: Sangeet Natak Akademi.

Vishveshvara, Acharya. 1998. *Kavyaprakasha*. Varanasi: Jnanamandala Limited.

Wadley, Susan and Priti Ramamurthy. 1995. *Spotlight on Ramayana, An Enduring Tradition*. New York: The American Forum For Global Education.

Zaheer, Mohammad. 1981. *The Temple at Bhitargaon*. Delhi: Agam Kala Prakashan.

Index